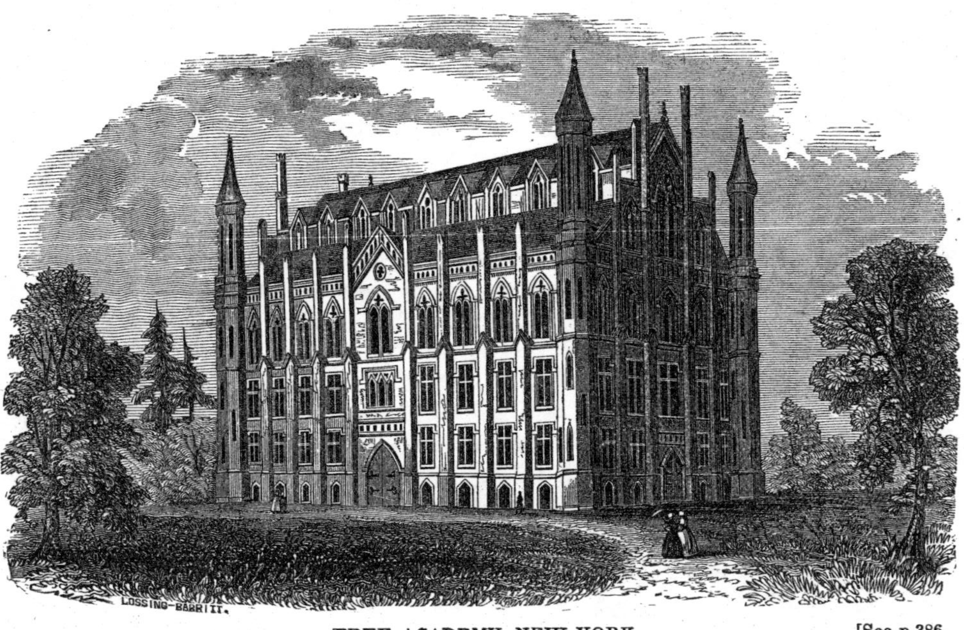

FREE ACADEMY, NEW YORK. [See p 386.

THE

MEANS AND ENDS

OF

UNIVERSAL EDUCATION.

BY IRA MAYHEW, A. M.,

Superintendent of Public Instruction of the State of Michigan,

AND

Author of a Practical System of Book-keeping.

NEW YORK:

PUBLISHED BY A. S. BARNES & Co.,

111 & 113 WILLIAM ST., COR JOHN.

PREFACE.

WHEN about to engage in enterprises of any kind, it is befitting that persons should first settle in their own minds THE ENDS they propose to attain, in order that they may wisely adapt THE MEANS to be pursued, to the accomplishment of these ends. If the responsibilities about to be assumed are delicate in their nature, and far-reaching in their consequences, it is eminently proper that the candidate should seek to be duly and truly prepared, and well qualified, that he may prove in some degree adequate to the task to which he thus voluntarily devotes himself.

But what relation is so delicate and responsible in its nature, and what so far reaching in its results, as that of the parent to his offspring? or that of the teacher to his pupils? And what positions are more thoughtlessly assumed, or sustained with less solicitude, than are these, in perhaps the great majority of cases! The consideration of these facts necessarily awakens deep and earnest solicitude in appreciating minds.

It is lamentable to consider how many parents there are—and how many teachers, even—who never thoughtfully consider *the ends* of human life, and *the means* which are necessarily connected therewith. Of those who are actually engaged in so developing the characters, and so establishing the habits of their children, and of their pupils, as materially to affect their weal or woe, for this life, not only, but while being endures—whether conscious of it or not—how few, comparatively, answer for themselves, or even seriously consider, these and like questions:

In what does a correct education consist? and, How can this education be best secured to the successive generations of men? What course of training is best calculated to fit *my children*, or *my pupils*, for the discharge of the various duties that will be incumbent on them as individuals, as social beings, as citizens of a free government, and as candidates for immortality? In considering these questions previously to the preparation of this volume, the author was led to treat the subject, in many respects, very differently from what most writers that preceded him had done.

In the present state of being, the *mind*, which constitutes the *real man*, dwells in a material body, for the purposes of development and culture, that it may thereby be prepared to enter most advantageously upon that higher life which awaits us in the future. The body, properly developed, with its five senses all in a state of healthy action, is the medium, and the *only* medium, through which a correct knowledge of God, as manifest in the material world, can be communicated to, and his likeness daguerreotyped upon, the mind. Hence the great prominence given in this volume to physical culture, and the right education of the senses, as constituting the true substratum for symmetrical and most successful mental development.

The author, in his present effort, has sought to awaken

a deeper interest with all classes of the community in behalf of *universal education*, and to inspire confidence in the redeeming power of improved Common Schools, which constitute the only reliable instrumentality for the proper training of the rising generation. He has endeavored so to present the subject of Education, which should have reference to the *whole man*—the body, the mind, and the heart—and so to unfold its nature, advantages, and claims, as to make it everywhere acceptable. Nay, more; he would have a *good common education* considered as the *inalienable right of every child in the community*, and have it placed *first among the necessaries of life.*

This work was first issued by Harper and Brothers, in 1850, under the title of "Popular Education;" but the right to publish having been recently transferred to A. S. Barnes & Company, who propose to add it to their valuable Teachers' Library, it has been deemed advisable to so change the title as to render it at once more specific, and more suggestive of the scope of its contents.

The author is not insensible to the favorable opinions which the press of our country, without regard to sect or party, have been pleased to express of the earlier editions of this work; nor to the cordial endorsement it has received from school officers and school teachers, from legislators, and from the earnest friends of education generally. These constitute the pleasing assurance that his efforts have not been entirely unsuccessful.

Hitherto this work has stood alone. But now, because of its appearing with a new name, with a new costume, and with new associates, it is hoped it may lose none of its old friends; for these changes are the result of circumstances not under its control. But, on the contrary, while it shall find new friends in persons possessing The Teachers' Library, as heretofore published, may it reciprocate the favor, and have the honor itself of extending, in turn, their favorable acquaintance among its early friends.

With this introduction we commend the work anew to the regards of the friends of the cause which it seeks to promote, while we suffer it again to go forth on its chosen mission, with the hope that it may contribute to a knowledge of *the means* which shall be instrumental in securing *the ends* attendant upon a correct *Universal Education.*

IRA MAYHEW.

ALBION, MICH., October, 1856.

CONTENTS.

UNIVERSAL EDUCATION.

CHAPTER I.

IN WHAT DOES A CORRECT EDUCATION CONSIST?

I call that education which embraces the culture of the whole man, with all his faculties—subjecting his senses, his understanding, and his passions to reason, to conscience, and to the evangelical laws of the Christian revelation.—De Fellenberg.

From the beginning of human records to the present time, the inferior animals have changed as little as the herbage upon which they feed, or the trees beneath which they find shelter. In one generation, they attain all the perfection of which their nature is susceptible. That Being without whose notice not even a sparrow falls to the ground, has provided for the supply of their wants, and has adapted each to the element in which it moves. To birds he has given a clothing of feathers; and to quadrupeds, of furs, adapted to their latitudes. Where art is requisite in providing food for future want, or in constructing a needful habitation, as in the case of the bee and the beaver, a peculiar aptitude has been bestowed, which, in all the inferior races of animals, has been found adequate to their necessities. The crocodile that issues from its egg in the warm sand, and never sees its parent, becomes, it has been well said, as perfect and as knowing as any crocodile.

Not so with man! "He comes into the world," says an eloquent writer, "the most helpless and dependent of living beings, long to continue so. If deserted by parents at an early age, so that he can learn only what the experience of one life may teach him—as to a few individuals has happened, who yet have attained matu rity in woods and deserts—he grows up in some respect inferior to the nobler brutes. Now, as regards many regions of the earth, history exhibits the early human inhabitants in states of ignorance and barbarism, not far removed from this lowest possible grade, which civilized men may shudder to contemplate. But these countries, occupied formerly by straggling hordes of miserable savages, who could scarcely defend themselves against the wild beasts that shared the woods with them, and the inclemencies of the weather, and the consequences of want and fatigue; and who to each other were often more dangerous than any wild beasts, unceasingly warring among themselves, and destroying each other with every species of savage, and even cannibal cruelty—countries so occupied formerly, are now become the abodes of myriads of peaceful, civilized, and friendly men, where the desert and impenetrable forest are changed into cultivated fields, rich gardens, and magnificent cities.

"It is the strong intellect of man, operating with the faculty of language as a means, which has gradually worked this wonderful change. By language, fathers communicated their gathered experience and reflections to their children, and these to succeeding children, with new accumulation; and when, after many generations, the precious store had grown until memory could contain no more, the arts of writing, and then of printing, arose, making language visible and permanent, and enlarging illimitably the repositories of knowledge. Language thus, at the present moment of the world's existence, may be said to bind the whole human race of uncounted millions into one gigantic rational being, whose memory reaches to the beginnings of written records, and retains imperishably the important events that have occurred; whose judgment, analyzing the treasures of memory, has discovered many of the sublime and unchanging laws of nature, and has built on them all the arts of life, and through them, piercing far into futurity, sees clearly many of the events that are to come; and whose eyes and ears, and observing mind at this moment, in every corner of the earth, are watching and recording new phenomena, for the purpose of still better comprehending the magnificence and beautiful order of creation, and of more worthily adoring its beneficent Author.

"It might be very interesting to show here, in minute detail, how the arts of civilization have progressed in accordance with the gradual increase of man's knowledge of the universe; but it would lead too far from the main subject." The preceding sketch may remind us of the low condition of man in a state of ignorance and barbarism, and of the high condition to which he may be brought by cultivation. We possess a material and an immaterial part, mutually dependent on each other. On one hand, we may well say to corruption, Thou art my father; and to the worm, Thou art my mother and my sister. On the other hand, the Psalmist says of man, Thou hast made him a little lower than the angels.

In the Scriptures we learn the origin and history of man—the subject of education. He was created in the image of his Maker. It was his delightful employment, in innocency, to dress the beautiful garden in which he dwelt. Presently we learn he transgressed. His subsequent career becomes infelicitous. In the earlier history of the human race, the days of his pilgrimage were protracted several hundred years. In process of time, because of the prevalence of sin, a universal deluge swept away the entire family of man, save *one*—a preacher of righteousness—and those of his household. Subsequently his days were shortened to three score years and ten. Much of this time is consumed in helpless infancy, in sleep, and in securing the necessary means of supporting animal life. This, it would seem, is calamity enough; but not so. Man finds himself beset with temptations on every side, to deepen and perpetuate his degradation, by giving reign to unbridled passion.

But a Light has shined upon his dark pathway, pointing him to a brighter country, and beckoning him thither. Under these adverse circumstances, it becomes the duty of the Educator to unfold the opening energies of his youthful charge; to mold their plastic character, and to assist their efforts in the recovery of that which was lost, and in the attainment of immortality and eternal life.

These are strong views, I am aware; but nothing less would be adequate to the nature and wants of man. In these views I am fully sustained by nearly every writer of any distinction in Europe and America. In a volume of prize essays on the expediency and means of elevating the profession of the educator in society, published in London, under the direction of the central society of education, one of the writers, introducing a quotation from an American author, says, I can not resist the pleasure of quoting a few of Alcott's brief sentences, by way of conclusion to the present division of the argument. The voice that has been sent athwart the Atlantic may find an echo in some British bosoms.

These are its words: "Education includes all those influences and disciplines by which the faculties of man are unfolded and perfected. It is that agency that takes the helpless and pleading infant from the hands of its Creator, and, apprehending its entire nature, tempts it forth, now by austere, and now by kindly influences and disciplines, and thus molds it at last into the image of a perfect man; armed at all points to use the body, nature, and life for its growth and renewal, and to hold dominion over the fluctuating things of the outward. It seeks to realize in the soul the image of the Creator. Its end is a perfect man. Its aim, through every stage of influence, is self-renewal. The body, nature, and life are its instruments and materials. Jesus is its worthiest ideal—Christianity its purest organ. The Gospels are its fullest text-book—genius is its inspiration—holiness its law—temperance its discipline—immortality its reward."

Says Dr. Howe, in a lecture before the American Institute of Instruction, "Education should have for its aim the development and greatest possible perfection of the whole nature of man: his moral, intellectual, and physical nature. My *beau ideal* of human nature would be a being whose intellectual faculties were active and enlightened; whose moral sentiments were dignified and firm; whose physical formation was healthy and beautiful: whoever falls short of this, in one particular—be it in but the least, beauty and vigor of body—falls short of the standard of perfection. To this standard, I believe, man is approaching; and I believe the time will soon be when specimens of it will not be rare."

The following thoughts are drawn from a treatise on the "Mental Illumination and Moral Improvement of Mankind," by that very judicious and celebrated writer, Dr. Dick, of Scotland. The education of human beings, considered in its most extensive sense, comprehends every thing which is requisite to the cultivation and improvement of the faculties bestowed upon them by the Creator. It ought to embrace every thing that has a tendency to strengthen and invigorate the animal system; to enlighten and expand the understanding; to regulate the feelings and dispositions of the heart; and, in general, to direct the moral powers in such a manner as to render those who are the subjects of instruction happy in themselves, useful members of society, and qualified for entering upon the scenes and employments of a future and more glorious existence.

It is a very common but absurd notion, and one that has been too long acted upon, that the education of youth terminates, or should terminate, about the age of thirteen or fourteen years. Hence, in an article on this subject in one of our encyclopedias, education is defined to be "that series of means by which the human understanding is gradually enlightened, between infancy and the period when we consider ourselves as qualified to take a part in active life, and, *ceasing to direct our views to the acquisition of new knowledge or the formation of new habits*, are content to act upon the principles we have already acquired."

This definition, though accordant with general opinion and practice, is certainly a very limited and defective view of the subject. In the ordinary mode of our scholastic instruction, education, so far from being *finished* at the age above stated, can scarcely be said to have *commenced*. The *key* of knowledge has indeed been put into the hands of the young; but they have never been taught to unlock the gates to the temple of science, to enter within its portals, to contemplate its treasures, and to feast their minds on the entertainments there provided. Several moral maxims have been impressed on their memories; but they have seldom been taught to appreciate them in all their bearings, or to reduce them to practice in the various and minute ramifications of their conduct. Besides, although every rational means were employed for training the youthful mind till the age above named, no valid reason can be assigned why regular instruction should cease at this early period.

Man is a progressive being ; his faculties are capable of an indefinite expansion ; the objects to which these faculties may be directed are boundless and infinitely diversified ; he is moving onward to an eternal world, and, in the present state, can never expect to grasp the universal system of created objects, or to rise to the highest point of moral excellence. His tuition, therefore, can not be supposed to terminate at any period of his terrestrial existence ; and the course of his life ought to be considered as nothing more than the course of his education. When he closes his eyes in death, and bids a last adieu to every thing here below, he passes into a more permanent and expansive state of existence, where his education will likewise be progressive, and where intelligences of a higher order may be his instructors ; and the education he received in this transitory scene, *if it was properly conducted,* will found the ground-work of all his future progressions in knowledge and virtue throughout the succeeding periods of eternity.

There are two very glaring defects which appear in most of our treatises on education. In the first place, the moral tuition of youthful minds, and the grand principles of religion which ought to direct their views and conduct, are either entirely overlooked, or treated of in so vague and general a manner, as to induce a belief that they are considered matters of very inferior moment ; and, in the business of teaching, and the superintendence of the young, the moral precepts of Christianity are seldom made to bear with particularity upon every malignant affection that manifests itself, and every minor delinquency that appears in their conduct, or to direct the benevolent affections how to operate in every given circumstance, and in all their intercourses and associations. In the next place, the idea that man is a being destined to an immortal existence, is almost, if not altogether overlooked. Volumes have been written on the best modes of training men for the profession of a soldier, of a naval officer, of a merchant, of a physician, of a lawyer, of a clergyman, and of a statesman; but I know of no treatise on this subject which, in connection with other subordinate aims, has for its grand object to develop that train of instruction which is most appropriate for man considered as a candidate for immortality. This is the more unaccountable, since, in the works alluded to, the eternal destiny of human beings is not called in question, and is sometimes referred to as a general position which can not be denied; yet the means of instruction requisite to guide them in safety to their final destination, and to prepare them for the employments of their everlasting abode, are either overlooked, or referred to in general terms, as if they were unworthy of particular consideration. To admit the doctrine of the immortality of the human soul, and yet to leave out the consideration of it, in a system of mental instruction, is both impious and preposterous, and inconsistent with the principle on which we generally act in other cases, which requires that affairs of the greatest moment should occupy our chief attention. If man is only a transitory inhabitant of this lower world; if he is journeying to another and more important scene of action and enjoyment; if his abode in this higher scene is to be permanent and eternal; and if the course of instruction through which he now passes has an important bearing on his happiness in that state, and his preparation for its enjoyments—if all this be true, then surely every system of education must be glaringly defective which either overlooks or throws into the shade the immortal destination of human beings.

If these sentiments be admitted as just, the education of the young becomes a subject of the highest importance. There can not be an object more interesting to Science, to Religion, and to general Christian society, than the forming of those arrangements, and the establishing of those institutions, which are calculated tc train the minds of all to knowledge and moral rectitude, and to guide their steps in the path which leads to a blessed immortality. In this process there is no period in human life that aught to be overlooked. We musi commence the work of instruction when the first dawning of reason begins to appear, and continue the process through all the succeeding periods of mortal existence, till the spirit takes its flight to the world unknown.

While we would bring clearly into view the nature of that education which is needful for man, considered as a candidate for immortality, we would by no means overlook those subordinate aims which have reference to his present condition, and the relations he sustains in this life. The two are so intimately connected, and sustain such a reciprocal relation to each other, that each is best secured by that system of training and in the use of those appliances by which the other is most successfully promoted. In training the rising generation for the proper discharge of their duty to themselves and to one another—as children, and subsequently as parents; as members of society and citizens of free and independent states—we at the same time best promote their interests as candidates for immortality. It is equally true that any system of education which omits to provide for man's highest and enduring wants as an immortal being, in a proportionate degree falls short of providing for his dearest interests and best good in this life.

The system of education which we should promote comprehends whatever may have any good influence in developing the mind, by giving direction to thought, or bias to motives of action. To lead infancy in the path of duty, to give direction to an immortal spirit, and to teach it to aspire by well-doing to the rewards of virtue, is the first step of instruction. To youth, education imparts that knowledge whose ways are usefulness and honor, and by due restraint and subordination, makes individual to intwine with public good in a just observance of laws, comprehending the path of duty. To manhood, it "leads him to reflect on the ties that unite him with friends, with kindred, and with the great family of mankind, and makes his bosom glow with social tenderness; it confirms the emotions of sympathy into habitual benevolence, imparts to him the elating delight of rejoicing with those who rejoice, and, if his means are not always adequate to the suggestions of his charity, soothes him at last with the melancholy pleasure of weeping with those who weep." To age, it gives consolation, by remembrance of the past, and anticipation of the future. Wisdom is drawn from experience, to give constancy to virtue; and amid all the vicissitudes of life, it enables him to repose unshaken confidence in that goodness which, by the arrangement of the universe, constantly incites him to perpetual progress in excellence and felicity. Education is the growth and improvement of the mind. Its great object is immediate and prospective happiness. That, then, is the best education which secures to the individual and to the world the greatest amount of permanent happiness, and that the best system which most effectually accomplishes this grand design. How far this is accomplished by the present systems of education is not easily determined, but that it fails in many important considerations can not admit of a doubt.

It is feared that, by a great majority, a wrong estimate is made of education. Is it not generally considered as a *means* which must be employed to accomplish *some other purpose*, and consequently made subservient and secondary to the employments of life? Is it not considered as being contained in books, and a certain routine of studies, which, when gone through with, is believed to be accomplished, and consequently laid by, to be used as interest may suggest or convenience demand? Education comprehends all the improvements of the mind from the cradle to the grave. Every man is what education has made him, whether he has drunk deep at the Pierian spring, or sipped at the humblest fountain. The philosopher, whose comprehensive mind can scan the universe, and read and interpret the phenomena of nature; whose heaven-aspiring spirit can soar beyond the boundaries of time, indulge in the anticipation of immortality, and discern in the past, the present, and the future the all-pervading spirit of benevolence, is equally the child of education with him whose soul proud science never taught to feel its wants, and know how little may be known.

As we have already said, man possesses a material and an immaterial part, mutually dependent on each other. These are so intimately connected, and sustain such a reciprocal relation to each other, that neither can be neglected without detriment to both. The body continually modifies the state of the mind, and the mind ever varies the condition of the body. Mental and physical training should, then, go together. That system of instruction which relates exclusively to either, is a partial system, and its fate must be that of a house divided against itself. Education has reference to the *whole man.* It seeks to make him a complete creature after his kind, giving to both mind and body all the power, all the beauty, and all the perfection of which they are capable.

Our systems of education have hitherto fallen far short of this high and only true standard. Education, in too many instances, has been confined, almost entirely, to either the physical, intellectual, or moral energies of men. With the greater part, it has been limited to the *physical powers.* No effort has been made to develop any but their bodily strength, animal passions, and instinctive feelings. Accordingly, the great mass of mankind are raised but little above inferior animals. They labor hard, and boast of their strength; gratify their passions, and glory in their shame; eat and drink, sleep and wake, supposing to-morrow will be like the present. They are scarcely aware of their rational, intellectual powers, much less of their ever-expanding and never-dying spirits; consequently they feel but imperfectly their responsibility, and are governed principally by the fear of human authority. They have been taught to fear or reverence nothing higher. Their education is confined to animal feeling—physical energies. They have no conception of any thing beyond. The whole intellectual world, and all hereafter, is narrowed down to the animal feeling of the present time. How erroneous! How badly educated! And what are we to anticipate when only the physical energies of men generally are thus developed? Why, surely, what we are beginning to witness—namely, physical power, trampling on all authority.

The education of others is confined principally to *intellect.* Not that their physical powers are not necessarily more or less developed, but that their attention is directed almost exclusively to intellectual attainments. From the earliest infancy their minds are taxed, though their bodies are neglected, and their souls forgotten. Nor is it unfrequent that their physical strength gives way under the constant pressure of intellectual studies. And thus they are subjected to all the evils of physical inability—the sufferings of living death, in consequence of an erroneous education. Besides, they are destitute of all those kinder feelings and sympathetic emotions which alone result from the cultivation of the moral susceptibilities, and become insensible to the more delicate affections of the soul, and elevating hopes of the truly virtuous. They have nothing on which to rest for enjoyment but intellectual attainments. And even these are small compared with what they might have been under a different course of education. Yet with what delight are the first developments of intellect discovered by the natural guardian of the infant mind! and with what anxious solicitude are they watched through advancing youth and manhood by those employed in their education. In either stage the development of intellect alone seems worthy of an effort. And yet, when carried to the utmost, what may we expect of one destitute of virtue, and without strength of body? Little to benefit himself or others. Like Columbus, Franklin, or La Place, he may employ his intellect in useful discoveries; or, like Hume, Voltaire, and Paine, to curse the world. In either case he may lead astray, and should never be trusted implicitly. As the bark on the ocean without compass or chart, that rides out the storm or sinks to the bottom, he may guide us in safety, or ruin us forever!

The education of others, again, is confined mostly to their *moral energies.* Those of the body are almost forgotten, only as nature forces their development upon the reluctant soul within. And those of intellect are deemed unworthy of a thought, except as necessary in the rudest stages of society; while the moral susceptibilities are cultivated to the utmost. They are brought into action in every situation. They are employed in private, in the social circle, and around the public altar. Nor are those employing them ever satisfied. They become fanatics—religious enthusiasts. They have zeal without knowledge, and seem resolved on bringing all to their standard. They enlist in the work all the sympathies of the soul—its tenderest sensibilities and most compassionate feelings. Without intellect to guide, and physical strength to sustain them, they sink under moral excitement, and become deranged: a result that might be anticipated from such an education; and one that is often developed, in some of its milder features, among the reformers of the day. Nor may you reason with them. Reckless of consequences and regardless of authority, they are not to be convinced or persuaded. They are right, and *know* they are right, for the plain reason that they know nothing else, and will not be diverted from their course. What degradation! Who would not shrink from such an education? the development of the moral energies merely? It never qualified men for the highest attainment—the utmost dignity of which they are susceptible.

Diversified as are the developments of human character, and dissimilar as they may appear to the careless observer, there are peculiar characteristics of men that render them similar to one another, and unlike every other being. In their natures, original susceptibilities, and ultimate destinies, they are alike. They are material, intellectual, and spiritual; animal, rational and immortal. On these uniform traits of character education should be based. It should develop and strengthen the animal functions; classify and improve the rational faculties; and purify and elevate the spiritual affections in harmonious proportion and perfect symmetry.

The animal functions of the human system are to be developed and strengthened by education. Hitherto they have been assigned to the province of nature, and deemed foreign to the objects of education. But a more unphilosophical and dangerous theory has seldom been embraced, as the melancholy results abundantly testify. We shall therefore devote a chapter to physical education, which seems to lie at the foundation of the great work of human improvement; for, as we have seen, in the present state the mind can manifest itself only through the body; after which we shall proceed to the consideration of the other grand divisions of the great work of education.

CHAPTER II.

THE IMPORTANCE OF PHYSICAL EDUCATION.

The influence of the physical frame upon the intellect, morals, and happiness of a human being, is now universally admitted. The extent of this influence will be thought greater in proportion to the accuracy with which the subject is examined. Bodily pain forms a large proportion of the amount of human misery. It is, therefore, of the highest importance that a child should grow up sound and healthy in body, with the utmost degree of muscular strength that education can communicate.—LALOR.

THE importance of the department of the great work of education which we now approach has not hitherto been duly appreciated by parents and teachers generally. I shall therefore devote more space to this subject than is usual in works on education, but not more, I trust, than its relative importance demands. Physical, intellectual, and moral education are so intimately connected, that, in order duly to appreciate the importance of either, we must not view it separate and alone merely, but in connection with both of the others. And especially is this true of physical education. However much value, then, we may attach to it on its own account, considering man as a corporeal being, we shall have occasion greatly to magnify its importance when we come to direct our attention to his intellectual culture, and still more when we view it in connection with his moral training. Then, and not till then, shall we be enabled, in some degree, properly to appreciate the importance of physical education.

It has been objected, says Dr. Combe,* that to teach any one how to take care of his own health, is sure to

* Principles of Physiology applied to the Preservation of Health.

do harm, by making him constantly think of this and the other precaution, to the utter sacrifice of every noble and generous feeling, and to the certain production of peevishness and discontent. The result, however, he adds, is exactly the reverse; and it would be a singular anomaly in the constitution of the moral world were it otherwise. He who is instructed in, and is familiar with grammar and orthography, writes and spells so easily and accurately as scarcely to be conscious of attending to the rules by which he is guided; while he, on the contrary, who is not instructed in either, and knows not how to arrange his sentences, toils at the task, and sighs at every line. The same principle holds in regard to health. He who is acquainted with the general constitution of the human body, and with the laws which regulate its action, sees at once his true position when exposed to the causes of disease, decides what ought to be done, and thereafter feels himself at liberty to devote his undivided attention to the calls of higher duties. But it is far otherwise with the person who is destitute of this information. Uncertain of the nature and extent of the danger, he knows not to which hand to turn, and either lives in the fear of mortal disease, or, in his ignorance, resorts to irrational and hurtful precautions, to the certain neglect of those which he ought to use. It is ignorance, therefore, and not knowledge, which renders an individual full of fancies and apprehensions, and robs him of his usefulness. It would be a stigma on the Creator's wisdom if true knowledge weakened the understanding, and led to injurious results. Those who have had the most extensive opportunities of forming an opinion on this subject from extensive experience, bear unequivocal testimony to the advantages which knowledge confers in saving health and life, time and anxiety

If, indeed, ignorance were itself a preventive of the danger, or could provide a remedy when it approached, then it might well be said that "ignorance is bliss;" but as it gives only the kind of security which shutting the eyes affords against the dangers of a precipice, and consequently leaves its victim doubly exposed, it is high time to renounce its protection, and to seek those of a more powerful and beneficent ally. Every medical man can testify that, natural character and other circumstances being alike, those whose knowledge is the most limited are the fullest of whims and fancies: the most credulous respecting the efficacy of every senseless and preposterous remedy; the most impatient of restraint, and the most discontented at suffering.

If any of my readers be still doubtful of the propriety or safety of communicating physiological knowledge to the public at large, continues the author from whom we last quoted, and think that ignorance is in all circumstances to be preferred, I would beg leave to ask him whether it was knowledge or ignorance which induced the poorer classes in every country of Asia and Europe to attempt to protect themselves from cholera by committing ravages on the medical attendants of the sick, under the plea of their having poisoned the public fountains? And whether it was ignorance or knowledge which prompted the more rational part of the community to seek safety in increased attention to proper food, warmth, cleanliness, and clothing? In both cases, the desire of safety and sense of danger were the same, but the modes resorted to by each were as different in kind as in result, the efficacy of the one having formed a glaring contrast to the failure of the other.

Dr. Southwood Smith, the able author of a volume

entitled "The Philosophy of Health," says, The obvious and peculiar advantages of this kind of knowledge are, that it would enable its possessor to take a more rational care of his health; to perceive why certain circumstances are beneficial or injurious; to understand, in some degree, the nature of disease, and the operation as well of the agents which produce it as of those which counteract it; to observe the first beginnings of deranged function in his own person; to give to his physician a more intelligible account of his train of morbid sensations, as they arise; and, above all, to co-operate with him in removing the morbid state on which they depend, instead of defeating, as is now, through ignorance, constantly the case, the best concerted plans for the renovation of health. It would likewise lay the foundation for the attainment of a more just, accurate, and practical knowledge of our *intellectual* and *moral nature*. There is a *physiology* of the *mind* as well as of the *body*, and both are so intimately united that neither can be well understood without the study of the other. The physiology of man comprehends both. Were even what is already known of this science and what might be easily communicated made a part of general education, how many evils would be avoided! how much light would be let in upon the understanding! and how many aids would be afforded to the acquisition of a sound body and a vigorous mind! prerequisites more important than are commonly supposed to the attainment of wisdom and the practice of virtue.

Human physiology, says Dr. Combe, in his admirable treatise on that subject, from which I have already quoted, is as important in its practical consequences as it is attractive to rational curiosity. In its widest sense, it comprehends an exposition of the functions of the various organs of which the human frame is composed; of the mechanism by which they are carried on; of their relations to each other, or the means of improving their development and action; of the purposes to which they ought severally to be directed, and of the manner in which exercise ought to be conducted, so as to secure for the organ the best health, and for the function the highest efficacy. A true system of physiology comes thus to be the proper basis, not only of a sound *physical*, but of a sound *moral* and *intellectual* education, and of a rational hygiene; or, in other words, it is the basis of every thing having for its object the physical and mental health and improvement of man; for, so long as life lasts, the mental and moral powers with which he is endowed manifest themselves through the medium of organization, and no plan which he can devise for their cultivation, that is not in harmony with the laws which regulate that organization, can possibly be successful.

Let it not be said that knowledge of this description is superfluous to the unprofessional reader; for society groans under the load of suffering inflicted by causes susceptible of removal, but left in operation in consequence of our unacquaintance with our own structure, and of the relation of different parts of the system to each other and to external objects. Every medical man must have felt and lamented the ignorance so generally prevalent in regard to the simplest functions of the animal system, and the consequent absence of the judicious co-operation of friends in the care and cure of the sick. From ignorance of the commonest facts in physiology, or from want of ability to appreciate their importance, men of much good sense in every other respect not only subject themselves unwittingly to the active causes of disease, but give their sanction to laws and practices destructive equally to life and to morality, and which, if they saw them in their true light, they would shrink from countenancing in the slightest degree.

Were the intelligent classes of society better acquainted with the functions of the human body and the aws by which they are regulated, continues this judicious writer, the sources of much suffering would be dried up, and the happiness of the community at large would be essentially promoted. Medical men would no longer be consulted so exclusively for the cure of disease, but would be called upon to advise regarding the best means of strengthening the constitution, from an early period, against any accidental or hereditary susceptibility which might be ascertained to exist. More attention would be paid to the *preservation* of health than is at present practicable, and the medical man would then be able to advise with increased effect, because he would be proportionally well understood, and his counsel, in so far, at least, as it was based on accurate observation and a right application of principles, would be perceived to be, not a mere human opinion, but, in reality, an *exposition of the will and intentions of a beneficent Creator*, and would therefore be felt as carrying with it an *authority* to which, as the mere dictum of a fallible fellow-creature, it could never be considered as entitled.

It is true that, as yet, medicine has been turned to little account in the way of directly promoting the physical and mental welfare of man. But the day is, perhaps, not far distant, when, in consequence of the improvements both in professional and general education now in progress, a degree of interest will be attached to this application of its doctrines far surpassing what those who have not reflected on the subject will be able to imagine as justly belonging to it, but by no means exceeding that which it truly deserves.

Every person should be acquainted with the organization, structure, and functions of his own body—the house in which he lives: he should know the conditions of health, and the causes of the numerous diseases that flesh is heir to, in order to avoid them, prolong his life, and multiply his means of usefulness. If these things are not otherwise learned, they should be taught—the elements of them at least—in our primary schools. This instruction would come, perhaps, most appropriately from the members of the medical profession. But either society generally, or physicians themselves, or both, have mistaken the true sphere of a physician's usefulness, and what ought to constitute the grand object of his profession, namely, the *prevention of disease,* and the *general improvement of the health,* and not the CURING of diseases merely. The physician, like the clergyman in his parish, should receive a salary; and he should be occupied, chiefly, in teaching the laws of health to his employers; in imparting to them instruction in relation to the means of avoiding the diseases to which they are more particularly exposed, and in laying before them such information as shall be needful, in order to the highest improvement of their physical organization, and the transmission to posterity of unimpaired constitutions. This he may do by public lectures, at suitable seasons of the year; and by visiting from house to house, and imparting such information as may be particularly needed. The physician should not allow any of his employers blindly to disregard the laws of health, or, knowing them, to violate them unreproved. ***He*** should be accounted the ***best physician,*** other things being equal, whose employers have the ***least sickness,*** and uniformly enjoy the ***best*** *health.* When the relation existing between the members of the medical profession and the well-being of society generally comes to be better understood, and physicians are employed in accordance with the principles just stated, their greatest usefulness to the communities they serve will be found to consist in teaching well men and women how to retain and improve their health, and rear a healthy offspring, and not in partially curing diseased persons who are constantly violating the laws of health. These views will doubtless be new to many of my readers, and seem to them very strange! But let me inquire of such what they would think of the clergyman who should neglect to instruct his parishioners in the ennobling doctrines of morality and religion, and should suffer them to go on in sin unrebuked, until they become a burden to themselves? who should wait until his counsels were solicited before he sounds the note of alarm, and points the guilty sinner to "the Lamb of God which taketh away the sin of the world?" and who should confine his labors almost entirely to *condemned criminals?* Such conduct on the part of clergymen would doubtless be regarded by these very persons as passing strange! The course commonly pursued in the employment of physicians is equally unphilosophical, and floods society with a legion of evils—physical and intellectual, social and moral—three fourths of which might be avoided, by the proper exercise of the medical profession, in *one generation;* and ultimately, nineteen twentieths, if not ninety-nine one hundredths of them. As I have already said, this instruction would come, perhaps, most appropriately from the members of the medical profession. But if these things are not taught elsewhere, I repeat it, they should be taught—the elements of them at least—in our primary schools.

I can not better enforce the importance of physica education than by quoting from a lecture "on the edu cation of the blind," by one of the most distinguished practical educators* in this country. "That the proportion of the blind to the whole population might be diminished by wise social regulations, and by the dissemination of knowledge of the organic laws of man, there is not a doubt; but whether the time has come, or ever will come, is another question. At any rate, to so enlightened a body† as I have the honor of addressing, suggestions of methods by which the extent of blindness may be limited will neither be misapplied, nor liable to offend a mawkish sensibility. That the blindness of a large proportion of society is a social evil will not be denied, nor will the right which society has to diminish that proportion be questioned. But how? in a very simple way; by preventing the transmission of an hereditary blindness to another generation; by preventing the marriage of those who are congenitally blind, or who have lost their sight by reason of hereditary weakness of the visual organs, which disqualifies them to resist the slightest inflammation or injury in childhood.

"I am aware that many people would condemn this proposition as cruel, because it might add to the sadness of the sufferers; and that the whole seven thousand five hundred blind in this country would rise up and scout it, as barbarous and unnatural; for I have experienced the effects of contradiction to the wills of individual blind persons in this respect. But my rule is, the good of the community before that of the individual; the good of the race before that of the com-

* Dr. Samuel G. Howe, director of the New England Institution for the Education of the Blind, 1836.

† The American Institute of Instruction.

munity. To give you an instance: the city of Boston, with a population of eighty thousand, is represented in the Institution for the Blind by two blind children only; and I know of but four in the whole population; while Andover, with but five thousand, is fully and ably represented by seven;* and it has three more growing up.

"Now how is this? Why, the blind of Andover are mostly from a common stock; three of them are born of one mother, who has had four blind children. Another of the pupils is cousin, in the first degree, to these three; and two other pupils are cousins in a remote degree. Then, from other places, there are two brothers, who have a third at home. There is one blind girl, who has two blind sisters at home. Then there are two pairs of sisters.

"In the immediate vicinity of Boston, I know of a family in which blindness is hereditary; the last generation there were five. Of these five one is married, and has four children, not one of whom can see well enough to read; and if the others marry, they may increase the number to twelve or twenty.

"Now apply this state of things to the whole country, and have you any difficulty in conceiving how it happens that there are seven thousand five hundred blind in the United States? And can you doubt whether or not this great proportion of blind to the whole community might not be considerably diminished, if men and women understood the organic laws of their nature? understood that, very often, blindness is the punishment following an infringement of the natural laws of God; and if they could be made to act upon the holy Christian principles, that we should deny

* This makes the ratio of representation in the institution from Andover *fifty six times greater* than from the city of Boston.

ourselves any individual gratification, any selfish desire, that may result in evil to the whole community?

"I would that every individual whom I have the honor to address would assist in the education of the blind, so far as to give them just and Christian views of this subject. I would that all should work for society; not for society to-day alone, but for the society of future ages; not in any one narrow, partial way, but upon a broad scale, and in every way in which they can be useful. If a person congenitally blind, or strongly predisposed to become so, or one who marries a person so born or so disposed, has blind offspring in consequence of it, I ask, is he not as responsible, in a moral point of view, for the infirmity of his children as though he had put out their eyes with his own hands?

"You may suppose, perhaps, that the infirmity of blindness would incapacitate sufferers from winning the affections of seeing persons; and that, with respect to two blind persons, the sense of incapacity to support a family would prevent them from uniting themselves. In the first place, I answer, that seeing people do no better than the blind. Even a blind man may perceive that many marriages are mere matters of course, resulting from juxtaposition of parties; and rarely matters where the purer affections and higher moral sentiments are consulted. And, in the second place, that incapacity of supporting a family will not weigh a feather in the balance with desire, unless the intellectual and moral nature is enlightened and cultivated. Do we not see, every day, cases of misery entailed upon whole families, because one of the parties had overlooked or disregarded *moral infirmity*, which ought to have been a greater objection than any *physical defect*—than even blindness or deafness?

"But no process of reasoning is required, for there stand the facts. The blind not only seek for partners in life, but are sometimes sought by seeing persons; and numerous instances have occurred within my knowledge. It is true, that despair of success in any other quarter, or an equally unworthy motive, may induce some to seek for partners among the blind, or the blind to unite with the blind; but still, there is the evil.

"My observation induces me to think that the blind, far more than seeing persons, are fond of social relations, and desirous of family endearments. A moment's thought would induce one to conclude that this would naturally be the case; a moment's observation convinces one that it is so. Now I have found among them some of the most pious, intelligent, and disinterested beings I ever knew; but hardly more than one who was prepared to forego the enjoyments of domestic relations. And how can we expect them to be so, more than seeing people? The fact is, but very few persons in the community give any attention to the laws of their organic nature, and the tendency to hereditary transmission of infirmities. Very few consider that they owe more to society than to their individual selves; that if we are to love our neighbor *as ourself*, we must, of course, love *all* our neighbors, collectively, more than the single unit which each one calls I.

"I would that considerations of this kind had more weight with the community generally. I would that the subject were more attended to, and that the violation of the laws of our organic nature were less frequent in our country. There is one great and crying evil in our system of education; it is, that but part of man's nature is educated, and that our colleges and schools doom young men for years to an uninterrupted and severe exercise of the intellectual faculties, to the comparative neglect of their moral, and still more of their physical nature. Nay, not only do they *neglect* their physical nature—they ABUSE it; they sin against themselves and against God; and though they sin in ignorance, they do not escape the penalties of His violated laws. Hence you see them pale, and wan, and feeble; hence you find them acknowledging, when too late, the effects of severe application. But do they acknowledge it humbly and repentingly, as with a consciousness of sin? No, they often do it with a secret exultation, with a lurking feeling that you will say or think, 'Poor fellow, his mind is too much for his body!' Nonsense! his mind is too weak; his knowledge too limited; he is an imperfect man; he knows not his own nature. But if he has no conscientiousness, no scruple about impairing his own health and sowing the seeds of disease, he has less about entailing them upon others. And a consumptive young man or woman—the son or daughter of consumptive parents—hesitates not to spread the evil in society, and entail puny faces, weakness, pain, and early death upon several individuals, and punish their children for their own sins.

"Is this picture too high-colored? Alas! no. And if I showed you satisfactorily that sin against the organic laws caused so great a proportion of blindness, how much more readily will you grant that the same sin gives to so many of our population the narrow chest, the hectic flush, the hollow cough, which makes the *victim doomed*, by his *parent*, to consumption and early death! Do you not see, every Sabbath, at church, the young man or woman, upon whose fair and delicate structure the peculiar impress of the EARLY DOOMED is stamped? and as a slight but hollow cough comes upon your ear, does it not recall the death-knell which rang in the same sad note before to the father or mother? Who of you has not followed some young friend to his long resting-place, and found that the grass had not grown rank upon the grave of his brother? that the row of white marbles, beneath which slept his parents and sisters, were yet glistering in freshness, and that the letters which told their names and their early death seemed clear as if cut but yesterday?

"They tell us that physical education is attended to in this country; and yet, where is the teacher, where is the clergyman even, who dares to step forth in these cases, and say to those who are *doomed*, you must not and shall not marry? and where are the young men and women who would listen to them if they did? It is not that they are wanting in conscientiousness; they may be conscientious and disinterested; but they do not know that they are doing wrong, because they are not acquainted with the organic laws of their nature. All that is done in schools or colleges toward physical education is the mere strengthening of the muscular system by muscular exercise; but this is not half enough. These remarks may be deemed irrelevant to my subject, but they can not be lost to an audience whose highest interest is the education of man; and if I am mistaken in supposing that little attention has been paid to the subject, its importance will guaranty its repetition."

Before dismissing this subject, I will introduce two additional quotations from American authors, whose opinions are received by the medical profession in this country not only, but throughout Europe. In both instances, I copy from works published in Great Britain, into which the opinions of these American writers have been quoted. In regard to hereditary transmission, Dr. Caldwell observes: "Every constitutional quality, whether good or bad, may descend, by inheritance, from parent to child. And a long-continued habit of drunkenness becomes as essentially constitutional as a predisposition to gout or pulmonary consumption. This increases, in a manifold degree, the responsibility of parents in relation to temperance. By habits of intemperance, they not only degrade and ruin *themselves*, but transmit the elements of like degradation and ruin to their posterity. This is no visionary conjecture, the fruit of a favorite and long-cherished theory. It is a settled belief resulting from observation—an inference derived from innumerable facts. In hundreds and thousands of instances, parents, having had children born to them while their habits were temperate, have become afterward intemperate, and had other children subsequently born. In such cases, it is a matter of notoriety that the younger children have become addicted to the practice of intoxication much more frequently than the older, in the proportion of five to one. Let me not be told that this is owing to the younger children being neglected, and having corrupt and seducing examples constantly before them. The same neglects and profligate examples have been extended to all, yet all have not been equally injured by them. The children of the earlier births have escaped, while those of the subsequent ones have suffered. The reason is plain. The latter children had a deeper animal taint than the former."—*Transylvania Journal.*

Physiologists in general coincide in the belief that a vigorous and healthy physical and mental constitution in the parents communicates existence in the most perfect state to their offspring, while impaired constitutions, from whatever cause, are transmitted to posterity. In this sense, all who are competent to judge are agreed that the Giver of life is a jealous God, visiting the iniquity of the fathers upon the children unto the third and fourth generation of them that hate him or violate his laws. Strictly speaking, it is not *disease* which is transmitted, but organs of such imperfect structure that they are unable to perform their functions properly, and so weak as to be easily put into a morbid state or abnormal condition by causes which unimpaired organs are able to resist.

My last quotation on this point is from a lecture delivered by Dr. Warren before the American Institute of Instruction, copied into the "Schoolmaster," a work published in London under the superintendence of the Society for the Diffusion of Useful Knowledge:

"Let me conclude by entreating your attention to a revision of the existing plans of education in what relates to the preservation of health. Too much of the time of the better educated part of young persons is, in my humble opinion, devoted to literary pursuits and sedentary occupations, and too little to the acquisition of the corporeal powers indispensable to make the former practically useful. If the present system does not undergo some change, I much apprehend we shall see a degenerate and sinking race, such as came to exist among the higher classes in France before the Revolution, and such as now deforms a large part of the noblest families in Spain;* but if the spirit of improvement, so happily awakened, continues—as I trust it will—to animate those concerned in the formation of the young members of society, we shall soon be able, I doubt not, to exhibit an active, beautiful, and wise generation, of which the age may be proud."

* I am informed by a lady who passed a long time at the Spanish court, in a distinguished situation, that the grandees have deteriorated by their habits of living, and the restriction of intermarriages to their own rank, to a race of dwarfs; and, though fine persons are sometimes seen among them, they, when assembled at court, appear to be a group of manikins.

CHAPTER III.

PHYSICAL EDUCATION. THE LAWS OF HEALTH.

If man is ever to be elevated to the highest and happiest condition which his nature will permit, it must be, in no small degree, by the improvement—I might say, the redemption—of his physical powers. But knowledge on any subject must precede improvement.—ALCOTT.

Physical and moral health are as nearly related as the body and the soul.—HUFELAND'S *Art of Prolonging Life*.

IF the reader is persuaded that the views presented in the last chapter on the importance of physical education are truthful—and they are concurred in by physiologists generally—he will naturally desire to become acquainted with the *laws of health*, that, by yielding obedience to them, he may improve his physical condition, and most successfully promote his intellectual and moral well-being. I might, then, here refer to some of the many excellent treatises on this subject; but I shall probably better accomplish the object for which this work has been undertaken by presenting, within as narrow limits as practicable, a summary of these laws.

In every department of nature, *waste* is invariably the result of *action*. In mechanics, we seek to reduce the waste consequent upon action to the lowest possible degree; but to prevent it entirely is beyond the power of man. Every breath of wind that passes over the surface of the earth, modifies the bodies with which it comes in contact. The great toe of the bronze statue of Saint Peter at Rome has been reduced, it is said, to less than half its original size by the successive kisses of the faithful.

In *dead* or *inanimate* matter, the destructive influence of action is constantly forced upon our attenticn by every thing passing around us, and so much human ingenuity is exercised to counteract its effects that no reflecting person will dispute the universality of its operation. But when we observe shrubs and trees waving in the wind, and animals undergoing violent exertion, year after year, and continuing to increase in size, we may be inclined, on a superficial view, to regard *living* bodies as constituting an exception to this rule. On more careful examination, however, it will appear that waste goes on in living bodies not only without intermission, but with a rapidity immeasurably beyond that which occurs in inanimate objects.

In the vegetable world, for instance, every leaf of a tree is incessantly pouring out some of its fluids, and every flower forming its own fruit and seed, speedily to be separated from, and lost to its parent stem; thus causing in a few months an extent of waste many hundred times greater than what occurs in the same lapse of time after the tree is cut down, and all its living operations are at a close.

The same thing holds true in the animal kingdom. so long as life continues, a copious exhalation from the skin, the lungs, the bowels, and the kidneys goes on without a moment's intermission, and not a movement can be performed which does not in some degree increase the circulation, and add to the general waste. In this way, during violent exertion, several ounces of the fluids of the body are sometimes thrown out by perspiration in a very few minutes; whereas, after life is extinguished, all the excretions cease, and waste is limited to that which results from ordinary chemical decomposition.*

* For the views presented in the preceding paragraph (as also in sev

So far, then, the law that waste is attendant on action applies to both dead and living bodies; but beyond this point a remarkable difference between them presents itself. In the physical or inanimate world, what is once lost or worn away *is lost forever;* but *living* bodies, whether vegetable or animal, possess the distinguishing characteristic of being able to *repair their own waste* and add to their own substance. The possession of such a power is essential to their existence But there is a wide difference between them in other respects. In surveying the respective modes of existence of vegetables and of animals, we perceive the fixity of position of the one, and the free locomotive power of the other. The vegetable grows, flourishes, and dies, fixed to the same spot of earth from which it sprang. However much external circumstances change around it, it must remain and submit to their influence. At all hours and at all seasons, it is at home, and in direct communication with the soil from which its nourishment is extracted. But it is otherwise with animals: these not only enjoy the privilege of locomotion, but are compelled to use it, and often to go a distance in search of food and shelter. The necessity for a constant change of place being imposed on them, a different arrangement became indispensable for their nutrition. The method which the Creator has provided is not less admirable than simple. To enable animals to move about, and at the same time to maintain a connection with their food, they are provided with a stomach. In this receptacle they can store up a supply of materials from which sustenance may be gradually

eral that follow) I would acknowledge my indebtedness to Dr. Andrew Combe's treatise on the "Physiology of Digestion." From the "Principles of Physiology," by the same author, I have already quoted. These admirable works will prove an invaluable treasure to persons desirous of becoming acquainted with the laws of health.

elaborated during a period of time proportioned to their necessities and mode of life. Animals thus *carry with them* nourishment adequate to their wants; and the small nutritive vessels imbibe their food from the internal surface of the stomach and bowels, where it is stored up, just as the roots or nutritive vessels of vegetables do from the soil in which they grow. The possession of a stomach or receptacle for food is accordingly a distinguishing characteristic of the animal system.

The sole objects of nutrition being to repair waste and to admit of growth, the Creator has so arranged that within certain limits it is always most vigorous when growth or waste proceeds with the greatest rapidity. Even in vegetables this provision is distinctly observable. It is also strikingly apparent in animals. Whenever growth is proceeding rapidly, or the animal is undergoing much exertion and expenditure of material, an increased quantity of food is invariably required. On the other hand, where no new substance is forming, and where, from bodily inactivity, little loss is sustained, a comparatively small supply will suffice. In endowing animals with the sense of *appetite*, including the sensation of hunger and thirst, the Creator has effectually provided against any inconvenience which might otherwise exist, and given to them a guide in relation to both the quality and quantity of food needful for them, and the times of partaking of it, with that beneficence which distinguishes all his works. He has not only provided an effectual safeguard in the sensations of hunger and thirst, but he has attached to their regulated indulgence a degree of pleasure which never fails to insure attention to their demands, and which, in highly-civilized communities, is apt to lead to excessive gratification. Their end is manifestly to proclaim that nourishment is required for the support of the system. When the body is very actively exercised, and a good deal of waste is effected by perspiration and exhalation from the lungs, the appetite becomes keener, and more urgent for immediate gratification; and if it is indulged, we eat with a relish unknown on other occasions, and afterward experience a sensation of internal comfort pervading the frame, as if every individual part of the body were imbued with a feeling of contentment and satisfaction; the very opposite of the restless discomfort and depression which come upon us, and extend over the whole system, when appetite is disappointed. There is, in short, an obvious and active sympathy between the condition and bearing of the stomach, and those of every part of the animal frame; in virtue of which, hunger is felt very keenly when the general system stands in urgent need of repair, and very moderately when no waste has been suffered.

We have seen that *waste* is every where attendant upon *action*, and that the object of nutrition is to repair waste and admit of growth. We come now to consider the ***Process of Digestion.***

All articles used for food necessarily undergo several changes before they are fitted to constitute a part of the body. In the process of digestion, four different changes should be noticed. More might be specified.

1. Mastication.—The first step in the preparation of food for imparting nourishment to the system consists in proper mastication, or chewing. Food should be thoroughly masticated before it is taken into the stomach. This is necessary in order to break it up and reduce it to a sufficient degree of fineness for the efficient action of the gastric juice. Besides, the action o. chewing and the presence of nutrient food constitute a healthful stimulus to the salivary glands, situated in

the mouth. By this means, also, the food not only becomes well masticated, but has blended with it a proper amount of saliva, upon both of which conditions the healthy action of the stomach depends. We have here another illustration of the beneficence of the Creator, who has kindly so arranged that the very act of mastication gratifies taste, the mouth being the seat of this sensation. But if we disregard these benevolent laws, and introduce unmasticated food into the stomach, the gastric juice can act only upon its surface, and changes of a purely chemical nature frequently commence in food thus swallowed before digestion can take place. Hence frequently arise—and especially in children and persons of delicate constitution—pains, nausea, and acidity, consequent on the continued presence of undigested aliment in the stomach.

2. Chymification.—As soon as food has been thoroughly masticated and impregnated with saliva, it is ready for transmission to the stomach. This interesting part of the process of digestion, called deglutition or swallowing, is most easily and pleasantly performed, when the alimentary morsel has been well masticated and properly softened, not by drink, which should never be taken at this time, but by saliva. When the food reaches the stomach, it is converted into a soft, pulpy mass, called *chyme;* and the process by which this change is effected is called *chymification.* This is the second principal step in digestion, and is effected immediately by the action of the *gastric juice.* This powerful solvent is secreted by the gastric glands, which are excited to action by the presence of food in the stomach. In health, the gastric secretion always bears a direct relation to the quantity of aliment required by the system. If too much food is taken into the stomach, indigestion is sure to follow, for the sufficient reason

that the gastric juice is unable to dissolve it. This is true even when food has been well masticated; but it becomes strikingly apparent when a full meal has been hastily swallowed, both mastication and insalivation having been imperfectly performed.

The time usually occupied in the process of chymification, when food has been properly masticated, varies from *three to four hours.* Digestion is sometimes effected in less time, as in the case of rice, and pigs' feet soused; but it more commonly requires a longer period, as in the case of salt pork and beef, and many other articles of food, both animal and vegetable.

By the alternate contraction and relaxation of the muscular coat of the stomach, which is excited to action by the presence of food, a kind of churning motion is communicated to its contents that greatly promotes digestion; for by this means every portion of food in turn is brought in contact with the gastric juice as it is discharged from the internal surface of the stomach. This motion continues until the contents of the stomach are converted into chyme, and conveyed into the first intestine, where they undergo another important change.

3. Chylification.—As fast as chyme is formed, it is expelled by the contractile power of the stomach into the *duodenum,* or first intestine. It there meets with the *bile* from the liver, and with the pancreatic juice. By the action of these agents, the chyme is converted into two distinct portions: a milky white fluid, called *chyle,* and a thick yellow residue. This process is called *chylification,* or *chyle-making.* The chyle is then taken up by the absorbent vessels, which are extensively ramified over the inner membrane or lining of the bowels. From the white color of the contents of these vessels, they have been named *lacteals* or *milk-bearers,* from *lac,*

which signifies milk. These lacteals ultimately converge into one trunk, called the *thoracic duct*, which terminates in the great vein under the clavicle or collar bone, hence called the *subclavian* vein, just before that vein reaches the right side of the heart. Here the chyle is poured into the general current of the venous blood, and, mingling with it, is exposed to the action of the air in the lungs during respiration. By this process, both the chyle and the venous blood are converted into red, arterial, or nutritive blood, which is afterward distributed by the heart through the arteries, to supply nourishment and support to every part of the body. The change which takes place in the lungs is called *sanguification*, or *blood-making*. The chyle is not prepared to impart nourishment to the system until this change takes place. *Respiration*, then, is, in reality, *the completion of digestion*. This interesting and vital part of the process of digestion will be considered more fully in the following chapter.

Before passing from this part of the subject, a few remarks of a more general nature seem called for. The *nerves of the stomach* have a direct relation to *undigested* but *digestible* substances. When any body that can not be digested is introduced into the stomach, distinct uneasiness is speedily excited, and an effort is soon made to expel it, either upward by the mouth or downward by the bowels. It is in this way, says Dr. Combe, that bile in the stomach excites nausea, and that tartar emetic produces vomiting. The *nerves of the bowels*, on the other hand, are constituted in relation to *digested* food ; and, consequently, when any thing escapes into them from the stomach in an *undigested* state, it becomes a source of irritative excitement. This accounts for the cholic pains and bowel-complaints which so commonly attend the passage through the intestinal canal of such indigestible substances as fat, husks of fruits, berries, and cherry-stones.

The process of digestion, which commences in the stomach, is completed in the intestines. Physiologists have hence sometimes called the former part of the process, or chymification, by the more simple term *stomach digestion ;* and the latter, or chylification, has been termed *intestinal digestion.* The bowels have distinct coats corresponding with those of the stomach. By the alternate contraction and relaxation of the muscular coat, their contents are propelled in a downward direction, somewhat as motion is propagated from one end of a worm to the other. It has hence been called vermicular, or *wormlike motion.* Some medicines have the power of *inverting* the order of the muscular contractions. Emetics operate in this manner to produce vomiting. Other medicines, again, excite the *natural* action to a higher degree, and induce a cathartic action of the bowels. When medicines become necessary to obviate that kind of costiveness which arises from imperfect intestinal contraction, physicians usually administer rhubarb, aloes, and similar laxatives, combined with tonics. But when the muscular coat of the bowels is kept in a healthy condition by a natural mode of life, and is aided by the action of the abdominal muscles, it rarely becomes necessary to administer laxative medicines.

The inner or mucous coat of the stomach and bowels is generally regarded by physiologists as a continuation of the skin. They greatly resemble each other in structure, and they are well known to sympathize with each other. Eruptions of the skin are very generally the result of disorders of the digestive organs. On the other hand, bowel complaints are frequently produced by a chill on the surface. The mucous coat and the skin are both charged with the double function of *excretion* and *absorption*. By the exercise of the *former* function, much of the waste matter of the system, requiring to be removed, is thrown into the intestines, and, mingling with the indigestible portion of the food, forms the common excrement; while by the exercise of the *latter* function the nutritive portion of their contents is taken up, and, as we have seen, passes into the general circulation, and contributes either to promote growth or to repair waste.

4. EVACUATION.—This is the fourth and last principal step in the process of digestion. After the chyle is separated from the chyme and passes into the circulation, the indigestible and refuse portion of the food, which is incapable of nourishing the system, passes off through the intestinal canal. In its course its bulk is considerably increased by the excretion of waste matter which has served its purposes in the system, and which, mingling with the innutritious and refuse part of the food, is thrown out of the body in the form of excrement. If the contents of the bowels are too long retained, uneasiness is produced. Hurtful matter, also, which should pass off by evacuation, is reabsorbed, passes again into the general circulation, and is ultimately thrown out of the system either by the lungs or through the pores of the skin.

This part of the process of digestion is *very important*, for it is impossible to enjoy good health while this function is imperfectly performed. To secure full and natural action in the intestinal canal, several principal conditions are necessary. These are, first, well-digested chyme and chyle; second, a due quantity and quality of secretions from the mucous or lining membrane of the bowels; third, a free and full contractile power of the muscular coat, and the unrestrained action of the abdominal and respiratory muscles; and, finally, a due nervous sensibility to receive impressions and communicate the necessary stimulus. The contractile power of the muscular coat, and the free passage of the intestinal contents from the stomach downward, are greatly aided by the constant but gentle agitation which the whole digestive apparatus receives during the act of breathing, and from exercise of every description. By free and deep inhalations of air into the lungs, the diaphragm is depressed and the bowels are pushed down. But when the air is thrown out from the lungs, the diaphragm rises into the chest, and the bowels follow, being pressed upward by the contractile power of the abdominal muscles. During exercise, breathing is deeper and more free, which gives additional pressure to the bowels from above. The abdominal muscular contraction is also, in turn, more vigorous and extensive, and thus the motion is returned from below. Persons that take little or no exercise, or who allow the chest and bowels to be confined by tight clothing, lose this natural stimulus, and frequently become subjects of immense suffering from habits of costiveness. These should be removed if possible, and they generally can be by a proper course of discipline. This should have reference to both diet and exercise. Such articles of food should be used as tend to keep open the bowels. This should be combined with the free exercise of the lungs and the abdominal muscles. In addition to these, there should be a determination to secure a natural evacuation of the bowels at least once a day. This is regarded by physiologists generally as essential to health. Efforts should be continued until the habit is established. Some definite period should be fixed upon for this purpose. Soon after breakfast is, on many accounts, generally preferable.

Time for Meals.—Before passing from the subject of digestion, I will submit a few thoughts in relation to the times for eating. It has already been observed that *three or four hours* are generally necessary for the digestion of a simple meal. Usually, perhaps, a greater length of time is required. It is also an established doctrine, based upon the results of careful examination and experiment, that *the stomach requires an interval of rest*, after the process of digestion is finished, to enable it to recover its tone before it can again enter upon the vigorous performance of its function. As a general rule, then, *five or six hours should elapse between meals*. If the mode of life is indolent, a greater time is required; if active, less time will suffice. Where the usages of society will allow the principal meal to be taken near the middle of the day, the following time for meals is approved by physiologists generally: breakfast at 7 o'clock, dinner at half past 12, and tea at 6. Luncheons and late suppers should be avoided; for the former will always be found to interfere with the healthful performance of the function of digestion, and the latter will induce restlessness, unpleasant dreams, and pain in the head. "A late supper," says the author of the Philosophy of Health, "generally occasions deranged and disturbed sleep; there is an effort on the part of the nerves to be quiet, while the burdened stomach makes an effort to call them into action, and between these two contending efforts there is disturbance—a sort of gastric riot—during the whole night. This disturbance has sometimes terminated in a fit of apoplexy and in death."

The Skin. — This membranous covering, which is spread over the surface of the body to shield the parts beneath, serves also as an excreting and secreting organ. By the great supply of blood which it receives, it is admirably fitted for this purpose. The whole animal system, as we have seen, is in a state of transition, decay and renovation constantly succeeding each other. While the stomach and alimentary canal take in new materials, the skin forms one of the principal outlets by which particles that are useless to the system are thrown out of the body. Every one knows that the skin perspires, and that checked perspiration is a powerful cause of disease and death; but few have any just notion of the extent and influence of this exhalation. When the body is overheated by exercise, a copious sweat breaks out, which, by evaporation, carries off the excess of heat, and produces an agreeable feeling of coolness and refreshment. The sagacity of Franklin led him to the first discovery of the use of perspiration in reducing the heat of the body, and to point out the anology subsisting between this process and that of the evaporation of water from a rough porous surface, so constantly resorted to in the East and West Indies, and in other warm countries, as an efficacious means of reducing the temperature of the air in rooms, and of wine and other drinks, much below that of the surrounding atmosphere. This is the higher and more obvious degree of the function of exhalation. But in the ordinary state of the system, the skin is constantly giving out a large quantity of waste materials by what is called *insensible perspiration;* a process which is of great importance to the preservation of health, and which is called *insensible*, because the exhalation, being in the form of vapor, and carried off by the surrounding air, is invisible to the eye. But its presence may often be made manifest, even to the sight, by the near approach of a dry cool mirror, on the surface of which it will soon be condensed so as to become visible. It is this which causes so copious deposites upon the windows of a crowded school-room in cold weather. A portion of these exhalations, however, proceed from the lungs.

There is an experiment that may be easily tried, which affords conclusive evidence that the amount of insensible perspiration is much greater than it is ordinarily supposed to be. Take a dry glass jar, with a neck three or four inches in diameter, and thrust the hand and a part of the forearm into it, closing the space in the neck about the arm with a handkerchief. After the lapse of a few minutes, it will be seen, by drawing the fingers across the inside of the jar, that the insensible perspiration even from the hand is very considerable. Many attempts have been made to estimate accurately the amount of exhaled matter carried off through the skin ; but many difficulties stand in the way of obtaining precise results. There is a great difference in different constitutions, and even in the same person at different times, in consequence of which we must be satisfied with an approximation to the truth.

Although the precise amount of perspiration can not be ascertained, it is generally agreed that the cutaneous exhalation is greater than the united excretions of both bowels and kidneys. Great attention has been given to this subject. Sanctorius, a celebrated medical writer, weighed himself, his food, and his excretions, daily, for thirty days. He inferred from his experiments that *five pounds* of every eight, of both food and drink, taken into the system, pass out through the skin. All physiologists agree that from twenty to forty ounces pass off through the skin of an adult in usual health every twenty-four hours. Take the lowest estimate, and we find the skin charged with the removal of *twenty ounces* of waste matter from the system *every day*. We can thus see ample reason why checked perspiration proves so detrimental to health; for every twenty-four hours during which such a state continues, we must either have this amount of useless and hurtful matter accumulating in the system, or some of the other organs of excretion must be greatly overtasked, which obviously can not happen without disturbing their regularity and well-being. It is generally known that continued exposure in a cold day produces either a bowel complaint or inflammation of some internal organ. Instead of expressing surprise at this, if people generally understood the structure and uses of their own bodies, they would rather wonder why one or the other of these effects is not *always* attendant upon so great a violation of the laws of health, *which are the laws of God.*

The lungs also excrete a large proportion of waste matter from the system. So far, then, their office is similar to that of the kidneys, the liver, and the bowels. In consequence of this alliance with the skin, these parts are more intimately connected with each other, in both healthy and diseased action, than with other organs. Whenever an organ is unusually delicate, it will be more easily affected by any cause of disease than those which are sound. Thus, in one instance, checked perspiration may produce a bowel complaint, and in another, inflammation of the lungs, and so on. Hence the fitness, in prescribing remedies, of adapting them not only to the *disease* itself, but of taking into the account the *cause* of the disease. A bowel complaint, for example, may arise either from overeating or from a check to perspiration. The thing to be cured is the same in both cases, but the *means* of cure ought obviously to be different. In one instance, an emetic or laxative, to carry off the offending cause, would be the most rational and efficacious remedy; in the other, a diaphoretic should be administered, to open the skin and restore it to a healthy action. Facts like these expose the ignorance and impudence of the quack, who undertakes to cure every form of disease by one remedy.

It has already been remarked that the skin is charged with the double function of *excretion* and *absorption.* We have a striking illustration of the exercise of the latter function in the vaccination of children and others, to protect them from small-pox. A small quantity of cow-pox matter is inserted under the external layer of the skin, where it is acted upon, and in a short time taken into the system by the absorbent vessels. In like manner, when the perspiration is brought to the surface of the skin, and confined there, either by injudicious clothing or by want of cleanliness, there is much reason to believe that its residual parts are again absorbed. It is established by observation that concentrated animal effluvia form a very energetic poison. We can, then, see why the absorption of the residual parts of perspiration produces fever, inflammation, and even death itself, according to its quantity and degree of concentration. This leads me to notice the importance of

Bathing.—The exhalation from the skin being so constant and extensive, and the bad effects of it when confined being so great, it becomes very important that we provide for its removal. This can be most easily and effectually accomplished by frequently bathing the whole body. This is a luxury within the reach of all, but one which is unappreciated by those who have not enjoyed it. An aged gentleman said to me recently, that in early life he "used to go a swimming frequently and enjoyed it much; but," he added, "I have not bathed or washed myself all over *for the last thirty years!*"

This, it is believed, is an extreme case. But it is to be feared there are not wanting instances in which persons do not bathe the entire person once a month, or once a year even! When the residual parts of the perspiration are not removed by washing or bathing, they at last obstruct the pores and irritate the skin. It is apparently for this reason that, in the Eastern and warmer countries, where perspiration is very copious, ablution and bathing have assumed the rank and importance of *religious observances.* Those who are in the habit of using the flesh-brush daily are at first surprised at the quantity of white dry scurf which it brings off; and those who take a warm bath for half an hour at long intervals can not have failed to notice the great amount of impurities which it removes, and the grateful feeling of comfort which its use imparts. It is remarked by an eminent physician, that the warm, tepid, cold, or shower bath, as a means of preserving health, ought to be in as common use as a change of apparel, for it is equally a measure of necessary cleanliness. Many, no doubt, neglect this, and enjoy health notwithstanding; but many more suffer from its omission; and even the former would be greatly benefited by employing it. Cleanliness, then, is as essential to health as to decency. Still more, it promotes not only physical health, but contributes largely to strengthen and invigorate the intellectual faculties, and to elevate and purify the affections. It comes, then, to be ranked among the *cardinal virtues.*

To secure the benefits of bathing or ablution, a great amount of apparatus is not necessary. A shower-bath, or plunge-bath, may not be best for all. Every one can procure a wash-bowl and one or two quarts of water, which are all that is necessary. To prevent the reduction of heat in the system by evaporation, and especially in cold weather, it will usually be found best to bathe the body *by sections*. It is generally agreed that the morning is the best time for bathing. Immediately on rising, then, the clothing being removed, let the head, face, and neck be washed as usual, and thoroughly dried by the use of a towel. Proceed to wash the chest and abdomen, which may be dried as before, after which a coarse towel or a flesh-brush should be vigorously applied, until the skin is perfectly dry, and there is a pleasant glow upon the surface. The back and limbs, in turn, should be washed, dried, and excited to a healthy and pleasant glow by friction. This last is of the utmost importance. If not easily secured, salt or vinegar may be added to the water, both of which are excellent stimulants to the skin.* When these are used, and care is taken to excite in the surface, by subsequent friction with a coarse towel, flesh-brush, or hair glove, the healthful glow of reaction, it will be found to contribute largely to both physical and mental comfort. The beneficial results will be more apparent if, while bathing and rubbing the chest and abdomen, pains are taken to throw back the shoulders, expand the lungs, and enlarge the chest.

By an act of the Legislature of the commonwealth of Massachusetts, passed in April last, it is required that "physiology and hygiene shall hereafter be taught in the schools of that commonwealth, in all cases in which the school committee shall deem it expedient."

When physiology is not made a study in school, the teacher should not fail to give familiar and instructive lectures on the subject. I know of instances where, by this simple means, the habits of a whole school,

* It will frequently be found more convenient, and will be well-nigh as serviceable, to wash in soft water as usual, and excite a reaction in the skin in the use of a towel that has been dipped in brine and dried.

composed of several hundred youth of both sexes, have been radically changed; and the practice of daily ablution has ceased to be the luxury of the few, having become the necessity not only of teachers and scholars, but of the families in which they reside. There is the most satisfactory evidence that cleanliness is conducive to health.* How important it is, then, that *habits of cleanliness* be formed at an early age.

Dr. Weiss, a distinguished German physician, in his remarks on this subject, says, the best time, undoubtedly, for these ablutions, is the morning. They are to be performed immediately after rising from the bed, when the temperature of the body is raised by the heat of the bed. The sudden change favors in a great measure the reaction which ensues, and excites the skin, rendered more sensitive by the perspiration during the night, to renewed activity. Cold ablutions, he adds, are fitted for all constitutions; they are best adapted for purifying and strengthening the body; for women, weak subjects, children, and old age. The room in which the ablution is performed may be slightly heated for debilitated patients in winter, to prevent colds in consequence of too low a temperature of the apartment; this exception is, however, only admissible

* The friends of educational reform may well take courage from the increased attention which the subject of physical education is of late receiving from the *pulpit* and the *press*, those mighty conservators of the public weal. Since the text was prepared for the press, the following remarks and pertinent inquiry have appeared in the Family Favorite for February, 1850. They are quoted from a Discourse by the editor, the Rev. James V. Watson, on the First Sabbath of the New Year:

"The true interpretation of the providence of God in Asiatic cholera perhaps has never yet fully been given. Is it not one of God's marked modes of rebuking intemperance, physical uncleanness, and social degradation—evils which result from perverted appetite, wrong forms of government, and a want of Christian benevolence? The reformer, the philanthropist, and the Christian may learn a lesson here."

for very weakly persons. Generally speaking, ablutions may be performed in a cold room, especially where persons get through the operation quickly, and can immediately afterward take exercise in the open air.

It is the opinion of Dr. Combe that bathing is a safe and valuable preservative of health, in ordinary circumstances, and an active remedy in disease. Instead of being dangerous by causing liability to cold, it is, he says, when well managed, so much the reverse, that he has used it much and successfully for the express purpose of diminishing such liability, both in himself and in others in whom the chest is delicate. In his own instance, in particular, he is conscious of having derived much advantage from its regular employment, especially in the colder months of the year, during which he has found himself most effectually strengthened against the impression of cold by repeating the bath at shorter intervals than usual. I shall conclude my remarks on bathing by presenting a paragraph from this transatlantic author.

If the bath can not be had at all places, soap and water may be obtained every where, and leave no apology for neglecting the skin. If the constitution be delicate, water and vinegar, or water and salt, used daily, form an excellent and safe means of cleansing and gently stimulating the skin. To the invalid they are highly beneficial, when the nature of the indisposition does not render them improper. A rough and rather coarse towel is a very useful auxiliary in such ablutions. Few of those who have steadiness to keep up the action of the skin by the above means, and to avoid strong and exciting causes, will ever suffer from colds, sore throats, or similar complaints; while, as a means of restoring health, they are often incalculably serviceable. If one tenth of the persevering attention and labor bestowed to so much purpose in rubbing down and currying the skins of horses were bestowed by the human race in keeping themselves in good condition, and a little attention were paid to diet and clothing, colds, nervous diseases, and stomach complaints would cease to form so large an item in the catalogue of human miseries. Man studies the nature of other animals, and adapts his conduct to their constitution; himself alone he continues ignorant of and neglects. He considers himself a being of superior order, and not subject to the laws of organization which regulate the functions of the lower animals; but this conclusion is the result of ignorance and pride, and not a just inference from the premises on which it is ostensibly founded.

Clothing.—The skin is very materially affected in the healthy performance of its functions by the nature and condition of the clothing. It is a very commonly received opinion that one principal object in clothing is to impart heat to the body. This, however, is an erroneous idea; the utmost that it can do is to *prevent the escape of heat.* All articles of clothing are not alike in this respect. Some conduct the heat from the body readily, and are hence much used in warm weather; as linen, for example. Others, again, have very little tendency to convey heat from the body, and are hence sought in cold weather. Of this nature are furs, and cloths manufactured from wool. I do not intend in this connection to speak of the merits of different kinds of clothing, but to remark simply upon the necessity of changing clothes often, or at least of ventilating them frequently. This remark applies particularly to all articles of clothing worn next to the skin, and to beds. Clothes worn next to the skin during the day should be removed on going to bed, and a fresh sleeping-gown should be put on. The former should be hung up in a situation that will allow the accumulated perspiration of the day to pass off by evaporation. By this means they will become sufficiently freshened and ventilated, by morning, to be worn another day, when the night-clothes, in turn, should be ventilated. Beds also should be thrown open and exposed to fresh air with open doors, or at least windows, several hours before being made. In our best-regulated boarding schools, and literary and benevolent institutions of all kinds, particular attention is now paid to this subject. In some instances, lodging rooms are furnished with frames for the express purpose of facilitating the ventilation of the bed-clothes. Immediately on rising in the morning, the clothes are removed from the beds, and exposed upon these frames to a current of fresh air for several hours, the windows being opened for that purpose. Notwithstanding care be taken to promote personal cleanliness by daily ablutions, if the ventilation of beds and clothing be neglected, and perspiration be suffered to accumulate in them, it may be reabsorbed, and, passing again into the circulation, produce all the mischief of which I have before spoken.

THE TEETH.—I have already spoken of the relation the teeth sustain to digestion. Their use in the proper mastication of food is essential to the healthy and vigorous performance of this important function. The proper use of a good set of teeth contributes largely to both the physical comfort, and the intellectual and moral well-being of their possessor; but when neglected, they very commonly decay and become useless; nay, more, they are not unfrequently a source of great and almost constant discomfort for years. In order to preserve the teeth, they must be *kept clean.* After every meal, they should be cleaned with a brush and water. A tooth-pick will sometimes be found necessary in the removal of particles of food that are inaccessible to the brush. Metallic tooth-picks injure the enamel, and should not be used. Those made of ivory, or the common goose-quill, are unobjectionable. The brush should be used, not only after each meal, but the last thing at night and the first thing in the morning. This will prevent the accumulation of *tartar*, which so commonly incrusts neglected teeth. If suffered to remain, it gradually accumulates, presses upon the gums, and destroys their health. By this means the roots of the teeth become bare, and thus deprived of their natural stimulus, they prematurely decay. Food or drink either very hot or very cold is exceedingly injurious to the teeth. Sour drops, acidulated drinks, and all articles of food that "set the teeth on edge," are injurious, and should be carefully avoided. Should it become necessary to take sour drops as a medicine, they should be given through a quill, and every precaution should be taken to prevent their coming in contact with the teeth. Even then the mouth should be well rinsed immediately after they are swallowed.

Disordered digestion is a great source of injury to the teeth both in childhood and in mature age. When digestion is vigorous, there is less deposition of tartar, and the teeth are naturally of a purer white. Especially is this true when the general health is good, and the diet plain, and contains a full proportion of vegetable matter. This accounts for the fact that many rustics and savages possess teeth that would be envied in town. Tobacco is sometimes used as a *preservative* of the teeth. It is, indeed, occasionally prescribed as a *curative* by ignorant physicians, and those who are willing to pander to the diseased appetites of their patients.

But there is the best medical testimony that the use of this *filthy weed* "*debilitates the vessels of the gums, turns the teeth yellow, and renders the appearance of the mouth disagreeable.*" Dr. Rush informs us that he knew a man in Philadelphia who *lost all his teeth* by smoking. In speaking of the *moral effects* of this practice, he adds, "Smoking and chewing tobacco, by rendering water and other simple liquors insipid to the taste, dispose very much to the stronger stimulus of ardent spirits; hence the practice of smoking cigars throughout our country has been followed by the use of brandy and water as a common drink." A dentist of extensive and successful practice in the Middle and Western States, after listening to the reading of this article, said to me, he had a patient, a young lady, two of whose front teeth had decayed through, laterally, in consequence of smoking. On removing the caries, he found it impossible to fill her teeth, because the openings continued through them. He thinks, as do many others, that the heat of the smoke is a principal cause of the injury.

Among the conditions upon which the healthy action of the voluntary organs depends is a due degree of *appropriate exercise.* This is a *general law,* and holds with reference to the *teeth* as well as to any other organ or set of organs. The proper mastication of healthful and nutritious food constitutes the appropriate exercise of the teeth, and is a condition upon which *their health,* and the healthy exercise of the function of *digestion,* alike depend. If from any cause the teeth of one jaw are removed, the corresponding teeth of the other jaw, being thus deprived of that exercise which is essential to their health, are pressed out of the jaw, appear to grow long, become loose in their sockets, and sometimes fall out. Hence the propriety and advantage of inserting *artificial teeth* where the natural ones fail ; an event which rarely happens when they are properly taken care of. I need hardly add that nuts, and other hard substances that break the enamel, are injurious to the teeth, and should be avoided.

THE BONES.—The bones constitute the frame-work of the system. They consist of two substances, being formed of both *animal* and *earthy* matter. To the former belongs every thing connected with their *life* and *growth*, while the latter gives to them *solidity* and *strength*. The proportions of the animal and earthy elements of which the bones are composed vary at different ages. In childhood and early youth, when but *little strength* is needed, and *great growth* of bone is required, the animal part preponderates. As growth advances the animal part *decreases*, and the earthy part *increases*. In middle life, when growth is finished and the strength is greatest, and when nutrition is required only to repair waste, the proportions are changed, and the solid or earthy part exceeds the vital or animal ; and in extreme old age, the earthy part so predominates as to cause the bones to become very brittle.

The bones, like other parts of the system, require exercise. If properly used, they increase in size and strength. But while a due degree of exercise is beneficial, it ought to be remarked that severe and continued labor should not be required of children and youth ; for its tendency is to increase the deposition of earthy matter to a hurtful extent. It is by this means that many children are made dwarfs for life, their bones being consolidated by an undue amount of exercise and excessive labor before they have attained their full growth. Multitudes of children in our country, from this and kindred causes, fail of attaining the size of their ancestors. These remarks may be turned to a practical account in the family and in the school. At birth, many of the bones are scarcely more than cartilage; yet children are frequently urged to stand and walk long before the bones become sufficiently strong to sustain the pressure; and, as a consequence, their legs become crooked, and they are perhaps other ways deformed for life. Children ought always, when seated, to be able to rest their feet upon the floor. When they occupy a seat that is too high, and especially when they are unable to reach their feet to the floor, the thigh bones very frequently become curved. If, in addition to high seats, the back is not supported, children become round shouldered, their chests contract, their constitutions become permanently enfeebled, and they become peculiarly susceptible to pulmonary disease. The back to the seat should afford a pleasant and agreeable support to the small of the back, but it ought not to reach to the shoulder blades.

Parents and teachers should never forget that children are as susceptible to physical training as to intellectual or moral culture. And here, especially, they should be "trained *up* in the way they should go." Physical uprightness is next to moral. If children are allowed to contract bad physical habits, they are liable not only to grow crooked, but to become deformed in various ways. But so great is the power of education, that by it even the physically crooked may be made straight; the chest may be enlarged, the general health may be improved, and much may be done in many ways to fortify those who have inherited feeble constitutions against the attacks of disease. The benefits resulting from maintaining an upright form, and a free and open chest, have already been considered, and I shall have occasion to refer to them again. The chest of most adults, although *incased with bone*, may be increased several inches by drawing the arms back in the use of *nature's own shoulder-braces*, and at the same time taking deep inhalations of air, and filling the lungs to their utmost capacity. Hundreds of individuals in different parts of the country have borne testimony to the efficacy of this treatment in the improvement of their health. The good results of such discipline in childhood are still more manifest.

A stooping posture is frequently induced by sitting at tables and desks that are too low. It has been erroneously maintained by some that the top of the desk should be on the same plane with the elbow when the arm hangs by the side. When the desk is higher, it has been said the tendency is to elevate one shoulder, to depress the other, and to produce a permanent curvature of the spinal column. Although this may have been frequently the result of sitting at a high desk, yet it is not a *necessary result.* To prevent the projection of one shoulder, and the consequent spinal curvature, *both of the arms must be kept on the same level.* For this purpose, there should be room to support them equally; and care should be taken to see that this support is regularly sought. If this be not done, the right arm will be apt to rise above the left, from its more constant use and elevation. A physician, highly celebrated for the success that has attended his treatment for lung affections, after dwelling upon the injury to the health that frequently results from sitting at too low desks, remarks, that "every parent should go to the school-rooms, and know for a certainty that the desks at which his children write or study are fully up to the arm-pits, and in no case allow them to sit stooping, or leaning the shoulders forward on the chest. If fatigued by this posture, they should be called to stand, or go out of doors and run about." The height of table

I find most conducive to comfort for my own use is midway between the two; that is, half way from the elbow (as the arm hangs by the side) to the arm-pit. It is necessary, however, to rest both arms equally upon the table. The secret of posture consists in avoiding all bad positions, and in not continuing any one position too long. The ordinary carriage of the body is an object worthy of the attention of every parent and instructor. The more favorable impression which a man of erect and commanding attitude is sure to make, should not be overlooked. But there is a greater good than this; for he who *walks erect*, enjoys better health, possesses increased powers of usefulness, realizes more that *he is a man*, and has more to call forth gratitude to a beneficent Creator, than he who adopts an *oblique* posture. It was just remarked that "physical uprightness is next to moral." Physical *obliquity*, it may be added, is akin to *moral*. If they are not German-cousins, there can be little doubt but that, considered in all its bearings, the tendency of the former is to induce the latter.

Important as an erect posture and a well-developed chest are to gentlemen, they are in some respects even more so to the fairer sex; for, in addition to the advantages already considered, which both enjoy in common, these impart to them a peculiar charm, that to men of sense is far greater than pretty faces, which Nature has not given to all. "For a great number of years, it has been the custom in France to give young females, of the earliest age, the habit of holding back the shoulders, and thus expanding the chest. From the observations of anatomists lately made, it appears that the clavicle or collar bone is actually longer in females of the French nation than in those of the English. As the two nations are of the same race, as there is no remarkable difference in their bones, and this is peculiar to the sex, it must be attributed, as I believe, to the habit above mentioned, which, by the extension of the arms, has gradually produced an elongation of this bone. Thus we see that habit may be employed to alter and improve the solid bones. The French have succeeded in the development of a part in a way that adds to health and beauty, and increases a characteristic that distinguishes the human being from the brute."*

THE MUSCLES.—The muscles consist of compact bundles of fleshy fibers, which are found in animals on removing the skin. They constitute the red fleshy part of meat, and give form and symmetry to the body. In the limbs they surround and protect the bones, while in the trunk they spread out and constitute a defensive wall for the protection of the vital parts beneath. The muscles have been divided into *three parts*, of which the middle and fleshy portion, called the *belly*, is most conspicuous. The other two parts are the opposite ends, and are commonly called the *origin* and *insertion* of the muscle. The *origin* is usually fastened to one bone, and the *insertion* is attached to another. By the contraction of the *belly* of the muscle, the *insertion*, which is *movable*, is drawn toward the *origin*, which is *fixed*, and brings with it the bone to which it is attached. This any one can see illustrated in bending the arm. The muscle which performs this function lies between the elbow and the shoulder. It is attached to the shoulder by its *origin*, and to one of the bones of the fore-arm, just below the elbow, by its *insertion*. By grasping the arm midway

* Quoted into the Schoolmaster (a work published in London under the superintendence of the Society for the Diffusion of Useful Knowledge) from a lecture delivered by Dr. J. C. Warren before the American Institute of Instruction, August, 1830.

between the shoulder and the elbow with the opposite hand, and then bending the arm, the enlargement of the belly of the muscle by the contraction will be at once perceived. Then, by moving the hand down on the inside of the arm toward the elbow, the lessening muscle may be readily traced until it terminates in a *tendon*, of much less size than the muscle, but of great strength, which is inserted into the bone just below the elbow. As the fore-arm is drawn up, and especially if there be a weight in the hand, the *tendon* may be felt just within the elbow-joint, running toward the point of insertion. Extend the arm at the elbow, and the muscle on the outside of the arm will swell and become firm, while the inside muscle, and its tendon at the elbow, will be relaxed. This example well illustrates the principle on which all the joints of the sys tem are moved. Those who are acquainted with mechanics will readily perceive that the action just described is an example of the "*third* kind of lever," where the power is applied between the weight and the fulcrum. The elbow is the fulcrum, the hand contains the weight, and the tendon, inserted into the bone just below the elbow, is the power. This kind of lever requires the power to be greater than the weight, and acts under what is called a *mechanical disadvantage.* What is lost in power, however, is compensated in increased velocity.

There are upward of four hundred muscles in the human body. Some of these are *voluntary* in their motions, as those I have described, while others are *involuntary*, as the action of the heart and the respiratory muscles. Had the action of these depended upon the will, as does the action of the muscles of locomotion, the circulation of the blood and the process of breathing would cease, and life would become extinct whenever sleep or any other cause should overcome the attention. Here, then, we have another beautiful illustration of the wisdom and beneficence of the Creator in so ordering that those muscles which are essential to the continuation of life shall perform their functions without the control or attention of the individual.

The study of the muscular system involves an exposition of the principles by which exercise should be regulated, and can scarcely fail to excite the attention of the general reader, and especially of those who, as parents or teachers, are interested in the education of the young.

The muscles enable us to move the frame-work of the system. Their chief purpose obviously is to enable us to carry into effect the various resolutions and designs which have been formed by the mind. But, while fulfilling this grand object, their active exercise is, at the same time, highly conducive to the well-being of many other important functions. By muscular contraction, the blood is gently assisted in its course through the smaller vessels to the more distant parts of the body; and by it the important processes of digestion, respiration, secretion, absorption, and nutrition are promoted; and by it the health of the whole body is immediately and greatly influenced. The mind itself is exhilarated or depressed by the proper or improper use of muscular exercise. It thus becomes a point of no slight importance to establish general principles by which that exercise may be regulated.

In every part of the animal economy, the muscles are proportioned in size and structure to the efforts required of them. Whenever a muscle is called into frequent use, its fibers increase in thickness within certain limits, and become capable of acting with greater force and readiness. On the other hand, when a muscle is little used, its volume and power decrease in a corresponding degree.

In order to secure the most beneficial results from exercise, reference should be had to the time at which it is taken. Those who are in perfect health may engage in it at almost any hour except immediately after a meal; but those who are not robust ought to confine their hours of exercise within narrower limits. To a person in full vigor, a good walk, or other brisk exercise before breakfast may be highly beneficial and exhilarating, while to an invalid or delicate person it will be likely to prove detrimental. In order to prove beneficial, exercise must be resorted to only when the system is sufficiently vigorous to be able to meet it. This is usually the case after a lapse of from two to four hours after a moderate meal. The forenoon, then, will generally be found the best time for exercise for persons whose habits are sedentary. If exercise be delayed till the system feels exhaustion from want of food, its tendency will be to dissipate the strength that remains and impair digestion; while, if taken at the proper time, it will invigorate the system and promote digestion. The reasons are obvious; for exercise of every kind causes increased action and waste in the organ, and if there be not materials and vigor enough in the system to keep up that action and supply the waste, nothing but increased debility can reasonably be expected.

Active exercise immediately *before* meals is injurious. The reasons are apparent, for muscular exercise directs a flow of blood and nervous energy to the surface and extremities; and it is an established law in physiology, that energetic action can not be kept up in two distant parts of the system at the same time. Hence, whenever a meal is taken immediately after vigorous exercise, the stomach is taken at disadvantage, and, from want of the necessary action in its vessels and nerves, is unable to carry on digestion with success. This is very obviously the case where the exercise has been severe or protracted.

Active exercise ought to be equally avoided immediately *after* a heavy meal, for then the functions of the digestive organs are in the highest state of activity. If the muscular system be called into vigorous action under such circumstances, it will cause a withdrawal of the vital stimuli of the blood and nervous influence from the stomach to the extremities, which can not fail greatly to retard the digestive process. In accordance with this well-established fact, there is a natural and marked aversion to active pursuits after a full meal. A mere stroll, which requires no exertion and does not fatigue, will not be injurious before or after eating; but exercise beyond this limit is at such times hurtful. All, therefore, who would preserve and improve their health, will find it to their advantage to observe faithfully this important law, otherwise they will deprive themselves of most of the benefits that are usually attendant upon judicious exercise. All, then, who are forced to much exertion immediately after eating, should satisfy themselves with partaking of a very moderate meal. These remarks apply to both physical and mental exercise; for if the intellect be intently occupied in profound and absorbing thought, the nervous energy will be concentrated in the brain, and any demands made on it by the stomach or muscles will be very imperfectly attended to. So, also, if the stomach be actively engaged in digesting a full meal, and some subject of thought be presented to the mind, considerable difficulty will be felt in pursuing it, and most probably both thought and digestion will be disturbed.

Another law of the muscular system requires that relaxation and contraction should alternate; or, in other words, that rest should follow exercise. In accordance with this law, it is easier to walk than to stand; and in standing, it is easier to change from one oot to the other than to stand still. To require a child to extend his arm and hold a book in his hand, or even to keep the arm extended but a short time, is a violation of this law which should never be permitted. Akin to this is the very injudicious practice, which is sometimes resorted to in schools, of requiring a boy to stoop over, and, placing his finger upon a nail in the floor, "hold it in." Teachers who are disposed to inflict punishments like these ought first to try the experiment themselves. Such protracted tension of the muscles enfeebles their action, and ultimately destroys their power of contraction.

These remarks sufficiently explain why small children, after sitting a while in school, become restless. Proper regard for this organic law requires that the smaller children in school be allowed a recess as often, at least, as once an hour; and that all be allowed and encouraged frequently to change their position. I fully concur in the opinion expressed by Dr. Caldwell, who says, "It would be infinitely wiser and better to employ suitable persons to superintend the exercises and amusements of children under seven years of age, in the fields, orchards, and meadows, and point out to them the richer beauties of nature, than to have them immured in crowded school-rooms, in a state of inaction, poring over torn books and primers, conning words of whose meaning they are ignorant, and breathing foul air."

A change of position calls into action a different set of muscles, and relieves those that are exhausted. The object of exercise is to employ all the muscles of the body, and especially to strengthen those that are weak. It ought hence to be frequently varied, and always adapted to the peculiarities of individuals. Different kinds of exercise will therefore be found to suit different constitutions. Sedentary persons best enjoy, and will be most profited by, that kind of exercise which brings into action the greatest number of muscles.

To give exercise its greatest value, it should be taken at the same hour every day. This is well-nigh as important as the rule that requires meals to be taken regularly. If exercise be taken irregularly, one day in the morning, another day at noon, and another day at night, if at all, it is possible that good may result from it, but its beneficial effects would be greatly increased if the same amount of exercise were taken every day at the same hours. Give the system an opportunity of establishing *good habits* in this respect, and it will derive great advantage from them; but it is difficult for it to derive any benefit from a *habit of irregularity*, if such may be called a habit. Students, teachers, and all persons who lead sedentary lives, should have their regular times for exercise as well as for meals, and if they find it necessary to do without one, they will generally find it advantageous to dispense with the other also.

Walking, it has been said, agrees with every body. But as it brings into play chiefly the lower limbs and muscles of the loins, and affords little scope for the play of the arms and muscles of the chest, it is of itself insufficient to constitute adequate exercise. To render it most beneficial, the shoulders should be drawn back, and the chest should be enlarged by taking deep inspirations of pure air. The muscles of the chest, and of every part of the body, should be free to move and unconfined by tight clothing. Fencing, shuttlecock, and such other useful sports as combine with them free movements of the upper part of the body, are doubly advantageous, for they not only exercise the muscles of the whole body, but possess the additional advantage of animating the mind and increasing the nervous stimulus, by which exercise is rendered easy, pleasant, and invigorating. For the purpose of developing the chest, physiologists generally concur in recommending *fencing* as a good exercise for boys. Shuttlecock is a very beneficial exercise for females, calling into play, as it does, the muscles of the chest, trunk, and arms. It ought to be practiced in the open air. When played with both hands, as it may be after a little practice, it is very useful in preventing curvature, and in giving vigor to the spine. It is an excellent plan to play with a battledore in each hand, and to strike with them alternately. The graces is another play well adapted for expanding the chest, and giving strength to the muscles of the back, and has the advantage of being practicable in the open air. It is very important that the muscles of the back be strengthened by due exercise, for their proper use contributes to both health and beauty.

When managed with due regard to the natural powers of the individual, and so as to avoid effort and fatigue, *reading aloud* becomes a very useful and invigorating exercise. In forming and undulating the voice, not only the chest, but also the diaphragm and abdominal muscles are in constant action, and communicate to the stomach and bowels a healthy and agreeable stimulus. Where the voice is raised and the elocution is rapid, the muscular effort becomes fatiguing; but when care is taken not to carry reading aloud so far at one time as to excite a sensation of soreness or fatigue in the chest, and the exercise is duly repeated, it is extremely useful in developing and giving tone to the organs of respiration and to the general system.

"Vocal music is also very useful, by its direct effect on the constitution. It was the opinion of Dr. Rush, that young ladies especially, who, by the custom of society, are debarred from many kinds of salubrious exercise, should cultivate singing, not only as an accomplishment, but as a means of preserving health. He particularly insists that it should never be neglected in the education of females; and states that, besides its salutary operation in enabling them to soothe the cares of domestic life, and quiet sorrow by the united assistance of the sound and sentiment of a properly chosen song, it has a still more direct and important effect. 'I here introduce a fact,' he remarks, 'which has been suggested to me by my profession, and that is, that the exercise of the organs of the breast by singing contributes very much to defend them from those diseases to which the climate and other causes expose them. The Germans are seldom afflicted with consumption, nor have I ever known but one instance of spitting blood among them. This, I believe, is in part occasioned by the strength which their lungs acquire by exercising them frequently in vocal music, for this constitutes an essential branch of their education. The music-master of our academy has furnished me with an observation still more in favor of this opinion. He informed me that he had known several instances of persons who were strongly disposed to consumption, who were restored to health by the exercise of their lungs in singing.'"*

Bathing or ablution, when conducted as recommended on pages 60 and 61, is not only a means of cleanliness and of exciting a healthy action in the skin, but it constitutes, at the same time, a most *admirable exercise.*

* Mr. Woodbridge's lecture before the American Institute of Instruction, 1830.

If a lodging-room has been properly ventilated by leav ing open windows, or otherwise, so that the air is pure and healthful in the morning, ten or fifteen minutes spent in bathing and friction, with a proper exercise of the muscles of the back and abdomen, will contribute more to invigorate the system and promote the general health than twice the amount of exercise taken at any other time or in any other way.

From the foregoing remarks, it appears that the most perfect of all exercises are those which combine the free play of all the muscles of the body, mental interest and excitement, and the unrestrained use of the voice.

CHAPTER IV.

THE LAWS OF HEALTH. PHILOSOPHY OF RESPIRATION.

We instinctively shun approach to the dirty, the squalid, and the diseased, and use no garment that may have been worn by another. We open sewers for matters that offend the sight or the smell, and contaminate the air. We carefully remove impurities from what we eat and drink, filter turbid water, and fastidiously avoid drinking from a cup that may have been pressed to the lips of a friend. On the other hand, we resort to places of assembly, and draw into our mouths air loaded with effluvia from the lungs, skin, and clothing of every individual in the promiscuous crowd—exhalations offensive, to a certain extent, from the most healthy individuals; but when arising from a living mass of skin and lungs in all stages of evaporation, disease, and putridity, they are in the highest degree deleterious and loathsome.—Birnan.

Respiration is usually defined as the process by which air is taken into the lungs and expelled from them. It explains the changes that take place in these organs, in the conversion of *chyle* and *venous*, or worn-out blood, into *arterial* or nutrient blood. In order to be clearly understood, I must premise a few observations on the circulation of the blood.* The blood circulating through the body is of two different kinds; the one *red* or *arterial*, and the other *dark* or *venous* blood. The former alone is capable of affording nourishment and supporting life. It is distributed from the *left* side of the heart all over the body by means of a great *artery*, which subdivides in its course, and ultimately terminates in myriads of very minute ramifications closely interwoven with, and in reality constituting a part of, the texture of every living part. On reaching this extreme point of its course, the blood passes into equally minute ramifications of the *veins*, which in their turn gradually coalesce, and form larger and larger trunks, till they at last terminate in two large veins, by which the whole current of the venous blood is brought back in a direction contrary to that of the blood in the arteries, and poured into the *right* side of the heart. On examining the quality of the blood in the arteries and veins, it is found to have undergone a great change in its passage from the one to the other. The florid hue which distinguished it in the arteries has disappeared, and given place to the dark color characteristic of venous blood. Its properties, too, have changed, and it is now no longer capable of sustaining life.

Two conditions are essential to the reconversion of venous into arterial blood, and to the restoration of its vital properties. The first is an adequate provision of *new materials* from the *food* to supply the place of those which have been expended in nutrition, and the second is the free exposure of the *venous blood* to the *atmospheric air*. The first condition is fulfilled by the chyle, or nutrient portion of the food, being regularly poured into the venous blood just before it reaches the right side of the heart, and the second by the import-

* Taken, with slight alterations, from the description of Dr. A. Combe.

ant process of *respiration*, which takes place in the air-cells of the lungs. The venous blood, having arrived at the right side of the heart, is propelled by the contraction of that organ into a large artery, leading directly, by separate branches, to the two lungs, and hence called the *pulmonary* artery. In the innumerable branches of this artery expanding themselves throughout the substance of the lungs, the dark blood is subjected to the contact of the air inhaled in breathing, and a change in the composition both of the blood and of the inhaled air takes place, in consequence of which the former is found to have reassumed its florid or arterial hue, and to have regained its power of supporting life. The blood then enters minute venous ramifications, which gradually coalesce into larger branches, and at last terminate in four large trunks in the left side of the heart, whence the blood, in its arterial form, is again distributed over the body, to pursue the same course and undergo the same change as before.

It will be perceived that there are two distinct circulations, each of which is carried on by its own system of vessels. The one is from the *left* side of the *heart* to *every part of the body*, and back to the *right* side of the *heart*. The other is from the *right* side of the *heart* to the *lungs*, and back to the *left* side of the *heart*. The former has for its object nutrition and the maintenance of life; and the latter, the restoration of the deteriorated blood, and the *animalization* or *assimilation* of the *chyle* from which the *blood* is formed. This process has already been referred to as the *completion of digestion;* for *chyle* is not fitted to nourish the system until, by its exposure to the atmospheric air in the lungs, it is converted into *arterial blood.*

As the food can not become a part of the living animal, or the venous blood regain its lost properties until they have undergone the requisite changes in the air-cells of the lungs, the function of respiration by which these are effected is one of pre-eminent importance in the animal economy, and well deserves the most careful examination. The term respiration is frequently restricted to the mere inhalation and expiration of air from the lungs, but more generally it is employed to designate the whole series of phenomena which occur in these organs. The term *sanguification* is occasionally used to denote that part of the process in which the blood, by exposure to the action of the air, passes from the venous to the arterial state. As the chyle does not become assimilated to the blood until it has passed through the lungs, this term, which signifies *blood-making*, is not unaptly used.

The *quantity* and *quality* of the blood have a most direct and material influence upon the condition of every part of the body. If the *quantity* sent to the arm, for example, be diminished by tying the artery through which it is conveyed, the arm, being then imperfectly nourished, wastes away, and does not regain its plumpness till the full supply of blood be restored. In like manner, when the *quality* of that fluid is impaired by deficiency of food, bad digestion, impure air, or imperfect sanguification in the lungs, the body and all its functions become more or less disordered. Thus, in consumption, death takes place chiefly in consequence of respiration not being sufficiently perfect to admit of the formation of proper blood in the lungs. A knowledge of the structure and functions of the lungs, and of the conditions favorable to *their* healthy action, is therefore very important, for on their welfare depends that of every organ of the body.

The exposure of the blood to the action of the air seems to be indispensable to every variety of animated creatures. In man and the more perfect of the lower animals, it is carried on in the lungs, the structure of which is admirably adapted for the purpose. In many animals, however, the requisite action is effected without the intervention of lungs. In fishes, for example, that live in water and do not breathe, the blood circulates through the gills, and in them is exposed to the air which the water contains. So necessary is the atmospheric air to the vitality of the blood in all animals, that the want of it inevitably proves fatal. A fish can no more live in water deprived of air, than a man could in an atmosphere devoid of oxygen, which is the element that unites with the blood in the lungs in sanguification.

In man the lungs are those large, light, spongy bodies which, along with the heart, completely fill up the cavity of the chest. They vary much in size in different persons ; and as the chest is formed for their protection, it is either large and capacious, or the reverse, according to the size of the lungs.

The substance of the lungs consists of bronchial tubes, air-cells, blood-vessels, nerves, and cellular membrane. The bronchial tubes are merely continuations and subdivisions of the windpipe, and serve to convey the external air to the air-cells of the lungs. The air-cells constitute the chief part of the lungs, and are the termination of the smaller branches of the bronchial tubes. When fully distended, they are so numerous as in appearance to constitute almost the whole lung. They are of various sizes, from the twentieth to the hundredth of an inch in diameter, and are lined with an exceedingly fine, thin membrane, on which the minute capillary branches of the pulmonary arteries and veins are copiously ramified. It is while circulating in the small vessels of this membrane, and there exposed to the air, that the blood undergoes the change from the venous to the arterial state. So numerous are these air-cells, that the aggregate extent of their lining membrane in man has been computed to exceed twenty thousand square inches, or about ten times the surface of the human body. Some writers place the estimate considerably higher.

A copious *exhalation* of moisture takes place in breathing, which presents a striking analogy to the exhalation from the surface of the skin already described. In the former as in the latter instance, the exhalation is carried on by the innumerable minute capillary vessels in which the small arterial branches terminate in the air-cells. Pulmonary exhalation is, in fact, one of the chief outlets of waste matter from the system; and the air we breathe is thus vitiated, not only by the subtraction of its oxygen and the addition of carbonic acid gas, but also by animal effluvia, with which it is loaded when returned from the lungs. In some individuals this last source of impurity is so great as to render their vicinity offensive, and even insupportable. It is this which gives the disagreeable, sickening smell to crowded rooms. The air which is expired from the lungs is rendered offensive by various other causes. When spirituous liquors are taken into the stomach, for example, they are absorbed by the veins and mixed with the venous blood, in which they are carried to the lungs to be expelled from the body. In some instances, when persons have drank copiously of spirits, their breath has been so saturated with them as actually to *take fire* and *burn*. An instance of this kind has recently been communicated to me by several reliable witnesses, in which the flame was extinguished by closing the mouth and nose, thus excluding the pure air that supported the combustion, until the unfortunate experimenter could remove the candle by which his breath had taken fire. This illustration will explain how the odor of different substances is frequently perceptible in the breath long after the mouth is free from them.

The lungs not only exhale waste matter, but *absorption* takes place from their lining membrane. In both of these respects there is a striking analogy between the functions performed by the lungs and the skin. When a person breathes an atmosphere loaded with the fumes of spirits, tobacco, turpentine, or of any other volatile substance, a portion of the fumes is taken up by the absorbing vessels of the lungs, and carried into the system, and there produces precisely the same effects as if introduced into the stomach. Dogs, for example, have been killed by being made to inhale the fumes of prussic acid for a few minutes. The lungs thus become a ready inlet to contagion, miasmata, and other poisonous influences diffused through the air we breathe.

From this general explanation of the structure and uses of the lungs, it is obvious that several conditions which it is our interest to know and observe are essential to the healthy performance of the important function of respiration. The first among these is a healthy original formation of the lungs. No fact in medicine is better established, says Dr. Combe, than that which proves the hereditary transmission, from parents to children, of a constitutional liability to pulmonary disease, and especially to consumption ; yet, continues he, no condition is less attended to in forming matrimonial engagements.

Another requisite to the well-being of the lungs, and to the free and salutary exercise of respiration, is a due supply of rich and healthy blood. When, from defective food or impaired digestion, the blood is impoverished in quality, and rendered unfit for adequate nutrition, the lungs speedily suffer, and that often to a fatal extent. The free and easy expansion of the chest is also indispensable to the full play and dilation of the lungs. Whatever interferes with or impedes it, either in dress or in position, is obviously prejudicial to health. On the other hand, whatever favors the free expansion of the chest equally promotes the healthy action of the respiratory organs. Stays and corsets, and tight vests and waistbands, operate most injuriously, compressing as they do the thoracic cavity, and interfering with the healthy dilation of the lungs.

The admirable harmony established by the Creator between the various constituent parts of the animal frame, renders it impossible to pay regard to the conditions required for the health of any one, or to infringe the conditions required therefor, without all the rest participating in the benefit or injury. Thus, while cheerful exercise in the open air and in the society of equals is directly and eminently conducive to the well-being of the muscular system, the advantage does not stop there, the beneficent Creator having kindly so ordered it that the same exercise shall be scarcely less advantageous to the important function of respiration. Active exercise calls the lungs into play, favors their expansion, promotes the circulation of the blood through their substance, and leads to their complete and healthy development. The same end is greatly facilitated by that free and vigorous exercise of the voice, which so uniformly accompanies and enlivens the sports of the young, and which doubles the benefits derived from them considered as exercise. The excitement of the social and moral feelings which children experience while engaged in play is another powerful tonic, the influence of which on the general health ought not to be overlooked; for the nervous influence is as indispensable to the right performance of respiration as it is to the action of the muscles or to the digestion of food.

The regular supply of pure fresh air is another essential condition of healthy respiration, without which the requisite changes in the constitution of the blood, as it passes through the lungs, can not be effected. To enable the reader to appreciate this condition, it is necessary to consider the nature of the changes alluded to.

It is ascertained by analysis that the air we breathe is composed chiefly of the two gases *nitrogen* and *oxygen*, united in the ratio of four to one by volume, with exceedingly small and variable quantities of carbonic acid and aqueous vapor. No other mixture of these, or of any other gases, will sustain healthy respiration. To be more specific—atmospheric air consists of about seventy-eight per cent. of nitrogen, twenty-one per cent. of oxygen, and not quite one per cent. of carbonic acid. Such is its constitution when taken into the lungs in the act of breathing. When it is expelled from them, however, its composition is found to be greatly altered. The quantity of nitrogen remains nearly the same, but eight or eight and a half per cent. of the oxgyen or vital air have disappeared, and been replaced by an equal amount of carbonic acid. In addition to these changes, the expired air is loaded with moisture. Simultaneously with these occurrences, the blood collected from the veins, which enters the lungs of a dark color and unfit for the support of life, assumes a florid hue and acquires the power of supporting life.

Physiologists are not fully agreed in explaining the processes by which these changes are effected in the lungs. All, however, agree that the change of the blood in the lungs is essentially dependent on the supply of oxygen contained in the air we breathe, and that air is fit or unfit for respiration in exact proportion as its quantity of oxygen approaches to, or differs from, that contained in pure air. If we attempt to breathe nitrogen, hydrogen, or any other gas that does not contain oxygen, the result will be speedy suffocation. If, on the other hand, we breathe air containing too great a proportion of oxygen, the vital powers will speedily suffer from excess of stimulus.

The chief chemical properties of the atmosphere are owing to the presence of *oxygen.* Nitrogen, which constitutes about four fifths of its volume, has been supposed to act as a mere diluent to the oxygen. *Increase* the proportion of oxygen in the atmosphere, and, as already stated, the vital powers will speedily suffer from excess of stimulus, the circulation and respiration become *too rapid*, and the system generally becomes highly excited. *Diminish* the proportion of oxygen, and the circulation and respiration become *too slow*, weakness and lassitude ensue, and a sense of heaviness and uneasiness pervades the entire system. As has been observed, air *loses* during each respiration a portion of its oxygen, and gains an equal quantity of *carbonic acid*, which is an *active poison.* When mixed with atmospheric air in the ratio of one to four, it extinguishes animal life. It is this gas that is produced by burning charcoal in a confined portion of common air. Its effect upon the system is well known to every reader of our newspapers. It causes dimness of sight, weakness, dullness, a difficulty of breathing, and ultimately *apoplexy* and *death.**

* Since the text was prepared for the press, I have noticed from the Syracuse (New York) Journal of January 3d, 1850, mention of the death of General Rensselaer Van Rensselaer, of that city, from breathing "the fumes of charcoal" burned in a "portable furnace." This, it should be remembered, is but *one* of the *many instances* that are constantly occurring all over our country, in which *immediate death* is the result of breathing this destructive agent.

Respiration produces the same effect upon air that the burning of charcoal does. It converts its oxygen, which is the aliment of animal life, into carbonic acid, which, be it remembered, is an active poison. Says Dr. Turner, in his celebrated work on chemistry, "An animal can not live in air which is unable to support combustion." Says the same author again, "An animal can not live in air which contains sufficient carbonic acid for extinguishing a candle." It will presently be seen why these quotations are made.

It is stated in several medical works that the quantity of air that enters the lungs at each inspiration of an adult varies from thirty-two to forty cubic inches. To establish more definitely some data upon which a calculation might safely be based, I some years ago conducted an experiment whereby I ascertained the medium quantity of air that entered the lungs of myself and four young men was thirty-six cubic inches, and that respiration is repeated once in three seconds, or twenty times a minute. I also ascertained that *respired air will not support combustion.* This truth, taken in connection with the quotations just made, establishes another and a *more important* truth, viz., that AIR ONCE RESPIRED WILL NOT FURTHER SUSTAIN ANIMAL LIFE. That part of the experiment by which it was ascertained that respired air will not support combustion is very simple, and I here give it with the hope that it may be tried at least in every *school-house,* if not in every family of our wide-spread country. It was conducted as follows:

I introduced a lighted taper into an inverted receiver (glass jar) which contained seven quarts of atmospheric air, and placed the mouth of the receiver into a vessel of water. The taper burned with its wonted brilliancy about a minute, and, growing dim gradually, became extinct at the expiration of three minutes. I then filled the receiver with water, and inverting it, placed its mouth beneath the surface of the same fluid in another vessel. I next removed the water from the receiver by *breathing into it.* This was done by filling the lungs with air, which, after being retained a short time in the chest, was exhaled through a siphon (a bent lead tube) into the receiver. I then introduced the lighted taper into the receiver of respired air, by which it was *immediately extinguished.* Several persons present then received a quantity of respired air into their lungs, whereupon the premonitory symptoms of apoplexy, as already given, ensued. The experiment was conducted with great care, and several times repeated in the presence of respectable members of the medical profession, a professor of chemistry, and several literary gentlemen, to their entire satisfaction.

Before proceeding further, I will make a practical application of the principles already established. Within the last ten years I have visited half of the states of the Union for the purpose of becoming acquainted with the actual condition of our common schools. I have therefore noticed especially the condition of school-houses. Although there is a great variety in their dimensions, yet there are comparatively few school-houses less than sixteen by eighteen feet on the ground, and fewer still larger than twenty-four by thirty feet, exclusive of our principal cities and villages. From a large number of actual measurements, not only in New York and Michigan, but east of the Hudson River and west of the great lakes, I conclude that, exclusive of entry and closets, when they are furnished with these appendages, school-houses are not usually larger than twenty by twenty-four feet on the ground, and seven feet in height. They are, indeed, more frequently smaller than larger. School-houses of these dimensions have a capacity of 3360 cubic feet, and are usually occupied by at least forty-five scholars in the winter season. Not unfrequently sixty or seventy, and occasionally more than a hundred scholars occupy a room of this size.

A simple arithmetical computation will abundantly satisfy any person who is acquainted with the composition of the atmosphere, the influence of respiration upon its fitness to sustain animal life, and the quantity of air that enters the lungs at each inspiration, that a school-room of the preceding dimensions contains quite too little air to sustain the healthy respiration of even *forty-five* scholars three hours—the usual length of each session ; and frequently the school-house is imperfectly ventilated between the sessions at noon, and sometimes for several days together.

Mark the following particulars: 1. The quantity of air breathed by forty-five persons in three hours, according to the data just given, is 3375 cubic feet. 2. *Air once respired will not sustain animal life.* 3. The school-room was estimated to possess a capacity of 3360 cubic feet—*fifteen feet less than is necessary to sustain healthy respiration.* 4. Were forty-five persons whose lungs possess the estimated capacity placed in an air-tight room of the preceding dimensions, and could they breathe pure air till it was all once respired, and then enter upon its second respiration, *they would all die with the apoplexy before the expiration of a three hours' session.*

From the nature of the case, these conditions can not conveniently be fulfilled. But numerous instances of fearful approximation exist. We have no air-tight houses. But in our latitude, comfort requires that rooms which are to be occupied by children in the winter season, be made very close. The dimensions of rooms are, moreover, frequently narrowed, that the *warm breath* may lessen the amount of fuel necessary to preserve a comfortable temperature. It is true, on the other hand, that the quantity of air which children breathe is somewhat less than I have estimated. But the derangement resulting from breathing impure air, in their case, is greater than in the case of adults whose constitutions are matured, and who are hence less susceptible of injury. It is also true in many schools that the number occupying a room of the dimensions supposed is considerably greater than I have estimated. Moreover, in many instances, a great proportion of the larger scholars will respire the estimated quantity of air.

Again, all the air in a room is not respired *once* before a portion of it is breathed the second, or even the *third* and *fourth* time. The atmosphere is not suddenly changed from purity to impurity—from a healthful to an infectious state. Were it so, the change, being more perceptible, would be seen and *felt* too, and a *remedy* would be sought and applied. But because the change is gradual, it is not the less fearful in its consequences. In a room occupied by *forty-five persons*, THE FIRST MINUTE, *thirty-two thousand four hundred cubic inches of air impart their entire vitality to sustain animal life, and, mingling with the atmosphere of the room, proportionately deteriorate the whole mass.* Thus are abundantly sown in early life the fruitful seeds of disease and premature death.

This detail shows conclusively sufficient cause for that uneasy, listless state of feeling which is so prevalent in crowded school-rooms. It explains why children that are amiable at home are mischievous in school, and why those that are troublesome at home are frequently well-nigh uncontrollable in school. It discloses the true cause why so many teachers who are justly considered both pleasant and amiable in the ordinary domestic and social relations, are obnoxious in the school-room, being there habitually sour and fretful. The ever-active children are disqualified for study, and engage in mischief as their only alternative. On the other hand, the irritable teacher, who can hardly look with complaisance upon good behavior, is disposed to magnify the most trifling departure from the rules of propriety. The scholars are continually becoming more ungovernable, and the teacher more unfit to govern them. Week after week they become less and less attached to him, and he, in turn, becomes less interested in them.

This detail explains, also, why so many children are unable to attend school at all, or become unwell so soon after commencing to attend, when their health is sufficient to engage in other pursuits. The number of scholars answering this description is greater than most persons are aware of. In one district that I visited a few years ago in the State of New York, it was acknowledged by competent judges to be emphatically true in the case of not less than *twenty-five scholars.* Indeed, in that same district, the health of more than *one hundred* scholars was materially injured every year in consequence of occupying an old and partially-decayed house, of too narrow dimensions, with very limited facilities for ventilation. The evil, even after the cause was made known, was suffered to exist for years, although the district was worth more than three hundred thousand dollars. And what *was* true* of this school, is now, with a few variations, true in the case

* In the district referred to there has since been erected a large and commodious union school house, which constitutes at once the pride and ornament of a beautiful and flourishing village.

of scores, if not hundreds of schools with which I am acquainted, from far-famed New England to the Valley of the Mississippi.

This detail likewise explains why the business of teaching has acquired, and *justly too*, the reputation of being unhealthy. There is, however, no reason why the health of either teacher or pupils should sooner fail in a well-regulated school, taught in a house properly constructed, and suitably warmed and ventilated, than in almost any other business. If this statement were not true, an unanswerable argument might be framed against the very *existence* of schools; and it might clearly be shown that it is *policy*, nay, DUTY, to close at once and forever the four thousand school-houses of Michigan, and the hundred thousand of the nation, and leave the rising generation to perish for lack of knowledge. But our condition in this respect is not hopeless. The evil in question may be effectually remedied by enlarging the house, or, which is easier, cheaper, and more effectual, by frequent and thorough ventilation. It would be well, however, to unite the two methods.

In the winter of 1841–2, I visited a school in which the magnitude of the evil under consideration was clearly developed. Five of the citizens of the district attended me in my visit to the school. We arrived at the school-house about the middle of the afternoon. It was a close, new house, eighteen by twenty-four feet on the ground—two feet less in one of its dimensions than the house concerning which the preceding calculation is made. There were present forty-three scholars, the teacher, five patrons, and myself, making fifty in all. Immediately after entering the school-house, one of the trustees remarked to me, "I believe our school-house is too tight to be healthy." I made no reply, but secretly resolved that I would sacrifice my comfort for the remainder of the afternoon, and hazard my health, and my life even, to test the accuracy of the opinions I had entertained on this important subject. I marked the uneasiness and dullness of all present, and especially of the patrons, who had been accustomed to breathe a purer atmosphere. School continued an hour and a half, at the close of which I was invited to make some remarks. I arose to do so, but was unable to proceed till I opened the outer door, and snuffed a few times the purer air without. When I had partially recovered my wonted vigor, I observed with delight the renovating influence of the current of air that entered the door, mingling with and gradually displacing the fluid poison that filled the room, and was about to do the work of death. It seemed as though I was standing at the mouth of a huge sepulcher, in which the dead were being restored to life. After a short pause, I proceeded with a few remarks, chiefly, however, on the subject of respiration and ventilation. The trustees, who had just tested their accuracy and bearing upon their comfort and health, resolved immediately to provide for ventilation according to the suggestions in the article on school-houses in the last chapter of this work.

Before leaving the house on that occasion, I was informed an evening meeting had been attended there the preceding week, which they were obliged to dismiss before the ordinary exercises were concluded, because, as they said, "We all got sick, and the candles went almost out." Little did they realize, probably, that the light of life became just as nearly extinct as did the candles. Had they remained there a little longer, both would have gone out together, and there would have been reacted the memorable tragedy of the *Black Hole* in Calcutta, into which were thrust a garrison of one hundred and forty-six persons, one hundred and twenty-three of whom perished miserably in a few hours, being suffocated by the confined air.

What has been said in the preceding pages on the philosophy of respiration was first given to the public nearly ten years ago, in a report of the author's in the State of New York. He has since seen the same sentiments inculcated by many of our most eminent practical educators, some of whom had written upon the subject at an earlier date. Allen and Pepy showed by experiment that air which has been once breathed contains eight and a half per cent. of carbonic acid, and that no continuance of the respiration of the same air could make it take up more than ten per cent. Air, then, when once respired, has taken up more than *four fifths* of the amount of this noxious gas that it can be made to by any number of breathings.

Dr. Clark, in his work on Consumption, remarks as follows: "Were I to select two circumstances which influence the health, especially during the growth of the body, more than others, and concerning which the public, ignorant at present, ought to be well informed, they would be the proper adaptation of food to difference of age and constitution, and the constant supply of pure air for respiration." Dr. William A. Alcott, who has given especial attention to this subject, after quoting the preceding remark of Dr. Clark, adds: "We believe this is the opinion of all medical men who have studied the constitution of man, and its relation to outward objects."

A distinguished surgeon* of Leeds, England, goes somewhat further in praising pure air than most of his contemporaries. "Be it remembered," says he, "that

* Dr. Thackrah, author of a most valuable work on the "Effects of Employments on the Health and Longevity of Mankind."

man subsists more upon air than upon his food and drink." There is some novelty in this remark, I admit; but is it not truthful? Men have been known to live *three weeks* without eating. But exclude the atmospheric air from the lungs for the space of *three minutes*, and death generally ensues. We thus see that life will continue with abstinence from food three thousand times as long as it is safe to protract an atmospheric fast.

Let us take another view of the subject. Men usually eat *three times* in twenty-four hours. This is all that is necessary to, or compatible with, the enjoyment of uninterrupted good health. But we involuntarily breathe nearly *thirty thousand times* in the same length of time. We need, then, fresh supplies of pure air ten thousand times as often as it is necessary to partake of meals. Is it not apparent, then, that *man subsists more upon* AIR *than upon his* FOOD *and* DRINK?

The atmosphere which we so frequently inhale, and upon which our well-being so much depends, surrounds the earth to the height of about forty-five miles. The surface of the earth contains about two hundred millions of square miles, and it is estimated that there dwell upon it eight hundred millions of inhabitants. This gives to each individual about eleven cubic miles of air. But the air is breathed by the inferior animals as well as by man. It is also rendered impure by combustion. If by both of these causes ten times as much air is consumed as by man, there is still left one cubic mile of uncontaminated atmospheric air to every human being dwelling upon the surface of the earth. This would allow him to live more than twice the age allotted to man, without breathing any portion of the atmosphere a second time. And still, as if to avoid the possibility of evil to man on this account, the beneficent Creator has wisely so ordered, that while we do not interfere with the laws of Nature, there is not even the possibility of rebreathing respired air until it has been purified and restored to its natural and healthful state; for carbonic acid, the vitiating product of respiration, although immediately *fatal* to *animals*, constitutes the very *life* of *vegetation*. When brought in contact with the upper surface of the green leaves of trees and plants, and acted upon by the direct solar rays, this gas is decomposed, and its carbon is absorbed to sustain, in part, the life of the plant, by affording it one element of its food, while the oxygen is liberated and restored to the atmosphere. Vegetables and animals are thus perpetually interchanging kindly offices, and each flourishes upon that which is fatal to the other. It is in this way that the healthful state of the atmosphere is kept up Its equilibrium seems never to be disturbed, or, if disturbed at all, it is immediately restored by the mutual exchange of poison for aliment, which is constantly going on between the animal and vegetable worlds. This interchange of kindly offices is constantly going on all over the earth, even in the highest latitudes, and in the very depths of winter; for air which has been respired is rarefied, and, when thrown from the lungs, *ascends*, and is thus not only out of our reach, whereby we are protected from respiring it a second time, but this (to us) deadly poison falls into the great aërial current which is constantly flowing from the polar to the tropical regions, where it is converted into vegetable growth. The oxygen which is exhaled in the processes of tropical vegetation, heated and rarefied by the vertical rays of the sun, mounts to the upper regions of the atmosphere, and, falling into a returning current, in its appointed time revisits the higher latitudes. So wisely has the Divine Author ordered these processes, that

air, in its natural state* in any part of the world, does not contain more than *one half of one per cent.* of carbonic acid gas, although, as already stated, air which has been once respired contains *eight and a half per cent.* of this gas, which is at least seventeen times its natural quantity.

There are other agencies than carbonic acid gas which in civic life render the atmosphere impure. Of this nature is carbureted hydrogen gas, which is produced in various ways. This, says Dr. Comstock, is immediately destructive to animal life, and will not support combustion. It exists in stagnant water, especially in warm weather, and is generated by the decomposition of vegetable products. Dr. Arnott expresses the conviction that the immediate and chief cause of many of the diseases which impair the bodily and mental health of the people, and bring a considerable portion prematurely to the grave, is the poison of atmospheric impurity, arising from the accumulation in and around their dwellings of the decomposing remnants of the substances used for food and in their arts, and of the impurities given out from their own bodies. If you allow the sources of aërial impurity to exist in or around dwellings, he continues, you are poisoning the people; and while many die at early ages of fevers and other acute diseases, the remainder will have their health impaired and their lives shortened.

There are many instances on record where the progress of an epidemic has been speedily arrested by ventilation. A striking instance is given by the writer last quoted. "When I visited Glasgow with Mr. Chadwick," says he, "there was described to us one vast

* It would be difficult to say whether carbonic acid gas is in the atmosphere constitutionally, or accidentally, or both.—*Dr. Wm. A. Alcott's Health Tracts.*

lodging-house, in connection with a manufactory there, in which formerly fever constantly prevailed, but where, by making an opening from the top of each room through a channel of communication to an air-pump common to all the channels, the disease had disappeared altogether. The supply of pure air obtained by that mode of ventilation was sufficient to dilute the cause of the disease, so that it became powerless."

Sulphureted hydrogen gas is also exceedingly poisonous to the lungs and to every part of the system. When pure, this gas is described as instantly fatal to animal life. Even when diluted with fifteen hundred times its bulk of air, it has been found so poisonous as to destroy a bird in a few seconds. "This gas," says Dr. Dunglison, in his Elements of Hygiene, "is extremely deleterious.* When respired in a pure state it kills instantly; and its deadly agency is rapidly exerted when put in contact with any of the tissues of the body, through which it penetrates with astonishing rapidity. Even when mixed with a portion of air, it has proved immediately destructive. Dr. Paris refers to the case of a chemist of his acquaintance, who was suddenly deprived of sense as he stood over a pneumatic trough in which he was collecting this gas. From the experiments of Dupuytren and Thenard, air that contains a thousandth part of sulphureted hydrogen kills birds immediately. A dog perished in air containing a hundredth part, and a horse in air containing a fiftieth part of it."

The preceding are far from being all the causes of atmospheric impurity. Besides these, there are numerous exhalations, as well as gases, that are poisonous.

* Sulphureted hydrogen gas is the deleterious agent exhaled from privies or vaults, which have been so fatal, at times, to night men, who have been employed to remove or cleanse them.—*Dr. Dunglison.*

Some of these exhalations are more abundant in the night, and about the time of the morning and evening twilight. "Hence the importance," says a writer on health, "to those who are feeble, of avoiding the air at all hours except when the sun is considerably above the horizon."

Although the atmosphere, in its natural state, is not at all times perfectly pure, still it is comparatively so, and especially in the daytime. All, therefore, who would retain and improve their health, should inhale the open air as much as possible, even though they can not, like Franklin's Methusalem,* be always in it. This remark is applicable to both sexes, and to every age and condition of life.

The following, from the pen of an American author† who has written much and well on physical education, is pertinent to the subject under consideration: "We breathe bad air principally as the production of our own bodies. Here is the source of a large share of human wo; and to this point must his attention be particularly directed who would save himself from disease, and promote, in the highest possible degree, his health and longevity. We must avoid breathing over the carbonic acid gas contained in the tight or unven-

* Dr. Franklin, in his usual humorous manner, but with his accustomed gravity, relates, in one of his essays, the following anecdote, for the purpose, doubtless, of showing the influence of pure air upon health, happiness, and longevity.

"It is recorded of Methusalem, who, being the longest liver, may be supposed to have best preserved his health, that he slept always in the open air; for when he had lived five hundred years, an angel said to him, Arise, Methusalem, and build thee a house, for thou shalt live yet five hundred years longer. But Methusalem answered and said, If I am to live but five hundred years longer, it is not worth while to build me a house. I will sleep in the air as I have been accustomed to do."

† From Dr. William A. Alcott's Tract on Breathing Bad Air.

tilated rooms in which we labor or remain for a long time, whether parlors, school-rooms, counting-rooms, bed-rooms, shops, or factories. The individual who lives most according to nature—who observes with most care the laws of life and health—must necessarily throw off much carbonic acid from his lungs, if not from his skin. It does not follow, however, that because this gas is formed we are obliged to inhale it. We may change our position, change our clothing, ventilate our rooms of all sorts, shake up our bed-clothing often and air our bed, and use clean, loose, and porous clothing by night and by day. We may thus very effectually guard against injuries from a very injurious agent.

"One thing should be remembered in connection with this subject which is truly encouraging. The more we accustom ourselves to pure air, the more easily will our lungs and nasal organs detect its presence. He who has redeemed his senses and restored his lungs to integrity, like him who has redeemed a conscience once deadened, is so alive to every bad impression made upon any of these, that he can often detect impurity around or within him, and thus learn to avoid it. It will scarcely be possible for such a person long to breathe bad air, or nauseous or unwholesome effluvia, without knowing it, and learning to avoid the causes which produce it. Such a person will not neglect long to remove the impurities which accumulate so readily on the surface of his body, or suffer himself to use food or drink which induces flatulence, and thus exposes either his intestines or his lungs, or the lungs of others, to that most extremely poisonous agent, sulphureted hydrogen gas. Nor will he be likely to permit the accumulation of filth, liquid or solid, around or in his dwelling. There are those whose senses will detect a very small quantity of stagnant water, or vinegar, or other liquids, or fruit, or changed food in the house, or even the presence of those semi-putrid substances, wine and cider. But some will indeed say that such integrity of the senses would be an annoyance rather than a blessing. On the same principle, however, would a high degree of conscientiousness in regard to right and wrong in moral conduct be a curse to us. If it be desirable to have our physical sense of right and wrong benumbed, it is so to have our moral sense benumbed also. Yet what person of sense ever complained of too tender a conscience, or too perfect a sense of right and wrong in morals?"

Exercise of the Lungs.—Judicious exercise of the lungs, in the opinion of that eminent physiologist, Dr. Andrew Combe, is one of the most efficacious means which can be employed for promoting their development and warding off their diseases. In this respect the organs of respiration closely resemble the muscles and all other organized parts. They are made to be used, and if they are left in habitual inactivity, their strength and health are unavoidably impaired; while, if their exercise be ill-timed or excessive, disease will as certainly follow.

The lungs may be exercised *directly* by the use of the voice in speaking, reading aloud, or singing, and *indirectly* by such kinds of bodily or muscular exertion as require quicker and deeper breathing. In general, both ought to be conjoined. But where the chief object is to improve the lungs, those kinds which have a tendency to expand the chest and call the organs of respiration into play ought to be especially preferred. Rowing a boat, fencing, quoits, shuttlecock, the proper use of skipping the rope, dumb-bells, and gymnastics are of this description, and have been recommended for this purpose. All of them employ actively the muscles of the chest and trunk, and excite the lungs themselves to freer and fuller expansion. Climbing up a hill is, for the same reason, an exercise of high utility in giving tone and freedom to the pulmonary functions. Where, either from hereditary predisposition or accidental causes, the chest is unusually weak, every effort should be made, from infancy upward, to favor the growth and strength of the lungs, by the habitual use of such of these exercises as can most easily be practiced. The earlier they are resorted to, and the more steadily they are pursued, the more certainly will their beneficial results be experienced.

If the *direct* exercise of the lungs in practicing deep inspiration, speaking, reading aloud, and singing, is properly managed and persevered in, particularly before the frame has become consolidated, it will exert a very beneficial influence in expanding the chest, and giving tone and imparting health to the important organs contained in it. As a preventive measure, Dr. Clark, in his treatise on Consumption and Scrofula, recommends the full expansion of the chest in the following manner: "We desire the young person, while standing, to throw his arms and shoulders back, and, while in this position, to inhale slowly as much air as he can, and repeat this exercise at short intervals several times in succession. When this can be done in the open air it is most desirable, a double advantage being thus obtained from the practice. Some exercise of this kind should be adopted daily by all young persons, more especially by those whose chests are narrow or deformed, and should be slowly and gradually increased."

In this preventive measure recommended by Dr. Clark, some of our most eminent physiologists heartily concur. They also express the opinion that, for the same reason, even the crying and sobbing of children, when not caused by disease, contribute to their future health. Dr. Combe says, "The loud laugh and noisy exclamations attending the sports of the young have an evident relation to the same beneficial end, and ought, therefore, to be encouraged." But beneficial as the direct exercise of the lungs is thus shown to be, in expanding and strengthening the chest, its influence extends still further, and, as we have already seen, contributes greatly to promote the important process of digestion. If, therefore, the lungs be rarely called into active exercise, not only do *they* suffer, but an important aid to digestion being withdrawn, the *stomach* and *bowels* also become weakened, and indigestion and costiveness ensue.

The exercise of what has not unaptly been called Vocal Gymnastics, and the loud and distinct speaking enforced in many of our schools, not only fortify the vocal organs against the attacks of disease, but tend greatly to promote the general health. For this purpose, also, as well as for its social and moral influences, vocal music should be introduced into all our schools. That by these and like exercises deep inspirations and full expirations are encouraged, any one may become convinced who will attend to what passes in his own body while reading aloud a single paragraph.

There is danger of exercising the lungs too much when disease exists in the chest. At such times, not only speaking, reading aloud, and singing, but ordinary muscular exertion, ought to be refrained from, or be regulated by professional advice. When a joint is sore or inflamed, we know that motion impedes its recovery. When the eye is affected, we, for a similar reason, shut out the light. So, when the stomach is disordered, we respect its condition, and are more careful about diet. The lungs demand a treatment founded on the same general principle. When inflamed, they should be exercised as little as possible. All violent exercise ought, therefore, to be refrained from during at least the active stages of a cold; but colds may often be entirely prevented at the time of exposure by a proper exercise of the lungs.

In conversing with an eminent physician recently on this subject, he expressed the conviction that one of the most effectual methods of warding off a cold, when exposed by wet feet or otherwise, is to take frequent deep inhalations of air. By this means the carbonic acid, which the returning circulation deposits in the lungs, is not only more effectually disengaged, but, at the same time, the greater amount of oxygen that enters the lungs and combines with the blood quickens the circulation and thus, imparting increased vitality to the system, enables it more effectually to resist any attack that may be induced by unusual exposure.

A late medical writer, who has become quite celebrated in this country for the successful treatment of pulmonary consumption,* expresses the opinion that, to the consumptive, air is a most excellent medicine, and "far more valuable than all other remedies." He thinks it "the grand agent in expanding the chest." In urging the importance of habitually maintaining an erect position, he expresses the conviction that "practice will soon make sitting or standing perfectly erect vastly more agreeable and less fatiguing than a stooping posture." To persons predisposed to consumption, these hints, he thinks, are of the greatest importance. While walking, he says, "the chest should be carried proudly erect and straight, the top of it pointing rather backward than forward." To illustrate the advantages of

* S. S. Fitch, M.D., author of "Consumption Cured."

habitually maintaining this position, he refers to the North American Indians, who never had consumption, and who are remarkable for their perfectly erect posture while walking. "Next to this," he adds, "it is of vast importance to the consumptive to breathe well. He should make a practice of taking long breaths, sucking in all the air he can, and holding it in the chest as long as possible." He recommends the repetition of this a hundred times a day, and especially with those who have a slight cold or symptoms of weak lungs. When practiced in pure cold air, its advantages are most apparent. To increase the benefits resulting from this practice, he recommends the use of the "inhaling tube." He thinks that inhaling tubes made of silver or gold are much better than those made of wood or India-rubber. In this opinion I fully concur, for I think with him that gold and silver tubes will not so readily "contract any impure or poisonous matter." But there is another and a stronger reason why I prefer *silver*, and especially GOLD inhaling tubes, to those made of wood or India-rubber. *They would be more highly prized* and MORE FREQUENTLY USED.

The same writer entertains the belief that about one third of all the consumptions originate from weakness of the abdominal belts. He hence, in such cases, recommends the use of the "abdominal supporter." In order to favor an erect posture and an open chest, he also recommends the use of "shoulder-braces." He says the proper use of these, with other remedies, will "entirely prevent the possibility of consumption, from whatever cause." The inhaling-tube, together with the shoulder-braces and supporter when needed, he says are perfect preventives, and should not be neglected; for if the shoulders are kept off the chest, and the abdomen is well supported, and then an inhaling tube is faithfully used, "the lungs can never become diseased. Any person in this way, who chooses to take the trouble, can have a large chest and healthy lungs."

When persons have contracted disease they may require these *artificial helps;* but it should be borne in mind that an all-wise and beneficent Creator has kindly given to each of his creatures *two inhaling tubes,* admirably adapted to their wants. He has also furnished them with a set of *abdominal muscles* which, when properly used, have generally been found to supersede the necessity of artificial "supporters." He has, moreover, in the plenitude of his goodness, furnished each member of the human family with a good pair of *shoulder-braces.* It should also be borne in mind that Nature's shoulder-braces *improve by use,* while the artificial ones not only soon fail, but their very use generally impairs the healthy action of the natural ones; for these, like all other muscles, improve by use and become enfeebled by disuse. Parents and teachers, then, and all who have the care of the young, should encourage the correct use of Nature's inhaling tubes, shoulder-braces, and abdominal supporters; for in this way they have it in their power not only to supersede the necessity of resorting to artificial ones later in life, but of preventing much of human misery, and contributing to the permanent elevation of the race.

CHAPTER V.

THE NATURE OF INTELLECTUAL AND MORAL EDUCATION.

In the cultivation and expansion of the faculties of the mind, we act altogether upon *organized matter*—and this, too, of the most delicate kind—which, while it serves as the mediator between *body* and *spirit*, partakes so largely of the nature, character, and essential attributes of the *former*, that, without its proper physical growth and development, all the manifestations of the *latter* sink into comparative insignificance; so that, without a perfect organization of the *brain*, the mental powers must be proportionally paralyzed; without *its* maintaining a healthy condition, *they* must be rendered proportionally weak and inactive.* —DR. J. L. PEIRCE.

IT has already been stated that there exists such an intimate connection between physical, intellectual, and moral education, that, in order duly to appreciate the importance of either, we must not view it separate and alone merely, but in connection with both of the others. However much value, then, we may attach to physical education on its own account, considering man as a corporeal being, we shall have occasion greatly to magnify its importance as we direct our attention to the cultivation and development of his mental faculties. We have no means of becoming acquainted with the laws which govern independent mind; but that mind separate from body is, from its very nature, all-knowing and intelligent, is an opinion that has obtained to a considerable extent. Be this as it may, it does not immediately concern us in the present state. This much we know, that embodied mind acquires knowledge

* From an Essay upon the Physical and Intellectual Education of Children, written by request of the Managers of the Pennsylvania Lyceum.

slowly, and with a degree of perfection depending upon the condition of the brain and the bodily organs of sense, through the medium of which mind communicates with the external world. We do not even know whether education modifies the mind itself; and, if at all, how it affects it in its disembodied state. Neither is it important that we should possess this knowledge. There is, however, much reason for believing that the mind of man in the future state will be permanently affected by, and enjoy the full benefit of, the preparatory training it has received in this life; that then, as now, it will be progressive in its attainments; and that the rapidity with which it will then acquire knowledge, and the nature of its pursuits, will depend upon the degree of cultivation, and the habits and character formed in this life.

From what we know of the beneficent and all-wise Creator, as manifested in his word and works, we have abundant reason for believing that our highest and enduring good will be best promoted by becoming acquainted with, and yielding a cheerful obedience to, the laws of organic mind. Whatever the effect of education upon independent mind may be, we may rest well assured that man's everlasting well-being in the future state will be most directly and certainly reached by a strict conformity to those laws which regulate mind in its present mode of being. It should be borne in mind, also, that just in proportion as man remains ignorant of those laws, or, knowing them, disregards them, will he fail to secure his best good in this life not only, but in that which is to come, to an extent corresponding with the influence which education may exert upon independent mind. In order, then, most successfully to carry forward the great work of intellectual and moral culture, and to secure to man the fullest benefits of education in the present life, and in that higher mode of being which awaits him in the future, we have only to acquaint him with the laws by which embodied mind is governed, and to induce him to yield a ready, cheerful, and uniform obedience to those laws. We shall therefore devote the following pages to an inquiry into the laws which must be observed by embodied mind in order to render it the fittest possible instrument for discovering, applying, and obeying the laws under which God has placed the universe, which constitutes the one great object of education, when considered in its widest and true sense.

All physiologists and philosophers regard the brain as the organ of the mind. Although it is not befitting here to give a particular description of this complicated organ, still it may be well further to premise that, by nearly universal consent, it is regarded as the immediate seat of the *intellectual* faculties not only, but of the passions and moral feelings of our nature, as well as of consciousness and every other mental act. It is also well established that the brain is the principal source of that nervous influence which is essential to vitality, and to the action of each and all of our bodily organs. As, then, its functions are the highest and most important in the animal economy, it becomes an object of paramount importance in education to discover the laws by which they are regulated, that by yielding obedience to them we may avoid the evils consequent on their violation.

Let no one suppose these evils are few or small; for, in the language of an eloquent writer, "the system of education which is generally pursued in the United States is unphilosophical in its elementary principles, ill adapted to the condition of man, practically mocks his necessities, and is intrinsically absurd The high excellences of the present system, in other respects, are fully appreciated. Modern education has indeed achieved wonders. It has substituted things for names, experiment for hypothesis, first principles for arbitrary rules. It has simplified processes, stripped knowledge of its abstraction and thrown it into visibility, made practical results rather than mystery the standard by which to measure the value of attainment, and facts rather than conjecture its circulating medium."*

A sound original constitution may be regarded as the first condition of the healthy action of the brain; for, being a part of the animal economy, it is subject to the same general laws that govern the other bodily organs. When a healthy brain is transmitted to children, and their treatment from infancy is judicious and rational, its health becomes so firmly established that, in after life, its power of endurance will be greatly increased, and it will be enabled most effectually to ward off the insidious attacks of disease. On the other hand, where this organ has either inherited deficiencies and imperfections, or where they have been subsequently induced by early mismanagement, it becomes peculiarly susceptible, and frequently yields to the slightest attacks. The most eminent physiologists of the age concur in the opinion that, of all the causes which predispose to nervous and mental disease, the transmission of hereditary tendency from parents to children is the most powerful, producing, as it does, in the children, an unusual liability to those maladies under which their parents have labored.

When both parents are descended from tainted families, their progeny, as a matter of course, will be more deeply affected than where one of them is from a pure stock. This sufficiently accounts for the fact that he-

* Report on Manual Labor, by Theodore D. Weld, 1833.

reditary predisposition is a more common cause of nervous disease in those circles that intermarry much with each other than where a wider choice is exercised. Fortunately, such is the constitution of society in this country, that there are fewer evils of this kind among us than are manifest in many of the European states, where intermarriages are restricted to persons of the same rank, as has already been illustrated by reference to the grandees of Spain, who have become a race of dwarfs intellectually as well as physically. But even in this country there are painful illustrations of the truth of the popular belief that when cousins intermarry their offspring are liable to be idiotic. The command of God not to marry within certain degrees of consanguinity is, then, in accordance with the organic laws of our being, and the wisdom of the prohibition is abundantly confirmed by observation.

What was said of hereditary transmission in the second chapter of this work applies here with increased force. It is of the highest possible importance that this subject should receive the especial attention of every parent, and of all who may hereafter sustain the parental relation; for posterity, to the latest generations, will be affected by the laws of hereditary transmission, whether those laws are understood and obeyed or not. The importance of this subject, already inconceivably vast, becomes infinitely momentous in view of the probability that the evils under consideration are not confined to this life, but must, from the nature of the case, continue to be felt while mind endures.

Unfortunately, it is not merely as a cause of disease that hereditary predisposition is to be dreaded. The obstacles which it throws in the way of permanent recovery are even more formidable, and can never be entirely removed. Safety is to be found only in avoiding the perpetuation of the mischief. When, therefore, two persons, each naturally of an excitable and delicate nervous temperament, choose to unite for life, they have themselves to blame for the concentrated influence of similar tendencies in destroying the health of their offspring, and subjecting them to all the miseries of nervous disease, melancholy, or madness.

There is another consideration that should be noticed here: it is this. Even where no hereditary defect exists, the state of the mother during pregnancy has an influence on the mental character and health of the offspring, of which even *few parents* have any adequate conception. "It is often in the maternal womb that we are to look for the true cause not only of imbecility, but of the different kinds of mania. During the agitated periods of the French Revolution, many ladies then pregnant, and whose minds were kept constantly on the stretch by the anxiety and alarm inseparable from the epoch in which they lived, and whose nervous systems were thereby rendered irritable in the highest degree compatible with sanity, were afterward delivered of infants whose brains and nervous systems had been affected to such a degree by the state of their parent, that, in future life, as children they were subject to spasms, convulsions, and other nervous affections, and in youth to imbecility or madness, almost without any exciting cause."*

* The testimony of M. Esquirol, whose talent, general accuracy, and extensive experience give great weight to all his well-considered opinions, quoted, also, and confirmed by the Physician Extraordinary to the Queen in Scotland, and consulting Physician to the King and Queen of the Belgians.

The same eminent author has recorded the following fact, illustrating the extent to which the temporary state of the mother, during gestation, may influence the *whole future life of the child.* A pregnant woman, otherwise healthy, was greatly alarmed and terrified by the threats of her husband when in a state of intoxication. She was after-

Dr. Caldwell, too, an able and philanthropic advocate of an improved system of physical, intellectual, and moral education in this country, is very urgent in enforcing rational care, during the period of gestation, on the part of every mother who values the future health and happiness of her offspring. Among other things, he insists on mothers taking more active exercise in the open air than they usually do. He also cautions them against allowing a feeling of false delicacy to keep them confined in their rooms for weeks and months together. At such times especially the mind ought to be kept free from gloom or anxiety, and in that state of cheerful activity which results from the proper exercise of the intellect, and especially of the moral and social feelings.

But if seclusion and depression be hurtful to the unborn progeny, surely thoughtless dissipation and late hours, dancing and waltzing, together with irritability of temper and peevishness of disposition, can not be less injurious. Every female that is about to become a mother should treasure up the remark of that sensible lady, the Margravine of Anspach, who says, "when a female is likely to become a mother, she ought to be doubly careful of her temper, and, in particular, to indulge no ideas that are not cheerful and no sentiments that are not kind. Such is the connection between the mind and the body, that the features of the face are moulded commonly into an expression of the internal disposition; and is it not natural to think that an infant,

ward delivered, at the proper time, of a very delicate child, which was so much affected by its mother's agitation that, up to the age of eighteen, it continued subject to panic terrors, and then became completely maniacal.

Many illustrative instances might be quoted from medical writers in this and other countries. The author might also refer to cases that have fallen under his own observation.

before it is born, may be affected by the temper of its mother?" If these things are true—and they are as well authenticated as any physiological facts are or can be—then not only *mothers*, but all with whom they associate, and especially *fathers*, are interested in knowing these important physiological laws; and they should aim, from the very beginning, so to observe them as to secure to posterity, physically and mentally, the full benefits that are connected with cheerful obedience.

A due supply of properly oxygenated blood is another condition upon which the healthy action of the brain depends. Although it may not be easy to perceive the effects of slight differences in the quality of the blood, still, when these differences exist in a considerable degree, the effects are too obvious to be overlooked. Withdraw entirely the stimulus of arterial blood, and the brain ceases to act, and sensibility and consciousness become extinct. When carbonic acid gas is inhaled, the blood circulating through the lungs does not undergo that process of oxygenation which is essential to life, as has been explained in a preceding chapter. As the venous blood in this unchanged state is unfit to excite or sustain the action of the brain, the mental functions become impaired, and death speedily ensues, as in the case of a number of persons breathing a portion of confined air, or inhaling the fumes of charcoal. On the other hand, if oxygen gas be inhaled instead of common air, the blood becomes too much oxygenated, and, as a consequence, the brain is unduly stimulated, and an intensity of action bordering on inflammation takes place, which also soon terminates in death.

These are extreme cases, I admit; but their consequences are equally remarkable and fatal. The slighter variations in the state of the blood produce equally sure, though less palpable effects. Whenever its vitality is impaired by breathing an atmosphere so vitiated as not to produce the proper degree of oxygenation, the blood can only afford an imperfect stimulus to the brain. As a necessary consequence, languor and inactivity of the mental and nervous functions ensue, and a tendency to headache, fainting, or hysteria makes its appearance. This is seen every day in the listlessness and apathy prevalent in crowded and ill-ventilated school-rooms, and in the headaches and liability to fainting which are so sure to attack persons of a delicate habit, in the contaminated atmospheres of crowded theaters, churches, and assemblies of whatever kind. The same effects, although less strikingly apparent, are perhaps more permanently felt by the inmates of cotton manufactories and public hospitals, who are noted for being irritable and sensitive. The languor and nervous debility consequent on confinement in ill-ventilated apartments, or in air vitiated by the breath of many people, are neither more nor less than minor degrees of the process of poisoning, which was particularly explained in the preceding chapter, while treating upon the philosophy of respiration.

That it is not real debility which produces these effects, is apparent from the fact, that egress to the open air almost instantly restores activity and vigor to both mind and body, unless the exposure has been very long. There is an interesting but fearful illustration of the truth of this statement at the 96th page of this work, to which I beg leave to refer. Where the exposure has been very long continued, more time is of course required to re-establish the exhausted powers of the brain. Indeed, we may not, in such cases, hope for complete recovery; for when persons remain several hours a day in a vitiated atmosphere, for weeks and months together, both mind and body become permanently diseased. It is well known to every person who has given attention to the subject, that hitherto this has been the condition of *public schools*, generally, in every part of the United States, and throughout the civilized world. This has, perhaps, tended more than all other causes combined, to render the profession of teaching disreputable, and to constitute the very name of schoolmaster, or pedagogue, a hissing and a by-word. And why is this? I can account for it in but one way. The school teacher is subject to the *same organic laws as other men;* and, either on account of the ignorance or parsimony of his employers, he has been shut up with *their* children several hours a day, in narrow and ill-ventilated apartments, where, whatever else they may have done, their principal business has of necessity been *to poison one another to death.* And, as if not satisfied with this, when the teacher has ruined his health in our employment, and become a mere wreck, physically and mentally, *we despise him.* This is a double injustice, and is adding insult to injury. And the consequences are hardly less fatal to the children. The situation of the majority of our schools, when viewed in connection with the physiological laws already explained, sufficiently accounts for that irritability, listlessness, and languor which have been so often observed in both teachers and pupils. Both irritability of the nervous system and dullness of the intellect are unquestionably the direct and necessary result of a want of pure air. The vital energies of the pupils are thus prostrated, and they become not only restless and *indisposed to study,* but absolutely *incapable of studying.* Their minds hence wander, and they unavoidably seek relief in mischievous and disorderly conduct. This doubly provokes the already exasperated teacher, who can hardly look with complaisance upon good behavior, and who.

from a like cause, is in the same irritable condition of both body and mind with themselves. He, too, must needs give vent to his irascible feelings some how. And what way is more natural, under such circumstances, than to resort to the use of the ferule, the rod, and the strap! We have already referred to a case, in which formerly fever constantly prevailed, but where disease disappeared altogether upon the introduction of *pure air*. Let the same prudential course be adopted in our schools, in connection with other appropriate means, and we shall readily see the superiority of the natural stimulus of oxygen over the artificial sedative of the rod.

The regular and systematic exercise of the functions of the brain is another condition upon which its healthy action depends. The brain is an organized part, and is subject to precisely the same laws of exercise that the other bodily organs are. If it is doomed to inactivity, its health decays, and the mental operations and feelings, as a necessary consequence, become dull, feeble, and slow. But let it be duly exercised after regular intervals of repose, and the mind acquires activity and strength. Too severe or too protracted exercise of the brain is as great a violation of the organic law just stated as inactivity is, and is sometimes productive of the most fearful consequences. By overtasking this organ, either in the force or duration of its activity, its functions become impaired, and irritability and disease take the place of health and vigor.

So important is the law under consideration, and so essential to the health of the brain and to the welfare of man, that I deem it advisable to explain more particularly the consequences of both inadequate and excessive exercise.

We have seen that by disuse the muscles become

emaciated and the bones soften. The blood-vessels, in like manner, become obliterated, and the nerves lose their characteristic structure. *The brain is no exception to this general rule.* Its tone is impaired by permanent inactivity, and it becomes less fit to manifest the mental powers with readiness and energy. Nor will this surprise any reflecting person, who considers that the brain, as a part of the same animal system, is nourished by the same blood, and regulated by the same vital laws as the muscles, bones, arteries, and nerves.

It is the withdrawal of the stimulus necessary to the healthy exercise of the brain, and the consequent weakening and depressing effect produced upon this organ, that renders solitary confinement so severe a punishment even to the most daring minds. It is a lower degree of the same cause that renders continuous seclusion from society so injurious to both mental and physical health. This explains why persons who are cut off from social converse by some bodily infirmity so frequently become discontented and morose, in spite of every resolution to the contrary. The feelings and faculties of the mind, which had formerly full play in their intercourse with their fellow-creatures, have no longer scope for sufficient exercise, and the almost inevitable result is irritability and weakness in the corresponding parts of the brain.

This fact is strikingly illustrated by reference to the deaf and blind, who, by the loss of one or more of the senses, are precluded from a full participation in all the varied sources of interest which their more favored brethren enjoy without abatement, and in whom irritability, weakness of mind, and idiocy are known to be much more prevalent than among other classes of people. "The deaf and dumb," says Andral, "presents, in intelligence, character, and the development of his passions certain modifications, which depend on his state of isolation in the midst of society. He remains habitually in a state of half childishness, is very credulous, but, like the savage, remains free from many of the prejudices acquired in society. In him the tender feelings are not deep; he appears susceptible neither of strong attachment nor of lively gratitude; pity moves him feebly; he has little emulation, few enjoyments, and few desires. This is what is commonly observed in the deaf and dumb; but the picture is far from being of universal application; some, more happily endowed, are remarkable for the great development of their intellectual and moral nature; but others, on the contrary, remain immersed in complete idiocy."

Andral adds, that we must not infer from this that the deaf and dumb are therefore constitutionally inferior in mind to other men. "*Their powers are not developed, because they live isolated from society. Place them, by some means or other, in relation with their fellow-men, and they will become their equals.*" This is the cause of the rapid brightening up of both mind and features, which is so often observed in blind or deaf children when transferred from home to public institutions, and there taught the means of converse with their fellows.

I have myself witnessed several striking illustrations of the benefits resulting from mental culture in persons who have lost one or more of their senses. Among these I would especially instance the American Asylum at Hartford for the education and instruction of the deaf and dumb, and the Perkins Institution and Massachusetts Asylum for the Blind, located at South Boston, to the accomplished principals and teachers of both of which institutions I would acknowledge my indebtedness for va'uable reports and the information of various kinds which they obligingly communicated to me at the time of my visits during the past summer.

Dr. Howe, the accomplished director of the Asylum for the Blind, after many years of experience and careful observation in this country and in Europe, expresses the conviction that *the blind, as a class, are inferior to other persons in mental power and ability.* The opinions put forth in almost every report of the institutions for the blind in this country, in almost all books on the subject, and even the doctor's earlier writings, may be brought to disprove this statement. He is now, nevertheless, fully convinced that it will be found true. This erroneous conviction, every where so prevalent, may be accounted for from the fact that none but intelligent parents of blind children could at first comprehend the possibility of their being educated, and even *they* would not think of trying the experiment except upon a child of more than ordinary ability. As soon, however, as the experiment proved successful, and institutions for the blind became generally known, the blind, without distinction—the bright and the backward, the bold and the timid—resorted to them, which gave an opportunity of judging of the *whole class.* The result is, that now, while the schools for the blind present a certain number of children who make more rapid progress in *intellectual studies* than the average of seeing children, they also present a much larger number who are decidedly inferior to them in both physical and mental vigor.

The loss of one sense makes us exercise the others so constantly and so effectually as to acquire a power quite unknown to common persons. This goes far to compensate the blind man who is in the pursuit of knowledge, and enables him to learn vastly more of *some* subjects than other men; but there are capacities of his nature which can never be developed. Perfect harmony in the exercise and development of his mental faculties he can never possess, any more than he can exhibit perfect physical beauty and proportion.

The proposition that the blind, *as a class*, are inferior in mental power and ability to ordinary persons, has been established beyond a doubt. Take an equal number of blind and seeing persons, of as nearly the same age and situation in life as may be, and it has been established by well authenticated data, that when all the blind have died, there will still be about half of the seeing ones alive. In other words, the chance of life among the blind is only about half what it is among the seeing. The standard of bodily health and vigor, then, being so much lower among the blind, the inevitable inference is that mental power and ability will be proportionably less also; for such is the dependence of the mind upon the body, that there can be no continuance of mental health and vigor without bodily health and vigor.

It is also true that *the deaf and dumb, as a class, are inferior to other persons in mental power and ability.* The general reasons for this are the same as those already given in the case of blind persons, and need not hence be repeated. The truth of this proposition is established beyond a doubt by the concurrent testimony of those who have had the greatest experience with this unfortunate class of persons both in this country and in Europe. The report of the directors of the American Asylum for the year 1845 shows that two pupils had died during the year. One of these had an affection of the lungs which terminated in consumption, and the disease of the other was dropsy on the brain. In a third, hereditary consumption was rapidly developing itself. Others, still, had been subject to more or less of bodily indisposition.

After speaking of the case of a young man in whom *hereditary consumption* had been rapidly developed, the following statement is introduced: "This great destroyer of our race is found extensively in Europe, as well as in our own country, to be a *common disease among the deaf and dumb.* It is brought on by scrofula, by fevers, by violent colds, and by various other causes; and there is often, no doubt, *a hereditary tendency to it in families connected by blood.*" If this is the effect of the loss of one of the senses upon the *bodily health,* keeping in view the principle already stated, we shall naturally enough be led to inquire what the influence is upon the *health of the mind.* A careful examination of the educational statistics of several states has convinced me that an unusually large proportion of the deaf and dumb—and perhaps an equally large proportion of the blind, and especially those who have remained uneducated and unenlightened—have been visited with mental derangement, and have *lived and died insane.*

This is easily accounted for. Uneducated persons, who are deprived of one or more of the senses, are isolated from the world in which they live. The book of nature is open before them, but they are unable to peruse it. The simplest operations constantly going on around them are locked in mystery. They are an enigma to themselves. Even those who are endowed with inquisitive minds are perplexed with the existing state of things. They know nothing of the physical organization of the planet we inhabit, of its political and civil divisions, and of the whole machinery of human society, and are profoundly ignorant of the past history and future destiny of the race to which they belong. It is not remarkable that mind so unnaturally and peculiarly circumstanced—with its usual inlets of knowledge so obstructed, and deprived of external objects to act upon—should prey upon itself, and thus superinduce insanity in its usual forms, and more especially when unaided and undirected by education.

Keeping the same principle in view, we shall not be surprised to find that *want of exercise* of the brain and nervous system, or, in other words, that inactivity of intellect and feeling, is a very frequent predisposing cause of every form of nervous disease, even with those who have not been deprived of any of their senses. For demonstrative evidence of this position, we have only to look at the numerous victims to be found among females of the middle and higher ranks, who have no call to exertion in gaining the means of subsistence, and no objects of interest on which to exercise their mental faculties, and who consequently sink into a state of mental sloth and nervous weakness, which not only deprives them of much enjoyment, but subjects them to suffering, both of body and mind, from the slightest causes.

In looking abroad upon society, we find innumerable examples of mental and nervous debility from this cause. When a person of some mental capacity is confined for a long time to an unvarying round of employment, which affords neither scope nor stimulus for one half of his faculties, and, from want of education or society, has no external resources, his mental powers. for want of exercise to keep up due vitality in their cerebral organs, become blunted, and his perceptions slow and dull. Unusual subjects of thought become to him disagreeable and painful. The intellect and feelings not being provided with interests external to themselves, must either become inactive and weak, or work upon themselves and become diseased.

But let the situation of such persons be changed;

bring them, for instance, from the listlessness of retirement to the business and bustle of a city; give them a variety of imperative employments, and place them in society so as to supply to their cerebral organs that extent of exercise which gives health and vivacity of action, and in a few months the change produced will be surprising. Health, animation, and acuteness will take the place of former insipidity and dullness. In such instances, it would be absurd to suppose that it is the *mind itself* which becomes heavy and feeble, and again revives into energy by these changes in external circumstances. The effects arise entirely from changes in the state of the *brain*, and the mental manifestations and the bodily health have been improved solely by the improvement of its condition.

The evils arising from excessive or ill-timed exercise of the brain, or any of its parts, are numerous, and equally in accordance with the ordinary laws of physiology. When we use the eye too long or in too bright a light, it becomes bloodshot, and the increased action of its vessels and nerves gives rise to a sensation of fatigue and pain requiring us to desist. If we turn away and relieve the eye, the irritation gradually subsides, and the healthy state returns; but if we continue to look intently, or resume our employment before the eye has regained its natural state by repose, the irritation at last becomes permanent, and disease, followed by weakness of sight, or even blindness, may ensue, as often happens to glass-blowers, smiths, and others who are obliged to work in an intense light.

Precisely analogous phenomena occur when, from intense mental excitement, the brain is kept long in a state of excessive activity. The only difference is, that we can always see what happens in the eye, but rarely what takes place in the brain. Occasionally, however, cases of fracture of the skull occur, in which, part of the bone being removed, we *can see* the quickened circulation in the vessels of the brain as easily as in those of the eye. Sir Astley Cooper had a young gentleman brought to him who had lost a portion of his skull just above the eyebrow. "On examining the head," says Sir Astley, "I distinctly saw that the pulsation of the brain was regular and slow; but at this time he was agitated by some opposition to his wishes, and directly the blood was sent with increased force to the brain, and the pulsation became frequent and violent." Sir Astley hence concludes that, in the treatment of injuries of the brain, if you omit to keep the mind free from agitation, your other means will be unavailing.

A still more remarkable case is said to have occurred in the hospital of Montpellier in 1821. The subject of it was a female who had lost a large portion of her scalp, skull-bone, and dura mater. A corresponding portion of her brain was consequently bare, and subject to inspection. When she was in a dreamless sleep, her brain was motionless, and lay within the cranium; but when her sleep was imperfect, and she was agitated by dreams, her brain moved and protruded without the cranium. In vivid dreams the protrusion was considerable; and when she was awake and engaged in active thought or sprightly conversation, it was still greater.

In alluding to this subject, Dr. Caldwell remarks, that if it were possible, without doing an injury to other parts, to augment the constant afflux of healthy arterial blood to the brain, the mental operations would be invigorated by it. This position is illustrated by reference to the fact that when a public speaker is flushed and heated in debate, his mind works more freely and powerfully than at any other time. And why? Because his brain is in better tune. What has thus suddenly improved its condition? An increased current of blood into it, produced by the excitement of its own increased action. That the blood does, on such occasions, flow more copiously into the brain, no one can doubt who is at all acquainted with the cerebral sensations which the orator himself experiences at the time, or who witnesses the unusual fullness and flush of his countenance, and the dewiness, flashing, and protrusion of his eye.

Indeed, in many instances, the increased circulation in the brain attendant on high mental excitement reveals itself by its effects when least expected, and leaves traces after death which are but too legible. Many are the instances in which public men have been suddenly arrested in their career by the inordinate action of the brain induced by incessant toil, and more numerous still are those whose mental power has been forever impaired by similar excess.

It is generally known that the eye, when tasked beyond its strength, becomes insensible to light, and ceases to convey impressions to the mind. The brain, in like manner, when much exhausted, becomes incapable of thought, and consciousness is well-nigh lost in a feeling of utter confusion. At any time in life, excessive and continued mental exertion is hurtful; but in infancy and early youth, when the structure of the brain is still immature and delicate, permanent injury is more easily produced by injudicious treatment than at any subsequent period. In this respect, the analogy is complete between the brain and the other parts of the body, as we have already seen exemplified in the injurious effects of premature exercise of the bones and muscles. Scrofulous and rickety children are the most usual sufferers in this way. They are generally remarkable for large heads, great precocity of understanding, and small, delicate bodies. But in such instances, the great size of the brain, and the acuteness of the mind, are the results of morbid growth, and even with the best management, the child passes the first years of its life constantly on the brink of active disease. Instead, how ever, of trying to repress its mental activity, as they should, the fond parents, misled by the promise of genius, too often excite it still further by unceasing cultivation and the never-failing stimulus of praise; and finding its progress, for a time, equal to their warmest wishes, they look forward with ecstasy to the day when its talents will break forth and shed a luster on their name. But in exact proportion as the picture becomes brighter to their fancy, the probability of its becoming realized becomes less; for the brain, worn out by premature exertion, either becomes diseased or loses its tone, leaving the mental powers feeble and depressed for the remainder of life. The expected prodigy is thus, in the end, easily outstripped in the social race by many whose dull outset promised him an easy victory.

To him who takes for his guide the necessities of the constitution, it will be obvious that the modes of treatment commonly resorted to should in such cases be reversed; and that, instead of straining to the utmost the already irritable powers of the precocious child leaving his dull competitors to ripen at leisure, a systematic attempt ought to be made, from early infancy, to rouse to action the languid faculties of the latter, while no pains should be spared to moderate and give tone to the activity of the former. But instead of this, the prematurely intelligent child is generally sent to school, and tasked with lessons at an unusually early age, while the healthy but more backward boy, who requires to be stimulated, is kept at home in idleness merely on acount of his backwardness. A double error is here committed, and the consequences to the active-minded boy are not unfrequently the permanent loss both of health and of his envied superiority of intellect.

In speaking of children of this description, Dr. Brigham, in an excellent little work on the influence of mental excitement on health, remarks as follows: "Dangerous forms of scrofulous disease among children have repeatedly fallen under my observation, for which I could not account in any other way than by supposing that the brain had been excited at the expense of the other parts of the system, and at a time in life when nature is endeavoring to perfect all the organs of the body; and after the disease commenced, I have seen, with grief, the influence of the same cause in retarding or preventing recovery. I have seen several affecting and melancholy instances of children, five or six years of age, lingering a while with diseases from which those less gifted readily recover, and at last dying, notwithstanding the utmost efforts to restore them. During their sickness they constantly manifested a passion for books and mental excitement, and were admired for the maturity of their minds. The chance for the recovery of such precocious children is, in my opinion, small when attacked by disease; and several medical men have informed me that their own observations had led them to form the same opinion, and have remarked that, in two cases of sickness, if one of the patients was a child of superior and highly-cultivated mental powers, and the other one equally sick, but whose mind had not been excited by study, they should feel less confident of the recovery of the former than of the latter. This mental precocity results from an unnatural development of one organ of the body at the expense of the constitution."

There can be little doubt but that ignorance on the part of parents and teachers is the principal cause that leads to the too early and excessive cultivation of the minds of children, and especially of such as are precocious and delicate. Hence the necessity of imparting instruction on this subject to both parents and teachers, and to all persons who are in any way charged with the care and education of the young. This necessity becomes the more imperative from the fact that the cupidity of authors and publishers has led to the preparation of "children's books," many of which are announced as purposely prepared "for children from *two* to *three* years old!" I might instance advertisements of "Infant Manuals" of Botany, Geometry, and Astronomy!

In not a few isolated families, but in many neighborhoods, villages, and cities, in various parts of the country, children *under three years of age* are not only required to commit to memory many verses, texts of Scripture, and stories, but are frequently sent to school for six hours a day. Few children are kept back later than the age of *four*, unless they reside a great distance from school, and some not even then. At home, too, they are induced by all sorts of excitement to learn additional tasks, or peruse juvenile books and magazines, till the nervous system becomes enfeebled and the health broken. "I have myself," says Dr. Brigham, "seen many children who are supposed to possess almost miraculous mental powers, experiencing these effects and sinking under them. Some of them died early, when but six or eight years of age, but manifested to the last a maturity of understanding, which only increased the agony of separation. Their minds, like some of the fairest flowers, were 'no sooner blown than blasted;' others have grown up to manhood, but with feeble bodies and disordered nervous system, which subjected them to hypochondriasis, dyspepsy, and all the Protean forms of nervous disease; others of the class of early prodigies exhibit in manhood but small mental powers, and are the mere passive instruments of those who in early life were accounted far their inferiors."

This hot-bed system of education is not confined to the United States, but is practiced less or more in all civilized countries. Dr. Combe, of Scotland, gives an account of one of these early prodigies whose fate he witnessed. The circumstances were exactly such as those above described. The prematurely developed intellect was admired, and constantly stimulated by injudicious praise, and by daily exhibition to every visitor who chanced to call. Entertaining books were thrown in its way, reading by the fireside encouraged, play and exercise neglected, the diet allowed to be full and heating, and the appetite pampered by every delicacy The results were the speedy deterioration of a weak constitution, a high degree of nervous sensibility, deranged digestion, disordered bowels, defective nutrition, and, lastly, *death*, at the very time when the interest excited by the mental precocity was at its height.

Such, however, is the ignorance of the majority of parents and teachers on all physiological subjects, that when one of these infant prodigies dies from erroneous treatment, it is not unusual to publish a memoir of his life, that other parents and teachers may see by what means such transcendent qualities were called forth. Dr. Brigham refers to a memoir of this kind, in which the history of a child, aged four years and eleven months, is narrated as approved by "several judicious persons, ministers and others, all of whom united in the request that it might be published, and all agreed in the opinion that a knowledge of the manner in which the child was treated, together with the results, would be profitable to both parents and children, and a benefit to the cause of education." This infant philosopher was "taught hymns before he could speak plainly;" "reasoned with" and constantly instructed until his last illness, which, "*without any assignable cause*," put on a violent and unexpected form, and carried him off!

As a *warning to others* not to force education too soon or too fast, this case may be truly profitable to both parents and children, and a benefit to the cause of education; but *as an example to be followed*, it assuredly can not be too strongly or too loudly condemned. While I speak thus strongly, I am ready to admit that infant schools in which physical health and moral training are duly attended to are excellent institutions, and are particularly advantageous where parents, from want of leisure or from other causes, are unable to bestow upon their children that attention which their tender years require.

In youth, too, much mischief is done by the long daily periods of attendance at school, and the continued application of mind which the ordinary system of education requires. The law of exercise already more than once repeated, that *long-sustained action exhausts the vital powers of an organ*, applies as well to the brain as to the muscles. Hence the necessity of varying the occupations of the young, and allowing frequent intervals of active exercise in the open air, instead of enforcing the continued confinement now so common. This exclusive attention to mental culture fails, as might be expected, even in its essential object; for all experience shows that, with a rational distribution of employment and exercise, a child will make greater progress in a given period than in double the time employed in continuous mental exertion. If the human being were made up of nothing but a brain and nervous system, we might do well to content ourselves with sedentary pursuits, and to confine our attention entirely to the mind. But when we learn from observation that we have numerous other important organs of motion, sanguification, digestion, circulation, and nutrition, all demanding exercise in the open air, as alike essential to their own health and to that of the nervous system, it is worse than folly to shut our eyes to the truth, and to act as if we could, by denying it, alter the constitution of nature, and thereby escape the consequences of our own misconduct.

Reason and experience being thus set at naught by both parents and teachers in the education of their children, young people naturally grow up with the notion that no such influences as the laws of organization exist, and that they may follow any course of life which inclination leads them to prefer without injury to health, provided they avoid what is called dissipation. It is owing to this ignorance that young men of a studious or literary habit enter heedlessly upon an amount of mental exertion, unalleviated by bodily exercise or intervals of repose, which is quite incompatible with the continued enjoyment of a sound mind in a sound body. Such, however, is the effect of the total neglect of all instruction in the laws of the organic frame during early education, that it becomes almost impossible effectually to warn an ardent student against the dangers to which he is constantly exposing himself. Nothing but actual experience will convince him of the truth.

Numerous are the instances in which young men of

the first promise have almost totally disqualified them selves for future useful exertion in consequence of long-protracted and severe study, who, under a more rational system of education, might have attained that eminence, the injudicious pursuit of which has defeated their own most cherished hopes, and ruined their general health. Such persons might be saved to themselves and to society by early instruction in the nature and laws of the animal economy. They mean well, but err from ignorance more than from headstrong zeal.

I shall conclude this chapter with a few rules relating to mental exercise, and the development and culture of the mind and brain. It is a law of the animal economy that two classes of functions can.not be called into vigorous action at the same time without one or the other, or both, sooner or later sustaining injury. Hence the important rule never to enter upon continued mental exertion or to rouse deep feeling immediately after a full meal, otherwise the activity of the brain is sure to interfere with that of the stomach, and disorder its functions. Even in a perfectly healthy person, unwelcome news, sudden anxiety, or mental excitement, occurring after eating, will put an entire stop to digestion, and cause the stomach to loathe the sight of food. In accordance with this rule, we learn by experience that the very worst forms of indigestion and nervous depression are those which arise from excessive mental application, or turmoil of feeling and distraction of mind, conjoined with unrestrained indulgence in the pleasures of the table. In such circumstances, the stomach and brain react upon and disturb each other, till all the horrors of nervous disease make their unwelcome appearance, and render life miserable. The tendency to inactivity and sleep, which besets most animals after a full meal, shows repose to be, in such circumstances, the evident intention of Nature The bad effects of violating this rule, although not in all cases immediately apparent, will most assuredly be manifest at a period less or more remote.

Dr. Caldwell, who has devoted much time and talent to the diffusion of sound physiological information and the general improvement of the race, and whose opportunities of observation have been very extensive, expressly states, that dyspepsy and madness prevail more extensively in the United States than among the people of any other nation. Of the amount of our dyspeptics, he says, no estimate can be formed; but it is immense. Whether we inquire in cities, towns, villages, or country places; among the rich, the poor, or those in moderate circumstances, we find dyspepsy more or less prevalent throughout the land.

The early part of the day is the best time for severe mental exertion. Nature has allotted the darkness of night for repose, and for the restoration by sleep of the exhausted energies of both body and mind. If study or composition be ardently engaged in toward the close of the day, and especially at a late hour of the evening, sound and invigorating sleep may not be expected until the night is far spent, for the increased action of the brain which always accompanies activity of mind requires a long time to subside. Persons who practice night study, if they be at all of an irritable habit of body, will be sleepless for hours after going to bed, and be tormented perhaps by unpleasant dreams, which will render their sleep unrefreshing. If this practice be long continued, the want of refreshing repose will ultimately induce a state of morbid irritability of the nervous system bordering on insanity. It is therefore of great advantage to engage in severer studies early in the day, and to devote the after part of the day and the evening to less intense application. It will be well to devote a portion of the evening, and especially the latter part of it, to light reading, music, or cheerful and amusing conversation. The excitement induced in the brain by previous study will be soothed by these influences, and will more readily subside, and sound and refreshing sleep will be much more likely to follow This rule is of the utmost importance to those who are obliged to perform a great amount of mental labor. It is only by conforming to it, and devoting their mornings to study and their evenings to relaxation, that many of our most prolific writers have been enabled to preserve their health. By neglecting this rule, others of the fairest promise have been cut down in the midst of their usefulness.

Regularity is of great importance in the development and culture of the moral and intellectual powers, the tendency to resume the same mode of action at stated times being peculiarly the characteristic of the nervous system. It is this principle of our nature which promotes the formation of what are called habits. By repeating any kind of mental effort every day at the same hour, we at length find ourselves entering upon it, without premeditation, when the time approaches. In like manner, by arranging our studies in accordance with this law, and taking up each regularly in the same order, a natural aptitude is soon produced, which renders application more easy than it would be were we to take up the subjects as accident might dictate. The tendency to periodical and associated activity sometimes becomes so strong, that the faculties seem to go through their operations almost without conscious effort, while their facility of action becomes so much increased as ultimately to give unerring certainty where at first great difficulty was experienced. It is not so much the soul or abstract principle of mind which is thus changed, as the organic medium through which mind is destined to act in the present mode of being.

The necessity of judicious repetition in mental and moral education is, in fact, too little adverted to, because the principle on which it is effectual has not hitherto been generally understood. Practice is as necessary to induce facility of action in the organs of the mind as in those of motion. The idea or feeling must not only be communicated, but it must be re-presented and reproduced in different forms till all the faculties concerned in understanding it come to work efficiently together in the conception of it, and until a sufficient impression is made upon the organ of mind to enable the latter to retain it. Servants and others are frequently blamed for not doing a thing at regular intervals when they have been but once told to do so. We learn, however, from the organic laws, that it is presumptuous to expect the formation of a habit from a single act, and that we must reproduce the associated activity of the requisite faculties many times before the result will certainly follow, just as we must repeat the movement in dancing or skating many times before we become master of it.

We may understand a new subject by a single perusal, but we can fully master it only by dwelling upon it again and again. In order to make a durable impression on the mind, repetition is necessary. It follows, hence, that in learning a language or science, six successive months of application will be more effectual in fixing it indelibly in the mind, and making it a part of the mental furniture, than double or even treble the time if the lessons are interrupted by long intervals. The too common practice of beginning a study, and, after pursuing it a little time, leaving it to be completed at a later period, is unphilosophical and very injurious. The fatigue of study is thus doubled, and the success greatly diminished. Studies should not, as a general thing, be entered upon until the mind is sufficiently mature to understand them thoroughly, and, when begun, they should not be discontinued until they are completely mastered. By this means the mind becomes accustomed to sound and healthy action, which alone can qualify the student for eminent usefulness in after life. Much of the want of success in the various departments of industry, and many of the failures that are constantly occurring among business men, are justly attributable to the fits of attention and the irregular modes of study they became habituated to in their school-boy days. Hence the mischief of long vacations, and the evil of beginning studies before the age at which they may be understood. Parents and teachers should hence, at an early period, impress indelibly upon the minds of their children and pupils the ever true and practical sentiment, that *what is worth doing at all is worth doing well.* Although, at first, their progress may *seem* to be retarded thereby, still, in the end, it will contribute greatly to accelerate their real advancement, and in after life, whether employed in literary or business pursuits, will be a means of augmenting their happiness and increasing their prospect of success in whatever department of labor they may be engaged.

In physical education most persons seem well aware of the advantages of repetition. They know, for instance, that if practice in dancing, fencing, skating, and riding is persevered in for a sufficient length of time to give the muscles the requisite promptitude and harmony of action, the power will be ever afterward retained, although rarely called into use. But if we stop short of this point, we may reiterate practice by fits and starts without any proportional advancement. The same principle is equally applicable to the moral and intellectual powers which operate by means of material organs.

The impossibility of successfully playing the hypocrite for any considerable length of time, and the necessity of being in private what we wish to appear in public, spring from the same rule. If we wish to be ourselves polite, just, kind, and sociable, or to induce others to become so, we must act habitually under the influence of the corresponding sentiments, in the domestic circle, in the school-room, and in every-day life, as well as in the company of strangers and on great occasions. It is the private and daily practice of individuals that gives ready activity to the sentiments and marks the real character. If parents or teachers indulge habitually in vulgarities of speech and behavior in the family or in the school, and put on politeness occasionally for the reception and entertainment of strangers, their true character will shine through the mask which is intended to conceal it. The habitual association to which the organs and faculties have been accustomed can not thus be controlled. Parents hence, in addition to correct personal influence in the family, should provide for their children teachers whose habits and character are in all respects what they are willing their children should form. If they neglect to do this, the utmost they can reasonably expect is that their children will become what the teacher is.

The principle that repetition is necessary in order to make a durable impression on the organ of the mind, and thus constitute a mental habit, explains how natural endowments are modified by external situation. The extent to which this modification may be carried, and is actually carried in every community, is much greater than most persons are aware of. Take a child, for example, of average propensities, sentiments, and intellect, and place him among a class of people in whom the selfish faculties are exclusively exercised—a class who regard gain as the end of life, and look upon cunning and cheating as legitimate means, and who never express disapprobation or moral indignation against either crime or selfishness—and his lower faculties, being exclusively exercised, will increase in strength, while the higher ones, remaining unemployed, will become enfeebled. A child thus situated will, consequently, not only act as those around him do, but insensibly grow up resembling them in disposition and character; for, by the law of repetition, the organs of the selfish qualities will have acquired proportionally greater aptitude and vigor, just as do the muscles of the fencer or dancer. But suppose the same individual placed, *from infancy*, in the society of a superiorly endowed moral and intellectual people, the moral faculties will then be habitually excited, and their organs invigorated by repetition, till a greater aptitude will be induced in them, or, in other words, till a higher moral character will be formed. The natural endowments of individuals set limits to these modifications of character; but where original dispositions and tendencies are not strongly marked, the range is very wide.

In the cultivation of the brain and mental faculties, each organ should be exercised directly upon its own appropriate objects, and not merely roused or addressed through the medium of another organ. When we wish to teach the graceful and rapid evolutions of fencing, we do not content ourselves with merely giving directions, but our chief attention is employed in making the muscles themselves go through the evolutions, till, by frequent repetition and correction, they acquire the requisite quickness and precision of action. So, when we wish to teach music, we do not merely address the understanding and explain the qualities of sounds. We train the ear to an attentive discrimination of these sounds, and the hand or the vocal organs, as the case may be, to the reproduction of the motions which call them into existence. We follow this plan, because the laws of organization require the direct practice of the organs concerned, and we feel instinctively that we can succeed only by obeying these laws. The purely mental faculties are connected during life with material organs, and are hence subjected to precisely the same laws. If, therefore, we wish to improve these faculties—the reasoning powers, for example—we must exercise them regularly in tracing the cause and relations of things. In like manner, if our aim is the development of the sentiments of attachment, benevolence, justice, or respect, we must exercise each of them directly and for its own sake, otherwise neither it nor its organ will ever acquire promptitude or strength.

It is the brain, or organ of the mind, more than the abstract immaterial principle itself, that requires cultivation, or can, indeed, receive it in this life. Education hence operates invariably in subjection to the laws of organization. In improving the *external* senses, we admit this principle readily enough ; but when we come to the *internal* faculties of thought and feeling, it is either denied or neglected. That the superior quickness of touch, sight, and hearing, consequent upon judicious exercise, is referable to increased facility of action in their appropriate organs, is readily admitted. But when we explain, on the same principle, the superior development of the reasoning powers, or the great er warmth of feeling produced by similar exercise in these and other internal faculties, few are inclined to listen to our proposition, or allow to it half the weight or attention its importance demands, although every fact in philosophy and experience concurs in supporting it. We see the mental powers of feeling and of thought unfolding themselves in infancy and youth in exact accordance with the progress of the organization. We see them perverted or suspended by the sudden inroad of disease. We sometimes observe every previous acquirement obliterated from the adult mind by fever or by accident, leaving education to be commenced anew, as if it had never been; and yet, with all these evidences of the organic influence, the proposition that the established laws of physiology, as applied to the brain, should be considered our best and surest guide in education, seems to many a novelty. Among the numerous treatises on education, there are very few volumes in which it is even hinted that these laws have the slightest influence over either intellectual or moral improvement.

As God has given us bones and muscles, and blood-vessels and nerves, for the purpose of being used, let us not despise the gift, but consent at once to turn them to account, and to reap health and vigor as the reward which he has associated with moderate labor. As he has given us lungs to breathe with and blood to circulate, let us at once and forever abandon the folly of shutting ourselves up with little intermission, whether engaged in study or other sedentary occupations, and consent to inhale, copiously and freely, that wholesome atmosphere which his benevolence has spread around us in such rich profusion. As he has given us appetites and organs of digestion, let us profit by his bounty, and earn their enjoyment by healthful exercise in some department of productive industry. As he has given us a moral and a social nature, which is invigorated by activity, and impaired by solitude and restraint, let us cultivate good feelings, and act toward each other on principles of kindness, justice, forbearance, and mutual assistance; and as he has given us intellect, let us exercise it in seeking a knowledge of his works and of his laws, and in tracing out the relation in which we stand toward him, toward our fellow-men, and toward the various objects of the external world. In so doing, we may be well assured we shall find a reward a thousand times more rich and pure, yea, infinitely more delightful and enduring, than we can hope to experience in following our own blind devices, regardless of his will and benevolent intentions toward us.

CHAPTER VI.

THE EDUCATION OF THE FIVE SENSES.

If the eye be obstructed, the ear opens wide its portals, and hears your very emotions in the varying tones of your voice; if the ear be stopped, the quickened eye will almost read the words as they fall from your lips; and if both be close sealed up, the whole body becomes like a sensitive plant—the quickened skin perceives the very vibrations of the air, and you may even write your thoughts upon it, and receive answers from the sentient soul within.—ANNUAL REPORT *of the Trustees of the Perkins Institution and Massachusetts Asylum for the Blind,* 1841.

HE who formed man of the dust of the earth, and breathed into his nostrils the breath of life, has honored his material organs by associating them with the immaterial soul. In this life *the senses* constitute the great conveyances of knowledge to the human mind. It then becomes not only a legitimate object of inquiry but one which commends itself to every human being, and especially to every parent and teacher, Can these senses be improved by human interference? And if so, how can that improvement be best effected?

The senses are the interpreters between the material universe without and the spirit within. Without the celestial machinery of sensation, man must have ever remained what Adam was before the Almighty breathed into his form of clay the awakening breath of life. The dormant energies of the mind can be aroused, and the soul can be put into mysterious communion with external nature only by the magical power of sensation.

The possession of all the corporeal senses, and their systematic and judicious culture by all proper appliances, are necessary in order to place man in such a relation to the material universe and its great Architect as most fully and successfully to cultivate the varied capabilities of his nature, and best to subserve the purposes of his creation. He who is deprived of the healthful exercise of one or more of his senses, or, possessing them all unimpaired, has neglected their proper culture, is, from the nature of the case, in a proportionate degree cut off from a knowledge of God as manifested in his works, and from that happiness which is the legitimate fruit of such knowledge.

Much light has been thrown upon this subject within a few years by the judicious labors of that class of practical educators who have devoted their lives to the amelioration of the condition of persons deprived of one or more of the senses. It is difficult to conceive the real condition of the minds of persons thus situated, and especially while they remain uneducated. He who is deprived of the sense of sight has the windows of his soul closed, and is effectually shut out from this world of light and beauty. In like manner, he who is deprived of the sense of hearing is excluded from the world of music and of speech. What, then, must be the condition of persons deprived of both of these senses? How desolate and cheerless! Yet some such there are.

While on a visit to the Asylum for the Blind, in Boston, a few months ago, I met two of this unfortunate class of persons—Laura Bridgman and Oliver Caswell. Laura has been several years connected with the institution.

LAURA BRIDGMAN, *the Deaf, Dumb, and Blind Girl.* —So remarkable is the case of this interesting girl, so full of interest, so replete with instruction, and in every way so admirably adapted to illustrate the subject of this chapter, that I proceed to give to my readers a sketch of the method pursued in her instruction, together with the results attendant upon it. My information in relation to her is derived from both personal acquaintance and the reports of her case, though principally from the latter source.

Laura was born in Hanover, New Hampshire, on the 21st of December, 1829. She is described as having been a very sprightly and pretty infant. During the first years of her existence she held her life by the feeblest tenure, being subject to severe fits, which seemed to rack her frame almost beyond the power of endurance. At the age of four years her bodily health seemed restored; but what a situation was hers! The darkness and silence of the tomb were around her. No mother's smile called forth her answering smile. No father's voice taught her to imitate his sounds. To her, brothers and sisters were but forms of matter which resisted her touch, but which hardly differed from the furniture of the house save in warmth and in the power of locomotion, and not even in these respects from the dog and the cat. But the immortal spirit implanted within her could not die, nor could it be maimed or mutilated; and, though most of its avenues of communication with the world were cut off, it began to manifest itself through the others. As soon as she could walk, she began to explore the room, and then the house. She thus soon became familiar with the form, density, weight, and heat of every article she could lay her hands upon. She followed her mother, and felt of her hands and arms, as she was occupied about the house, and her disposition to imitate led her to repeat every thing herself. She even learned to sew a little and to knit.

Her affections, too, began to expand, and seemed to be lavished upon the members of her family with peculiar force. But the means of communication with her were very limited. She could be told to go to a place only by being pushed, or to come to one by a sign of drawing her. Patting her gently on the head signified approbation, on the back disapprobation. She showed every disposition to learn, and manifestly began to use a natural language of her own. She had a sign to express her idea of each member of the family, as drawing her fingers down each side of her face to allude to the whiskers of one, twirling her hand around in imitation of the motion of a spinning-wheel for another, and so on. But, although Laura received all the aid a kind mother could bestow, she soon began to give proof of the importance of language in the development of human character. By the time she was seven years old the moral effects of her privation began to appear, for there was no way of controlling her will but by the absolute power of another, and at this humanity revolts.

At this time, Dr. Samuel G. Howe, the distinguished and successful director of the asylum, learned of her situation, and hastened to see her. He found her with a well-formed figure, a strongly-marked nervous-sanguine temperament, a large and beautifully shaped head and the whole system in healthy action. Here seemed a rare opportunity of trying a plan for the education of a deaf and blind person, which the doctor had formed on seeing Julia Brace at Hartford. The parents readily consented to her going to the institution in Boston, where Laura was received in October, 1837, just before she had completed her eighth year. For a while she was much bewildered. After waiting about two weeks, and until she became acquainted with her new locality, and somewhat familiar with the inmates, the attempt was made to give her a knowledge of arbitrary signs, by which she could interchange thoughts with others. One of two methods was to be adopted. Either the language of signs, on the basis of the natural language she had already commenced herself, was to be built up, or it remained to teach her the purely arbitrary language in common use. The former would have been easy, but very ineffectual. The latter, although very difficult, if accomplished, would prove vastly superior. It was therefore determined upon.

The *blind* learn to read by means of raised letters, which they gain a knowledge of by the sense of feeling. *The ends of the fingers*, resting upon the raised letters, thus constitute, in part, *the eyes of the blind.* This, although apparently difficult, becomes comparatively easy when the blind person possesses the *sense of hearing*, and is thus enabled to become acquainted with spoken language. On the contrary, the *deaf*, and consequently *dumb*, are unable to acquire a knowledge of spoken language so as to use it with any degree of success. In their education, hence, the *language of signs*, which can be addressed to the eye, is substituted for spoken language. In communicating with one another, by means of the *manual alphabet,* they substitute positions of the hand, which they can both make and see, for letters and words, which they can neither pronounce nor hear.

To be deprived of either sight or hearing was formerly regarded as an almost insuperable obstacle in the way of education. Persons deprived of both these senses have heretofore been considered by high legal authorities,* as well as by public opinion, as occupying, of necessity, a state of irresponsible and irrecoverable idiocy. By the education of the remaining senses, however, this formidable and heretofore insuperable barrier has been overleaped, or, rather, the obstacle has been met and overcome. The experiment has been successfully tried, once and again, in our own country. The deaf and blind mute has not only acquired a knowledge of reading and writing, and of the common branches of education, but has been enabled successfully to prosecute the study of natural philosophy, of mental science, and of geometry. The accomplishment of all this has resulted from the successful cultivation of the sense of touch or of feeling. The raised letter of the blind has been used for written language, and the manual language of the mute, taken by the *finger-eyes* of the blind, has been successfully substituted for spoken language.

Laura's mind dwelt in darkness and silence. In order, therefore, to communicate to her a knowledge of the arbitrary language in common use, it was neces-

* A man is not an idiot if he hath any glimmering of reason, so that he can tell his parents, his age, or the like matters. But a man who is born deaf, dumb, and blind, is looked upon by the law as in the same state with an idiot, he being supposed incapable of any understanding, as wanting all the senses which furnish the human mind with ideas.—*Blackstone's Commentaries,* vol. i., p. 304.

sary to combine the methods of instructing the blind and the deaf. The first experiments in instructing her were made by taking articles in common use, such as knives, forks, spoons, keys, etc., and pasting upon them labels with their names printed in *raised letters*. These she felt of very carefully, and soon, of course, distinguished that the crooked lines *spoon* differed as much from the crooked lines *key*, as the spoon differed from the key in form. Small detached labels, with the same words printed upon them, were then put into her hands, and she soon observed that they were similar to those pasted on the articles. She showed her perception of this similarity by laying the label *key* upon the key, and the label *spoon* upon the spoon. When this was done she was encouraged by the natural sign of approbation—patting on the head.

The same process was then repeated with all the articles which she could handle, and she very easily learned to place the proper labels upon them. After a while, instead of labels, the individual letters were given to her, on detached bits of paper. These were at first arranged side by side, so as to spell *book*, *key*, etc. They were then mixed up, and a sign was made for her to arrange them herself, so as to express the words *book*, *key*, etc., and she did so.

The process of instruction, hitherto, had been mechanical, and the success attending it about as great as that in teaching a very knowing dog a variety of tricks. The poor child sat in mute amazement, and patiently imitated every thing her teacher did. Presently the truth began to flash upon her; her intellect began to work; she perceived that here was a way by which she could herself make up a sign of any thing that was in her own mind, and show it to another mind, and at once her countenance lighted up with a human expression! her immortal spirit eagerly seizing upon a new link of union with other spirits! Dr. Howe says he could almost fix upon the moment when this truth dawned upon her mind and spread its light to her countenance. He saw at once that nothing but patient and persevering, but judicious efforts were needed in her instruction, and that these would most assuredly be crowned with success.

It is difficult to form a just conception of the amount of labor bestowed upon Laura thus far. In communicating with her, spoken language could not be used for she was destitute of hearing. Neither are signs of any use when addressed to the eyes of the blind. When, therefore, it was said that "a sign was made," we are to understand by it that the action was performed by her teacher, she feeling of his hands, and then imitating the motion. The next step in the process of her instruction was to procure a set of metal types, with the different letters of the alphabet cast upon their ends; also a board, in which were square holes, into which she could set the types so that the letters on the end could alone be felt above the surface. Then, on any article being handed to her whose name she had learned—a pencil or a watch, for instance—she would select the component letters and arrange them on her board, and read them with apparent pleasure.

When she had been exercised in this way for several weeks, and until her knowledge of words had become considerably extensive, the important step was taken of teaching her how to represent the different letters by the position of her fingers, instead of the cumbrous apparatus of the board and types. This she accomplished speedily and easily, for her intellect had begun to work in aid of her teacher, and her progress was rapid.

Six months after Laura had left home her mother went to visit her. The scene of their meeting was full of interest. The mother stood some time gazing with overflowing eyes upon her unfortunate child, who, all unconscious of her presence, was playing about the room. Presently Laura ran against her, and at once began feeling of her hands, examining her dress, and trying to find out if she knew her; but, not succeeding in this, she turned away as from a stranger, and the poor woman could not conceal the pang she felt at finding her beloved child did not know her. She then gave Laura a string of beads which she used to wear at home. These were at once recognized by the child, who gave satisfactory indications that she understood they were from home. The mother now tried to caress her; but Laura repelled her, preferring to be with her acquaintances.

Other articles from home were then given to Laura, and she began to look much interested; she examined the stranger much closer, and gave the doctor to understand she knew they came from Hanover; she now even endured her mother's caresses, but would leave her with indifference at the slightest signal. After a while, on the mother taking hold of her again, a vague idea seemed to flit across Laura's mind that this could not be a stranger; she therefore felt of her hands very eagerly, while her countenance assumed an expression of intense interest; she became very pale, and then suddenly red; hope seemed struggling with doubt and anxiety, and never were contending emotions more strongly painted upon the human face. At this moment of painful uncertainty, the mother drew Laura close to her side, and kissed her fondly, when at once the truth flashed upon the child, and all distrust and anxiety disappeared from her face. With an expression of exceeding joy, Laura nestled to the bosom of her parent, and yielded herself to her fond embraces. After this the beads were all unheeded, and the playthings which were offered to her were utterly disregarded. Her playmates, for whom she but a moment before left the stranger, now vainly strove to pull her from her mother. The meeting and subsequent parting showed alike the affection, the intelligence, and the resolution of the child as well as of her mother.

The following facts are drawn from the report made of her case at the end of the year 1839, after she had been a little more than two years under instruction. Having mastered the manual alphabet of the deaf mutes, and having learned to spell readily the names of every thing within her reach, she was then taught words expressive of positive qualities, as hardness and softness. This was a very difficult process. She was next taught those expressions of relation to place which she could understand. A ring, for example, was taken and placed *on* a box; then the words were spelled to her, and she repeated them from imitation. The ring was afterward placed *on* a hat, desk, etc. In a similar manner she learned the use of *in*, *into*, etc. She would illustrate the use of these and other words as follows: She would spell *o n*, and then lay one hand *on* the other; then she would spell *i n t o*, and inclose one hand *within* the other.

Laura very easily acquired a knowledge and use of active verbs, especially those expressive of *tangible action*, as to walk, to run, to sew, to shake. In acquiring a knowledge of language, she used the words with which she had become acquainted in a general sense, and according to the order of *her sense of ideas*. Thus, in asking some one to give her bread, she would first use the word expressive of the leading idea, and say,

Bread, give, Laura. If she wanted water, she would say, *Water, drink, Laura.*

Having acquired the use of substantives, adjectives verbs, prepositions, and conjunctions, it was thought time to make the experiment of trying to teach her to *write*, and to show her she might communicate her ideas to persons not in contact with her. It was amusing to witness the mute amazement with which she submitted to the process; the docility with which she imitated every motion, and the perseverance with which she moved her pencil over and over again in the same track, until she could form the letter. But when at last the idea dawned upon her that by this mysterious process she could make other people understand what she thought, her joy was boundless! Never did a child apply more eagerly and joyfully to any task than she did to this; and in a few months she could make every letter distinctly, and separate words from each other.

At this time Laura actually wrote, unaided, a legible letter to her mother, in which she expressed the idea of her being well, and of her expectation of going home in a few weeks. It was, indeed, a very rude and imperfect letter, couched in the language which a prattling infant would use. Still, it shadowed forth and expressed to her mother the ideas that were passing in her own mind. She had attained about the same command of language as common children three years of age. But her power of expression was, of course, by no means equal to her power of conception; for she had no words to express many of the perceptions and sensations which her mind doubtless experienced. In the spring of 1840, when she had been under instruc tion about two and a half years, returning fatigued from her journey home, she complained of a pain in her side, and on being asked what caused it, she replied as follows: "Laura did go to see mother, ride did make Laura side ache, horse was wrong, did not run softly." Her improvement in the use of language was very rapid, and she soon became, in some respects, quite a critic. When one of the girls had the mumps, Laura learned the name of the disease; soon after she had it herself, but she had the swelling only on one side; and some one saying to her, "You have got the mumps," she replied quickly, "*No, no; I have mump.*"

About this time Laura learned the difference between the present and past tense of the verb. And here her simplicity rebukes the clumsy irregularities of our language. She learned *jump, jumped—walk, walked,* etc., until she had an idea of the mode of forming the imperfect tense of regular verbs; but when she came to the word *see,* she insisted that it should be *seed* in the imperfect; and upon going down to dinner, she asked if it was *eat, eated;* but being told it was *eat,* ATE, she seemed to try to express the idea that this transposition of the letters was not only wrong, but ludicrous, for she laughed heartily. She continued this habit of forming words analogically. When she had become acquainted with the meaning of the word restless, she seemed to understand that *less* at the end of a word means without, destitute of, or wanting, as rest-less, fruit-less; also that *ful* at the end of a word expresses abundance of what is implied by the primitive, as bliss-ful, play-ful. This is clearly illustrated in the following expressions. One day, feeling weak, she said, "I am very strongless." Being told this was not right, she said, "Why, you say restless when I do not sit still." Then she said, "I am very weakful."

My primary object in referring to Laura has been to illustrate, in a striking manner, the practicability of the education of the senses to an extent not heretofore generally known. To such an extent has the sense of touch been cultivated in her, that her fingers serve as very good substitutes for both eyes and ears. I will mention one or two instances which strikingly illustrate the acuteness of Laura's sense of touch. When I was at the institution a few months ago, she was told a person was present whom she had never met, and who wished an introduction to her. She reached her hand, expecting to meet a *stranger*. By mistake (for her teachers design never to allow her to be deceived), she took the hand of another gentleman, whom she recognized immediately, though she had never met him but twice before. She recognizes her acquaintances in an instant by touching their hands or their dress, and there are probably hundreds of individuals who, if they were to stand in a row, and hold out each a hand to her, would be recognized by that alone. The memory of these sensations is very vivid, and she will readily recognize a person whom she has once thus touched. Many cases of this kind have been noticed; such as a person shaking hands with her, and making a peculiar pressure with one finger, and repeating this on his second visit, after a lapse of many months, being instantly known by her. She has been known to recognize persons with whom she had thus simply shaken hands but once, after a lapse of six months. But this is hardly more wonderful than that one should be able to recall impressions made upon the mind through the organ of sight, as when we recognize a person of whom we have had but one glimpse a year before; but it shows the exhaustless capacity of those organs which the Creator has bestowed, as it were, in reserve against accidents, and which we too commonly allow to lie unused and unvalued.

OLIVER CASWELL.—Had I not devoted so much space to this subject already, it would be interesting to consider the case of Oliver, who, like Laura, is deaf, dumb, and blind. His experience is full of interest, though less striking than that already presented. His progress in learning language, and in acquiring intellectual knowledge, is comparatively slow, because he has not that fineness of fiber and that activity of temperament which enable Laura to struggle so successfully against the immense disadvantages under which they both labor. Oliver is a boy of rather unfavorable organization; he had been deaf and blind from infancy; he received no instruction until he was twelve years old, and consequently lost the most precious years for learning; he has nevertheless been taught to express his thoughts both by the finger language and by writing; he has also become acquainted with the rudiments of the common branches of education, and is intelligent and morally responsible. His case proves, therefore, very clearly, that the success of the attempt made to instruct Laura Bridgman was not owing solely to her uncommon capacity.

Oliver's natural ability is small, and his acquired knowledge very limited; but his sense of right and wrong, his obedience to moral obligations, and his attachment to friends, are very remarkable.* He never willfully violates the rights or injures the feelings of

* I have omitted much in the case of Laura that I should have retained but for want of room. The moral qualities of her nature have developed themselves most clearly. She is honest to a proverb, having never been known to take any thing belonging to another. That she is a Christian there can be no doubt. It is said in the report of her case for 1846, that "on the last occasion of her manifesting any impatience, she said to Miss Wight, her teacher, '*I felt cross, but in a minute I thought of Christ, how good and gentle he was, and my bad feelings went away.*'"

others, and seldom shows any signs of temper when his own seem to be invaded. He even bears the teasing of little boys with gentleness and patience. He is very tractable, and always obeys respectfully the requests of his teacher. This shows the effect which kind and gentle treatment has had upon his character, for when he first went to the institution in Boston he was sometimes very willful, and showed occasional outbursts of temper which were fearfully violent. "It seems hardly possible," says Dr. Howe, "that the gentle and affectionate youth, who loves all the household and is beloved by all in return, should be the same who a few years ago scratched and bit, like a young savage, those who attempted to control him."

We regard it as a fact fully established that the sense of touch may be cultivated to a much greater extent than most persons are aware of. The same remark will apply to the cultivation of all the senses. We shall consider them separately.

The Sense of Touch.—The remarks already made apply chiefly to this sense. The nerves that supply it proceed from the anterior half of the spinal cord. This sense is most delicate where there are the greatest number of nervous filaments, and those of the largest size. The hands, and especially the fingers, have a most delicate and nice sense of touch, though the sense is extended over the whole body, in every part of which it is less or more acute. In this respect, then, this sense is unlike the others, which are confined to small spaces, as we shall see when we come to consider them. The action of the sensitive nerves depends upon the state of the brain, and the condition of the system generally. In sound and perfect sleep, when the brain is inactive, ordinary impressions made upon the skin are unobserved. Fear and grief diminish the impressibility of this tissue, while hope and joy increase it. The quantity and quality of the blood also influence sensation. If this vital fluid becomes impure, or its quantity is diminished, the sensibility of the skin will be impaired thereby. Whatever affects the general health affects the healthy action of this sense. It is also much affected by sudden changes in temperature. If the skin is wounded while under the influence of cold, the pain will be slight. By carrying this chilling influence too far, the surface becomes entirely destitute of sensation. This is produced by the contraction of the blood-vessels upon the surface. On the contrary, when the chilled extremities are suddenly exposed to heat, the rapid enlargement of the contracted blood-vessels excites the nerves unduly, which causes the pain experienced on such occasions.

The sensibility of the nerves depends much upon the habits of persons. Suppose two boys go out to play when the thermometer stands at the freezing point, and that one of them has been accustomed to exercise in the open air, and to practice daily ablution, while the other one has been confined most of the time to a warm room, and has been accustomed to wash only his hands and face. The skin of the former, other things being equal, will be active and healthy, while that of the latter will be enfeebled and diseased. The organs of touch diffused over the body at the surface will be very differently affected in these two boys, and the perceptions of their minds will be alike dissimilar. One will be roused to action, and will feel just right for some animating game. Both body and mind will be elastic and joyous. He will bound like the roe, make the welkin ring with his merry shout, and return to the bosom of his family with a gladdened heart, ready to impart and receive pleasure, while the other boy will be too keenly affected by the contact of the air, and think it too cold to stay out of doors. He will thrust his hands into his pockets, and curl himself up like one decrepit with age. His teeth will chatter and his whole frame tremble. Of course, very different reflections will be awakened in his mind. He will hurry back to the fireside, thinking winter a very dismal season, and will be apt to fret himself and all about him, because of the confinement from which he has not the resolution to break out.

The sensibility of the cutaneous nerves in these two cases depends upon the habits of the persons. If the latter would practice frequent ablutions, and excite a healthy action in the skin by friction and exercise, and conform to other laws of health, he would experience all that gladness of heart, and elasticity of body and mind, which the other is supposed to enjoy. Hence the advantages resulting from a strict conformity to the laws of health in this particular as well as in others that are generally regarded as more important.

The general law that the exercise of a faculty in creases its power is applicable to the senses. We have referred to the blind, who read as rapidly as seeing persons by passing their fingers over raised letters, the sense of touch being substituted by them for that of vision. Nor is the education of this sense useful to the blind merely. It may frequently be appealed to with great advantage by all who have cultivated it. The miller, for example, can judge more accurately of the quality of flour and meal, by passing some between his fingers than by the exercise of vision. The cloth-dresser, also, by the aid of this sense, not only marks the nicest shades of texture in examining cloths of different qualities, but in many instances learns to distinguish *colors* by the sense of touch with perhaps greater accuracy than is common with seeing persons.

THE SENSE OF TASTE.—The sense of taste bears the greatest resemblance to the sense of feeling. The upper surface of the tongue is the principal agent in tasting, though the lips, the palate, and the internal surface of the cheeks participate in this function, as does the upper part of the œsophagus. The multitude of points called papillæ, scattered over the upper surface of the tongue, constitute the more immediate seat of this sense. It is in these sensitive papillæ that the ramifications of the gustatory or tasting nerves terminate. When fluids are taken into the mouth, and especially those whose taste is pungent, these papillæ dilate and erect themselves, and the particular sensation produced is transmitted to the brain through the medium of the minute filaments of the gustatory nerves.

In order fully to gratify the taste in eating dry, solid food, it is necessary that the food be first reduced to a liquid state, or, at least, that it be thoroughly moistened. Nature has made full provision for this in furnishing the mouth with salivary glands, whose secretions are most abundant when engaged in masticating dry, hard substances. These quickened secretions contribute to gratify the taste and increase the pleasure of eating, and, at the same time, materially aid in the important processes of mastication and digestion. Nature, also, with her accustomed bounty, has furnished man with a great variety of articles for food. By this means the various tastes of different persons may be gratified, although, in many instances, those articles of food which are most agreeable to some persons are extremely disagreeable to others.

Many persons can not eat the most nourishing food, as fruits, butter, etc., because to them the taste of these articles is disagreeable. But this is very easily accounted for, as in the mouth the food mixes with various fluids that differ in different persons, and in the same person at different times. These fluids, and particularly the saliva, assist in the formation and change of taste. This accounts not only for the different tastes of different persons, but also for the varying taste of the same persons, and for that fickleness of taste which is so common in sickness, when the fluids of the mouth, in a disordered and deranged state, mix with the food, and produce the disagreeable taste so often complained of at such times, and which, moreover, occasionally create a permanent dislike for food that was previously much relished.

This sense was given to men and animals to guide them in the selection of their food, and to enable them to guard against the use of articles that would be injurious if introduced into the stomach. In the inferior animals, the sense of taste still answers the original design of its bestowment; but in man, it has been abused and perverted by the use of artificial stimulants, which have created an acquired taste that, in most persons, is very detrimental to health. This sense is so modified by habit, that, not unfrequently, articles which were at first exceedingly offensive, become, at length, highly agreeable. It is in this manner that many persons, whose sense of taste has been impaired or perverted, have formed the disgusting and ruinous habits of smoking and chewing tobacco, and of using stimulating and intoxicating drinks. But these pernicious habits, and all similar indulgences, lessen the sensibility of the gustatory nerve, and ultimately destroy the natural relish for healthful food and drink. By this means, also, the digestive powers become disordered, and the general health is materially impaired. All persons, then, should seek to preserve the natural integrity of this sense, and to restore it immediately to healthy action when at all depraved, for upon this depends much of health and longevity, of happiness and usefulness.

This sense may be rendered very acute by cultivation, as is illustrated by persons who are accustomed to taste medicines, liquors, teas, etc. It ought, however, to be chiefly exercised in partaking of those simple articles of food and drink which are most conducive to health. In its natural state it prefers these, and if depraved it will soon recover a healthy tone, if not continually tempted by stimulating substances. This is beautifully illustrated in thousands of instances all over our country by persons who were once accustomed to use strong drink, but who have substituted for it sparkling water, a beverage prepared by God himself to nourish and invigorate his creatures, and beautify his footstool.

The Sense of Smell.—The sense of taste has received a faithful companion in that of smell. The beneficent Creator, with that wisdom which characterizes all his works, has very wisely placed the organ of this sense just above the mouth, in order that the scent of many things that are hurtful may warn us from partaking of them before they reach the mouth. The air-passages of the nose, in which this sense is located, are lined with a thin skin, called the mucous membrane, which is continuous with the lining membrane of the parts of the throat and of the external skin. Upon this membrane the olfactory nerve ramifies. The odoriferous particles of matter that float in the air come in contact with these fine and sensitive nerves as the air rushes through the nostrils, and the impression is conveyed to the brain by the olfactory nerve. The mucous membrane, upon which this ramifies, is of considerable extent in man. In the lower animals it is less or more extensive, according to the degree of acuteness of this sense. This membrane is full of little glands that are continually giving off thick mucus, and especially when the membrane is inflamed. There is a small canal leading from the eyes to the nose, through which a fluid, that also forms tears, is constantly passing when the passage is clear. It is the office of this fluid to moisten and thin the mucus of the nose. When this mucous is too abundant, as in some stages of a cold, and especially if it becomes dry from the closing of the canal leading from the eyes, or from any other cause, as fever, the sense of smell will be greatly impaired, if not entirely suspended. It is, indeed, not unfrequently permanently injured in this way, and sometimes is irrecoverably lost.

The sensation of smell, it should be borne in mind, is produced by a kind of odoriferous vapor, very fine and invisible, that flies off from nearly all bodies. The air which contains this vapor is drawn into the nose, and is in this way brought into contact with the very delicate nerves of smell that ramify the membrane which lines the air-passages of this organ. It is only when the exceedingly small particles of which the odor of various bodies is composed come in contact with the minute ramifications of the olfactory nerve that this sensation is produced. In order to protect these sensitive nerves, as well as to prevent the introduction into the lungs of injurious substances, the air-passages of the nose are furnished with hairy appendages, which are less or more abundant according to the size of these passages. These intercept any foreign substances that enter the nose, and thus irritate the mucous membrane, and cause a quick and powerful contraction of the diaphragm, by which the offending matter is immediately expelled. This phenomenon, which is called sneezing, depends upon a connection of the olfactory with the respiratory nerves.

This sense not only comes in to the aid of taste in enabling man and the lower animals to select proper food, and avoid that which is injurious, but it also gives us positive and varied pleasure by the inhalation of agreeable odors, while, at the same time, it enables us to avoid an infectious atmosphere, and all objects whose odors are offensive and hurtful.

It is true that man can accustom himself to nearly all kinds of odor, even to those that at first are very disagreeable. He indeed not unfrequently so vitiates the sense of smell as actually to prefer those scents which, to persons who have preserved the integrity of this sense, are regarded as exceedingly offensive, and even filthy. But why, let me ask, did the Creator give us the sense of smell? Was it to be thus perverted? No, indeed: it was, without doubt, that we might enjoy the refreshing fragrance of flowers and herbs, of food and drink; and also that we might distinguish between air that is pure and healthful, and that which is impure and infectious. As most articles of food which are agreeable to the smell are wholesome, and as those which are disagreeable are generally unwholesome, so, also, those states of the atmosphere which are grateful to this sense are salubrious, and those odors which are pleasant are healthful, while air which is ungrateful will generally be found injurious to health, as will also all those odors which are unpleasant to this sense when in a healthful state. He who has had occasion to enter a crowded court-room, lecture-room, church, or assembly-room of whatever kind, which has been occupied for a considerable time without adequate ventilation, can not fail to remember the unwelcome impression made upon his nasal organs when first he inhaled the vitiated atmosphere within, though by degrees he might have become accustomed to it, did he remain, so as ultimately to become well-nigh insensible to its noisome influence. But let such and all others be well assured that, however offensive such a fetid atmosphere may be to the smell, it is equally injurious to the health. And let those who, having returned from a morning walk or healthful exercise in a salubrious atmosphere, have had occasion to revisit the small and unventilated lodging-room in which they spent a restless night without refreshing sleep, perceive, in the sickening smell, a sufficient cause for all their pains and aches, and wonder how they survived such a gross violation of the organic laws.

All of the senses may be improved by education. The sense of smell constitutes no exception to this rule. Let none be discouraged, then; for the more we accustom our lungs and nasal organs to pure air, the more will they require it, and the more readily will they detect the presence of the least impurity.

This sense becomes very acute in deaf persons, and even more so in the case of those that are blind. The reason is obvious; for, as they are led of necessity to rely upon it more than persons who have all the senses, it becomes thereby developed, and is enabled more accurately to judge of the properties of whatever is submitted to its scrutiny. Seeing persons rarely partake of any article of food, and especially of any thing new, without first smelling it, and blind persons never; for this is the only means by which they can judge of its wholesomeness or unwholesomeness without tasting it.

Whatever stupefies the brain, impairs the healthy action of the nerve of smell, or thickens the membrane that lines the nasal cavities, and thus diminishes the sensibility of the nerves ramified upon it, injures this sense. All these effects are produced by the habitual use of snuff, which, when introduced into the nose, diminishes the sensibility of the nerves, and thickens the lining membrane. By its use the air-passages through the nostrils sometimes become completely obstructed. It is on this account that most habitual snuff-takers are compelled to open their mouths in order to breathe freely. It has been well said, that if Nature had intended that the nose should be used as a snuff-hole, she would doubtless have put it on the other end up.

THE SENSE OF HEARING.—The external ear, although curiously shaped, is not the most important part of the organ whose function it is to take cognizance of sounds. In the transmission of sound to the brain, the vibrations of the air produced by the sonorous body are collected by the external ear, and conducted through the auditory canal to the drum of the ear, which is so arranged that it may be relaxed or tightened like the head of an ordinary drum. That its motion may be free, the air contained within the drum has free communication with the external air by an open passage, called the Eustachian tube, leading to the back of the mouth. This tube is sometimes obstructed by wax, when a degree of deafness ensues. But when the obstruction is removed in the effort of sneezing or otherwise, a crack or sudden noise is generally experienced, accompanied usually with an immediate return of acute hearing.

The ear-drum performs a two-fold office; for while it aids in the transmission of sound from without to the internal ear, it at the same time modifies the intensity of sound. This softening of the sound is effected by the relaxation of a muscle when sounds are so acute as to be painful; but when listening to low sounds, the drum is rendered tense by the contraction of this muscle, and the sounds become, by this means, more audible. The vibrations made on the drum are transmitted by the tympanum—an irregular bony cavity—to the internal ear, which is filled with a watery fluid. In his fluid the filaments of the auditory nerve terminate, which receive and transmit the sound to the brain.

The ear has the power of judging of the direction from which sound comes, as is strikingly exemplified in the fact that when horses or mules march in company at night, those in front direct their ears forward, and those in the rear turn them backward, while those in the center turn them laterally or across, the whole troop seeming to be actuated by a feeling to watch the common safety. This is also illustrated by four or six horse teams, and is a fact with which coachmen are familiar. It is further illustrated by the dog, and many other animals. The external ear of man is likewise furnished with muscles; and savages are said to have the power of moving or directing their ears at pleasure, like a horse, to catch sounds as they come from different directions; but few men in civilized life retain this power.

The acuteness of this sense in men and animals, other things being equal, depends upon the size of the ear. In timid animals, as the hare and the rabbit, the ear is very large. They are thus apprized of the approach of an enemy in time to flee to a place of safety.

The ear-trumpet—which is a tube wide at one end, where the sound enters, and narrow at the other, where the ear is applied—is constructed on this principle, its sides being so curved that, according to the law of reflection, all the sound which enters it is brought to a focus in the narrow end. It thus increases many fold the intensity of a sound which reaches the ear through it, and enables a person who has become deaf to common conversation to mix again with pleasure in society. The concave hand held behind the ear answers in some degree the purpose of an ear-trumpet.

The Ear of Dionysius, in the dungeons of Syracuse, was a notorious instance of a sound-collecting surface. The roof of the prison was so formed as to collect the words, and even whispers, of the unhappy prisoners, and to direct them along a hidden conduit to where the tyrant sat listening.

Acuteness of hearing requires the healthy action of the brain, and particularly of that portion of it from which the auditory nerve proceeds, combined with perfection in the structure and functions of the different parts of the ear. The best method, then, of retaining and improving the hearing, is to observe well the general laws of health, and particularly to avoid every thing that will in the least impair the structure or healthy action of the parts immediately concerned in the exercise of this function. Inflammatory fevers, affections of the brain, and injuries upon the head, are among the more common causes of imperfect hearing. Hence the impropriety of striking children upon the head in correcting them, whether in the family or in the school. The instances are not few in which deafness, and the impairing of the mental faculties, have resulted from that barbarous practice familiarly known as "boxing the ears." This inhuman practice is likely to result in injury to the drum of the ear, either in thickening this membrane, or in diminishing its vibratory character. Inflammation of the ear-drum, either acute or chronic, is the common cause of its increased thickness. How often this is produced by blows, the reader may judge. Diminution of the vibratory character of the ear-drum may result from an accumulation of wax upon its outer surface. In such cases chronic inflammation of the parts is not unfrequently the result of the injudicious practice of attempting its removal by introducing the heads of pins into the ear.

This wax, it should be known, is designed to subserve an important end; for the tube leading from the external ear, being, like the nose, constantly open, is liable to the entrance of foreign bodies, such as dust, insects, and the like. But, fortunately, it is not left without the means of defense; for on its inside there are numerous fine bristles, which, interlacing each other, interpose a barrier to the entrance of every thing but sound. Moreover, between the roots of these hairs there are numerous little glands, that secrete a nauseous, bitter wax, which, by its offensiveness, either deters insects from entering, or entangles them and prevents their advance in case they do enter. This wax, then, is very serviceable. But its usefulness does not stop here. When the ear becomes dry from a deficiency of it, the hearing becomes imperfect, as also when it is thin and purulent. This wax not unfrequently becomes hard and obstructs the tube, causing less or more deafness. But this form of deafness may be easily cured, even though it has existed for years; for, having softened the accumulations of viscid wax by dropping animal oil into the ear, they may be removed by the injection of warm soap-suds, which is an effectual and safe remedy.

The sense of hearing is perhaps as susceptible of cultivation as any of the senses. The Indian in the forest, who is accustomed to listen to the approach of his enemies or of his prey, acquires such acuteness of hearing as to be able to detect sounds that would be inaudible to persons living amid the din of civilized life. The blind, also, who of necessity are led to rely more upon this sense than seeing persons, excel in the acuteness of their hearing. They recognize their acquaintances by the exercise of this sense as readily as persons usually do by that of sight, an attainment which very few seeing persons make, and yet one that is perhaps within the reach of ninety-nine persons in every hundred. The blind judge with great accuracy the distance of persons in conversation, of carriages in motion, and of all sonorous bodies whose vibrations reach their ears. They even estimate with remarkable correctness the distance and height of buildings by the reflection or interception of sound. It is in consequence of the acuteness of this sense, acquired by careful cultivation, that the blind, as a class, have become so generally and justly distinguished for their pre-eminence in instrumental music. This enables them also to cultivate vocal music with more than ordinary success.

The due cultivation of the sense of hearing will contribute vastly to promote our intellectual and moral well-being. If it be true, as we are told it is by those who have been engaged in teaching both the deaf and the blind, that the absence of hearing is even a more formidable impediment to the communication of knowledge than that of sight, we must infer that all imperfections of the organ of hearing itself, or in the manner of using it, must correspondingly lessen the accuracy of the knowledge we receive through that organ. The meaning of language very often is conveyed not so much by the words themselves as in the tones of voice in which the words are uttered. If, therefore, the hearing be indistinct, or there be no habit formed of careful attention to the inflections of sound, the impressions received from what we hear must often be inaccurate. Our speech, too, will be far less agreeable, and be inefficient, even if it be not positively inarticulate. We owe it to others, no less than to ourselves, then, to cultivate the powers of the voice—the common instrument that God has given us for the interchange of thought, sentiment, and feeling, and which, though so common, is the most perfect of all instruments for the transmission of sound. Yet how deplorably is it neglected! how shamefully is it misused! It can be fully developed and made what it is capable of being only through the influence of the ear. If this organ be neglected, the voice must needs be imperfect. And the voices of many persons are through life imperfect and disagreeable, because they were not carefully trained in early life to articulate distinctly, much less to utter *musical* sounds. The opinion is confidently expressed by those who are best qualified to decide the matter, that nearly all children might be taught to sing, if proper attention were paid early enough to the use they make of their ears and their organs of sound. The careful training of these should be considered an indispensable part of a school-teacher's as well as of a parent's duty.

The ear will find appropriate discipline in distinguishing, without aid from the eye, the causes of various sounds, as the opening of a door, the shutting of a knife, the dropping of various coins, the moving of different articles of furniture, etc. It may also find appropriate exercise in determining the direction from which various sounds proceed; in recognizing acquaintances by their natural voices, and in detecting the counterfeit voices of companions; in arranging and classifying the elementary sounds of the language, and in determining all the different musical tones; in judging of the genus and species of birds by their chirping, of the distance and nature of sonorous bodies of various kinds, etc., etc. These are some of the direct means of improving this sense: others will suggest themselves to the thoughtful reader

THE SENSE OF SIGHT.—The sense of sight, which is the most refined and admirable of all the senses, still remains to be considered. The senses generally serve as interpreters between the material universe without and the spirit within. But it is more especially by the sense of sight that we are enabled to hold converse with the external world. Without it we should be deprived of a large portion of the pleasures of life not only, but even of the means of maintaining our existence. It is through the sense of vision that the wisdom, power, and benevolence of the Deity are chiefly manifested to us.

I shall describe the apparatus of vision only so far as is necessary in order to subserve my leading object, which is the preservation and improvement of this sense, and the means of rendering it tributary to intellectual and moral culture. The eye, which is the organ of vision, is an optical instrument of the most perfect construction. It is surrounded by *coats*, which contain refracting mediums, called *humors*. There are three coats, called the *sclerotic*, the *choroid*, and the *retina*; and three humors, called the *aqueous*, the *crystalline*, and the *vitreous*.

The *sclerotic* or outer coat, called also the white of the eye, is an opaque, fibrous membrane. It has almost the firmness of leather, possesses little sensibility, and is rarely exposed to inflammation or other diseases. It invests the eye on every side except the front, and besides maintaining its globular form and preserving its internal and delicate structure, serves for the attachment of those muscles which move this organ. The opening in the fore part of this opaque coat is filled by the transparent *cornea*, which resembles a watch crystal in shape, and is received into a groove in the front part of the sclerotic coat in the same manner that a watch-glass is received into its case. But for this arrangement light could not gain admission to the eye.

The *choroid coat*, which constitutes the second investing membrane of the eye, is of a dark brown color upon its outer surface, and of a deep black within. The internal surface of this membrane secretes a dark substance resembling black paint, upon which the retina is spread out, and which is of great importance in the function of vision, as it seems to absorb the rays of light immediately after they have struck upon the sensible surface of the retina.

The *retina*, which is the third and innermost membrane of the eye, is the expansion of the optic nerve, and constitutes the immediate seat of vision. Such is the arrangement of the humors of the eye, and so perfectly are they adapted to the functions they are called upon to perform, that in the healthy state of this organ, the light entering the pupil is so refracted as to paint upon the retina an exact image of the objects from which it proceeds. The optic nerve, whose expansion forms the retina, receives this image and transmits it to the mind.

Arnott has well remarked, that "a whole printed sheet of a newspaper may be represented on the retina on less surface than that of a finger nail; and yet not only shall every word and letter be separately perceivable, but even any imperfection of a single letter. Or, more wonderful still, when at night an eye is turned up to the blue vault of heaven, there is portrayed on the little concave of the retina the boundless concave of the sky, with every object in its just proportions. There a moon in beautiful miniature may be sailing among her white-edged clouds, and surrounded by a thousand twinkling stars, so that to an animalcule supposed to be within and near the pupil, the retina might appear another starry firmament with all its glory."

Besides these three coats, and the cornea which constitutes about one fifth of the anterior portion of the outer coat, it is necessary to notice the *iris*, so called from its variety of color in different persons, and upon which alone the color of the eye depends. The iris is a circular membrane situated just behind the cornea, and is attached to one of the coats at its circumference. In its center is a small round hole, called the *pupil;* and sometimes spoken of familiarly as the sight of the eye, as no light can enter the eye except through it. The iris possesses the power of dilating and contracting, so as to admit more or less light, as it may be needed. This change in the size of the pupil is effected by two sets of muscular fibers. The first set converge from the circumference of the iris to the circular margin of the pupil, and constitute the *radiated muscle.* The outer ends of these fibers are attached to the sclerotic coat, which is unyielding; hence, when they contract, the pupil *enlarges* to receive more light. The other set is composed of circular fibers, which go round in the iris from the border to the pupil, and constitute the *orbicular muscle,* the contraction of which *diminishes* the size of the pupil. When too much light enters the eye, the excited and sensitive retina immediately gives warning of the danger, and the nerves, which are plentifully distributed to the iris, stimulate the orbicular muscle to contract, and the radiated one to relax, by which the size of the pupil is lessened. But when the light which enters the pupil is insufficient to transmit a distinct image of objects to the brain, the orbicular muscle relaxes, and the radiated one contracts, so as to enlarge the pupil. The contraction of the pupil is readily seen when a person passes from a darkened room into a bright sunlight, or when a light is first brought into a room in the twilight of evening. Any person may notice this contraction in his own eye by beholding himself in a glass immediately after passing from a dark to a well-lighted room. So, also, when a person looks at an object near the eye, the pupil contracts, but when he looks at an object more remote, it dilates. The muscles of the iris are somewhat under the control of the will; for most persons can contract or dilate the pupil, in some degree, at pleasure. Some persons possess this faculty to a great extent.

The three *humors of the eye* have been compared to the glasses of a telescope, and the coats to the tube, which keeps them in their places. The *aqueous* humor is situated in the fore part of the eye, and is divided by the iris into what are called the anterior and posterior chambers of the eye. The *crystalline* humor, or lens, is situated immediately behind the aqueous humor, a short distance back of the pupil, and is a perfectly transparent double convex lens, closely resembling in shape the common burning glass. This resemblance does not stop here; for this lens, like the burning glass, possesses the property of converging the rays of light which fall upon it, and bringing them to a focus. When this lens becomes so opaque as to obstruct the passage of light, either partially or entirely, a person is said to have a *cataract*. This can be cured only by a surgical operation. The *vitreous* humor, situated back of the other two, forms the principal part of the globe of the eye. It differs from the aqueous in one important particular. When that is discharged in extracting the crystalline lens for cataract or otherwise, it will be restored again in a few hours, and the eye will continue to perform its function. But if this be discharged by accident, the eye is irrecoverably lost. This, however does not often occur; for, as we shall presently see, the eye is admirably fortified.

The eye is a perfect optical instrument, infinitely surpassing all specimens of human skill. This is true, view it in what light we may. It not only possesses the power of so adjusting its parts as to adapt it to the examination of objects at different distances, and in light of different degrees of intensity, but we are enabled to direct it at will to objects above, beneath, or around us.

The various motions of the eye are produced by six little muscles. These are attached at one extremity to the immovable bones of the orbit, while at the other extremity they are inserted into the sclerotic coat, four of them near its junction with the cornea, by broad, thin tendons, which give to the white of the eye its pearly appearance. These muscles are so arranged by the matchless skill of the Architect as to enable the beholder to direct the eye to any object he chooses, and to hold it there for any length of time that is compatible with the laws by which muscular exercise should be regulated. By the slight or intense action of four of these, called the straight muscles, the eye is less or more compressed, and the relative positions of its humors are by this means so nicely adjusted as to enable us to view objects near by or at a distance. The other two are called oblique muscles, one of which, with its long tendon passing through a cartilaginous loop, acts upon the principle of the fixed pulley, and turns the eye in a direction contrary to its own action. When the external muscle becomes too short, the eye turns out; but if the internal muscle is unduly contracted, the eye turns inward, toward the nose. One eye is sometimes turnea up or down, but this is of less frequent occurrence.

It would be interesting to notice the protecting organs of the eye, consisting of the *orbit*, which is a deep bony socket, in which the eye securely rests; of the *eye-brows*, which are two projecting arches, covered with hair, and so arranged as to prevent the moisture that accumulates upon the forehead, in free perspiration, from flowing into the eye; of the *eye-lids*, which are two movable curtains for the protection of the eye, and which secrete a fluid that moistens and lubricates it; of the *lachrymal gland*, with its ducts, which keeps the eye constantly moist, and whose secretions go on while we wake and when we sleep, etc., etc.; but the preceding must suffice.

With this brief description of the apparatus of vision, we proceed to the consideration of the means of pre serving and improving this sense, and of rendering i tributary to intellectual and moral culture.

The rule requiring that *action should alternate wit.i rest*, which has been so often stated, and which applies to all the organs of both body and mind, should be especially observed in relation to the eye. This organ requires exercise, and light is its appropriate stimulus; but injury is the inevitable consequence of keeping it too constantly employed, or too intently fixed for a long time on any object. Whenever the eye is fixed for any length of time upon an object which it distinguishes with difficulty, it experiences a painful sensation, which is a sure indication that it has been overtaxed. The sight is also impaired when the eye is too little used, or when its natural stimulus is shut out, as is strikingly illustrated in the case of persons confined in dungeons. A distinguished oculist has said that many men daily impair or destroy their eyes by immoderate use, and that not a few have done the same by too little use of them.

The exposure of the eyes to *sudden transitions from weak to strong light* is very injurious. This may be regarded as one of the most prolific causes of weak ness of sight. The injury is generally gradual, it is true, but it is none the less fatal on that account. The immediate sensation of pain, when a strong light is brought into a dark room, should be a sufficient warning to avoid such sudden extremes. The iris dilates and contracts, and thus enlarges or diminishes the size of the pupil as the light that falls upon the eye is faint or strong; but this dilation and contraction are not instantaneous. There are numerous instances on record in which total blindness has resulted from a sudden transition from darkness to the brilliancy of day. The habit of looking at a bright light of any kind, and especially of watching flashes of lightning, which is practiced by many, is exceedingly dangerous. The practice which many students and others indulge in, of resting their eyes as the twilight of evening advances, and allowing the pupil to dilate until it is quite dark, and then suddenly introducing a bright light, is a palpable violation of this rule, and one that is sure, sooner or later, sensibly to injure the eyes. The exposure of the eyes suddenly to a strong light upon waking from sleep, and all sudden changes of whatever kind from darkness to intense light, should be carefully avoided by persons who would preserve their sight unimpaired.

The strength of light used should be regulated *according to the powers of the eye.* This is a general though a very important rule. Both the amount and the distribution of light should be such as to produce no unpleasant sensations. The eye possesses a certain degree of adaptation to light, according as it is intense or feeble. Some eyes require a stronger light than others, but all eyes are injured by being used in light that is too intense or too feeble. Reading by a strong sunlight, and by moon or star light, may be adduced as illustrations which are alike painful and injurious.

Too little light is well-nigh as injurious as too much, as he can not fail to have noticed who has had occasion to travel a difficult road in a dark night. The injury, in such cases, is two-fold; for while, on the one hand, the radiated muscle of the iris is unduly contracted for a length of time, in order sufficiently to enlarge the pupil to render objects visible, the sensitive retina, on the other hand, is overtaxed to gain a knowledge of them in too feeble light. The pain which the strained eye thus experiences is only an indication and a warning to the individual of the permanent injury he is inflicting upon this delicate organ.

Rooms should be well and evenly lighted. The irregular and flickering light of common lamps and candles is very injurious, and should be avoided in the study, and in all mechanical pursuits where the eye is much taxed. The best oculists concur in the opinion that reflected and concentrated light are highly injurious. Several cases of actual blindness are recorded as having occurred within a few years from exposure to concentrated light, and weakness of sight that has unfitted the individual for usefulness through life has often been thus produced. The rays of the sun are considered as peculiarly injurious when reflected from an opposite building or wall, or even when they pass through a window, and, descending to the floor, are thence reflected to the eyes. What, then, shall we say of the habit of constructing school-rooms in such a manner that perhaps a majority of the scholars are obliged to write and study at desks upon which the direct rays of the sun shine for a considerable portion of the day unbroken unless it be by a passing cloud! And yet thousands of school-houses are situated in such a manner as to create this very necessity all over our country. At a moderate estimate, the eyes of one hundred thousand children are taxed in this manner in the schools of the United States every passing year. A vast amount of discomfort and unhappiness is produced in this way that might easily be avoided, would parents and teachers take the trouble. Any exposure of this kind should be immediately obviated, either by blinds, or by curtains of some soft color. A few newspapers are much better than nothing. The desks and furniture should be of such a color that the eye may repose upon them with agreeable sensations. Nature is clothed with drapery whose color is refreshing to the eye; and it is false taste, as well as false philosophy, which attempts to dazzle in order to please it.

The use of side lights is injurious. The eye will accommodate itself to light of different degrees of intensity within a limited range, but both eyes should be exposed to an equal degree of light. The sympathy between the eyes is so great, that if the pupil of one eye is dilated by being kept in the shade, as must, of course, be the case where the light is on one side, the eye which is exposed can not contract itself sufficiently for protection, and is almost inevitably injured.

When viewing objects, we should avoid, as far as possible, *all oblique positions of the eye.* By neglecting this rule, an unnatural and permanent contraction of the muscle is liable to be produced, as is illustrated in the numerous instances of strabismus, or cross-eye, which are every where too common.

We should accustom the eye to viewing objects at different distances. The muscles upon which the form of the eye and the size of the pupil depend are subject to the general laws of muscular action. Their strength and flexibility, which are increased by healthful exercise, are impaired by disuse. Hence students who have neglected this rule, and have accustomed themselves for a long time to view objects near by, lose the powei of adjusting the eye so as to view things at a distance. As a consequence, they become near-sighted, and put on glasses, when, by a proper use of the eye, their vision might have been preserved unimpaired many long years. I know some students upon whom this habit became so firmly fixed before they were twenty years of age, that they felt compelled to put on glasses, but who, unwilling to contract so pernicious a habit in early life, commenced a course of discipline in accordance with the suggestions here given. By perseverance, their eyes not only recovered their former healthful action, but became so improved that they now possess the sense of vision unimpaired not only, but in a very high state of cultivation.

Persons become near or long sighted as the objects to which they are accustomed to direct the eye are near or remote. This is illustrated in the case of students, watch-makers, and engravers, who are accustomed to examine minute objects near the eye, and, as a consequence, become near-sighted ; and of surveyors, hunters, and sailors, who, being accustomed to view objects at a distance, become long-sighted. By a proper discipline of the eye, persons may attain and retain the power of viewing objects near by and at a distance, as is illustrated in the case of those gunsmiths who are accustomed to manufacture guns, and to try them in shooting at a mark at a great distance. The preceding principles being borne in mind in their various applications, I need, perhaps, state but one more rule.

He who would secure clear and distinct vision, must observe all those rules which are necessary to keep the body in health. The sympathy of the eyes with all the other organs of the body is wonderful and intimate. There is no other organ whose strength depends so much on the general vigor of the system. Strict temperance in eating and drinking may be regarded as an indispensable requisite for the preservation of healthy eyes. To this may be attributed the clear heads of the ancient philosophers, who, unlike most students of the present day, exercised their bodies and limbs as well as their minds. Their works are not the production of congested brains, for these were not oppressed with blood belonging to other parts of the body. They studied and thought, and exercised both body and mind in the open air, and thus observed the laws of health. But among the multitudes of close students of the present day, who complain of weakness of the eyes, the misfortune is generally attributable to an almost total neglect of the first principles of health.

While we reproach and loathe the man whose eyes are red and weeping with the effects of intemperate drinking, we cordially pity purblind students, as in some sense martyrs to the cause of learning. Dr. Reynolds, a distinguished American oculist, administers a rebuke to such which we fear is too often merited: "A closer examination of their history presents a very different result. Our sympathy may grow cool if we regard them with a physiologic eye. It is a love of the flesh, more than a love of the spirit, that too often clouds their vision. It is too much food, crowding with unnecessary blood the tender vessels of the retina. It is too little exercise, allowing these accumulated fluids to settle down into fatal congestion. It is positions wholly at variance with the freedom of the circulation, and various other imprudences, which are the results of carelessness or unjustifiable ignorance. 'The day laborer may eat what he will, provided it is wholesome, and his eyes will not suffer. But let the student, who is called upon to devote not only his eyes, but his brain, to severe labor, live upon highly nutritious food, and such as is difficult of digestion, and we shall soon see how his vision will be impaired, through the vehement and persevering determination of blood to the head, which such a course must inevitably occasion.' So speaks Beer, whose extensive opportunities of observation have perhaps never been exceeded. The daily practice of every observing oculist is filled with coincident experience."

Among the prevalent habits of students by which the eyes are injured, the same writer mentions the irritation produced by rubbing them on awaking in the morning, a practice which has in some cases occasioned permanent and incurable disease; reading while the body is in a recumbent position; using the eyes too early after the system has been affected with serious disease; exercising them too much in the examination of minute objects; the popular plan of *using green spectacles*, and *the use of tobacco.*

Light which is sufficient for distinct vision, and which falls over the shoulder in an oblique direction, from above, upon the book or study table, is generally regarded, and with great propriety, as best suited to the eyes. Some oculists prefer to have the light fall over the *left* shoulder.

The acuteness of this sense and the extent of its cultivation are very much greater in some individuals and classes of men than in others. This is a fact that has been remarked by observing persons. Its consequences should not be overlooked, for they are neither few nor unimportant. Those persons who have been long accustomed, either by the necessity of their situation, the example of those about them, or the judicious care of parents and teachers, to observe attentively the relations of parts, the symmetry of forms, or the shades of color, have eyes that are perpetually soliciting their minds to notice some beautiful or grand perceptions. Wherever they turn, they espy some new, and, therefore, curious arrangement of the elements of shape, some striking combination of light and shade, or some delicious peculiarity of coloring. The multiplicity and variety of their perceptions must and do increase the number of their thoughts, or give to their thoughts greater compass and definiteness. Such persons are likely to become poets, or painters, or sculptors, or architects. At any rate, they will appreciate and enjoy the productions of others who have devoted themselves to these delightful arts. And will not such persons be most readily awakened to descry and adore the power, the skill, and the beneficence of the Great Architect who reared the stupendous fabric of the universe, who devised the infinite variety of forms which diversify creation, and whose pencil has so profusely decked every work with myriads of mingling dyes, resulting all from a few parent colors? To an unpracticed eye, the beauties and wonders of creation are all lost. The surface of the earth is a blank, or, at best, but a confused and misty page. Such an eye passes over this scene of things, and makes no communication to the mind that will awaken thought, much less enkindle the spirit of devout adoration, and fill the soul with love to Him "whose universal love smiles every where."

Mr. May speaks no less sensibly than eloquently when he says, "I may be extravagant in my estimation of the importance of the culture of the eye and the ear, but so it is, that while I have been reading the writings of the Hebrew Prophets, and of those other gifted bards who communed so intently with nature and with nature's God, it has seemed to me impossible that any one could enter fully into all the tenderness, beauty, and sublimity of their language, or receive into his heart all its peculiarity of meaning, unless his own eye had been used to trace the skill of that hand which framed and fashioned every thing that is, and to descry the delicacy of that pencil which has painted all the flowers of the field, nor unless his own ear has learned to perceive the melody and harmony of sounds."

We can discipline the sight directly, and to a very great extent; and we can have the satisfaction of perceiving the progressive improvement of the faculty. For this purpose, every school should be furnished with appropriate apparatus. A set of measures is indispensable. I will illustrate by an example. For the benefit of the primary department connected with a seminary of learning that was formerly for several years under my supervision, I constructed a set of rules for linear measurement. Their breadth and thickness were uniform, each being an inch wide and half an inch thick. The set consisted of nine rules, whose lengths were as follows: four were each one foot long; one, a foot and a half long; two, two feet; one, two and a half feet; and one, three feet. Every rule had a small hole bored through each end. I had also a number of small pins turned just the right size to fit these holes. I have since submitted to several hundred teachers, in institutes and elsewhere, my mode of combining and using these measures; and from the deep interest which a large number of intelligent parents and teachers in different localities have manifested in the subject, I venture to refer to it in this connection. I first tried the experiment ten years ago, with a class of about twenty children from four to seven years of age. Several of these could not read. and some of them had not learned the alphabet. The children were first led to observe carefully the length of these several rules, until they could determine at sight the length of each. For several of the first lessons some of them would misjudge. They would, for instance, call a two foot rule one and a half or two and a half feet long. In such cases their judgments were immediately corrected by the application of two one foot rules. They were then led to observe with care, tables, desks, etc., and to estimate their length, and were afterward permitted to measure them, and discover the degree of accuracy in their decisions. After obtaining the opinions of the children in relation to the length or height of an object, I would measure it myself in the presence of the class. When the class became a little experienced, we examined the length, breadth, and height of rooms, of houses, and of churches; and then the distance of objects less or more remote, correcting or confirming their estimates by the application of the rule or measure, which gave a permanent interest to the exercise. By exercising the class in this manner, not to exceed half an hour a day, they would, at the end of the first quarter, judge of each other's height, of the height of persons generally, of the length of various objects, of the size of buildings, and of the dimensions of yards, gardens, and fields, with greater accuracy than the average of adult persons, as was tested by actual measurement in some instances where there was a disagreement in opinion.

By holding these rules in different positions, the children readily became familiar with the meaning and practical application of the terms perpendicular, horizontal, and oblique. They would also tell which term is applicable to the different parts of the stove-pipe; to the different parts of the furniture of the school-room; to the floor, sides of the room, roof, etc.; and to all objects with which they were familiar.

But the reader may inquire, what is the use of the holes and the pins? By pinning two rules together, one resting upon the other, and then turning one of them around, the class will readily gain a correct idea of the use of the term *angle;* also of the terms acute angle, right angle, and obtuse angle. By pinning three of these rules together at their ends, the children not only *see*, but can *handle* the simplest form of geometrical figures. When this figure is *defined*, they are enabled permanently to possess themselves of the meaning of the word *triangle*, by the simultaneous exercise of *three senses.* By combining rules of the same and different lengths, they become familiar with equilateral, isosceles, scalene, right, and obtuse angled triangles. By combining, in this way, such a set of rules as I have described, the child readily becomes familiar with the names and many of the properties of more than half a score of geometrical figures, with less effort on the part of the teacher than would be required to teach the child the names of the same number of letters. These exercises, then, may well precede the learning of the alphabet, or, at least, proceed simultaneously with it By this means the child's interest in the school is increased; his senses are cultivated; he is enabled better to fix his attention; he progresses more rapidly and thoroughly in his juvenile studies, and at the same time lays the foundation for future excellence in penmanship and drawing, and other useful arts.

The child may also be taught to discriminate the varieties of green in leaves and other things; of yellow, red, and blue, in flowers and paints; and to distinguish not only the shades of all the colors, but their respective proportions in mixtures of two or more. Many persons, for want of such early culture, have grown to years without the ability of distinguishing between colors, as others have who have neglected the culture of the ear without the ability of distinguishing between tunes.

Drawing, whether of maps, the shape of objects, or of landscapes, is admirably adapted to discipline the sight. Children should be encouraged carefully to survey and accurately to describe the prominent points of a landscape, both in nature and in picture. Let them point out the elevations and depressions; the mowing, the pasture, the wood, and the tillage land; the trees, the houses, and the streams. Listen to their accounts of their plays, walks, and journeys, and of any events of which they have been witnesses. In these and all other exercises of the sight, children should be encouraged to be strictly accurate; and whenever it is practicable, the judgment they pronounce and the descriptions they give should, if erroneous, be corrected by the truth. Children can not fail to be interested in such exercises; and even where they have been careless and inaccurate observers, they will soon become more watchful and exact.

It is by the benign influences of education only that the senses can be improved. And still their culture has been entirely neglected by perhaps the majority of parents and teachers, who in other respects have manifested a commendable degree of interest in this subject. That by judicious culture the senses may be educated to activity and accuracy, and be made to send larger and purer streams of knowledge to the soul, has been unanswerably proved by an accumulation of unquestionable testimony. Most persons, however, allow the senses to remain uneducated, except as they may be cultivated by fortuitous circumstances. Eyes have they, but they see not; ears have they, but they hear not; neither do they understand. It is not impossible, nor perhaps improbable, that he who has these two senses properly cultivated will derive more unalloyed pleasure in spending a brief hour in gazing upon a beautiful landscape, in examining for the same length of time a simple flower, or in listening to the sweet melody of the linnet as it warbles its song of praise, than those who have neglected the cultivation of the senses experience during their whole lives!

This subject commends itself to all who regard their individual happiness, or who desire to render their usefulness as extensive as possible. Upon parents, teachers, and clergymen, who are more immediately concerned in the correct education of the rising generation, its claims are imperative. Let them be met, in connection with other appropriate means now in use and hereafter to be put in requisition, and our schools can not fail to become increasingly attractive; truancy, hence, will be less frequent, and the benign influences resulting from the correct education of the *whole man* will inspire the benevolent and philanthropic to renewed and increased efforts to secure the right education of *all men*, a condition upon which the maximum of human happiness depends.

CHAPTER VII.

THE NECESSITY OF MORAL AND RELIGIOUS EDUCATION.

The exaltation of talent, as it is called, above virtue and religion, is the curse of the age. Education is now chiefly a stimulus to learning, and thus men acquire power without the principles which alone make it a good. Talent is worshiped; but if divorced from rectitude, it will prove more of a demon than a god.—CHANNING.

Religion ought to be the basis of education, according to often-repeated writings and declamations. The assertion is true. Christianity furnishes the true basis for raising up character; but the foundation must be laid in a very different manner from that which is commonly practiced. * * * We can, indeed, scarcely conceive of the purity, the self-denial, and the power that might be given to human character by systematic development.—LALOR.

WE have now reached a department of our subject of surpassing importance, for however judiciously physical and intellectual cultivation may have been conducted, if we make a mistake here, all is lost. Knowledge is *power*, it is true; but we should bear in mind that it is potent for evil as well as for good; and that, whether its effects be good or ill, depends entirely upon the dispositions and sentiments by which it is impelled and guided. Numerous have been the instances illustrative of the fact that the greatest scourges of our race are men of gigantic *cultivated* intellect. Where knowledge but qualifies its possessor for inflicting misery, ignorance would indeed be bliss.

I find my views on this important subject so admirably expressed in the writings of some of the most eminent men of the age, that I feel it both a privilege and a duty to enforce the sentiments I would inculcate by the introduction of their testimony.

Dr. Humphrey observes,* that "it must strike every one who is capable of taking a just and comprehensive view of the subject, that the common idea of a good education—of such an education as every child in the state ought to receive—is exceedingly narrow and defective. Most men leave out, or regard as of very little importance, some of the essential elements. They seem to forget that the child has a *conscience* and a *heart* to be educated as well as an *intellect.* If they do not lay too much stress on mental culture, which, indeed, is hardly possible, they lay by far too little upon that which is moral and religious. They expect to elevate the child to his proper station in society, to make him wise and happy, an honest man, a virtuous citizen, and a good patriot, by furnishing him with a comfortable school-house, suitable class-books, competent teachers, and, if he is poor, paying his quarter bills, while they greatly underrate, if they do not entirely overlook, that high moral training, without which knowledge is the power of doing evil rather than good. It may possibly nurture up a race of intellectual giants, but, like the sons of Anak, they will be far readier to trample down the Lord's heritage than to protect and cultivate it.

"Education is not a talismanic word, but an *art,* or rather a *science;* and, I may add, the most important of all sciences. It is the right, the proper training of the *whole man,* the thorough and symmetrical cultivation of all his noble faculties. If he were endowed with a mere physical nature, he would need, he would *receive* none but a physical training. On the other hand if he were a purely intellectual being, intellectual culture would comprehend all that could be included in a

* In a lecture before the American Institute of Instruction, on the Moral and Religious Training of Children.

perfect education. And were it possible for a moral being to exist without either body or intellect, there would be nothing but the heart or affections to educate. But man is a complex, and not a simple being. He is neither all body, nor all mind, nor all heart. In popular language, he has three natures, a corporeal, a rational, and a moral. These three, mysteriously united, are essential to constitute a perfect man; and as they all begin to expand in very early childhood, the province of education is to watch, and assist, and shape the development; to train, and strengthen, and discipline neither of them alone, but each according to its intrinsic and relative importance.

"When it is said that 'man is a religious being,' we should carefully inquire in what respects he is so. In a guarded and limited sense the proposition is undoubtedly true. Terrible as was the shock which his moral nature received by 'the fall,' it was not wholly buried in the ruins. Though blackened and crushed to the effacing of that glorious image in which he was created, his moral susceptibilities were not destroyed. The capacity of being restored, and of infinite improvement in knowledge and virtue, was left. In the lowest depths of ignorance and debasement, the human soul feels that it must have some religion, some support, some refuge 'when flesh and heart fail.' There is a natural dread of annihilation, a longing after immortality, a starting back from the last leap in the dark. Men, if they have not true religion, will cling to the greatest absurdities as substitutes. Hence the pagan world is full of idols. Tribes and nations seemingly destitute of all moral sense, nevertheless have 'gods many and lords many.' If there are any cold-blooded, incorrigible atheists in the world, you must look for them not in heathen lands. You must go where the altars of the true God have been thrown down. In this view, *man is a religious being*. He has a moral nature. He is susceptible of deep and controlling religious impressions. He can, at a very early period of life, be made to see and feel the difference between right and wrong—between good and evil. He can, while yet a child, be influenced by hope and by fear—by reason, by persuasion, and by the word of God; and all this shows that religion was intended to be a prominent part of his education. There can be no mistake in this. It is plainly the will of God that the moral as well as the intellectual faculties should be cultivated. Every child, whether in the family or the school, is to be treated by those who have the care of him as a moral and accountable being. His religious susceptibilities invite to the most diligent culture, and virtually enjoin it upon every teacher. The simple study of man's moral nature, before we open the Bible, unavoidably leads to the conclusion that any system of popular education must be extremely defective which does not make special provision for this branch of public instruction.

"Even if there had been no fatal lapse of our race—if our children were not naturally depraved, nor inclined to evil in the slightest degree, still they would need religious as well as physical and intellectual guidance and discipline. It is true, the educator's task would be infinitely easier and pleasanter than it now is, but they would need instruction. They would enter the world just as ignorant of their immortal destiny as of letters. They would have every thing to learn about the being and perfections of God; every thing about his rightful claims as their Creator, Preserver, and moral Governor; and every thing touching their duties and relations to their fellow-men. Moreover, there is every reason to believe that moral and religious training would be necessary *to strengthen the principle of virtue* in the rising generation, and confirm them in habits of obedience and benevolence. As, notwithstanding their bodies are perfect bodies, and their minds perfect minds at their creation, no member or faculty being wanting, still they need all the helps of education; so, if they had a perfectly upright moral nature, they would need the same helps. There is no more reason to think, had sin never entered into the world, every child would have grown up to the 'fullness of the stature of a perfect man' in a religious sense, without an appropriate education, than that he would have become a scholar without it. But the little beings that are all the while springing into life around us to be educated are the sinful offspring of apostate parents. How deeply depraved, how strongly inclined to sin from the cradle, this is not the place to inquire. All agree that they show an early bias in the wrong direction; and that, left to grow up without moral culture and restraint, the great majority would go far astray, and become bad members of society. This is sufficient for our present argument. The evil bias must be counteracted. For the safety of the state, as well as for their own sakes, all its children must be brought under the forming and sanative influence of religious education. No adequate substitute was ever devised, or ever can be. 'Train up a child in the way he should go, and when he is old he will not depart from it.' This is divine; and the opposite is equally true. Train up a child in the way he should *not* go, or—which comes to about the same thing—leave him to take the wrong way of his own accord, and when he is old he will not depart from that. His tread will be heavier and heavier upon the broad and beaten track. 'Men do not gather grapes of thorns, nor figs of thistles.' 'Can the Ethiopian change his skin, or the leopard his spots? Then may those also do good who are accustomed to do evil.'

"Moral and religious training ought, undoubtedly, to be commenced in every family much earlier than children are sent to school, and no parent can throw off upon the school-master the responsibility of bringing them up in the 'nurture and admonition of the Lord.' He must himself teach them the good way, and lead them along in it by his own example. But few parents, however, have the leisure and ability to do all that is demanded in this vitally essential branch of education. All are entitled to the aid of their pastors and religious teachers; and every good shepherd will feel a tender concern for the lambs of his flock, and will feed them with the sincere milk of the word both in the sanctuary and at the fireside. But the work should not stop here. There ought to be a co-operation of good influences in all the seminaries of learning, and especially in the primary schools. This co-operation would be necessary if moral and religious household instruction were universally given, and if all the children of the state regularly attended public worship, and enjoyed the benefits of catechetical and Sabbath-school teaching. But those who would banish religion from our admirable systems of popular education by the plea that it belongs exclusively to the family and the Church, ought to remember what multitudes of children this exclusion would deprive of their birthright as members of a Christian community. There are tens of thousands in our own heaven-blessed New England, and hundreds of thousands in these United States, who receive no religious instruction whatever at home, and whose parents are connected with no religious denomination. What is to be done? We can neither compel ignorant and graceless fathers and mothers to teach their children the fear of the Lord, nor to send them to any place of worship or Sabbath-school. I ask again, what is to be done? These neglected children are in the midst of us. Our cities swarm with them. They are scattered every where over our beautiful hills and valleys. Grow up they will among our own children, without principle and without morals, to breathe mildew upon the young virtues which we have sown in our families, and to prey upon the dearest interests of society, unless somebody cares for their moral and religious education. And where shall they receive this education, if not in the school-house? You will find them there, if in any place of instruction, and multitudes of them you can reach nowhere else.

"A more Utopian dream never visited the brain of a sensible man than that which promises to usher in a new golden age by the diffusion and thoroughness of what is commonly understood by popular education. With all its funds, and improved school-houses, and able teachers, and grammars, and maps, and black-boards, such an education is essentially defective. Without moral principle at bottom to guide and control its energies, education is a sharp sword in the hands of a practiced and reckless fencer. I have no hesitation in saying, that if we could have but one, moral and religious culture is even more important than a knowledge of letters; and that the former can not be excluded from any system of popular education without infinite hazard. Happily, the two are so far from being hostile powers in the common domain, that they are natural allies, moving on harmoniously in the same right line, and mutually strengthening each other. The more virtue you can infuse into the hearts of your pupils, the better they will improve their time and the more rapid will be their proficiency in their common studies. The most successful teachers have found the half hour devoted to moral and religious instruction more profitable to the scholar than any other half hour in the day; and there are no teachers who govern their schools with so much ease as this class. Though punishment is sometimes necessary where moral influence has done its utmost, the conscience is, in all ordinary cases, an infinitely better disciplinarian than the rod. When you can get a school to obey and to study because it is right, and from a conviction of accountability to God, you have gained a victory which is worth more than all the penal statutes in the world; but you can never gain such a victory without laying great stress upon religious principle in your daily instructions.

"There is, I am aware, in the minds of some warm and respectable friends of popular education, an objection against incorporating religious instruction into the system as one of its essential elements. It can not, they think, be done without bringing in along with it the evils of sectarianism. If this objection could not be obviated, it would, I confess, have great weight in my own mind. It supposes that if any religious instruction is given, the distinctive tenets of some particular denomination must be inculcated. But is this at all necessary? Must we either exclude religion altogether from our common schools, or teach some one of the many creeds which are embraced by as many different sects in the ecclesiastical calendar? Surely not. There are certain great moral and religious principles in which all denominations are agreed; such as the ten commandments, our Savior's golden rule—every thing, in short, which lies within the whole range of duty to God and duty to our fellow-men. I should be glad to know what sectarianism there can be in a schoolmaster's teaching my children the first and second tables of the moral law; to 'love the Lord their God with all their heart, and their neighbor as themselves;' in teaching them to keep the Sabbath holy, to honor their parents, not to swear, nor drink, nor lie, nor cheat, nor steal, nor covet. Verily, if this is what any mean by sectarianism, then the more we have of it in our common schools the better. 'It is a lamentation, and shall be for a lamentation,' that there is so little of it. I have not the least hesitation in saying, that no instructor, whether male or female, ought ever to be employed who is not both able and willing to teach morality and religion in the manner which I have just alluded to. Were this faithfully done in all the primary schools of the nation, our civil and religious liberties, and all our blessed institutions, would be incomparably safer than they are now. The parent who says, I do not send my child to school to learn religion, but to be taught reading, and writing, and grammar, knows not 'what manner of spirit he is of.' It is very certain, that such a father will teach his children any thing but religion at home; and is it right that they should be left to grow up as heathens in a Christian land? If he says to the schoolmaster, I do not wish you to make my son an Episcopalian, a Baptist, a Presbyterian, or a Methodist, very well. That is not the schoolmaster's business. He was not hired to teach sectarianism. But if the parent means to say, I do not send my child to school to have you teach him to fear God and keep his commandments, to be temperate, honest, and true, to be a good son and a good man, then the child is to be pitied for having such a father; and with good reason might we tremble for all that we hold most dear, if such remonstrances were to be multiplied and to prevail.

"In this connection I can not refrain from earnestly recommending the daily reading of the Scriptures, and prayer,* in all our schools, as eminently calculated to exert a powerful moral influence upon the scholars. It is melancholy to think what swarms of children are growing up even in Massachusetts—and what multitudes of them in every one of these United States—who will seldom, if ever, hear the voice of prayer if they do not hear it in the schools, and to whom the Bible will remain a sealed book if it be not opened there. I would not insist that *every* primary teacher should be absolutely required to open or close the school daily with prayer. Great and good as I think the influence of such an arrangement would be, it might be impossible, at present, to find a sufficient number of instructors otherwise well qualified who are fitted to lead in this exercise. The number, however, I believe is steadily increasing. It is probably too late for me, but I hope that some of you, gentlemen, may live to see the time when the voice of prayer, and of praise too, will be heard in every school-house of the land. Could I know that this would be the case, it would give me a confidence in the perpetuity of our civil and religious liberties which I should exceedingly rejoice to cherish as I pass off from the stage."

It would seem that these patriotic sentiments, enforced by such persuasive eloquence by this venerable

* I would not be understood to recommend that any person who does not love the Bible, and the doctrines which it inculcates, and who does not seek after that purity of heart which it every where enjoins, should conduct devotional exercises in school; but I would respectfully inquire whether any who do not *delight* in such exercises, and who do not esteem it a *privilege* to lead the devotions of those under their charge, do not lack an *essential* qualification to teach school. Our laws generally require that the school-teacher be, among other things, *well qualified in respect to moral character* TO INSTRUCT *a Primary School.*

man, can hardly fail to find a permanent lodgment in every truly American bosom. The great principles of natural and revealed religion, in which all are agreed, ought to be inculcated in our common school-books,* just as every teacher ought orally to instill these principles into the minds of his pupils. That will be a happy day, especially to the children of ignorant and vicious parents, when they shall learn more of that "fear of the Lord which is the beginning of knowledge" in the school-house than they have ever yet done. Nor is it discovered that the practice of teaching morals according to the Christian code, and using the Bible for that purpose, the great majority adopting it, is any infringement whatever on the religious rights and liberty of any individual.

The anecdote of the Indian touching this subject may arrest the attention of some reader who would otherwise peruse these paragraphs without profit, and fix indelibly in his mind the sentiment I would inculcate, and I therefore insert it. The Indian inquires of the white man what religion he professes. The white man replies, "*Not any.*" "*Not any?*" says the Indian, in astonishment; "then you are *just like my dog;* he's got no religion." We have *men* enough like the Indian's dog, without teaching our *children* to be like him.

* The day of writing the above, a lady mentioned to me the following gratifying illustration of my idea. The subject of it is a little girl only five years of age, who has never attended school, but has learned to read at home, under her mother's tuition. After reading in the first number of one of our excellent series of reading books, the story of "the honest boy" who never told a lie, for perhaps the twentieth time, the little girl said to her mother, "Mother, I like to read this story, for it always makes me feel very happy." Similar instances I have witnessed scores of times, in the family and in the school. Teachers may almost invariably lead their scholars to admire and copy the examples of good children about whom they read, and to dislike and avoid those of bad ones. This power over children should always be exercised for good.

The French, in the days of the Revolution, voted God from his throne. They abolished the Sabbath, and declared that Christianity was a nullity. They set apart one day in ten, not for religion, but for idleness and licentiousness. History informs us that the goddess of Reason, personified by a naked prostitute, was drawn in triumph through the streets of Paris, and that the municipal officers of the city, and the members of the National Convention of France, joined publicly in the impious parade. We need not wonder, then, that even the forms of religion were destroyed, and that licentiousness and profligacy walked forth unveiled. How unlike this is the state of things in these United States! We are professedly a Christian nation. We recognize the existence of a superior and superintending power in all our institutions.

The New World was early sought by a Christian people, that fled from oppression in order to find a home where they might worship God unmolested, and bequeath to posterity the same inestimable privilege and inalienable right. In the days of the Revolution, Washington and his coadjutors were accustomed to invoke the blessing of the God of battles; and without His favor, they looked not for victory. In the Congress of this Great Nation, and in our State Legislatures, we are accustomed to acknowledge our dependence upon God in employing chaplains with whom we unite in daily devotions.

The Constitution of the United States requires that all legislative, executive, and judicial officers in the United States, and in the several states, shall be bound by oath or affirmation to support the Constitution. The Constitution of each of the several states requires a similar oath or affirmation; and some of them further provide that, in addition to the oath of office, all persons appointed to places of profit or trust shall, before entering upon the same, subscribe a declaration of their faith in the Christian religion.

In our Penitentiaries even, we employ chaplains for the social, moral, and religious improvement of criminals confined within them; for our object is, not merely to *deter others* from vice by the punishment of offenders, but, if possible, *to reform the offenders themselves*, and, bringing them back to virtue, make them useful members both of Christian and of civil society. Should we not, then, recognize God in our common schools—the primary training-places of our country's youth—by reading His word, and familiarizing the juvenile mind of the nation with the precepts of the Great Teacher, whose code of morals is acknowledged, even by infidels, to be infinitely superior to any of human origin? And should we not humbly invoke His aid in our efforts to learn and to do his will? and His blessing to attend those efforts? A Paul may plant, and Apollos water; but God giveth the increase.

The instruction in our common schools, I repeat, should be Christian, but not sectarian. There is sufficient common ground which all true believers in Christianity agree in, to effect an incalculable amount of good, if honestly and faithfully taught. Which of the various religious sects in our country would take exceptions to the inculcation of the following sentiments, and kindred ones expressed in every part of the Scriptures?

"Thou shalt love the Lord thy God with all thy heart, and with all thy soul, and with all thy mind. This is the first and great commandment. And the second is like unto it, Thou shalt love thy neighbor as thyself." "As ye would that men should do to you, do ye also to them likewise." "Love your enemies, bless them that curse you, do good to them that hate you, and pray for them which despitefully use you and persecute you."

If there is a single instance in which a sect of professing Christians would take exceptions to the inculcation of these and kindred sentiments in all the schools of our land, I have yet to learn it. On the contrary, I have received and accepted invitations from scores of clergymen, representing not less than eight different denominations, to address their congregations on the subject of "Moral and Religious Education in Common Schools;" and, having expressed the sentiments herein advocated, I have, in every instance, received letters of approval and encouragement; and their hearty prayers and active co-operation have confirmed me in the belief that they are ready and willing to "work together" upon this common platform, in advancing the interests of this glorious cause.

I have spoken of the Christian religion as the most important branch of a common school education. The cultivation of the intellectual faculties alone constitutes no sufficient guaranty that the subject of it will become either a virtuous man, a good neighbor, or a useful citizen. But where physical education has been properly attended to, if we combine with the cultivation of the intellectual faculties of a child a good moral and religious education, we have the highest and most unquestionable authority for believing that, in after life, he will "do justly, love mercy, and walk humbly with God."

"The Bible, in several expressive texts," says Dr. Stowe,* "gives emphatic utterance to the true principle of all right education. For example, 'The fear of the Lord is the beginning of wisdom, and a knowledge

* In a lecture before the American Institute of Instruction, on the Religious Element in Education.

of the Holy is understanding.' Religion must be the basis of all right education; and an education without religion is an education for perdition. Religion, in its most general sense, is the union of the soul to its Creator; a union of sympathy, originating in affection, and guided by intelligence. The word is derived from the Latin terms *re* and *ligo*, and signifies to *tie again*, or *reunite*. The soul, sundered from God by sin, by grace is *reunited* to Him; and this is *religion*."

I might present many and substantial reasons why instruction in the principles of religion should be given in our common schools and in all our institutions of learning, and why those heaven-given principles should be exemplified wherever taught.

The nature of the human mind requires it, as is clearly shown by the writer last quoted. "The mind is created, and God is its creator. Every mind is conscious to itself that it is not self-existent or independent, but that its existence is a derived one, and its condition one of entire, uniform, unceasing dependence. This feeling is as truly a part of the essential constitution of the mind as the desire for food is of the body, and it never can be totally suppressed. If it ever seems to be annihilated, it is only for a very brief interval; and any man who would persist in affirming himself to be self-existent and independent, would be universally regarded as insane. The sympathy which attracts the sexes toward each other is not more universal nor generally stronger than that inward want which makes the whole human race feel the need of God; and, indeed, the feelings are, in many respects, so analogous to each other, that all ancient mysteries of mythology, and the Bible itself, have selected this sympathy as the most expressive, the most unvarying symbol of the relation between the soul and God.

"Till men can be taught to live and be healthy and strong without food; till some way is discovered in which the social state can be perpetuated and made happy, with a total separation of the sexes; till the time arrives when these things can be done, we can not expect to relieve the human mind from having some kind of religious faith. This being the fact, a system of education which excludes attention from this part of the mental constitution is as essentially incomplete as a system of military tactics that has no reference to fighting battles; a system of mechanics which teaches nothing respecting machinery; a system of agriculture that has nothing to do with planting and harvesting; a system of astronomy which never alludes to the stars; a system of politics which gives no intimation on government; or any thing else which professes to be a system, and leaves out the very element most essential to its existence. The history of all ages, of all nations, and of all communities is a continued illustration of this truth. Where did the nation ever exist untouched either by religion or superstition? which never had either a theology or a mythology? When you find a nation that exists without food of some sort, then you may find a nation that subsists without religion of some sort; and never, *never* before. How unphilosophical, how absurd it is, then, to pretend that a system of education may be complete, and yet make no provision for this part of the mental constitution! It is one of the grossest fooleries which the wickedness of man has ever led him to commit. But it is not only unphilosophical and foolish, it is also exceedingly mischievous; for where religion is withheld, the mind inevitably falls to superstition, as certainly as when wholesome food is withheld the sufferer will seek to satisfy his cravings with the first deleterious substance which comes within his reach. The only remedy against superstition is sound religious instruction. The want exists in the soul. It is no factitious, no accidental or temporary want, but an essential part of our nature. It is an urgent, imperious want; it must and will seek the means of satisfaction, and if a healthful supply be withheld, a noxious one will be substituted."

THE BIBLE IN SCHOOLS.—Having taken the liberty of recommending the devotional reading of the Scriptures in all the public schools as eminently calculated to make them what they ought to be—nurseries of morality and religion as well as of good learning—I am now prepared to express the strong conviction, to adopt the language of Dr. Humphrey, "*that the Bible ought to be used in every primary school as a class-book.* I am not ignorant of the objections which even some good men are wont to urge against its introduction. The Bible, it is said, is too sacred a volume to be put on a level with common school-books, and to be thumbed over and thrown about by dirty hands. This objection supposes that if the Bible is made a school-book, it must needs be put into such rude hands; and that it can not be daily read in the classes without diminishing the reverence with which it ought to be regarded as the book of God. But I would have it used chiefly by the older scholars, who, if the teachers are not in the fault, will rarely deface it. A few words now and then, reminding them of its sacred contents, will be sufficient to protect it from rough and vulgar usage.

"The objection that making the Bible a common school-book would detract from its sacredness in the eyes of the children, and thus blunt rather than quicken their moral susceptibilities, is plausible; but it will not, I am confident, bear the test of examination and experience. What were the Scriptures given us for, if not to be read by the old and the young, the high and the low? Is the common use of any good thing which a kind Providence intended for all, calculated to make men underrate it? The best of Heaven's gifts, it is true, are *liable* to be perverted and abused; but ought this to deter us from using them thankfully and properly? We, the descendants of the Puritans, are so far from regarding the Bible as too sacred for common use, that, however we may differ among ourselves in other respects, we cordially unite in efforts to put the sacred treasure in the hands of all the people. It is one of our cardinal principles, as Protestants, that the more they read the Scriptures the better. Are we right or are we wrong here? Let us bring the question to the test of experience. Who are the most moral and well-principled class in the community? those who have been accustomed from childhood to read the Bible, till it has become the most familiar of all books, or those who read it but little? Of two schools, of equal advantages in other respects, which is best regulated and most easily governed? which has most of the fear of God in it, the deepest reverence for his word, that where the Bible is read or from which it is excluded? It is easy for ingenious men to reason plausibly, and tell us that such and such injurious effects *must* follow from making sacred things too familiar to the youthful mind; but who ever heard of such effects following from the use of the Bible as a school-book? It will be time enough to listen to this objection when a solitary example can be adduced to sustain it.

"How do all other men out of the Protestant communion, Papists, Mohammedans, Jews, and Gentiles, reason and act in the education of their children? Do they discard their sacred books from the schools as too holy for common and familiar use? No. They understand the influence of such reading far too well, and are too strongly attached to their respective religions to exclude it. The Romanists, indeed, forbid the use of the Scriptures to the common people; but the Missal and the Breviary, which they hold to be quite as sacred, are their most familiar school-books. A large portion of the children's time is taken up with reading the lessons and reciting the prayers; and what are the effects? Do they become disgusted with the Missal and Breviary by this daily familiarity? We all know the contrary. The very opposite effect is produced. It is astonishing to see with what tenacity children thus educated cling to the superstitions and absurdities of their fathers; and it is because their religion is wrought into the very texture of their minds, in the schools as well as in the churches. Go to Turkey, to Persia, to all the lands scorched and blighted by the fiery train of the Crescent, and what school-books will you find but portions of the Koran? Pass to Hindostan, and there you will find the Vedas and Shasters wherever any thing like popular education is attempted. Enter the great empire of China, and, according to the best information we can obtain, their sacred books are the school-books of that vast and teeming population. Inquire among the Jews, wherever in their various dispersions they have established schools, and what will you find but the Law and the Prophets, the Targums and the Talmud.

"Now when and where did ever Protestant children grow up with a greater reverence for the Bible, a stronger attachment to their religion, than Jewish, Mohammedan, and Pagan children cherish for their school-books, to the study of which they are almost exclusively confined, in every stage of their education? It is opposing theory, then, to great and undeniable facts, to say that using the Christian Scriptures in this manner would detract from their sacredness in the eyes of our children. If this is ever the case, it must be where the teacher himself is a Gallio, and lacks those moral qualifications which are essential to his profession. Another objection which is sometimes brought against the use of the Bible is, that considerable portions of it—though all true, and important as a part of our great religious charter—are not suitable for common and promiscuous reading. My answer is, we do not suppose that any instructor would take all his classes through the whole Bible, from Genesis to Revelation. The genealogical tables, and some other things, he would omit of course, but would always find lessons enough to which the most fastidious could make no objection.

"The way is now prepared to take an affirmative attitude, and offer some reasons in favor of using the Bible as a school-book. In the first place, *it is the cheapest school-book in the world.* It furnishes more reading for *fifty cents* than can be obtained in common school-books for *two dollars.* This difference of cost is, to the poor, an important consideration. With large families on their hands, they often find it extremely difficult to meet the demands of teachers and committees for new books. Were the Scriptures generally introduced, they would take the place of many other reading-books which parents are now obliged to purchase at four-fold expense. This would be a cogent argument on the score of economy, even if the popular school-books of this year were sure of maintaining their ground the next. But so busy is the press in bringing forward new claimants to public favor, that they rapidly supplant each other, and thus the burden is greatly increased.

"In the next place, *the Bible furnishes a far greater variety of the finest reading-lessons than any other book whatever.* This is a point to which my attention has been turned for many years, and the conviction grows upon me continually. There is no book in which children a little advanced beyond the simplest monosyllabic lessons will learn to read faster, or more readily catch the proprieties of inflection, emphasis, and cadence, than the Bible. I would by no means put it into the hands of a child to spell out and blunder over the chapters before he has read any thing else. The word of God ought not to be so used by mere beginners. But it contains lessons adapted to all classes of learners, after the first and simplest stage. Let any teacher who has never made the trial put a young class into the first chapter of John, and he will be surprised to find how easy the reading is, and with what pleasure and manifest improvement they may be carried through the whole Gospel; and as few are too young to read with advantage in the Bible, so none are too old. It is known to every body, that the very best reading lessons in our most popular school-books for the higher classes are taken from the Scriptures. Just open the Sacred Volume with reference to this single point, and turn over its thousand pages. As a history, to interest, instruct, and improve the youthful mind, what other book in the world can compare with it? Where else will you find such exquisitely finished pieces of biography? such poetry? such genuine and lofty eloquence? such rich and varied specimens of tenderness, pathos, beauty, and sublimity? I regret that I have not room for a few quotations. I can only refer, in very general terms, to the history of the creation; of Joseph and the forty years' wandering in the wilderness; to the book of Job; to the Psalms of David; to Isaiah; to the Gospels; and to the visions of John in the Isle of Patmos.

"Now if the primary qualities of a good school-book are to teach the art of reading, and to communicate instruction upon the most interesting and important subjects, I have no hesitation in saying that the Bible stands pre-eminently above every other. If I were again to become a primary instructor, or to teach the art of reading in any higher seminary than the common school-house, I would take the Bible in preference to any twenty 'Orators' or 'English Readers' that I have ever seen. Indeed, I would scarcely want any other. Milton and Shakspeare I would not reject, but I would do very well without them, for they are both surpassed by Isaiah and John. Let enlightened teachers, and members of any of the learned professions, read over aloud, in their best manner, such portions of Scripture as they may easily select, and see if they have ever found any thing better fitted to bring out and discipline the voice, and to express all the emotions in which the soul of true eloquence is bodied forth. Why do the masters of oratory, who charm great audiences with their recitations, take so many of their themes from the Bible? The reason is obvious. They can find none so well suited to their purpose. And why should not the common schools, in which are nurtured so many of the future orators, and rulers, and teachers of the land, have the advantage of the best of all reading-lessons? Moreover, since so much of the sense of Scripture depends upon the manner in which it is read, why should not the thousands of children be taught the art in school, who will never learn it at home? The more I study the Bible, the more does it appear to me to excel all other reading-books. You may go on improving indefinitely, without ever making yourself a perfect scriptural reader, just as you might, with all the help you can command, spend your whole life in the study of any one of its great truths without exhausting it. Let it not be said that we have but few instructors who are capable of entering into the spirit of the Sacred Volume, so as to teach their scholars to read it with propriety. Then let more be educated. It ought to be one of the daily exercises in our Normal Schools, and other seminaries for raising up competent teachers, to qualify them for this branch of instruction."

I remark again, that were the Bible made a school-book throughout the commonwealth and throughout the land, *an amount of scriptural knowledge would be insensibly treasured up, which would be of inestimable value in after life.* Every observing teacher must have been surprised to find how much the dullest scholar will learn by the ear, without seeming to pay any attention to what others are reading or reciting. The boy that sits half the time upon his little bench nodding or playing with his shoe-strings, will, in the course of a winter, commit whole pages and chapters to memory from the books he hears read, when you can hardly beat any thing into him by dint of the most diligent instruction. Indeed, I have sometimes thought that children in our common schools learn more by the ear, without any effort, than by the study of their own class-books; and I am quite sure this is the case with the most of the younger scholars. Let any book be read for a series of years in the same school, and half of the children will know most of it by heart. Wherever there are free schools—and the free school system is now becoming extensively adopted in every part of the United States—the great mass of the children are kept at school from four or five years of age, to nine or ten, through the year; and in the winter season, from nine or ten to fifteen or sixteen. The average of time thus devoted to their education is from eight to ten years. Now let the Bible be read daily as a class-book during all this time, in every school, and how much of it will, without effort, and without interfering in the least with other studies, be committed to memory. And who can estimate the value of such an acquisition? What pure morality; what maxims of supreme wisdom for guidance along the slippery paths of youth, and onward through every stage of life; what bright examples of early piety, and of its glorious rewards, even in the present world; what sublime revelations of the being and perfections of God; what incentives to love and serve him, and to discharge with fidelity all the duties which we owe to our fellow-men! and all these enforced by the highest sanctions of future accountability. Let any man tell, if he can, how much all this store of divine knowledge, thus insensibly acquired, would be worth to the millions of children who are growing up in these United States of America. They might not be at all sensible of its value at the time, but how happily and safely would it contribute to shape their future opinions and characters, both as men and as citizens.

Another cogent reason for using the Bible as a common school-book is, that *it is the firmest basis, and, indeed, the only sure basis of our free institutions, and, as such, ought to be familiar to all the children in the state from their earliest years.* While it recognizes the existence of civil governments, and enjoins obedience to magistrates as ministers of God for the good of the people, it regards all men as free and equal, the children of one common Father, and entitled to the same civil and religious privileges. I do not believe that any people could ever be enslaved who should be thoroughly and universally educated in the principles of the Bible.

It was no less truly than eloquently said by Daniel Webster, in his Bunker Hill address, that "the American colonists brought with them from the Old World a full portion of all the riches of the past in science and art, and in morals, religion, and literature. The *Bible* came with them. And it is not to be doubted that to the *free* and *universal* use of the Bible it is to be ascribed that in that age men were much indebted for right views of civil liberty. The Bible is a book of faith and a book of doctrine; but it is also a book which teaches man his individual responsibility, his own dignity, and equality with his fellow-men."

These sentiments of the great American statesman are worthy to be engraved in golden capitals upon the monument under whose shade they were uttered! Yes, it was the free and universal use of the Bible which made our Puritan fathers what they were; and it is because, in these degenerate times, multitudes of children will be taught to read it nowhere else, that I am so anxious to have it read as a school-book. One other, and the only additional reason which I shall suggest, is that, as the Bible is *infinitely the best*, so it is the only decidedly *religious book* which can be introduced into our popular systems of early education. So jealous are the different sects and denominations of each other, that it would be hardly possible to write or compile a religious school-book with which all would be satisfied. But here is a book prepared to our hands, which we all receive as the inspired record of our faith, and as containing the purest morality that has ever been taught in this lower world. Episcopalians can not object to it, because they believe it teaches the doctrines and polity of their own church; and this is just what they want. Neither Congregationalists, Presbyterians, Baptists, Methodists, Universalists, nor any other denomination, can object to it for the same reason. Every denomination believes, so far as it differs from the rest, that the Bible is on its side, and, of course, that the more it is read by all, the better.

For me to object to having the Bible read as a common school-book on account of any doctrine which those who differ from me suppose it to teach, would be virtually to confess that I had not full confidence in my own creed, and was afraid it would not bear a scriptural test. It seems to me an infinite advantage, for which we are bound devoutly to thank the Author of all good, that he has given us a religious book of incomparable excellence, which we may fearlessly put into the hands of all the children in the state, with the assurance that it is able to make them "wise unto salvation," and will certainly make them better children, better friends, and better members of society, so far as it influences them at all. But some persons who highly approve of daily scriptural reading in common schools are in favor of using *selections* rather than the whole Bible. I should certainly prefer this, provided the selections are judiciously made, to excluding the Scriptures altogether; but I think there are weighty and obvious reasons why the *whole* Bible should be taken rather than a part. The whole is cheaper than half would be in a separate volume; and when the whole is introduced, "without note or comment," there can be no possible ground for sectarian jealousy.

Doctors of divinity not only, but the most eminent statesmen in the country, hold the views here presented. The bold and noble stand taken by the Legislature of New York more than ten years ago (1838), has revived the hopes and infused fresh courage into the minds of those who believe that the safety and welfare of our country are essentially dependent on the prevalence of a "*religious* morality and a *moral* religion." The representatives of this great state, whose system of education is becoming increasingly an object of imitation in all the rest, at one and the same session doubled the amount of the public money for the purpose of improving the education given in the common schools—which, to the praise of that state, be it said, are *now free*—and in reply to the petition of sundry persons, praying that all religious exercises and the use of the Bible might be prohibited in the public schools, decided by a vote of *one hundred and twenty-one* to ONE! that the request of the petitioners be not granted. For the purpose of corroborating the doctrines of this volume, I will introduce a paragraph from the report of the Hon. Daniel D. Barnard on the occasion referred to, which was sustained by the noble, unequivocal, and almost unanimous testimony of the representatives of the most powerful member of the American states.

"Moral instruction is quite as important to the object had in view in popular education as intellectual instruction; it is indispensable to that object. But, to make instruction effective, it should be given according to the best code of morals known to the country and the age; and that code, it is universally conceded, is contained in the Bible. Hence the Bible, as containing that code, so far from being arbitrarily excluded from our schools, ought to be in common use in them. Keeping all the while in view the object of popular education, the fitting of the people by *moral* as well as by *intellectual* discipline for self-government, no one can doubt that any system of instruction which overlooks the training and informing of the moral faculties must be wretchedly and fatally defective. Crime and intellectual cultivation merely, so far from being dissociated in history and statistics, are unhappily old acquaintances and tried friends. To neglect the moral powers in education is to educate not quite half the man. To cultivate the intellect only is to unhinge the mind and destroy the essential balance of the mental powers ; it is to light up a recess only the better to see how dark it is. And if this is all that is done in popular education, then nothing, literally nothing, is done toward establishing popular virtue and forming a moral people."

This is but a specimen of an invaluable document, which does honor to the heart and head of him who penned it, and to the Legislature of the commonwealth by which it was adopted by almost unparalleled unanimity.

The Hon. Samuel Young, the eminently distinguished superintendent of common schools in the same state, in a report made in 1843, inculcates sentiments which so well accord with my own views of the importance of weaving scriptural reading into the very warp and woof of popular education, that I gladly add his testimony. "I regard the New Testament as in all respects a suitable book to be daily read in our common schools, and I earnestly recommend its general introduction for this purpose. As a mere reading-book, intended to convey a practical knowledge of the English language, it is one of the best text-books in use ; but this, although of great use to the pupils, is of minor importance when the moral influences of the book are duly considered. Education consists of something more than mere instruction. It is that training and discipline of all the faculties of the mind which shall symmetrically and harmoniously develop the future man for usefulness and for happiness in sustaining the various relations of life. It must be based upon knowledge and virtue ; and its gradual advancement must be strictly subordinated to those cardinal and elementary principles of morality, which are nowhere so distinctly and beautifully inculcated as in that book from whence we all derive our common faith. The nursery and family fireside may accomplish much; the institutions of religion may exert a pervading influence; but what is commenced in the hallowed sanctuary of the domestic circle, and periodically inculcated at the altar, must be daily and hourly recognized in the common schools, that it may exert an ever-present influence, enter into and form a part of every act of life, and become thoroughly incorporated with the rapidly expanding character. The same incomparable standard of moral virtue and excellence, which is expounded from the pulpit and the altar, and which is daily held up to the admiration and imitation of the family circle, should also be reverently kept before the mind and the heart in the daily exercises of the school."

I will add the testimony of another whom we all delight to honor. Never were sentiments uttered more worthy to be remembered and repeated through all generations, than those which fell from the Father of his Country in his Farewell Address to the American people. "Of all the dispositions and habits which lead to political prosperity, religion and morality are indispensable supports. In vain would that man claim the tribute of patriotism who should labor to subvert these great pillars of human happiness, these firmest props of the duties of men and citizens. The mere politician, equally with the pious man, ought to respect and cherish them. A volume could not trace all their connections with private and public felicity. Let it simply be asked, Where is the security for property, for reputation, for life, if a sense of religious obligation desert the oaths which are the instruments of investigation in courts of justice? And let us with caution indulge the supposition that *morality* can be maintained *without religion.* Whatever may be conceded to the influence of refined education on minds of peculiar structure, reason and experience both forbid us to expect that national morality can prevail in exclusion of religious principles." How noble, how elevated, how just these parting words.

Washington was an enlightened Christian patriot, as well as a great general and a wise statesman. The oracles which he consulted in all his perils, and in the perils of his country, were the oracles of God.* No one of the fathers of the Revolution knew better than he did that religion rests upon the Bible as its main pillar, and that as a knowledge and belief of the Bible are essential to true religion, so they are to private and public morality. I can not doubt, says the venerable President of Amherst College, that could the greatest among the great men of his day add a codicil to his invaluable legacy, it would be, "Teach your children early to read and love the Bible. Teach them to read it in your families; teach them in your schools; teach them every where, that the first moral lesson indelibly enstamped upon their hearts may be to 'fear God and keep his commandments.' 'The fear of the Lord, that is wisdom; and to depart from evil is understanding.'"

How few are aware of what the Bible has done for mankind, and still less of what it is destined to accomplish. "Quench its light, and you blot out the brightest luminary from these lower heavens. You bring back 'chaos and old night' to reign over the earth, and leave man, with all his immortal energies and aspirations, to 'wander in the blackness of darkness forever.'

* John Quincy Adams, during his long and eventful life, was accustomed to read daily portions of the Scriptures in several languages.

It was by constantly reading it that our Puritan fathers imbibed that unconquerable love of civil and religious liberty which sustained them through all the 'perils of the sea and perils of the wilderness.' It was from the Bible they drew those free and admired principles of civil government that were so much in advance of the age in which they lived. It was this book by which they 'resolved to go till they could find some better rule.'"

The Bible has built all our churches, and colleges, and school-houses; it has built our hospitals and retreats for the insane, the deaf, and the blind; it has built the House of Refuge, the Sailors' Home, and the Home for the Friendless. To it we are indebted for our homes, for our property, and for all the safeguards of our domestic relations and happiness. It is under its broad shield that we lie down in safety, without bolts or bars to protect us. It has given us our free constitutions of civil government, and with them all the statutes and ordinances of a great and independent people, whose territory extends from the Atlantic to the Pacific. It is the industry, sobriety, and enterprise, which nothing but the Bible could ever inspire and sustain, that have dug our canals, and built our thousand factories, and "clothed the hills with flocks, and covered over the valleys with corn;" that have laid down our railways and established telegraph lines, bringing the East into the neighborhood of the West, and enabling the North to hold converse with the South. The Bible has directly and indirectly done all this for us, and infinitely more. Let not, then, the book which has given to us sweet homes, and happy families, and systems of public instruction, and has thus constituted us a great and prosperous people—the book which diminishes our sorrows and multiplies our joys, and gives to those who obey its precepts a "hope big with immortality"—let not this book be excluded from the common schools of our country. In the name of patriotism, of philanthropy, and of our common Christianity, let me, in behalf of the millions of youth in our country who will otherwise remain ignorant of it, ask that, whatever else be excluded from our schools, there be retained in them this Book of books, the Bible.

CHAPTER VIII.

THE IMPORTANCE OF POPULAR EDUCATION.

Education, as the means of improving the moral and intellectual faculties, is, under all circumstances, a subject of the most imposing consideration. To rescue man from that state of degradation to which he is doomed unless redeemed by education; to unfold his physical, intellectual, and moral powers, and to fit him for those high destinies which his Creator has prepared for him, can not fail to excite the most ardent sensibility of the philosopher and philanthropist. A comparison of the savage that roams through the forest with the enlightened inhabitant of a civilized country would be a brief but impressive representation of the momentous importance of education.—*Report of School Commissioners, New York*, 1812.

He who has carefully perused the preceding chapters of this work is already aware that we regard the subject of popular education as one of paramount importance. The object of devoting a chapter to the special consideration of this subject at this time is, if possible, to remove from the mind any remaining doubts in relation to it. The reader will bear in mind that we regard education as having reference to the *whole man*—the body, the mind, and the heart; and that its object, and, when rightly directed, its effect, is to make him a complete creature after his kind. To his frame it should give vigor, activity, and beauty; to his intellect, power and thoughtfulness; and to his heart, virtue and felicity.

We shall be the better prepared to appreciate the importance and necessity of a judicious system of training and instruction if we consider that, in its absence, every individual will be educated by circumstances. Let it be borne in mind, then, that all the children in every community will be educated somewhere and somehow; and that it devolves upon citizens and parents to determine whether the children of the present generation shall receive their training in the *school-house* or in the *streets;* and if in the former, whether in good or poor schools.

In the discharge of my official duties in this state, I had occasion to visit two counties in 1846 in which there were no organized common schools.* They were not, however, without places of instruction, for in the shire town of each of those counties there were a billiard-room, bar-rooms, and bowling-alleys. I was forcibly impressed with the remark of an Indian chief residing in one of those counties. As he was passing along the streets one day, he discovered a second bowling-alley in process of erection. He paused, and, surveying it attentively, remarked to those at work upon it as follows: "You have here another long building going up rapidly; and," he added, "*is this the place where our children are to be educated?*" Such keen and well-merited rebuke rarely falls from human lips. Those two bowling-alleys, with their bars—indispensable appendages—were thronged from six o'clock in the morning until past midnight, six days in the week. They were, moreover, the very places where many of the youth of that village were receiving their education. And who were their teachers? Idlers, tipplers, gam-

* Common schools have since been organized in both of those counties.

blers, profane persons, Sabbath-breakers. Mark well this truth: *as is the teacher, so will be the school.* Those pupils will graduate, it may be, at our poor-houses, at our county jails, or at the state penitentiary. These debasing and corrupting appendages of civilization spent not all their influence upon the white man; and this is what gave pungency to the withering satire of the chief. They were at once working the ruin of the red man and of his pale neighbor.

The rudest nations or individuals can not be said to be wholly without education. Even the wildest savage is taught by his superiors not only the best mode of procuring food and shelter known to his race, but also the most adroit manner of defending himself and destroying his enemy. But we use the term in a higher, broader, and more capacious sense, as having reference to the whole man, and the whole duration of his being. A volume might be filled in stating and illustrating the advantages of education. We have only space to state and elucidate a few propositions. We remark, then, first, that

EDUCATION DISSIPATES THE EVILS OF IGNORANCE.

Ignorance is one principal cause of the want of virtue, and of the immoralities which abound in the world. Were we to take a survey of the moral state of the world as delineated in the history of nations, or as depicted by modern voyagers and travelers, we should find abundant illustration of the truth of this remark. We should find, in almost every instance, that ignorance of the character of the true God, and false conceptions of the nature of the worship and service he requires, have led, not only to the most obscene practices and immoral abominations, but to the perpetration of the most horrid cruelties.—Dr. Dick.

The evils of ignorance are not few in number nor small in magnitude. The whole history of the world justifies the statement that ignorant and uncultivated mind is prone to sensuality and cruelty. In what countries, let me ask, are the people most given to the lowest forms of animal gratification, and most regardless of the lives and happiness of others? Is it not in pagan lands, over which moral and intellectual darkness broods, and where men are vile without shame, and cruel without remorse? And if from pagan we pass to Christian countries, we shall find that those in which education is least prevalent are the very ones in which there is the most immorality, and the greatest indifference to the sufferings of animated and sentient beings. Spain—in which, until recently, there was but one newspaper printed, and in which only about one in thirty-five of the people are instructed in schools—has a population about equal to that of England and Wales. Popular education in the latter countries, although much behind several of the other European states, is still greatly in advance of what it is in Spain, and there is an equally marked difference in the state of morals in the people of these countries. In England and Wales the whole number of convictions for murder in the year eighteen hundred and twenty-six was *thirteen*, and the number convicted for wounding, etc., with intent to kill, was *fourteen;* while in Spain, the number convicted during the same year was, for murder, *twelve hundred and thirty-three!* and for maiming with intent to kill, *seventeen hundred and seventy-three!* or a more than one hundred fold greater number than in the former countries. Facts like these speak volumes in favor of the elevating influences of popular education, while they show most conclusively the low and degraded condition to which people will sink in countries in which education is neglected.

Spain affords an apt illustration of the truth of the statement just made, that ignorant and uncultivated people are prone to sensuality and cruelty. Scenes of cruelty and blood constitute the favorite amusement of the Spaniards, their greatest delight being in bull-fights. An eye-witness describes the manner in which they conduct themselves during these appalling scenes in the following language. "The intense interest which they feel in this game is visible throughout, and often loudly expressed. An astounding shout always accompanies a critical moment. Whether it be the *bull* or *man* who is in danger, their joy is excessive; but their greatest sympathy is given to the feats of the BULL! If the picador receives the bull gallantly and forces him to retreat, or if the matadore courageously faces and wounds the bull, they applaud these acts of science and valor; but if the bull overthrow the horse and his rider, or if the matadore miss his aim and the bull seems ready to gore him, their delight knows no bounds. And it is certainly a fine spectacle to see thousands of spectators rise simultaneously, as they always do when the interest is intense. The greatest and most crowded theater in Europe presents nothing half so imposing as this. But how barbarous, how brutal is the whole exhibition! Could an English audience witness the scenes that are repeated every week in Madrid, a universal burst of '*shame!*' would follow the spectacle of a horse gored and bleeding, and actually treading upon his own entrails while he gallops round the arena. Even the appearance of the goaded bull could not be borne, panting, covered with wounds and blood, lacerated by darts, and yet brave and resolute to the end.

"The spectacle continued two hours and a half, and during that time there were seven bulls killed and six horses. When the last bull was dispatched, the people immediately rushed into the arena, and the carcass was dragged out amid the most deafening shouts."—*Spain in* 1830, vol. i., p. 191.

The same writer, after describing another fight, in

which one bull had killed three horses and one man, and remained master of the arena, remarks, that "this was a time to observe the character of the people. When the unfortunate picador was killed, in place of a general exclamation of horror and loud expressions of pity, the universal cry was 'Que es bravo ese toro!' ('Ah, the admirable bull!') The whole scene produced the most unbounded delight; the greater the horror, the greater was the shouting, and the more vehement the expressions of satisfaction. I did not perceive a single female avert her head or betray the slightest symptom of wounded feeling."—Vol. i., p. 195.

A correct system of public instruction develops a character widely different from that here brought to light. Instead of a love for vicious excitement, it cultivates a taste for simple and innocent pleasures, and gives to its subjects a command over their passions, and a disposition habitually to control them. It acquaints them with their duty, and enables them to find their highest pleasure in its discharge. They order their pursuits and choose their employments with reference to their own advantage, it is true; but still, a higher, and the controlling motive with them is, the promotion of the best good of the community in which they live. In short, their supreme desire is to co-operate with the beneficent Creator in advancing the permanent interests of the whole human family; in themselves obeying, and leading others to obey, all the laws which God has ordained for the government and well-being of his creatures.

Education, we said, dissipates the evils of ignorance. But in this country we hardly know what popular ignorance is. The most illiterate among us have derived many and inestimable advantages from our systems of public instruction. Occasionally persons are found among us who can neither read nor write. But even such persons insensibly imbibe ideas and moral influences from the more cultivated society about them which, in countries less favored, are denied to multitudes. Individuals who have had no early advantages for learning, who have never even entered a school-house, but have grown up amid a generally intelligent population, trained by the institutions established by our fathers, have in many instances acquired a mental character and influence which, but for these fortuitous circumstances, they could not have attained. The very excellence of our systems of education in many states of the Union, and the vital and pervading influence of the schools upon the public mind, reaching as they do, and improving even those that remain ignorant of letters, do not allow us to see the full extent of our obligation to them. This remark applies to all civilized countries where any systems of general education are adopted, but perhaps not to so great an extent in any other country as in our own.

The evils which flow from ignorance are deplorable enough in the case of individuals, although, as we have seen, the disastrous consequences are limited in the case of those who live surrounded by an intelligent community. But the general ignorance of large numbers and entire classes of men, unreached by the elevating influence of the educated, acting under the unchastened stimulus of the passions, and excited by the various causes of discontent which are constantly occurring in the progress of human affairs, is not unfrequently productive of scenes, the contemplation of which makes humanity shudder. The following extract from a foreign journal affords a pertinent illustration of the evils which flow from popular ignorance. It relates to the outrages committed by the peasantry in a part of Hungary in consequence of the ravages of the cholera in that region.

"The suspicion that the cholera was caused by poisoning the wells was universal among the peasantry of the counties of Zips and Zemplin, and every one was fully convinced of its truth. The first commotion arose in Klucknow, where, it is said, some peasants died in consequence of taking the preservatives; whether by an immoderate use of medicine, or whether they thought they were to take chloride of lime internally, is not known. This story, with a sudden and violent breaking out of the cholera at Klucknow, led the peasants to a notion of the poisoning of the wells, which spread like lightning. In the sequel, in the attack of the estate of Count Czaki, a servant of the chief bailiff was on the point of being murdered, when, to save his life, he offered to disclose something important. He said that he received from his master two pounds of poisonous powder, with orders to throw it into the wells, and, with an ax over his head, took oath publicly, in the church, to the truth of his statement. These statements, and the fact that the peasants, when they forcibly entered the houses of the land-owners, every where found chloride of lime, which they took for the poisonous powder, confirmed their suspicions, and drove the people to madness. In this state of excitement, they committed the most appalling excesses. Thus, for instance, when a detachment of thirty soldiers, headed by an ensign, attempted to restore order in Klucknow, the peasants, who were ten times their number, fell upon them; the soldiers were released, but the ensign was bound, tortured with scissors and knives, then beheaded, and his head fixed on a pike as a trophy. A civil officer in company with the military was drowned, his carriage broken, and, chloride of lime being found in the carriage, one of the inmates was compelled to eat it till he vomited blood, which again confirmed the notion of poison. On the attack of the house of the lord at Klucknow, the countess saved her life by piteous entreaties; but the chief bailiff, in whose house chloride of lime was unhappily found, was killed, together with his son, a little daughter, a clerk, a maid, and two students who boarded with him. So the bands went from village to village; wherever a nobleman or a physician was found death was his lot; and in a short time it was known that the high constable of the county of Zemplin, and several counts, nobles, and parish priests, had been murdered. A clergyman was hanged because he refused to take an oath that he had thrown poison into a well; the eyes of a countess were put out, and innocent children cut to pieces. Count Czaki, having first ascertained that his family was safe, fled from his estate at the risk of his life; but he was stopped at Kirtchtrauf, pelted with stones, and wounded all over, torn from his horse, and only saved by a worthy merchant who fell on him, crying, 'Now I have got the rascal.' He drew the count into a neighboring convent, where his wounds were dressed, and a refuge afforded him. His secretary was struck from his horse with an ax, but saved in a similar manner, and in the evening conveyed with his master to Leutschau."*

A little knowledge on the part of the peasantry would have prevented these horrible scenes. Had they learned even the elements of physiology and chemistry, they would have known that cleanliness is essential to health at all times, and that during the prevalence of a malignant epidemic it is doubly needful. They would have known, also, that chloride of lime is not a medicine to be taken internally, but that it is very useful for dis-

* Quoted from an address delivered in Boston by Edward Everett

infecting offensive apartments, and that its tendency, when properly used, would be to counteract the cause of the disease which they so much dreaded.

Among all nations, and in all ages of the world, ig norance has not only debarred mankind from many ex quisite and sublime enjoyments, but has created innumerable unfounded alarms, which greatly increase the sum of human misery. In the early ages of the world, a total eclipse of the sun or of the moon was regarded with the utmost consternation, as if some unusual catastrophe had been about to befall the universe. Believing that the moon in an eclipse was sickening or dying, through the influence of enchanters, the trembling spectators had recourse to the ringing of bells, the sounding of trumpets, the beating of brazen vessels, and to loud and horrid exclamations, in order to break the enchantment, and to drown the muttering of witches, that the moon might not hear them. Nor are such foolish opinions and customs yet banished from the world.

Comets, too, with their blazing tails, were long regarded, and still are by many, as harbingers of divine vengeance, presaging famines and inundations, or the downfall of princes and the destruction of empires. The northern lights have been frequently gazed at with similar apprehensions, whole provinces having been thrown into consternation by the fantastic coruscations of these lambent meteors. Some pretend to see in these harmless lights armies mixing in fierce encounter and fields streaming with blood, while others behold states overthrown, earthquakes, inundations, pestilences, and the most dreadful calamities. Because some one or other of these calamities formerly happened soon after the appearance of a comet or the blaze of an aurora, therefore they are considered either as the causes or the prognostics of such events.

Popular ignorance has given rise to the practice of *judicial astrology;* an art which, with all its foolish notions so fatal to the peace of mankind, has been practiced in every period of time. Under a belief that the characters and the fates of men are dependent on the various aspects of the stars and conjunctions of the planets, the most unfounded apprehensions, as well as the most delusive hopes, have been excited by the professors of this fallacious science. Such impositions on the credulity of mankind are founded on the grossest absurdity and the most palpable ignorance of the nature of things; still, in the midst of the light of science which the present century has shed upon the world, the astrologer meets with a rich support* even in the metropolis of Great Britain; and soothsayers, if not astrologers, get great gain by their craft in various portions of the United States. The extensive annual sale of hundreds of thousands of copies of almanacs that abound in astrological predictions in the United States and in Great Britain, and the extent to which they are consulted, affords a striking proof of the belief which is still attached to the doctrines of this fallacious science, and of the ignorance and credulity from which such a belief proceeds.

Shooting stars, fiery meteors, lunar rainbows, and other atmospherical phenomena, have likewise been considered by some as ominous of impending calamities, but they are regarded in a very different light by scientific observers. The most sublime phenomenon of shooting stars of which the world has furnished any record was witnessed throughout the United States on the morning of the 13th of November, 1833. This astonishing exhibition covered no inconsiderable portion of the earth's surface. The first appearance was every

* See Appendix to Dick's Improvement of Society, p. 338.

where that of fire-works of the most imposing grandeur, covering the entire vault of heaven with myriads of fire-balls resembling sky-rockets; but the most brilliant sky-rockets and fire-works of art bear less relation to the splendors of this celestial exhibition than the twinkling of the most tiny star to the broad glare of the noonday sun. Their coruscations were bright, gleaming, and incessant, and they fell thick as the flakes in the early snows of December. The whole heavens seemed in motion, and suggested to some the awful grandeur of the image employed in the Apocalypse upon the opening of the sixth seal, when "the stars of heaven fell unto the earth, even as a fig-tree casteth her untimely figs when she is shaken of a mighty wind."

While these scenes of grandeur were viewed with unspeakable delight by enlightened scientific observers, the ignorant and superstitious were overpowered with horror and dismay. The description which a gentleman of South Carolina gave of the effect produced by this phenomenon upon his ignorant blacks will apply well to many hardly better informed white persons. "I was suddenly awakened," said he, "by the most distressing cries that ever fell upon my ears. Shrieks of horror and cries of mercy I could hear from most of the negroes of three plantations, amounting in all to about six or eight hundred. While earnestly listening for the cause, I heard a faint voice near the door calling my name: I arose, and, taking my sword, stood at the door. At this moment I heard the same voice still beseeching me to rise and saying, 'O! my God, the world is on fire!' I then opened the door, and it is difficult to say which excited me most, the awfulness of the scene or the distressed cries of the negroes. Upward of one hundred lay prostrate on the ground, some speechless, and some with the bitterest cries, but most with their hands raised, imploring God to save the world and them. The scene was truly awful, for never did rain fall much thicker than the meteors fell toward the earth; east, west, north, and south, it was the same."

Those harmless meteors, the *ignes fatui*, which hover above moist and fenny places in the night-time, emitting a glimmering light, have been regarded by the ignorant as malicious spirits endeavoring to deceive the bewildered traveler and lead him to destruction. The plaintive note of the mourning dove, the ticking noise of the little insect called the death-watch, the howling of a dog in the night-time, the meeting of a bitch with whelps, or a snake lying in the road, the breaking of a looking-glass, and even the falling of salt from the table, and the curling of a fiber of wick in a burning candle, together with many other equally harmless incidents, have been regarded with apprehensions of terror, being considered as unfailing signs of impending disasters or of approaching death.

Dr. Dick remarks, that in the Highlands of Scotland—and it should be borne in mind that the Scotch are, as a nation, better instructed, and more moral and religious in their habits, than any other people in Europe—the motions and appearances of the clouds were, not long ago, considered ominous of disastrous events. On the evening before new year's day, if a black cloud appeared in any part of the horizon, it was thought to prognosticate a plague, a famine, or the death of some great man in that part of the country over which it seemed to hang; and in order to ascertain the place threatened by the omen, the motions of the clouds were often watched through the whole night. In the same country, the inhabitants regard certain days as *unlucky*, or ominous of bad fortune. The day of the week on which the third of May falls is deemed unlucky throughout the year.

With a very slight change, a part of this description would apply well to our own country, even up to the present time. How many thousands of days are lost annually in the United States in consequence of superstitious fears in relation to setting out upon a journey, entering upon a new pursuit of any kind, or even beginning to plant or plow on Friday, the unlucky day of the Americans. How many persons have had misfortunes attend them all their lives because they were born, or christened, or married on Friday! How many houses have been burned because they were begun, raised, or moved into on Friday! How many steamboats and vessels have been burned or wrecked because they were launched or sailed on Friday! And yet, strange as it may seem, this is the very day on which Columbus set sail on a voyage that resulted in the discovery of the New World.

Many people, and in some instances whole communities, always commence plowing, sowing, and reaping on Tuesday, though by this rule the most favorable weather for these purposes is frequently lost. Others, again, will not, on any account, perform certain kinds of labor on Friday. The age of the moon is also much attended to in many parts of the world. Among the vulgar Highlanders, an opinion prevails, that if a house takes fire while the moon is in the decrease, the family will from that time decline in its circumstances and sink into poverty. In this country, equally unfounded and ridiculous opinions are entertained. Passing by the more commonly received opinions that if swine are killed in the old of the moon, the pork will shrink in the pot; that seed sown at this time will be less likely to do well. etc., etc., I will mention one or two instances of opinions which, although equally well founded, are less commonly received, and which may therefore more forcibly impress the popular mind. A few years ago, I spent some months in a neighboring state, in a community where the belief was commonly entertained that shingles should not be laid nor stakes driven in the old of the moon, because the former would be more likely to warp, and the latter to be thrown by the frost. The same and kindred opinions are extensively held in various portions of the United States.

These are a few, and but a very few, of the superstitious notions and vain fears by which the great majority of the human race, in every age and country, have been enslaved, as he who will take the pains to peruse Dr. Dick's admirable treatise on the improvement of society by the diffusion of knowledge can not fail to be convinced. That such absurd notions should ever have prevailed is a most grating and humiliating thought, when we consider the noble faculties with which man is endowed. That they still prevail to a great extent, even in our own country, is a striking proof that as yet we are, as a people, but just emerging from the gloom of intellectual darkness. The prevalence of such opinions is to be regretted, not only on account of the groundless alarms they create, but chiefly on account of the false ideas they inspire with regard to the nature of the Supreme Ruler of the universe, and of his arrangements in the government of the world. He whose mind is enlightened with true science perceives throughout all nature the most striking evidences of benevolent design, and rejoices in the benignity of the Great Parent of the universe, discovering nothing in the arrangements of the Creator, in any department of his works, which has a direct tendency to produce pain to any intelligent or sensitive being. The superstitious man, on the contrary, contemplates the sky, the air, the waters, and the earth as filled with malicious beings, ever ready to haunt him with terror or to plot his destruction. The former contemplates the Deity directing the movements of the material world by fixed and invariable laws, which none but himself can counteract or suspend. The latter views these movements as continually liable to be controlled by capricious and malignant beings to gratify the most trivial passions. How very different, of course, must be their conceptions and feelings respecting the attributes and government of the Supreme Being! While the one views him as the infinitely wise and benevolent Father, whose paternal care and goodness inspire confidence and affection, the other must regard him, in a certain degree, as a capricious being, and offer up his adorations under the influence of fear.

These and like notions have also an evident tendency to habituate the mind to false principles and processes of reasoning which unfit it for legitimate conclusions in its researches after truth. They manifestly chain down the understanding, and unfit it for the appreciation of those noble and enlarged views which revelation and modern science exhibit of the order, extent, and economy of the universe. It is lamentable to reflect that so many thousands of beings endowed with the faculty of reason, who can not by any means be persuaded of the motion of the earth, and the distances and magnitudes of the heavenly bodies, should swallow, without the least hesitation, opinions ten thousand times more improbable. Notwithstanding the mathematical certainty of the truth of the Copernican system of astronomy, I have never yet become extensively acquainted with any community in which I have not found many persons professing a respectable degree of intelligence.

and even official members of orthodox churches, who entirely discredit its sublime teachings; and yet some of these very persons find little difficulty in believing that an old woman can transform herself into a hare, and wing her way through the air on a broomstick. What contracted notions such persons must have of the almightiness of the Deity, and of the infinite depth of meaning of the following and like passages of Scripture: The heavens declare the glory of God, and the firmament showeth his handy work. Day unto day uttereth speech, and night unto night showeth knowledge.—*Ps.* xix., 1–2.

It has been already remarked, that the whole history of the world justifies the statement that ignorant and uncultivated mind is prone to sensuality and cruelty. Spain and Hungary were referred to in illustration. We are now prepared to remark, what is worse still, that where such superstitious notions as we have been considering are held, even by persons who are somewhat educated, they almost invariably lead to the perpetration of deeds of cruelty and injustice. Many of the barbarities committed in pagan countries, both in their religious worship and their civil polity, and most of the cruelties inflicted on the victims of the Romish Inquisition, have flowed from this source.* Nor are the annals of Great Britain and the United States deficient in examples of this kind. About the commencement of the last century, the belief in witchcraft, which was almost universal throughout Christendom, was held in both of these countries. The laws of England, which admitted its existence and punished it with death, were

* In the Duchy of Lorraine, nine hundred females were delivered over to the flames for being *witches*, by one inquisitor alone. Under this accusation, it is reckoned that upward of *thirty thousand women* have perished by the hands of the Inquisition.—Quoted by Dr. Dick from "*Inquisition Unmasked.*"

adopted by the Puritans of New England, and in less than twenty years from the founding of the colony, one individual was tried and executed for the supposed crime. Half a century later the delusion broke out in Salem. A minister, whose daughter and niece were subject to convulsions accompanied by extraordinary symptoms, supposing they were bewitched, cast his suspicions on an Indian woman who lived in the house, and who was whipped until she confessed herself a witch; and the truth of the confession, although obtained in this way, was not doubted. During the same year more than fifty persons were terrified into the confession of witchcraft, twenty of whom were put to death. Neither age, sex, nor station afforded any safeguard against a charge for this supposed crime. Women and children not only were its victims, but magistrates were condemned, and a clergyman of the highest respectability was among the executed. So late as 1722 a woman was burned for witchcraft in Scotland, which was among the last executions in that country.

It appears that these superstitious notions, so far from being innocent and harmless speculations, lead to the most deplorable results; they ought, therefore, to be undermined and thoroughly eradicated by all persons who wish to promote the happiness and well-being of general society. This duty is especially incumbent upon parents and teachers, and can be effected only by rendering correct early education universal. Ignorance of the laws and economy of nature is the one great source of these absurd opinions. They have not only no foundation in nature or experience, but are directly opposed to both. In proportion, then, as we advance in our researches into Nature's economy and laws, shall we perceive their futility and absurdity. As in other cases, take away the cause, and the effect will be removed.

Education will dissipate all these evils. It is true that an acquaintance with a number of dead languages, with Roman and Grecian antiquities, with the subtleties of metaphysics, with pagan mythology, and with politics and poetry, may coexist with these superstitions, as was true in the case of the late Dr. Samuel Johnson, who believed in ghosts and in the *second sight.* However important in other respects these departments of an extensive and varied education may be, they do not form an effectual barrier against the admission of superstitious opinions. In order to do this, the mind must be directed to the study of the material universe, to contemplate the various appearances it presents, and to mark well the uniform results of those invariable laws by which it is governed. In particular, the attention should be directed to those discoveries which have been made by philosophers in the different departments of nature and art during the last two centuries. For this purpose, the study of natural history, as recording the various facts respecting the atmosphere, the waters, the earth, and animated beings, combined with the study of natural philosophy and astronomy, as explaining the causes of the phenomena of nature, will have a happy tendency to eradicate from the mind superstitious and false notions, and at the same time will present to view objects of delightful contemplation. Let a person be once thoroughly convinced that nature is uniform in her operations, and governed by regular laws impressed by an all-wise and benevolent Being, and he will soon be inspired with confidence, and will not easily be alarmed at any occasional phenomena which at first sight might appear as exceptions to the general rule.

Let persons be taught, for example, that eclipses are occasioned merely by the shadow of one opaque body falling upon another ; that they are the necessary result of the inclination of the moon's orbit to that of the earth ; that, if these orbits were in the same plane, there would be an eclipse of the sun and of the moon every month, the former occurring at the change, and the latter at the full of the moon ; that the times when they do actually take place depend on the new or full moon happening at or near the points of intersection of the orbits of the earth and moon, and that other planets which have moons experience eclipses of a similar nature. Let them also be taught that the *comets* are regular bodies belonging to our system, which finish their revolutions and appear and disappear in stated periods of time ; that the northern lights, though seldom seen in southern climes, are frequent in the regions of the North, and supply the inhabitants with light in the absence of the sun, and have probably a relation to the magnetic and electric fluids ; that the *ignes fatui* are harmless lights, formed by the ignition of a certain species of gas produced in the soils above which they hover; and that the notes of the death-watch, so far from being presages of death, are ascertained to be the notes of *love* and presages of hymeneal intercourse among these little insects.

Let rational information of this kind be imparted to people generally, and they will learn to contemplate nature with tranquillity and composure. A more beneficial effect than this will at the same time be produced, for those very objects which were formerly beheld with alarm will now be converted into sources of enjoyment, and be contemplated with emotions of delight.

To remove the groundless apprehensions which arise from the fear of invisible and incorporeal beings, let persons be instructed in the various optical illusions to which we are subject, arising from the intervention of fogs, and the indistinctness of vision in the night-time, which makes us frequently mistake a bush that is near us for a large tree at a distance, and let them be taught that under the influence of these illusions a timid imagination will transform the indistinct image of a cow or a horse into a terrific phantom of a monstrous size. Let them also be taught, by a selection of well-authenticated facts, the powerful influence of the imagination in creating ideal forms, especially when under the dominion of fear; the effects produced by the workings of conscience when harassed by guilt; let them be taught the effects produced by lively dreams, by strong doses of opium, by drunkenness, hysteric passions, madness, and other disorders that affect the mind. Let the experiments of optics, and the striking phenomena produced by electricity, galvanism, magnetism, and the different gases, be exhibited to their view, together with details of the results which have been produced by various mechanical contrivances. In fine, let their attention be directed to the foolish, whimsical, and extravagant notions attributed to apparitions, and to their inconsistency with the wise and benevolent arrangements of the Governor of the universe.

There is no rational foundation for entertaining any doubts but that, could such instructions as I have suggested be universally given, the effect would be the banishment of superstitions of the nature contemplated from among mankind; for *they have uniformly produced this effect on every mind which has been thus enlightened.* Where is the man to be found whose mind is enlightened by the doctrines and discoveries of modern science, and who yet remains the slave of superstitious notions and vain fears? Of all the philosophers of America and Europe, is there one who is alarmed at an eclipse, at a comet, at an *ignis fatuus*, or at the notes of a death-watch? or who postpones his experiments on account of what is called an unlucky day? Who ever heard of a specter appearing to such a person, dragging him from bed at the dead hour of midnight, to wander through the forest, trembling with fear? Such beings appear only to the ignorant and illiterate, at least to those who are unacquainted with natural science, and we never hear of their appearing to any who did not previously believe in their existence. But should philosophers be freed from such terrific visions, if substantial knowledge has not the power of banishing them from the mind? Why should supernatural beings feel so shy in conversing with men of science? These would, indeed, be the fittest persons to whom they might impart their secrets, and communicate information respecting the invisible world; but it never falls to their lot to be favored with such visits. It may therefore be concluded that the diffusion of useful knowledge among mankind would infallibly dissipate those groundless fears which have banished much of happiness from the human family, and particularly among the lower orders of society.*

* Dr. Dick, to whom I have frequently referred, and whose writings I have freely consulted, expresses in a note a sentiment in which I fully concur. "It would be unfair," says he, "to infer, from any expression here used, that the author denies the possibility of supernatural visions and appearances. We are assured from the records of sacred history that beings of an order superior to the human race have 'at sundry times and in divers manners' made their appearance to men. But there is the most marked difference between vulgar apparitions and the celestial messengers to which the records of revelation refer. They appeared not to old women and clowns, but to patriarchs, prophets, and apostles. They appeared not to frighten the timid and to create unnecessary alarm, but to declare 'tidings of great joy.' They appeared not to reveal such paltry secrets as the place where a pot of gold or silver is concealed, or where a lost ring may be found, but to communicate intelligence worthy of a God to reveal, and of the utmost importance for man to receive. In these and many other

I might, perhaps, safely dismiss this subject, and proceed to the consideration of other topics; but, before doing so, it may be well to state that many of the views here presented, and all that come within the range of the subjects discussed by him, are fully sustained by Dr. Lardner, whose popular lectures on science and art have been so well received both in Europe and America. His publishers justly remark, that "probably no public lecturer ever continued, for the same length of time, to collect around him so numerous audiences." The author himself states, in the preface to his Lectures,* that from November, 1841, when he commenced his public lectures in the lecture-room of Clinton Hall, in New York, to the close of the year 1844, when he concluded his public labors in this country, he "visited every considerable city and town of the Union, from Boston to New Orleans, and from New York to St. Louis. Most of the principal cities were twice visited, and several courses were given in Boston, New York, and Philadelphia. Nor did the appetite for this species of intellectual entertainment appear to flag by repetition."

I can not forbear making a few quotations from the preface to the work under consideration, which are creditable to the comparative intelligence of the American people, and show the avidity with which they seek instruction and useful knowledge. Dr. Lardner observes, that "it was usual on each evening to deliver from two to four of the essays which compose the contents of the present volumes, and the duration of the

respects, there is the most striking contrast between popular ghosts and the supernatural communications and appearances recorded in Scripture."

* In two large volumes, published by Greeley and McElrath, New York.

entertainment was from two to three hours. On every occasion the most profound interest was evinced on the part of the audience, and the most unremitting and silent attention was given. These assemblies consisted of persons of both sexes, of every age, from the elder classes of pupils in the schools to their grandfathers and grandmothers. Frequently the audiences amounted to twelve hundred, and sometimes, as at the Philadelphia Museum, they exceeded two thousand. Nor was the manifestation of this interest confined, as might be imagined, to the northern Atlantic cities, where education is known to be attended to, and where, as in New England, the diffusion of useful knowledge is regarded as a paramount duty of the state. The same crowded assemblies were collected, for a long succession of nights, in the largest theaters of each of the southern and western cities; in the Charleston Theater; the Mobile Theater; the St. Charles Theater, New Orleans; the Vicksburg and Jackson Theaters, Mississippi; the St. Louis Theater, Missouri; and in the theaters of Cincinnati, Pittsburg, and other western and central cities.

"It can not be denied that such facts are symptomatic of a very remarkable condition of the public mind, more especially among a people who are admitted to be, more than any other nation, engrossed by money-getting and by the more material pursuits of life. The less pretension to eloquence and the attractive graces of oratory the lecturer can offer, the more surprising is the result, and the more creditable to the intelligence of the American people. It is certain that a similar intellectual entertainment, clogged, as it necessarily was, with a pecuniary condition of admission, would fail to attract an audience even in the most polished and enlightened cities of Europe."

While these statements are highly creditable to the

American people, the lectures themselves contain paragraphs which show that the popular mind even in our own country is not sufficiently enlightened to eradicate the superstitions just considered.

THE MOON AND THE WEATHER.—Dr. Lardner, in a lecture on the moon, in answer to the question, Does the moon influence the weather? says,* It is asserted, first, that at the epochs of new and full moon, and at the quarters, there is generally a change of weather; and, secondly, that the phases of the moon, or, in other words, the relative position of the moon and sun in regard to the earth, is the cause of these changes. Now these and kindred opinions are very extensively held in this country. But the doctor refers to meteorological tables, constructed in various countries after the most extensive and careful observation, and the result is that no correspondence exists between the condition of the weather and the phases of the moon. He hence, after a full examination, comes to the conclusion that "*the condition of the weather as to change, or in any other respect, has, as a matter of fact, no correspondence whatever with the lunar phases.*"

In another lecture on the moon and the weather, the following decisive opinion is expressed: "From all that has been stated, it follows then, conclusively, that the popular notions concerning the influence of the lunar phases on the weather have no foundation in the theory, and no correspondence with observed facts."†

TIME FOR FELLING TIMBER.—In another lecture on lunar influences, Dr. Lardner observes that "there is an opinion generally entertained that timber should be felled only during the decline of the moon; for if it be cut down during its increase, it will not be of a good or

* See Lectures on Science and Art, vol. i., p. 315.

† Ibid., p. 419–420.

durable quality. This impression prevails in various countries. It is acted upon in England, and is made the ground of legislation in France. *The forest laws of the latter country interdict the cutting of timber during the increase of the moon.* In the extensive forests of Germany, the same opinion is entertained and acted upon, with the most undoubting confidence in its truth. Sauer, a superintendent of some of these districts, assigns what he believes to be its physical cause. According to him, the increase of the moon causes the sap to ascend in the timber, and, on the other hand, the decrease of the moon causes it to descend. If the timber, therefore, be cut during the decrease of the moon, it will be cut in a dry state, the sap having retired, and the wood, therefore, will be compact, solid, and durable. But if it be cut during the increase of the moon, it will be felled with the sap in it, and will therefore be more spongy, more easily attacked by worms, more difficult to season, and more readily split and warped by changes of temperature.

"Admitting for a moment the reality of this supposition concerning the motion of the sap, it would follow that the proper time for felling the timber would be *the new moon*, that being the epoch at which the descent of the sap would have been made, and the ascent not yet commenced. But can there be imagined, in the whole range of natural science, a physical relation more extraordinary and unaccountable than this supposed correspondence between the movement of the sap and the phases of the moon? Assuredly theory affords not the slightest countenance to such a supposition; but let us inquire as to the fact whether it be really the case that the quality of timber depends upon the state of the moon at the time it is felled.

"M. Duhamel Monceau, a celebrated French agri

L 2

culturist, has made direct and positive experiments for the purpose of testing this question, and has clearly and conclusively shown that the qualities of timber felled in different parts of the lunar month are the same. M. Duhamel felled a great many trees of the same age, growing from the same soil, and exposed to the same aspect, and never found any difference in the quality of the timber, when he compared those which were felled in the decline of the moon with those which were felled during its increase: in general, they have afforded timber of the same quality. He adds, however, that by a circumstance which was doubtless fortuitous, a slight difference was manifested in favor of timber which had been felled between the new and full moon, *contrary to popular opinion.*"

Supposed Lunar Influences.—It is an aphorism received by all gardeners and agriculturists in Europe, remarks the same author, that vegetables, plants, and trees, which are expected to flourish and grow with vigor, should be planted, grafted, and pruned during the increase of the moon. This opinion, however, he thinks is altogether erroneous; for the experiments and observations of several French agriculturists have clearly established the fact that the increase or decrease of the moon has no appreciable influence on the phenomena of vegetation.

This erroneous prejudice prevails also on the American continent. A French author states that, in Brazil, cultivators plant during the *decline* of the moon all vegetables whose *roots* are used as food, and that, on the contrary, they plant during the *increasing* moon the sugar-cane, maize, rice, beans, etc., and those which bear the food upon their *stocks* and *branches*. Experiments, however, were made and reported by M. de Chauvalon, at Martinique, on vegetables of both kinds, planted at different times in the lunar month, and no appreciable difference in their qualities was discovered.

There are some traces of a principle adopted by the South American agronomes (farmers), according to which they treat the two classes of plants distinguished by the production of fruit on their roots or on their branches differently; but there are none in the European aphorisms. The directions of Pliny are still more specific: he prescribes the time of the full moon for sowing beans, and that of the new moon for lentils. "Truly," says M. Arago, "we have need of a robust faith to admit, without proof, that the moon, at the distance of two hundred and forty thousand miles, shall, in one position, act advantageously upon the vegetation of *beans*, and that in the opposite position, and at the same distance, she shall be propitious to *lentils*."

Dr. Lardner gives numerous and extended illustrations of the supposed influence of the moon on the growth of grain, on wine-making,* on the color of the complexion, on putrefaction, on the size of shell-fish, on the quantity of marrow in the bones of animals, on the number of births, on mental derangement, and other human maladies, etc., etc.

The influence on the phenomena of human maladies imputed to the moon is very ancient. Hippocrates had so strong a faith in the influence of celestial objects upon animated beings, that he expressly recommends no physician to be trusted who is ignorant of astronomy. Galen, following Hippocrates, maintained the same opinion, especially of the influence of the moon. The critical days, or *crises*, were the seventh, fourteenth, and twenty-first of the disease, corresponding to the intervals between the moon's principal phases. While the

* On this subject the prevailing opinions in different countries disagree, as they do also on some of the others.

doctrine of alchemists prevailed, the human body was considered as a microcosm, or an epitome of the universe, the heart representing the sun, and the brain the moon. The planets had each his proper influence: Jupiter presided over the lungs, Saturn over the spleen, Venus over the kidneys, and Mercury over the organs of generation. The term *lunacy*, which still designates unsoundness of mind, is a relic of these grotesque notions, and is defined by Dr. Webster as "a species of insanity or madness, formerly supposed to be influenced by the moon, or periodical in the month." But even this term may now be said, in some degree, to be banished from the nomenclature of medicine; it has, however, taken refuge in that receptacle of all antiquated absurdities of phraseology—the law—lunatic being still the term for the subject who is incapable of managing his own affairs.

Sanctorius, whose name is celebrated in physics for the invention of the thermometer, held it as a principle that a healthy man gained two pounds' weight at the beginning of every lunar month, which he lost toward its completion. This opinion appears to have been founded on experiments made upon himself, and affords another instance of a fortuitous coincidence hastily generalized.

For all the progress that has been made in this country toward the removal from the popular mind of the numerous corrupting and debasing absurdities which have hitherto enslaved it, we are indebted to our enlightened and chastened systems of popular education; and to these, and to these only, may we confidently look for entire freedom from the thraldom.

EDUCATION INCREASES THE PRODUCTIVENESS OF LABOR.

Education has a power of ministering to our personal and material wants beyond all other agencies, whether excellence of climate, spontaneity of production, mineral resources, or mines of silver and gold. Every wise parent, every wise community, desiring the prosperity of its children even in the most worldly sense, will spare no pains in giving them a generous education.—HORACE MANN.

The best educated are always the best paid.—*Foreign Report.*

The desirableness of education is manifest, view it in what light we may, and whether as affecting individuals or communities. We have already seen that education, and that alone, will dissipate the evils of ignorance. We now propose to discuss the equally tenable proposition that education increases the productiveness of labor.

That knowledge is power has become a proverb. If it be asked why the labor of a man is more valuable than the same amount of physical effort put forth by a brute, the ready answer is, It is because man combines *intelligence* with his labor. A single yoke of oxen will do more in one day at plowing than forty men; yet the oxen may be had for fifty cents a day, while each of the men can earn a dollar. Physical exertion in this case, combined with ordinary skill, is eighty times more valuable than the same amount of brute force. The strength of the ox is of no account without some one to guide and apply it, while the power of man is guided by intelligence within.

In proportion as man's intelligence increases is his labor more valuable. A small compensation is the reward of mere physical power, while skill, combined with a moderate amount of strength, commands high wages. The labor of an ignorant man is scarcely more valuable than the same amount of brute force;

but the services of an intelligent, skillful person are a hundred fold more productive. I will pause and illustrate, for I wish to have every person who arises from the perusal of these pages do so with the fullest conviction that mental culture is of the highest importance even in the ordinary departments of human industry. It is, indeed, hardly less important for the man of business, the farmer, or the mechanic, than for statesmen, legislators, and members of the so-called learned professions.

An intelligent farmer of my acquaintance having a piece of greensward to break up, and having three work-horses, determined to employ them all. He hence, possessing some mechanical skill, himself constructed a three-horse whipple-tree, by means of which he advantageously combined the strength of his horses. A less intelligent neighbor, pleased with the novel appearance of three horses working abreast, resolved to try the experiment himself. But not possessing the skill requisite to construct such a whipple-tree, he waited till his better-informed and more expert neighbor had got through with his, and then, borrowing it, tried the experiment with his own team. Early one morning, and full of expectation, aided by his two sons and a hired man, he harnessed his three horses to the plow. But one of them, for the first time, refused to draw. After several fruitless attempts to make the team work as first harnessed, the relative position of the horses was changed, when, lo! although *this* horse would draw as formerly, one of the others would not. By and by another change was made, and the third horse, in turn, refused to draw. The farmer could not understand it, nor his sons, nor his hired man. His three horses, for the first time, were each fickle in turn. And, what was most surprising, they would all work 'n either of two positions, but in the third none of them would draw. The honest farmer thought the age of witchcraft had not yet passed. At the conclusion of the forenoon he gave up the undertaking in disgust, and, carrying the whipple-tree home, told the story of his unsuccessful and vexatious experiment.

"And how did you harness the horses to the whipple-tree?" inquired the more intelligent farmer. "Why, one at the short end, and two at the long end, where there is the most room for them, to be sure!" was the frank reply.

The power at the short end, I need not say, should be twice that at the long end; whereas he had it reversed. One horse drew against two with a double purchase. He then would have to draw twice as much as both of them, or four times as much as one of them. The fickleness of the horses, then, instead of being the result of *witchcraft*, as he was inclined to believe, was chargeable solely to the *ignorance* of their hardly more intelligent master. A knowledge of the first principles of mechanics, or, in the absence of this, an ordinary degree of active, available common sense, would teach the proper use of such a whipple-tree. For want of this knowledge, the farmer suffered much chagrin, lost the time of four men, and did great injury to his team.

After mentioning this circumstance on a certain occasion, a gentleman present gave a parallel case, that occurred under his immediate observation. His neighbor had a yoke of oxen, one of which was large, strong, and beautiful. One day, as the neighbor was passing the residence of the gentleman, the latter remarked to him, "You have one very fine-looking ox." "Yes," replied the neighbor, with apparent satisfaction, "and a bonny fellow he is too. He can carry the *long end of the yoke, and grow fat under it.*" Here, again, the weaker ox had to tax his strength doubly on account of the advantage which the ignorance of his kind master had unintentionally given to his superior yoke-fellow.

A farmer, or laborer of any kind, who possesses a knowledge of the merest elements of science, and is accustomed to think and investigate, can not only work more advantageously with his team, but he can do more work himself, and do it easier too, than his neighbor of superior physical strength, though of inferior mental capacity. The correctness of this statement may be satisfactorily proved and amply illustrated in loading timber, in moving buildings, in plowing, and in almost every kind of work done on a farm or among men, either on land or at sea. The ignorant man will spend more time in running after help to do a supposed difficult job, than it will require for a skillful one to do it alone. This is true in carpentry, and in all of the mechanic arts. Increase the practical and available education of the laborer, and you enable him to do more work, and better work too, than his less informed associate. The following is a striking illustration.

A practical teacher employed some mechanics to build him a barn. The day after the frame was raised, the teacher discovered that it needed to be turned a few inches upon its foundation, to range properly with other buildings. While the mechanics went in several directions to procure what they regarded as necessary help, the teacher, who was familiar with the various combinations of the lever, effected the work alone, and before their return! Other equally striking illustrations might be cited.

But education increases the productiveness of labor in a wider and more extended sense. By its omnipotent influence, man is enabled to lay the elements under tribute. The water and the wind, by its mysterious power, are made to propel his machinery for various purposes. The utmost skill of the untutored savage enables him to construct a rude canoe which two can carry upon their shoulders by land, which is barely capable of plying upon our rivers and coasting our inland seas, and which can be propelled only by human muscles, but the *educated man* erects a magnificent vessel, a floating palace, and, spreading his canvas to the breeze, aided by the mariner's compass, can traverse unknown seas in safety. To such perfection has he attained in the science and art of navigation, that he contends successfully with wind and tide, and makes headway against both, even when he depends upon the former for his motive power. Yes, education enables man even to tax the gentle breeze to urge a proud ship, heavily laden, up an inclined plane, thousands of miles, against the current of a mighty river.

I can not, perhaps, so satisfactorily establish the proposition which I am now endeavoring to elucidate, nor so well maintain the universality of its application, as by referring to the writings of the most indefatigable and successful laborer in the department of popular education of which our country can boast. I refer to the Hon. Horace Mann,* who, a few years ago, in his official capacity, opened a correspondence, and availed himself of all opportunities to hold personal interviews with many of the most practical, sagacious, and intelligent business men in our country, who for many years had had large numbers of persons in their employment. His object was to ascertain the difference in the productive ability, where natural capacities were

* Late Secretary of the Massachusetts Board of Education. Reference is here especially made to his Fifth Annual Report, bearing date January 1, 1842, from which, with his consent, what follows under this head has been substantially drawn.

equal, between the educated and the uneducated; between a man or a woman whose mind has been awakened to thought, and supplied with the rudiments of knowledge by a good common school education, and one whose faculties have never been developed, or aided in emerging from their original darkness and torpor by such a privilege. For this purpose he conferred and corresponded with manufacturers of all kinds—with machinists, engineers, railroad contractors, officers in the army, etc.; classes which have means of determining the effects of education on individuals equal in their natural abilities that other classes do not possess.

A farmer hiring a laborer for one season who has received a good common school education, and the ensuing season hiring another who has not enjoyed this advantage, although he may be personally convinced of the relative value or profitableness of their services, yet he will rarely have any exact data or tests to refer to by which he can measure the superiority of the former over the latter. They do not work side by side, so that he can institute a comparison between the amounts of labor they perform. They may cultivate different fields, where the ease of tillage or the fertility of the soils may be different. They may rear crops under the influence of different seasons, so that he can not discriminate between what is referable to the bounty of nature and what to superiority in judgment or skill.

Similar difficulties exist in estimating the amount and value of female labor in the household. And as to the mechanic also—the carpenter, the mason, the blacksmith, the tool-maker of any kind—there are a thousand circumstances, which we call accidental, that mingle their influence in giving quality and durability to their work, and prevent us from making a precise estimate of the relative value of any two men's handicraft. Individual differences, too, in regard to a single article or a single days' work, may be too minute to be noticed or appreciated, while the aggregate of these differences at the end of a few years may make all the difference between a poor man and a rich one. No observing man can have failed to notice the difference between two workmen, one of whom, to use a proverbial expression, always "hits the nail on the head," while the other loses half his strength and destroys half his nails by the awkwardness of his blows; but perhaps few men have thought of the difference in the results of two such men's labor at the end of twenty years.

But when hundreds of men or women work side by side in the same factory, at the same machinery, in making the same fabrics, and, by a fixed rule of the establishment, labor the same number of hours each day; and when, also, the products of each operative can be counted in number, weighed by the pound, or measured by the yard or cubic foot, then it is perfectly practicable to determine, with arithmetical exactness, the productions of one individual and class as compared with those of another individual and class.

So, where there are different kinds of labor, some simple, others complicated, and of course requiring different degrees of intelligence and skill, it is easy to observe what class of persons rise from a lower to a higher grade of employment.

This, too, is not to be forgotten, that in a manufacturing or mechanical establishment, or among a set of hands engaged in filling up a valley or cutting down a hill, where scores of people are working together, the absurd and adventitious distinctions of society do not intrude. The capitalist and his agents are looking for the greatest amount of labor or the largest income in money from their investments, and they do not promote a dunce to a station where he will destroy raw material or slacken industry because of his name, or birth, or family connections. The obscurest and humblest person has a fair field for competition. That he proves himself capable of earning more money for his employers is a testimonial better than a diploma from all the colleges.

Now many of the most intelligent and valuable men in the community, in compliance with Mr. Mann's request, examined their books for a series of years, and ascertained both the quality and the amount of work performed by persons in their employment, and the result of the investigation is a most astonishing superiority in productive power on the part of the educated over the uneducated laborer. The hand is found to be another hand when guided by an intelligent mind. Processes are performed not only more rapidly, but better, when faculties which have been exercised in early life furnish their assistance. Individuals who, without the aid of knowledge, would have been condemned to perpetual inferiority of condition, and subjected to all the evils of want and poverty, rise to competence and independence by the uplifting power of education. In great establishments, and among large bodies of laboring men, where all services are rated according to their pecuniary value; where there are no extrinsic circumstances to bind a man down to a fixed position after he has shown a capacity to rise above it; where, indeed, men pass by each other, ascending or descending in their grades of labor just as easily and certainly as particles of water of different degrees of temperature glide by each other—under such circumstances it is found, as an almost invariable fact, other things being equal, that those who have been blessed with a good common school education rise to a higher and a higher point in the kinds of labor performed, and also in the rate of wages received, while the ignorant sink like dregs, and are always found at the bottom.

James K. Mills, Esq., of Boston, who has been connected with a house that has had for the last ten years the principal direction of cotton-mills, machine shops, and calico-printing works, in which are constantly employed about three thousand persons, and whose opinions of the effects of a common school education upon a manufacturing population are the result of personal observation and inquiries, and are confined to the testimony of the overseers and agents who are brought into immediate contact with the operatives, expresses the conviction that the rudiments of a common school education are essential to the attainment of skill and expertness as laborers, or to consideration and respect in the civil and social relations of life; that very few who have not enjoyed the advantages of a common school education ever rise above the lowest class of operatives, and that the labor of this class, when it is employed in manufacturing operations which require even a very moderate degree of manual or mental dexterity, is unproductive; that a large majority of the overseers and others employed in situations which require a high degree of skill in particular branches—which oftentimes require a good general knowledge of business, and *always* an unexceptionable moral character—have made their way up from the condition of common laborers, with no other advantage over a large proportion of those they have left behind than that derived from a better education.

A statement made from the books of one of the manufacturing companies will show the relative number of the two classes, and the earnings of each; and this mill, we are assured, may be taken as a fair index of all the others. The average number of operatives employed for the last three years is twelve hundred. Of this number there are forty-five unable to write their names, or about three and three fourths per cent. The average of women's wages, in the departments requiring the most skill, is two dollars and fifty cents per week, exclusive of board. The average wages of the lowest departments is one dollar and twenty-five cents per week.

Of the forty-five who are unable to write, twenty-nine, or about two thirds, are employed in the lowest department. The difference between the wages earned by the forty-five and the average wages of an equal number of the better-educated class is about twenty-seven per cent. in favor of the latter. The difference between the wages earned by twenty-nine of the lowest class and the same number in the higher is sixty-six per cent. Of seventeen persons filling the most responsible stations in the mills, ten have grown up in the establishment from common laborers or apprentices.

This statement does not include an importation of sixty-three persons from Manchester, in England, in 1839. Among these persons there was scarcely one who could read or write; and although a part of them had been accustomed to work in cotton-mills, yet, either from incapacity or idleness, they were unable to earn sufficient to pay for their subsistence, and at the expiration of a few weeks not more than half a dozen remained in the employment of the company.

In some of the print-works a large proportion of the operatives are foreigners. Those who are employed in the branches which require a considerable degree of skill are as well educated as our people in similar situations. But the common laborers, as a class, are without any education, and their average earnings are about two thirds only of those of *our* lowest classes, although the prices paid to each are the same for the same amount of work.

Among the men and boys employed in the machine shops, the want of education is quite rare. Mr. Mills does not know an instance of a person so employed who is unable to read and write; and many have a good common school education. To this, he thinks, may be attributed the fact that a large proportion of persons who fill the higher and more responsible situations come from this class of workmen. From these statements the reader will be able to form some estimate, in dollars and cents, at least, of the advantages of even a little education to the operative; and *there is not the least doubt,* says the same authority, that *the employer is equally benefited.* He has the security for his property that intelligence, good morals, and a just appreciation of the regulations of his establishment always afford. His machinery and mills, which constitute a large part of his capital, are in the hands of persons who, by their skill, are enabled to use them to their utmost capacity, and to prevent any unnecessary depreciation.

Each operative in a cotton-mill, according to the estimate of Mr. Mills, may be supposed to represent from one thousand to twelve hundred dollars of the capital invested in the mill and its machinery. It is only from the most diligent and economical use of this capital that the proprietor can expect a profit. A fraction less than one half of the cost of manufacturing common cotton goods when a mill is in full operation, is made up of charges which are permanent. If the product is reduced in the ratio of the capacity of the two classes of operatives mentioned in this statement, it will be seen that the cost will be increased in a compound ratio. Mr. Mills expresses the opinion "that the best cotton-mill in New England, with such operatives only as the forty-five mentioned above, who are unable to write their names, would never yield the proprietor a profit; that the machinery would be soon worn out, and he would be left, in a short time, with a population no better than that which is represented by the importation from England. I can not imagine any situation in life," he continues, "where the want of a common school education would be more severely felt, or be attended with worse consequences, than in manufacturing villages; nor, on the other hand, is there any where such advantages can be improved with greater benefit to all parties. There is more excitement and activity in the minds of people living in masses, and if this expends itself in any of the thousand vicious indulgences with which they are sure to be tempted, the road to destruction is traveled over with a speed exactly corresponding to the power employed."

H. Bartlett, Esq., of Lowell, who has been engaged ten years in manufacturing, and has had the constant charge of from four hundred to nine hundred persons during that time, has come in contact with a very great variety of character and disposition, and has seen mind applied to production in the mechanic and manufacturing arts possessing different degrees of intelligence, from gross ignorance to a high degree of cultivation, and he has no hesitation in affirming that he finds the best educated to be the most profitable help. *Even those females who merely tend machinery give a result somewhat in proportion to the advantages enjoyed in early life for education*, those who have a good common school education giving, as a class, invariably a better production than those brought up in ignorance.

In regard to the domestic and social habits of persons in his employ, the same gentleman adds, "I have never considered mere knowledge, valuable as it is to the laborer, as the only advantage derived from a good common school education. I have uniformly found the better educated, as a class, possessing a higher and better state of morals, more orderly and respectful in their deportment, and more ready to comply with the wholesome and necessary regulations of an establishment. And in times of agitation, on account of some change in regulations or wages, I have always looked to the most intelligent, best educated, and the most moral for support, and have seldom been disappointed; for, while they are the last to submit to imposition, they *reason*, and if your requirements are reasonable, they will generally acquiesce, and exert a salutary in-influence upon their associates. But the ignorant and uneducated I have generally found the most turbulent and troublesome, acting under the influence of excited passion and jealousy.

"The former appear to have an interest in sustaining good order, while the latter seem more reckless of consequences. And, to my mind, all this is perfectly natural. The better educated have more and stronger attachments binding them to the place where they are. They are generally neater in their persons, dress, and houses; surrounded with more comforts, with fewer of 'the ills flesh is heir to.' In short, I have found the educated, as a class, more cheerful and contented, devoting a portion of their leisure time to reading and intellectual pursuits, more with their families, and less in scenes of dissipation. The good effect of all this is seen in the more orderly and comfortable appearance of the whole household, but nowhere more strikingly than in the children. A mother who has a good com mon school education will rarely suffer her children to grow up in ignorance. As I have said, this class of persons are more quiet, more orderly, and, I may add, more regular in their attendance upon public worship, and more punctual in the performance of all their duties."

Mr. Bartlett thinks it would be very difficult, if not impossible, for a young man, who has not an education equal to a good common school education, to rise from grade to grade until he should obtain the berth of an overseer, and that, in making promotions, as a general thing, it would be unnecessary to make inquiry as to the education of the young men from whom you would select. Very seldom indeed, he says, would an uneducated young man rise to "*a better place and better pay.* Young men who expect to resort to manufacturing establishments for employment, can not prize too highly a good education. *It will give them standing among their associates, and be the means of promotion among their employers.*"

The final remark of this gentleman, in a lengthy letter, showing the advantages of education in a pecuniary, social, and moral point of view, is, that "*those who possess the greatest share in the stock of worldly goods are deeply interested in this subject, as one of mere insurance;* that the most effectual way of making insurance on their property would be *to contribute from it enough to sustain an efficient system of common school education, thereby educating the whole mass of mind, and constituting it a police more effectual than peace officers and prisons.*" By so doing he thinks they would bestow a benefaction upon those who, from the accident of birth or parentage, are subjected to the privations and temptations of poverty, and would do much to remove the prejudice and to strengthen the bands of union between the different and extreme portions of society. He very justly regards it a wise provision of Providence which connects so intimately, and, as he thinks, so indissolubly, the greatest good of the many with the highest interest of the few; or, in other words, which unites into one brotherhood all the members of the community, and in the existing partnership connects inseparably the interests of Labor and Capital.*

John Clark, Esq., of Lowell, who has had under his superintendence for eight years about fifteen hundred persons of both sexes, gives concurrent testimony. He has found, with very few exceptions, the best educated among his hands to be the most capable, intelligent, energetic, industrious, economical, and moral, and that they produce the best work, and the most of it, with the least injury to the machinery. They are, in short, in all respects the most useful, profitable, and the safest operatives; and as a class, they are more thrifty, and more apt to accumulate property for themselves. "I am very sure," he remarks, "that neither men of property nor society at large have any thing to fear from a more general diffusion of knowledge, nor from the extension and improvement of our system of common schools. On our pay-roll for the last month are borne the names of twelve hundred and twenty-nine female operatives, forty of whom receipted for

* The New York Free School State Convention, held in Syracuse the 10th and 11th of July inst. (1850), *unanimously* adopted an Address to the People of the State, written by Horace Greeley, in which the following passage occurs, inculcating the same sentiment: "Property is deeply interested in the Education of All. There is no farm, no bank, no mill, no shop—unless it be a grog-shop—which is not more valuable and more profitable to its owner if located among a well-educated than if surrounded by an ignorant population. *Simply as a matter of interest, we hold it to be the duty of Property to itself to provide Education for All.*"

their pay by 'making their mark.' Twenty-six of these have been employed in job work; that is, they are paid according to the quantity of work turned off from their machines. The average pay of these twenty-six falls eighteen and one half per cent. below the general average of those engaged in the same departments.

"Again: we have in our mills about one hundred and fifty females who have at some time been engaged in *teaching schools.* Many of them teach during the summer months, and work in the mills in winter. The average wages of these ex-teachers I find to be seventeen and three fourths per cent. *above the general average of our mills, and about forty per cent. above the twenty-six who can not write their names.* It may be said they are generally employed in the higher departments, where the pay is better. This is true; but this again may be, in most cases, fairly attributed to their better education, which brings us to the same result. If I had included in my calculations the remaining fourteen of the forty, who were mostly sweepers and scrubbers, and who are paid by the day, the contrast would have been still more striking; but, having no well-educated females in this department with whom to compare them, I have omitted them altogether. In arriving at the above results, I have considered the *net wages* merely, the price of board being in all cases the same. I do not consider these results as either extraordinary or surprising, but as a part only of the legitimate and proper fruits of a better cultivation, and fuller development of the intellectual and moral powers."

Mr. Mann gives the entire letters from which I have so freely drawn, and also introduces into his report extracts from a letter of Jonathan Crane, Esq., who has been for many years a large rail-road contractor, and has had several thousand men in his employment.

The testimony of this gentleman is corroborative of that already presented. Testimony similar to the preceding might be introduced from the proprietors and superintendents of the principal manufacturing establishments in America not only, but from every part of the civilized world. Before concluding this chapter, I shall, for another purpose, refer to statements made by extensive manufacturers in England and Switzerland.

These are no more than a fair specimen of a mass of facts which Mr. Mann obtained from the most authentic sources. They seem to prove incontestably that education is not only a moral renovator, and a multiplier of intellectual power, but that it is also the most prolific parent of material riches. It has a right, therefore, not only to be included in the grand inventory of a nation's resources, but to be placed at the very head of that inventory. It is not only the most honest and honorable, but the surest means of amassing property. Considering education, then, as a producer of wealth, it follows that the more educated a people are, the more will they abound in all those conveniences, comforts, and satisfactions which money will buy; and, other things being equal, *the increase of competency and the decline of pauperism will be measurable on this scale.*

Education and Agriculture.—The healthful and praiseworthy employment of agriculture requires knowledge for its successful prosecution. In this department of industry we are in perpetual contact with the forces of nature. We are constantly dependent upon them for the pecuniary returns and profits of our investments, and hence the necessity of knowing what those forces are, and under what circumstances they will operate most efficiently, and will most bountifully reward our original outlay of money and time.

Our country yields a great variety of agricultura. productions, and this brings into requisition all that chemical and experimental knowledge which pertains to the rotation of crops and the enrichment of soils. If rotation be disregarded, the repeated demands upon the same soil to produce the same crop will exhaust it of the elements on which that particular crop will best thrive. If the chemical ingredients and affinities of the soil are not understood, an attempt may be made to re-enforce it by substances with which it is already surcharged, instead of renovating it with those of which it has been exhausted by previous growths. But for these arrangements and adaptations knowledge is the grand desideratum, and the addition of a new fact to a farmer's mind will often increase the amount of his harvests more than the addition of acres to his estate.

Why is it that, if we except Egypt, all the remaining territory of Africa, containing nearly ten millions of square miles, with a soil most of which is incomparably more fertile by nature, produces less for the sustenance of man and beast than England, whose territory is only fifty thousand square miles? In the latter country, knowledge has been a substitute for a genial climate and an exuberant soil; while in the former, it is hardly a figurative expression to say that all the maternal kindness of nature, powerful and benignant as she is, has been repulsed by the ignorance of her children. Doubtless industry as well as knowledge is indispensable to productiveness; but knowledge must precede industry, or the latter will work to so little effect as to become discouraged, and to relapse into the slothfulness of savage life. This is illustrated by the condition of the inhabitants of Lower California, as described by an intelligent friend of the author, who left this country a year ago. He says this is a "most beau tiful country, with the finest climate in the world. But its inhabitants, who are principally Spaniards and Indians, are in a state of semi-barbarism, and consequently its resources are, to a certain extent, undeveloped. The land, which is generally level and of the richest quality, is divided into ranchos or plantations, the largest of which are twenty miles square, and feed twenty or thirty thousand head of wild cattle, with horses and mules in proportion. But these are all. The arts are in the lowest state imaginable. Their houses are mere pens, without pen floors ; their plows are pointed logs ; their yokes are straight sticks, which they tie to the horns of their oxen ; and every implement of industry shows an equal want of ingenuity and enterprise. They are too indolent to raise much grain, though the soil will yield, I am told, eighty bushels of wheat to an acre ; consequently, wheat is sold to the immigrants at three dollars per bushel, while the finest beef cattle in the world bring from eight to ten dollars per head. Butter, cheese, and even milk, you can not obtain at all, for they are too lazy to tame their cows. A few Americans, who own large ranchos, have American plows, and are doing better than the rest. Many ranchos have been abandoned, and their owners have gone to the mines. This state of things the energetic Anglo-Saxon will soon change. The immigration for the next few years will be immense, and the whole community will yield to American customs. The large ranchos will be cut up into farms, and their products will supply the wants of a dense population. Property will rapidly change hands, and it will be easy for the shrewd Yankee to reap the benefit of the change."

But, without further exposition, it may be remarked generally, that the spread of intelligence, through the instrumentality of good books, and the cultivation in our children of the faculties of observing, comparing, and reasoning, through the medium of good schools, would add millions to the agricultural products of nearly every state of the Union, without imposing upon the husbandman an additional hour of labor.

Education and the Useful Arts.—For the successful prosecution among us of the manufacturing and mechanic arts, if not for their very existence, there must be not only the exactness of science, but also exactness or skill in the application of scientific principles throughout the whole processes, either of constructing machinery, or of transforming raw materials into finished fabrics. This ability to make exact and skillful applications of science to an unlimited variety of materials, and especially to the subtile but most energetic agencies of nature, is one of the latest attainments of the human mind. It is remarkable that astronomy, sculpture, painting, poetry, oratory, and even ethical philosophy, had made great progress thousands of years before the era of the manufacturing and mechanic arts. This era, indeed, has but just commenced; and already the abundance, and, what is of far greater importance, the *universality* of the personal, domestic, and social comforts it has created, constitute one of the most important epochs in the history of civilization.

The cultivation of these arts is conferring a thousand daily accommodations and pleasures upon the laborer in his cottage, which, only two or three centuries ago, were luxuries in the palace of the monarch. Through circumstances incident to the introduction of all economical improvements, there has hitherto been great inequality in the distribution of their advantages; but their general tendency is greatly to ameliorate the condition of the mass of mankind. It has been estimated that the products of machinery in Great with a population of eighteen millions, is equal to the labor of hundreds of millions of human hands. This vast gain is effected without the conquest or partitioning of the territory of any neighboring nation, and without rapine or the confiscation of property already accumulated by others. It is an absolute creation of wealth—that is, of those articles, commodities, and improvements which we appraise and set down as of a certain moneyed value alike in the inventory of a deceased man's estate and in the grand valuation of a nation's capital. These contributions to human welfare have been derived from knowledge; from knowing how to employ those natural agencies which from the beginning of the race had existed, but had lain dormant or run uselessly away. For mechanical purposes, what is wind, or water, or the force of steam worth, until the ingenuity of man comes in, and places the wind-wheel, the water-wheel, or the piston *between* these mighty agents and the work he wishes them to perform? But after the intervention of machinery, how powerful they become for all purposes of utility! In a word, these great improvements, which distinguish our age from all preceding ages, have been obtained from Nature by addressing her in the language of Science and Art, the only language she understands, yet one of such all-pervading efficacy that she never refuses to comply to the letter with all petitions for wealth or physical power, if they are preferred to her in that dialect.

Now it is easy to show, from reasoning, from history, and from experience, that an early awakening of the mind is a prerequisite to success in the useful arts. But it must be an awakening to thought, not to feeling merely. In the first place, a clearness of perception must be acquired, or the power of taking a correct mental transcript, copy, or image of whatever is seen. This, however, though indispensable, is by no means sufficient.

The talent of improving upon the labors of others requires not only the capability of receiving an exact mental copy or imprint of all the objects of sense or reasoning; it also requires the power of reviving or reproducing at will all the impressions or ideas before obtained, and the power of changing their collocations, of re-arranging them into new forms, and of adding something to or removing something from the original perceptions, in order to make a more perfect plan or model. If a ship-wright, for instance, would improve upon all existing specimens of naval architecture, he would first examine as great a number of ships as possible; this done, he would revive the image which each had imprinted upon his mind, and, with all the fleets which he had inspected present to his imagination, he would compare each individual vessel with all others, make a selection of one part from one, and of another part from another, apply his own knowledge of the laws of moving and of resisting forces to all, and thus create, in his own mind, the complex idea or model of a ship more perfect than any of those he had seen.

Now every recitation in a school, if rightly conducted, is a step toward the attainment of this wonderful power. With a course of studies judiciously arranged and diligently pursued through the years of minority, all the great phenomena of external nature, and the most important productions in all the useful arts, together with the principles on which they are evolved or fashioned, would be successively brought before the understanding of the pupil. He would thus become familiar with the substances of the material world, and with their manifold properties and uses; and he would learn the laws, comparatively few, by which results infinitely diversified are produced. When such a student goes out into life, he carries, as it were, a plan or model of the world in his own mind. He can not, therefore, pass, either blindly or with the stupid gaze of the brute creation, by the great objects and processes of nature; but he has an intelligent discernment of their several existences and relations, and their adaptation to the uses of mankind. Neither can he fasten his eye upon any workmanship or contrivance of man without asking two questions: first, How is it? and, secondly, How can it be improved?

Hence it is that all the processes of nature and the contrivances of art are so many lessons or communications to an instructed man; but an uninstructed one walks in the midst of them like a blind man among colors, or a deaf man among sounds. The Romans carried their aqueducts from hill-top to hill-top, on lofty arches erected at immense expenditure of time and money. One idea—that is, a knowledge of the law of the equilibrium of fluids; a knowledge of the fact that water in a tube will rise to the level of the fountain—would have enabled *a single individual* to do with ease what, *without that knowledge*, it required the *wealth of an empire to accomplish.*

It is in ways similar to this—that is, by accomplishing greater results with less means; by creating products at once cheaper, better, and by more expeditious methods; and by doing a vast variety of things otherwise impossible—that the cultivation of mind may be truly said to yield the highest pecuniary requital.

Intelligence is the great money-maker, not by *extortion*, but by PRODUCTION. There are ten thousand things in every department of life which, if done in season, can be done in a minute, but which, if not seasonably done, will require hours, perhaps days or weeks for their performance. An awakened mind will see and seize the critical juncture; the perceptions of the sluggish one will come too late, if they come at all.

A general culture of the faculties, also, gives versatility of talent, so that, if the customary business of the laborer is superseded by improvements, he can readily betake himself to another kind of employment. But an uncultivated mind is like an automaton, which can do only the thing for which its wheels or springs were made. Brute force expends itself unproductively. It is ignorant of the manner in which Nature works, and hence it can not avail itself of her mighty agencies. Often, indeed, it attempts to oppose Nature. It throws itself across the track where her resistless car is moving. But knowledge enables its possessor to employ her agencies in his own service, and he thereby obtains an amount of power, without fee or reward, which thousands of slaves could not give.

Every man who consumes a single article in whose production or transportation the power of steam is used, has it delivered to him cheaper than he could otherwise have obtained it. Every man who can avail himself of this power in traveling, can perform the business of three days in one, and so far add two hundred per cent. to the length of his life as a business man. What innumerable millions has the invention of the cotton-gin, by Whitney, added, and will continue to add, to the wealth of the world! a part of which is already realized, but vastly the greater part of which is yet to be received, as each successive day draws for an installment which would exhaust the treasury of a nation. The instructed and talented man enters the rich domains of Nature not as an *intruder*, but, as it were, a PROPRIETOR, and makes her riches his own.

Why is it that, so far as the United States are concerned, four fifths of all the improvements, inventions, and discoveries in regard to machinery, to agricultural implements, to superior models in ship-building, and to the manufacture of those refined instruments on which accuracy in scientific observations depends, have originated in New England? I believe no adequate reason can be assigned but the early awakening and training of the power of thought in her children. Improvements, inventions, and discoveries have been made in other states of the Union to an extent commensurate with the progress they have made in perfecting their systems of public instruction, and these improvements will ever keep pace with the attentions which a people bestow upon their common schools.

Mr. Mann remarks that, in conversing with a gentleman who had possessed most extensive opportunities for acquaintance with men of different countries and of all degrees of intellectual development, he observed that he could employ a common immigrant or a slave, and, if he chose, could direct him to shovel a heap of sand from one spot to another, and then back into its former place, and so to and fro through the day; but, added he, neither love nor money would prevail on a New Englander to prosecute a piece of work of which he did not see the utility.

There is scarcely any kind of labor, however simple, pertaining to the farm, to the work-shop, or to domestic employments, and whether performed by male or female, which can be so well done without knowledge in the workman or domestic as with it. It is impossible for an overseer or employer at all times to supply mind to the laborer. In giving directions for the shortest series or train of operations, something will be omitted or misunderstood; and without intelligence in the workman, the omission or mistake will be repeated in the execution.

It is a fact of universal notoriety, that the manufacturing population of England, as a class, work for half, or less than half the wages of our own. The cost of machinery there, also, is about half as much as the cost of the same articles with us; while our capital, when loaned, produces nearly double the rate of English interest; yet against these grand adverse circumstances our manufacturers, with a small per centage of tariff, successfully compete with English capitalists in many branches of manufacturing business. No explanation can be given of this extraordinary fact which does not take into the account the difference of education between the operatives in the two countries.

One of our most careful and successful manufacturers remarks that, on substituting in one of his cotton-mills a better for a poorer educated class of operatives, he was enabled to add twelve or fifteen per cent. to the speed of his machinery, without any increase of damage or danger from the acceleration. How direct and demonstrative the bearing which facts like this have upon the wisdom of our laws respecting the education of children in manufacturing establishments.*

* In Connecticut the statutes provide "that no child under the age of fifteen years shall be employed to labor in any manufacturing establishment, or in any other business in the state, unless such child shall have attended some public or private day school where instruction is given by a teacher qualified to instruct in orthography, reading, writing, English grammar, geography, and arithmetic, at least three months of the twelve months next preceding any and every year in which such child shall be so employed. And the owner, agent, or superintendent of any manufacturing establishment who shall employ any child in such establishment contrary to the provisions of this act, shall forfeit and pay for each offense a penalty of twenty-five dollars to the treasurer of the state." In Massachusetts the forfeiture is fifty dollars. Similar provisions exist in other American, and in several European states.

The number of females in the State of Massachusetts engaged in the various manufactures of cotton, straw-platting, etc., has been estimated at forty thousand, and the annual value of their labor at one hundred dollars each on an average, or four millions of dollars for the whole. From the facts stated in the letters of Messrs. Mills and Clark above cited, it appears there is a difference of not less than fifty per cent. between the earnings of the least educated and of the best educated operatives—between those who make their marks instead of writing their names, and those who have been acceptably employed in school-keeping. Now suppose the whole forty thousand females engaged in the various kinds of manufactures in that commonwealth to be degraded to the level of the lowest class, it would follow that their aggregate earnings would fall at once to two millions of dollars. But, on the other hand, suppose them all to be elevated by mental cultivation to the rank of the highest, and their earnings would rise to the sum of six millions of dollars annually.

There can be no doubt but that education, or the want of it, affects the pecuniary value of female labor in the ordinary domestic employments of the sex not less than in manufactures. If, then, the females of the thirty states of the Union be estimated at eight millions—and the number sustaining the relations of daughters, wives, and mothers must exceed the supposition—the effect of giving them all an education equal to the best would at once raise their earnings, annually, two hundred millions of dollars! But this is the lowest sense in which we can estimate the value of education, even in the sterner sex. This sum, vast as it may seem, is as dross to gold when compared with the refining and elevating influence which eight millions of educated females would exert upon the domestic and social institutions of our country, in uplifting our national character and improving the condition of the race.

Not more than thirty years ago it was uncommon for a glazier's apprentice, even after having served an apprenticeship of seven years, to be able to cut glass with a diamond without spending much time and destroying much of the glass upon which he worked. But the invention of a simple tool has put it into the power of the merest tyro in the trade to cut glass with facility, and without loss. A man who had a *mind*, as well as *fingers*, observed that there was one direction in which the diamond was almost incapable of abrasion or wearing by use. The tool not only steadies the diamond, but fastens it in that direction.

The operation of tanning leather consists in exposing a hide to the action of a chemical ingredient, called tannin, for a length of time sufficient to allow every particle of the hide to become saturated with the solution. In making the best leather, the hides used to lay in the pit for six, twelve, or eighteen months, and sometimes for two years, the tanner being obliged to wait all this time for a return of his capital. By the modern process, the hides are placed in a close pit, with a solution of the tannin matter, and the air being exhausted, the liquid penetrates through every pore and fiber of the skin, and the whole process is completed in a few days.

The bleaching of cloth, which used to be effected in the open air, and in exposed situations where temptation to theft was offered, and in England hundreds and probably thousands of men have yielded and forfeited their lives, is now performed in an unexposed situation, and in a manner so expeditious, that cloth is bleached as much more rapidly than it formerly was as hides are tanned.

It is stated by Lord Brougham, in his beautiful Discourse on the Advantages of Science, that the inventor of the new mode of refining sugar made more money in a shorter time, and with less risk and trouble, than perhaps was ever realized from any previous invention.

Intelligence also *prevents loss* as well as *makes profits.* How much time and money have been squandered in repeated attempts to invent machinery, after a principle had been once tested and had failed through some defect inherent and natural, and therefore insuperable! Within thirty years not less than five patents have been taken out, in England and the United States, for a certain construction of paddle-wheels for a steamboat, which construction was tested and condemned as early as 1810.* A case once came within my own knowledge, says Mr. Mann, of a person who spent a fortune in mining for coal, when a work on geology, which would have cost but a dollar, and might have been read in a week, would have informed him that the stratum where he began to excavate belonged to a formation lower down in the natural series than coal ever is, or, according to the constitution of things, ever can be found. He therefore worked into a stratum which must have been formed before a particle of coal, or even a tree, or a vegetable existed on the planet. Numerous similar and equally striking illustrations might be cited, but this is not necessary.

These are a few specimens, on familiar subjects, taken almost at random, for the purpose of showing the inherent superiority of any association or community, whether small or great, where *mind* is a member of the partnership. What is true of the above-mentioned cases is true of the whole circle of those arts by which

* This statement was made eight years ago. More such patents may have been taken out within this time.

human life is sustained and human existence comforted, elevated, and embellished. Mind has been the improver, for matter can not improve itself, and improvement has advanced in proportion to the number and culture of the minds excited to activity and applied to the work.

Similar advancements have been effected throughout the whole compass of human labor and research; in the arts of Transportation and Locomotion, from the employment of the sheep and the goat as beasts of burden, to the steam-engine and the rail-road car; in the art of Navigation, from the canoe clinging timidly to the shore, to steam-ships which boldly traverse the ocean; in Hydraulics, from carrying water by hand in a vessel or in horizontal aqueducts, to those vast conduits which supply the demands of a city, and to steam fire-engines which throw a column of water to the top of the loftiest buildings; in the arts of Spinning and Rope-making, from the hand distaff to the spinning-frame, and to the machine which makes cordage or cables of any length, in a space ten feet square; in Horology or Time-keeping, from the sun-dial and the water-clock to the watch, and to the chronometer, by which the mariner is assisted in measuring his longitude, and in saving property and life; in the extraction, forging, and tempering of Iron and other ores having malleability to be wrought into all forms and used for all purposes, and supplying, instead of the stone hatchet or the fish-shell of the savage, an almost infinite variety of instruments, which have sharpness for cutting or solidity for striking; in the art of Vitrification or Glass-making, giving not only a multitude of commodious and ornamental utensils for the household, but substituting the window for the unsightly orifice or open casement, and winnowing light and warmth from the outward and the cold atmosphere; in the arts of Induration by Heat, from bricks dried in the sun to those which withstand the corrosion of our climate for centuries or resist the intensity of the furnace; in the arts of Illumination, from the torch cut from the fir or pine tree to the brilliant gas-light which gives almost a solar splendor to the nocturnal darkness of our cities; in the arts of Heating and Ventilation, which at once supply warmth for comfort and pure air for health; in the art of Building, from the hollowed trunk of a tree or the roof-shaped cabin, to those commodious and lightsome dwellings which betoken the taste and competence of our villages and cities; in the art of Copying or Printing, from the toilsome process of hand-copying, where the transcription of a single book was the labor of months or years, and sometimes almost of a life, to the power printing-press, which throws off sixty printed sheets in a minute; in the art of Paper-making, from the preparation of the inner bark of a tree, cleft off and dried at immense labor, to machinery from which there jets out an unbroken stream of paper with the velocity and continuousness of a current of water; in the art of Painting, from the use of the crayon, and artificial colors imperfectly blended, requiring whole days to present an incomplete picture, to the production, as by enchantment, of perfect likenesses in nature's own penciling, executed in a few seconds; in the art of Telegraphing, from communicating information by signs which may be seen from one station to another, to conveying intelligence to any given distance with the velocity of lightning; and, in addition to all these, in the arts of Moulding and Casting, of Designing and Engraving, of Preserving materials and of Changing their color, of Dividing and Uniting them, etc., etc., an ample catalogue, whose very names and processes would fill volumes.

Now, for the perfecting of all these operations, from the tedious and bungling process to the rapid and elegant; for the change of an almost infinite variety of crude and worthless materials into useful and beautiful fabrics, *mind* has been the agent. Succeeding generations have outstripped their predecessors just in proportion to the superiority of their mental cultivation. When we compare different people or different generations with each other, the diversity is so great that all must behold it. But there is the same kind of difference between contemporaries, fellow-townsmen, and fellow-laborers. Though the uninstructed man works side by side with the intelligent, yet the mental difference between them places them in the same relation to each other that a *past age* bears to the *present*. If the ignorant man knows no more respecting any particular art or branch of business than was generally known during the last century, *he belongs to the last century*, and he must consent to be outstripped by those who have the light and knowledge of the present. Though they are engaged in the same kind of work, though they are supplied with the same tools or implements for carrying it on, yet, so long as one has only an *arm*, but the other has an arm and a MIND, their products will come out stamped and labeled all over with marks of contrast; inferiority and superiority, both as to quantity and quality, will be legibly written on their respective labors.

It is related by travelers among savage tribes that when, by the aid of an ingeniously devised instrument or apparatus, they have performed some skillful manual operation, the savages have purloined from them the instrument they had used, supposing there was some magic in the apparatus itself, by which the seeming miracle had been performed; but, as they could not steal *the art of the operator* with the instrument which he employed, the theft was fruitless. Any person who expects to effect with less education what another is enabled to do with more, ought not to smile at the delusion of the savage or the simplicity of his reasoning.

On a cursory inspection of the great works of art—the steam-engine, the printing-press, the power-loom, the mill, the iron foundery, the ship, the telescope, etc., etc.—we are apt to look upon them as having sprung into sudden existence, and reached their present state of perfection by one, or, at most, by a few mighty efforts of creative genius. We do not reflect that they have required the lapse of centuries and the successive application of thousands of minds for the attainment of their present excellence; that they have advanced from a less to a more perfect form by steps and gradations almost as imperceptible as the growth by which an infant expands to the stature of a man; and that, as later discoverers and inventors had first to go over the ground of their predecessors, so must future discoverers and inventors first master the attainments of the present age before they will be prepared to make those new achievements which are to carry still further onward the stupendous work of improvement.

EDUCATION DIMINISHES PAUPERISM AND CRIME.

Education is to be regarded as one of the most important means of eradicating the germs of pauperism from the rising generation, and of securing in the minds and in the morals of the people the best protection for the institutions of society.—DR. JAMES PHILLIPS KAY, *Assistant Poor-Law Commissioner, and Secretary to the Committee of Council on Education.**

The different countries of the world, if arranged according to the state of education in them, will be found to be arranged also according to WEALTH, MORALS, and GENERAL HAPPINESS; at the same time, THE CONDITION OF THE PEOPLE, AND THE EXTENT OF CRIME AND VIOLENCE AMONG THEM, FOLLOW A LIKE ORDER.—NATIONAL EDUCATION, *by Fred. Hill, London.*

That education increases the productiveness of labor has been already conclusively established. It has also been incidentally shown that mere knowledge, valuable as it is to the laborer, is not the only advantage derived from a good common school education, but that the better educated, as a class, possess a higher and better state of morals, and are more orderly and respectful in their deportment than the uninstructed; and that for those who possess the greatest share in the stock of worldly goods, the most effectual way of making insurance on their property would be, to contribute from it enough to sustain an efficient system of common school education, thereby educating the whole mass of mind, and constituting it a police more effective than peace officers or prisons. If, then, *poverty is at once a cause and an effect of crime*, as is stated by a late writer,† who has made an extended survey of the relative state of instruction and social welfare in the leading nations of the world, it is directly inferable that ed-

* Quoted from the Report to the Secretary of State for the Home Department, on the Training of Pauper Children, London, 1841.

† Fred. Hill, author of National Education, whose testimony is quoted at the head of this article.

ucation will, and, from the nature of the case, *must* act in a compound ratio in diminishing both pauperism and crime.

This proposition is not received by a few individuals merely in comparatively unimportant communities: it is one which is generally adopted by enlightened practical educators and by liberal-minded capitalists of both hemispheres. The views of several of our principal American manufacturers have been already presented. Let us now direct our attention to the testimony of enlightened and liberal-minded capitalists residing in some of the transatlantic states.

William Fairbrain, Esq., the sole proprietor of a manufactory in Manchester, and part owner of another establishment in London, and who has between eleven and twelve hundred persons in his employ, remarks in relation to the habits of the educated and uneducated as follows: There is no doubt that the educated are more sober and less dissipated than the uneducated. During the hours of recreation, the younger portion of the educated workmen indulge more in reading and mental pleasures; they attend more at reading-rooms, and avail themselves of the facilities afforded by libraries, by scientific lectures, and by lyceums. The older of the more educated workmen spend their time chiefly with their families, reading and walking out with them. The time of the uneducated classes is spent very differently, *and chiefly in the grosser sensual indulgences.* Mr. Fairbrain has given his own time as president of a lyceum for the use of the working classes, which furnishes the means of instruction in arithmetic, mathematics, drawing, and mensuration, and by lectures. In these institutions liberal provision is very properly made, not only for the occupation of the leisure hours of the laborers themselves, and for their intellectual and social improvement, but for that of their wives and families, in order "to make the home comfortable, and to minister to the household recreation and amusement: this is a point of view in which the education of the wives of laboring men is really of very great importance, that they may be rational companions for men."*

Albert G. Escher, Esq., one of the firm of Escher, Wyss, and Co., of Zurich, Switzerland, remarks as follows: We employ from six to eight hundred men in our machine-making establishment at Zurich: we also employ about two hundred men in our cotton-mills there, and about five hundred men in our cotton manufactories in the Tyrol and in Italy. I have occasionally had the control of from five to six hundred men engaged in engineering operations as builders, masons, etc., and men of the class called navigators in England.

After giving a list of the different countries from which his laborers are drawn, classifying the workmen of various nations "in respect to such natural intelligence as may be distinguished from any intelligence imparted by the labors of the schoolmaster," and remarking in relation to the influence of education upon the value of labor—where his testimony corroborates that of manufacturers in New England, already quoted—the same gentleman makes a statement which is applicable to the subject under consideration.

"*The better educated workmen, we find, are distinguished by superior moral habits in every respect.* In the first place, they are entirely sober; they are discreet in their enjoyments, which are of a more rational and refined kind; they are more refined themselves, and they have a taste for much better society, which they

* See evidence taken by Edwin Chadwick, Esq., Secretary to the Poor-Law Commissioners, a quotation from whose report heads this article.

approach respectfully, and consequently find much readier admittance to it; they cultivate music; they read; they enjoy the pleasures of scenery, and make parties for excursions into the country; they are economical, and their economy extends beyond their own purse to the stock of their master; they are consequently honest and trustworthy."

Scotland affords a very striking illustration of the power of education in diminishing pauperism and crime, and in improving the morals and increasing the wealth of a country. Indeed, it would be difficult to find another instance in the history of nations of a country which has made such rapid progress in the diminution of crime, the increase of public wealth, and the diffusion of comforts, as Scotland. And this gratifying change—this remarkable instance of progress in the scale of being, has been concurrent with increased and increasing attention to the education of the people.

At the beginning of the last century, Scotland swarmed with gipsies and other vagabonds, who lived chiefly by stealing, and who often committed violent robberies and murders. Of these pests to society it was estimated that there were not less than two hundred thousand. Besides these, there were the more gentlemanly, though less tolerable robbers, such as the notorious Rob Roy, who made no more ado about seizing another man's cattle than a grazier does of driving from market a drove of oxen for which he has paid every shilling demanded.

But now, the laying aside of a sum sufficient for the education of his children is an object which a Scotchman seldom loses sight of, both when he thinks of marrying and settling in life, and at every future period; and it is to this habit, handed down from father to son, that the Scotch owe their morality. One of their own writers says, "we have scarcely any rural population who are not perfectly aware of the importance of education, and not willing to make sacrifices to secure it to their children."

Having seen something of the excellence of education in improving the social and moral habits of a community, and in banishing pauperism and crime from among those who become the happy subjects of its uplifting power, let us, for the purpose of becoming more alive to its importance, consider the condition of a people where the masses are not brought under its benign influence.

Spain, which has been already referred to in illustration of the evils of ignorance, affords a striking illustration for our present purpose. Until after the lapse of one third of the present century, there was but ONE newspaper published in this country! "Yes, one miserable government gazette was the sole channel through which twelve or fourteen millions of people, spread over a vast territory, were to be supplied with information on the momentous affairs of their own country, and of the whole external world."—*National Education*, vol. ii., p. 136.

"The most authentic return of the number of children receiving education in Spain was made in the year 1803, and it is believed that but little change has taken place since that time. According to the returns, the number of children receiving education, exclusive of those brought up in convents and monasteries, was only one in every three hundred and forty-six of the population! M. Jonnés estimates the population at about fourteen millions and a half, and assuming, as he does, that about the same fraction of the population is receiving education as in 1803, he estimates the present number of children in school in the whole of Spain at not more than about forty-three thousand; and, pursuing his calculations, he shows that, if his data be correct, not more than one child in thirty-five ever goes to school. He further states that the children thus favored are exclusively from the middle and upper classes."*—*National Education*, vol. ii., p. 130–1.

How far the education given to the favored few is of a practical and useful kind, may be conjectured from the following extract from M. Jonnés's work. After speaking of the many libraries, schools, colleges, and universities, the creation of past times, but which still exist, he remarks, that "these institutions were intended for a state of society which had nothing in common with that of the present day. The kind of instruction afforded in them, confined as it is to prayer, church discipline, and the dogmas of theology, has no connection with the interests and wants of the existing generation.

"What every enlightened man in Spain has long called for is a national, popular, gratuitous education, extending to all classes, as well in the towns as in the rural districts. Up to the present time, the people have received no other instruction than that offered by the clergy, which has had scarcely any other object than the performance of religious ceremonies."

In addition to what has been already stated, it may be remarked, that even with those who know how to read, "books and study are almost out of the question, because, unless in the principal cities, public libraries are nowhere to be found, and private libraries are luxuries that few possess."

If education is conducive to virtue, and ignorance

* The writer would here remark, in reference to extracts made from various authors, that, for the sake of abridging, he has often, as in this case, left out parts of a paragraph, but never so as to modify the meaning. Some ideas, not connected with the subject in hand, are omitted, but none are changed.

fosters crime, what must be the social and moral state of a country in which ignorance is so prevalent! "The amount of crime in Spain is appalling. We have before us a return of convictions for the year 1826, from which we shall make some extracts. Our reason for taking this year is simply because we are unable to procure any return for a later one. The number of convictions for murder in England and Wales in the year 1826 was thirteen, and the number convicted of wounding, etc., with intent to kill, was fourteen. These numbers are lamentably large. That the horrible crime of murder should ever be perpetrated is a most melancholy fact; and that so many as thirteen murders should be committed in one year must fill the mind of every moral man and lover of his country with grief and shame. But great as this number is absolutely, it sinks into insignificance when compared with the number of murders perpetrated in Spain; for in that unhappy country, in the single year of 1826, the number of convictions for murder reached the frightful height of TWELVE HUNDRED AND THIRTY-THREE! in addition to which, there were seventeen hundred and seventy-three convictions on charges of maiming with intent to kill, and sixteen hundred and twenty persons were convicted of robbery under aggravated circumstances. We doubt not for an instant THIS MASS OF CRIME IS THE OFFSPRING OF IGNORANCE."—*National Education*, vol. ii., p. 144.

It has been well remarked that the truest proofs of a good government are just laws, and that the best evidence of a well-organized government is to be found in the strict execution of these laws. "Judging the Spanish government by these tests, it will appear the worst and weakest government that ever held together. Justice of no kind has any existence; there is the most lamentable insecurity of person and property; redress is never certain, because both judgment and the execution of the laws are left to men so inadequately paid that they must depend for their subsistence upon bribery. Nothing is so difficult as to bring a man to trial who has any thing in his purse, except to bring him to execution: this, unless in Madrid and Catalonia, is impossible, for *money will always buy indemnity.*

"I can state, upon certain information received in Madrid, that the principal Spanish diligences pay black mail to the banditti for their protection. This arrangement was at first entered into with some difficulty; and from a gentleman who was present at the interview between the person employed to negotiate on behalf of the diligences and the representative of the banditti, I learned a few particulars. The diligences in question were those between Madrid and Seville, and the sum offered for their protection was not objected to, but another difficulty was started. 'I have nothing to say against the terms you offer,' said the negotiator for the banditti, 'and I will at once insure you against being molested by robbers of consequence! but as for the *small fry*, I can not be responsible! we respect the engagements entered into by each other, *but there is nothing like honor among the petty thieves.*' The proprietors of the diligences, however, were satisfied with the assurance of protection against the great robbers, and the treaty was concluded; but not long afterward one of the coaches was stopped and rifled by the petty thieves: this led to an arrangement which has ever since proved effectual; one of the chiefs accompanies the coach on its journey, and overawes, by his name and reputation, the robbers of inferior degree."—*Spain in* 1830, vol. i., p. 2.

A volume might be filled with similar testimony,

showing the great insecurity of person and property in various parts of this unhappy country. Even "a woman who dares prosecute the murderer of her husband speedily receives a private intimation that effectually silences her; and it has not been uncommon for money to be put into the hands of an escrivano* previous to the commission of a murder, in order to insure the services and protection of a person so necessary to one who meditates crime."

Spain abounds in poverty. Ignorance conduces to crime, which, as we have seen, is at once a cause and an effect of poverty. In view of what has already been said of the ignorance and immorality of the Spaniards, one would readily enough infer that poverty exists among them to a deplorable extent, and it is even so. In this country "every thing, indeed, appears to have conspired to paralyze industry, and to render of no avail the natural fertility of the soil. The havoc of war; the plunder committed by organized and powerful bodies of robbers; the rapacity of government and of its army of officers; the exclusion of foreign goods, and the consequent shutting up of the foreign market; the ignorance of the people as to the best modes of agriculture; and, last of all, the want of capital—all these

* The *escrivanos*, who figure so largely in Spain, are the representatives of the lowest class of attorneys. Nothing can be done without them, and they are not unfrequently almost the sole authority in a place capable of reading and writing. Notwithstanding the miserable state of the rural districts, they contrive to make money, and many of them rise from this humble office to much higher places in the state. Their wretched appointments are, consequently, objects of competition. I witnessed the execution of one at Seville by accidentally entering the Plaza, where the Capuchins were bawling out the last words for his repetition, announcing to the crowd that they had done their duty, and he died in the true faith. He had been superseded in some village in the vicinity, and assassinated his rival.—*Cook's Sketches in Spain*, vol. i., p. 197.

combine to produce squalid poverty in a land which ought to," and, with a good system of popular education, most assuredly would, "ABOUND IN WEALTH."

Scotland and Spain have been referred to, not to bring out a few facts in history merely, but to illustrate an important truth. Where a good system of popular education is well administered in a country, and, as a consequence, intelligence, industry, and morality become universal among its citizens, they will eventually become a wealthy, and a highly-prosperous and happy community, even though they derive their subsistence from a naturally unfruitful soil; but, on the contrary, where popular education is neglected in a commonwealth, and its future citizens, as a consequence, grow up in ignorance, idleness, and vice, squalid poverty and flagrant crime will become prevalent throughout a wretched and degenerate community, that is scarcely able to gain a mere subsistence from a naturally productive soil.

In further confirmation of the truth of the proposition that education diminishes crime, I will introduce the following statistics, gleaned from various official documents respecting prisons. According to returns to the British Parliament, the commitments for crimes in an average of nine years in proportion to population are as follows: In Manchester, the most infidel city in the nation, 1 in 140; in London, 1 in 800; in all Ireland, 1 in 1600; and in Scotland, celebrated for learning and religion, 1 in 20,000!

The Rev. Dr. Forde, for many years the Ordinate of Newgate, London, represents *ignorance* as the first great cause, and *idleness* as the second, of all the crimes committed by the inmates of that celebrated prison. Sir Richard Phillips, sheriff of London, says that, on the memorial addressed to the sheriffs by 152 criminals in the same institution, 25 only signed their names in a fair hand, 26 in an illegible scrawl, and that 101, two thirds of the entire number, were *marksmen*, signing with a cross. Few of the prisoners could read with facility; more than half of them could not read at all; the most of them thought books were useless, and were totally ignorant of the nature, object, and end of religion.

The Rev. Mr. Clay, chaplain to the House of Correction in Lancashire, represents that out of 1129 persons committed, 554 could not read; 222 were barely capable of reading; 38 only could read well; and only 8 or 1 in 141, could read and write well. One half of the 1129 prisoners were quite ignorant of the simplest truths; 37 of these, 1 in 20 of the entire number, were occasional readers of the Bible; and only *one* out of this large number was familiar with the Holy Scriptures and conversant with the principles of religion. Among the 516 represented as entirely ignorant, 125 were incapable of repeating the Lord's Prayer.

In the New York State Prisons, as examined a few years ago, more than three fourths of the convicts had either received no education or a very imperfect one. Out of 842 at Sing Sing, 289 could not read or write, and only 42—less than 1 in 20—had received a good common school education. Auburn prison presents similar statistics. Out of 228 prisoners, only 59 could read, write, and cipher, and 60 could do neither.

The chaplain of the Ohio penitentiary remarks that not only in the prison of that state, but in others, depraved appetites and corrupt habits, which have led to the commission of crime, are usually found with the ignorant, uninformed, and duller part of mankind. Of 276 at one time in that institution, nearly all were below mediocrity, and 175 are represented as grossly ignorant, and, in point of education, scarcely capable of transacting the ordinary business of life.

The preceding, it is believed, is no more than a fair specimen of the criminal statistics of this country and of the civilized world. I will conclude this dark catalogue by introducing a statement in relation to education and crime in a state which, according to the last general census, contained fewer persons in proportion to the whole population who were unable to read and write than any other state in the Union. From this statement it appears that as a people become more generally intelligent and moral, a greater proportion of their criminals will be found among the ignorant and neglected classes.

The chaplain of the Connecticut State Prison states that, out of 190 prisoners, not one was liberally educated, or a member of either of the learned professions. Of the whole number, 109 were natives of Connecticut; and of these, many of them could not understand the plainest sentences which they read, and their moral culture had been more neglected than their intellectual. From the investigations of this officer, it appears that out of every 100 prisoners only two could be found who could read, write, and were temperate, and only four who could read, write, and followed any regular trade.

It is evident, then, that while education increases the wealth and general happiness of a community, the want of it will reduce a people to a state of poverty and wretchedness; or, to repeat a sentiment placed at the head of this article, the different countries of the world, if arranged according to the state of education in them, will be found to be arranged also according to wealth, morals, and general happiness; at the same time, the condition of the people, and the extent of crime and violence among them, follow a like order.

I might appropriately add under this head that a proper attention to the subject of education would greatly diminish the number of *fatal accidents;* that it would save *many lives*, prevent much of *idiocy* and *insanity*, and a multitude of evils that ordinarily result from ignorance of the organic laws.

Fatal Accidents.—He who understands the laws of motion knows that a man jumping from a carriage at speed is in great danger of falling after his feet reach the ground, for his body has the same forward velocity as if he had been running with the speed of the carriage, and unless he continues to advance his feet as in running to support his advancing body, he must as certainly be dashed to the ground as a runner whose feet are suddenly arrested. If, then, there is danger in leaping from a carriage in motion, how much greater is the hazard in jumping from a rail-road car under full headway. And yet many do this, jumping off sidewise, so that it is impossible to advance; and some even jump in the opposite direction from the motion of the car, which increases the already imminent hazard. From statistics recently collected, it appears that the great majority of accidents on the rail-roads of this country have happened in this way, a want of practical conformity to this one law of motion being the prevailing cause of fatality along these thoroughfares. This is but a specimen of the fatal accidents that are continually occurring in the every-day transactions of life, which might be prevented as easily as this by the practical application of a single scientific principle.

Loss of Life.—In a single hospital at Dublin, during four years, 2944 children out of 7650, about 40 in 100, died within a fortnight after their birth. Dr. Clark the attending physician, suspecting a want of pure air to be the cause, provided for the ventilation of all the apartments; and by means of pipes six inches in diameter, introduced into every room a current of fresh pure air, which is essential to vitality, and allowed that which was vitiated by respiration to escape. The consequence was, that during the three succeeding years only 165 out of 4243 children died within the first two weeks, or less than 4 in 100. As there was no other known cause of improvement in the health of these children, it may be justly inferred that, during the four years first mentioned, 2650 children, nine tenths of the whole number, had perished for want of pure air.

It has been estimated that about 40 in every 100 of the deaths annually occurring in Great Britain and the United States are of children under five years of age. To avoid every possibility of exaggeration, we will place the number in this country at 30 in 100. At this rate we lose about 200,000 children under five years of age every year. Now, if nine tenths of the mortality among infants in the Dublin Hospital were caused by breathing bad air, we may reasonably infer that at least one half of the deaths in the United States of children under the age of five years proceed from the same fatal cause. And those who have noticed what pains are taken by excessively careful mothers* and ignorant nurses to exclude from the lungs of infants the "free, pure, unadulterated air of heaven," and, by means of many thicknesses of enveloping shawls and blankets, require them to re-respire portions at least of their own breath, until it becomes a virulent and deadly poison,

* It would seem that the great majority of "educated mothers" do not realize the necessity of supplying pure air to the new-born child. Before birth, the blood of the fetus is purified in the maternal lungs; after birth, in the lungs of the child, if at all; and for this purpose pure air is necessary.

will think with me that this is a low estimate, and wonder that the swaddling-cloths of more infants do not become their winding-sheets. But, even according to this estimate, 100,000 children in the United States annually fall victims to the ignorance of their fond mothers. Many thousands more are subsequently sacrificed in consequence of occupying small and unventilated bed-rooms and school-rooms, which, by a practical knowledge of the principles of physiology, might be saved. Perhaps as many more become sufferers for life from the same cause, for a thousand forms of disease, as it manifests itself in every stage of life, either owe their existence or their severity to breathing bad air. These, then, who drag out a miserable existence in consequence of this cruel treatment, are to be more pitied than those who fall its ready victims.

If so many thousand deaths occur annually in the United States from this one cause, in addition to the vast amount of misery which is entailed upon the wretched survivors, how many hundred thousand precious lives might be saved, and what untold wretchedness might be prevented, by a strict conformity to those physiological laws of our being which might and should be generally taught in the common schools of the land

Education and Idiocy.*—The education of idiots has hitherto been regarded as paradoxical, and still is by the mass of mankind; but that it is possible to improve the condition of this most wretched and helpless class of persons none need longer doubt. The experiment has succeeded in both Europe and America.

* The statements under this head are drawn from Dr. Howe's Report on Idiocy, made in February last, and communicated by the governor to the Legislature of the Commonwealth of Massachusetts. The author visited the Institution in South Boston during the past summer, and derived much information on the subject from personal observation and inquiry.

Massachusetts has the honor of taking the lead in this country; and it is meet that it should be so, for she has long, like a wise parent, been accustomed to care for all her children. She had most readily and generously seconded the efforts of humane men for the relief of the insane, the deaf mutes, and the blind, and made provision for their care and instruction. She extended her maternal love to the *bodies* of those who were in hopeless idiocy, but as for *minds*, they seemed to have none; they were, therefore, kept out of sight of the public as much as possible until the year 1846, when a board of commissioners were appointed "to inquire into the condition of the idiots of the commonwealth, to ascertain their number, and whether any thing can be done in their behalf."

In their report the commissioners say that, "by diligent and careful inquiries in nearly one hundred towns in different parts of the state, we have ascertained the existence and examined the condition of *five hundred and seventy-five* human beings who are condemned to hopeless idiocy, who are considered and treated as idiots by their neighbors, and left to their own brutishness. They are also idiotic in a legal sense; that is, they are regarded as incapable of entering into contracts, and are irresponsible for their actions."

The commissioners conclude that, "if the other parts of the state contain the same proportion of idiots to their whole population, the total number in the commonwealth is between *fourteen and fifteen hundred!*" Now if we make the same estimate in proportion to the entire population, it will appear that in the United States there are upward of *thirty-five thousand* persons in the most wretched and helpless condition of idiocy.

In view of the great number of idiots in the commonwealth, the commissioners say, "it appeared to us certain that the existence of so many idiots in every gen eration must be the consequence of some violation of the *natural laws;* that where there was so much suffering there must have been sin. We resolved, therefore, to seek for the *sources* of the evil, as well as to gauge the depth and extent of the misery."

Some of the causes of idiocy are set forth in the report, two of which are as follows: first, *the low condition of the physical organization* of one or both parents, induced often by *intemperance;* second, *the intermarriage of relatives.*

The report states that out of 420 cases of congenital idiocy which were examined, some information was gained respecting the condition of the progenitors of 359. Now in all these cases, save only four, it was found that one or the other, or both, of the immediate progenitors of the unfortunate sufferer had in some way widely departed from the normal condition of health, and violated the natural laws. That is to say, one or the other, or both of them, had been very unhealthy or scrofulous; or hereditarily predisposed to affections of the brain, causing occasional insanity; or had intermarried with blood relatives; or had been intemperate; or had been guilty of sensual excesses which impair the constitution.*

INTEMPERANCE AND IDIOCY.—Out of the three hundred

* The subject of hereditary transmission of diseased tendency is of vast importance, but it is a difficult one to treat, because a squeamish delicacy makes people avoid it; but if ever the race is to be relieved of a tithe of the bodily ills which flesh is now heir to, it must be by a clear understanding of, and a willing obedience to, the law which makes the parents the blessing or the curse of the children; the givers of strength, and vigor, and beauty, or the dispensers of debility, and disease, and deformity. It is by the lever of enlightened parental love, more than by any other power, that mankind is to be raised to the highest attainable point of bodily perfection.—DR. S. G. HOWE.

and fifty-nine idiots, the condition of whose progenitors was ascertained, *ninety-nine were the children of drunkards.* But this does not tell the whole story by any means. By drunkard is meant a person who is a notorious and habitual sot. Many persons who are habitually intemperate do not get this name *even now;* much less would they have done so twenty-five or thirty years ago. By a pretty careful inquiry, with an especial view of ascertaining the number of idiots of the lowest class whose parents were known to be *temperate* persons, it is found that *not one quarter* can be so considered.

From the pretty uniform action of a physiological law, which is now becoming well understood, it appears that idiots, fools, and simpletons, either in the first or second generation, are common among the progeny of intemperate persons, and may be considered as an effect of the *habitual* use of alcohol, even in moderate quantities. If, moreover, one considers how many children of intemperate parents there are who, without being idiots, are deficient in bodily and mental energy, and predisposed by their very organization to have cravings for alcoholic stimulants, it will be seen what an immense burden the drinkers of one generation throw upon the succeeding one.

Idiocy and the Marriage of Relatives.—Out of the three hundred and fifty-nine cases of congenital idiocy already referred to, in which the parentage was ascertained, "seventeen were *known* to be the children of parents nearly related by blood; but, as many of these cases were adults, it was impossible to ascertain, in some cases, whether their parents, who were dead, were related or not before marriage. From some collateral evidence, we conclude that at least three more cases should be added to the seventeen. This would show that more than one twentieth of the idiots examined are offspring of the marriage of relations. Now, as marriages between near relations are by no means in the ratio of one to twenty, nor even, perhaps, as one to a thousand to the marriages between persons not related, it follows that the proportion of idiotic progeny is vastly greater in the former than in the latter case. Then it should be considered that idiocy is only *one* form in which Nature manifests that she has been offended by such intermarriages. It is probable that blindness, deafness, imbecility, and other infirmities, are more likely to be the lot of the children of parents related by blood than of others. The probability, therefore, of unhealthy or infirm issue from such marriages becomes fearfully great, and the existence of the law against them is made out as clearly as though it were written on tables of stone.

"The statistics of the seventeen families, the heads of which, being blood relatives, intermarried, tells a fearful tale. Most of the parents were intemperate or scrofulous; some were both the one and the other; of course, there were other causes to increase chances of infirm offspring besides that of the intermarriage. There were born unto them ninety-five children, of whom forty-four were idiotic, twelve others were scrofulous and puny, one was deaf, and one was a dwarf! In some cases, all the children were either idiotic, or very scrofulous and puny. In one family of eight children, five were idiotic."

Condition of Idiots.—From what has been said of the character of parents to whom are born the greatest proportion of this most wretched and helpless class of persons, their condition and treatment might be inferred. To rear healthy children properly, a knowledge of the principles of physiology and mental science is essentially necessary. This knowledge is still more important in the treatment of idiots. Dr. Howe is of the opinion that it requires a rarer and higher kind of talent to teach an idiot than a youth of superior talent. When the time comes that schools for idiots are established all over the country, he thinks "it will be found more difficult to get good teachers for them than to get good professors for our colleges."

After excepting five or six alms-houses in which the idiots are treated both kindly and wisely, the commissioners say, "the general condition of those at the public charge is most deplorable. They are filthy, gluttonous, lazy, and given up to abominations of various kinds. They not only do not improve, but they sink deeper and deeper into bodily depravity and mental degradation. Bad, however, as is the condition of the idiots who are at public charge, and gross as is the ignorance of those who take the charge of them about their real wants and capabilities, we are constrained to say that the condition of those in private houses is, generally speaking, still worse, and the ignorance of the relatives and friends who support them is still more profound."

This is not to be wondered at when we consider that idiots are generally born of a very poor stock—of persons who are subject to some disorders of the brain, or who are themselves scrofulous and puny to the last degree. Such persons are, generally, very feeble in intellect, poor in purse, and intemperate in habits. A great many of them are hardly able to take care of themselves. They are unfit to teach or train common children; how much less to take the charge of idiots, whose education is the most difficult of all!

The commissioners ascertained, mainly by personal observation, the condition of three hundred and fifty-five idiotic persons who are not town or state paupers.

Of these there may be, at the most, five who are treated very judiciously; who are taught by wise and discreet persons, and whose faculties and capabilities are developed to their fullest extent but the remaining three hundred and fifty are generally "in a most deplorable condition as it respects their bodily, mental, and moral treatment."*

The commissioners come to the unquestionable conclusion in their report that "nothing can afford a stronger argument in favor of an institution for the proper training and teaching of idiots, and the dissemination of information upon the subject, than the striking difference manifested in the condition of the few children who are properly cared for and judiciously treated, and those who are neglected or abused. There are cases in our community of youths who are idiotic from birth, but who, under proper care and training, have become cleanly in person, quiet in deportment, industrious in habits, and who would almost pass in society for persons of common intelligence; and yet their natural capacity was no greater than that of others, who, from ignorance or neglect of their parents, have be-

* One would hardly be credited if he should put down half the instances of gross ignorance manifested by parents in this enlightened community [the State of Massachusetts] in the treatment of idiotic children. Sometimes they find that the children seem to comprehend what they hear, but soon forget it; hence they conclude that the brain is soft, and can not retain impressions, and then they cover the head with cold poultices of oak-bark in order to tan or harden the fibers. Others, finding that it is exceedingly difficult to make any impression upon the mind, conclude that the brain is too hard, and they torture the poor child with hot and *softening* poultices of bread and milk; or they plaster tar over the whole skull, and keep it on for a long time. *These are innocent applications compared with some, which doubtless render weak-minded children perfectly idiotic.*—DR. S. G. HOWE.

What a striking illustration have we here of the necessity of diffusing correct physiological information more widely among the masses than has yet been done even in enlightened Massachusetts!

come filthy, gluttonous, lazy, vicious, depraved, and are rapidly sinking into driveling idiocy. This fact alone should be enough to encourage the state to take measures at once for the establishment of a school or institution for teaching or training idiots, if it were but a matter of experiment."

Massachusetts is the only state in the Union that as yet has attempted to do any thing for the education and training of this hitherto neglected class of persons. The result of the first year's experiment has been most gratifying and encouraging. Of the whole number received, there was not one who was in a situation where any great improvement in his condition was probable, or hardly possible; they were growing worse in habits, and more confirmed in their idiocy. But the process of deterioration in the pupils has been entirely stopped, and that of improvement has commenced; and though a year is a very short time in the instruction of such persons, yet its effects are manifest in all of them. They have improved in personal appearance and habits, in general health, in vigor, and in activity of body. Some of them can control their appetites in a considerable degree; they sit at the table with their teachers, and feed themselves decently. Almost all of them have improved in the understanding and the use of speech. Some of them have made considerable progress in the knowledge of language; they can select words printed on slips of paper, and a few can read simple sentences. But, what is most important, THEY HAVE MADE A START FORWARD.

"There is ground for confidence that the reasonable hopes of the friends of the experiment will be satisfied. All that they promised has been accomplished, so far as was possible in the period of a year. It has been demonstrated that idiots are CAPABLE OF IMPROVEMENT.

and that they can be raised from a state of *low degradation* to a HIGHER CONDITION. How far they can be elevated, and to what extent they may be educated, can only be shown by the experience of the future. The result of the past year's trial, however, gives confidence that each succeeding year will show even more progress than any preceding one."

EDUCATION AND INSANITY.—It is well established that a defective and faulty education through the period of infancy and childhood is one of the most prolific causes of insanity. Such an education, or rather miseducation, causes a predisposition in many, and excites one where it already exists, which ultimately renders the animal propensities of our nature uncontrollable. Appetites indulged and perverted, passions unrestrained, propensities rendered vigorous by indulgence, and subjected to no salutary restraint, bring persons into a condition in which both moral and physical causes easily operate to produce insanity, if they do not produce it themselves.

We must look to well-directed systems of popular education, having for their object physical improvement, no less than mental and moral culture, to relieve us from many of the evils which "flesh is heir to," and nothing can so effectually secure us from this most formidable disease (as well as from others not less appalling) as that system of instruction which teaches us how to preserve the normal condition of the body and the mind; to fortify the one against the catalogue of physical causes which every where assail us, and to elevate the other above the influence of the trials and disappointments of life, so that the host of moral causes which affect the brain, through the medium of the mind, shall be inoperative and harmless.

Those first principles of physical education which

teach us how to avoid disease are all-important to all liable to insanity from hereditary predisposition. The physical health must be attended to, and the training of the faculties of the mind be such as to counteract the over-active propensities of our nature—correcting the bias of the mind to wrong currents and to too great activity by bringing into action the antagonizing powers, and thus giving a sound body and a well-balanced mind. Neglect of this early training entails evils upon the young which are felt in all after life.

These positions are stated and amplified in the able reports of Dr. S. B. Woodward, superintendent of the State Lunatic Asylum, Worcester, Mass., to which the reader is referred. They are also corroborated by persons who have had the care of the insane in other institutions. In the eighteenth annual report of the physician and superintendent of the Connecticut Retreat for the Insane, Dr. Brigham says, "a knowledge of the nature of the disease would frequently lead to its prevention. Insanity, in most cases, arises from undue excitement and labor of the brain; for even if a predisposition to it is inherited, an exciting cause is essential to its development. Hence every thing likely to cause great excitement of the brain, especially in early life, should be avoided.

"The records of cases at this institution and my own observation justify me in saying that the neglect of moral discipline, the too great indulgence of the passions and emotions in early life, together with the excessive and premature exercise of the mental powers, are among the most frequent causes that predispose to insanity. But these causes are in no other way operative in producing insanity than by unduly exciting the brain. By neglect of moral discipline, a character is formed subject to violent passions, and to extreme emotions and anxiety from the unavoidable evils and disappointments of life, and thus the brain, by being often and violently agitated, becomes diseased; and by too early exercising and prematurely developing the mental powers, this organ is rendered more susceptible and liable to disease.

"I am confident there is too much mental labor imposed upon youth at our schools and colleges. There have been several admissions of young ladies at this institution direct from boarding-schools, and of young men from college, where they had studied excessively. Should such intense exertion of the mind in youth not lead to insanity or immediate disease, it predisposes to dyspepsy, hysteria, hypochondriasis, and affections allied to insanity, and which are often its precursors. Should that portion of the community who now act most wisely in obtaining a knowledge of the functions of the digestive organs, and in carefully guarding them from undue excitation, be equally regardful of the brain, they would do a very great service to society, and, in my opinion, do much toward arresting the alarming increase of insanity, and all disorders of the nervous system."*

* In the education of many, very many, I fear, the same mistake is made as in the case of Lord Dudley, thus described in a late number of the London Quarterly Review: "The irritable susceptibility of the brain was stimulated at the expense of bodily power and health. His foolish tutors took a pride in his precocious progress, which they ought to have kept back. They watered the forced plant with the blood of life; they encouraged the violation of Nature's laws, which are not to be broken in vain; they infringed the condition of conjoint moral and physical existence; they imprisoned him in a vicious circle, where the overworked brain injured the stomach, which reacted to the injury of the brain. They watched the slightest deviation from the rules of logic, and neglected those of dietetics, to which the former are a farce. They thought of no exercises but Latin; they gave him a Gradus instead of a cricket-bat, until his mind became too keen for its mortal coil, and the foundation was laid for ill health, derangement of stomach, moral

EDUCATION INCREASES HUMAN HAPPINESS.

What is a man
If his chief good and market of his time
Be but to sleep and feed? a beast, no more.
Sure He that made us with such large discourse,
Looking before and after, gave us not
That capability and godlike reason
To rust in us unused.—SHAKSPEARE.

All the happiness of man is derived from discovering, applying, or obeying the laws of his Creator; and all his misery is the result of ignorance or disobedience.—DR. WAYLAND.

If the doctrines taught and the sentiments inculcated in the preceding chapters of this work, but more especially in the preceding sections of this chapter, are true; if it is established that education dissipates the evils of ignorance; that it increases the productiveness of labor; that it diminishes pauperism and crime—if all this is true, it may seem a work of supererogation to attempt the establishment of the proposition that education increases human happiness. I admit this seeming impropriety; for that the proposition is true may be legitimately inferred from what has gone before. But I wish to amplify and extend this thought, and to show that education has, if possible, still higher claims upon our attention than have yet been presented; that it not only has the power of removing physical and moral evils, and of multiplying and augmenting personal and social enjoyments, but that, when rightly understood, it constitutes our chief good; that to it, and to it only, we may safely look for man's highest and enduring joys, and for the permanent elevation of the race.

MAN IN IGNORANCE.—That we may be the better pre-

pusillanimity, irresolution, lowness of spirits, and all the Protean miseries of nervous disorders, by which his after life was haunted, and which are sadly depicted in almost every letter before us."

pared to appreciate the advantages of education, and its usefulness as a means of increasing human happiness, let us consider the state and the enjoyments of the man whose mind is shrouded in ignorance. He grows up to manhood like a vegetable, or like one of the lower animals that are fed and nourished for the slaughter He exerts his physical powers because such exertion is necessary for his subsistence. Were it otherwise, we should most frequently find him dozing over the fire with a gaze as dull and stupid as his ox, regardless of every thing but the gratification of his appetites. He has, perhaps, been taught the art of reading, but has never applied it to the acquisition of knowledge. His views are chiefly confined to the objects immediately around him, and to the daily avocations in which he is employed. His knowledge of society is circumscribed within the limits of his neighborhood, and his views of the world are confined within the range of the country in which he resides, or of the blue hills which skirt his horizon.

Of the aspect of the globe in other countries, of the various tribes with which these are peopled, of the seas and rivers, continents and islands, which diversify the landscape of the earth, of the numerous orders of animated beings which people the ocean, the atmosphere, and the land, of the revolutions of nations, and the events which have taken place in the history of the world, he has almost as little conception as have the animals which range the forest.

In regard to the boundless regions that lie beyond him in the firmament, and the bodies that roll there in magnificent grandeur, he has the most confused and inaccurate ideas; indeed, he seldom troubles himself with inquiries in relation to such subjects. Whether the stars are great or small, whether they are near us or at a distance, and whether they move or stand still, are to him matters of trivial importance. If the sun gives him light by day and the moon by night, and the clouds distil their watery treasures upon his parched fields, he is contented, and leaves all such inquiries and investigations to those who have leisure and inclination to engage in them. He views the canopy of heaven as merely a ceiling to our earthly habitation, and the starry orbs as only so many luminous tapers to diversify its aspect, and to afford a glimmering light to the benighted traveler.

Such a person has no idea of the manner in which the understanding may be enlightened and expanded by education; he has no relish for intellectual pursuits, and no conception of the pleasures they afford; and he sets no value on knowledge but in so far as it may increase his riches and his sensual gratifications. He has no desire for making improvements in his trade or domestic arrangements, and gives no countenance to those useful inventions and public improvements which are devised by others. He sets himself against every innovation, whether religious, political, mechanical, or agricultural, and is determined to abide by the "good old customs" of his forefathers, even though they compel him to carry his grist to mill in one end of a bag, with a stone in the other to balance it. Were it dependent upon him, the moral world would stand still, as the material world was supposed to in former times; all useful inventions would cease; existing evils would never be remedied; ignorance and superstition would universally prevail; the human mind would be arrested in its progress to perfection, and man would never arrive at the true dignity of his intellectual nature.

It is evident that such an individual—and the world contains thousands and millions of such characters—

can never have his mind elevated to those sublime objects and contemplations which enrapture the man of science, nor feel those pure and exquisite pleasures which cultivated minds so frequently experience; nor can he form those lofty and expansive conceptions of the Deity which the grandeur and magnificence of his works are calculated to inspire. He is left as a prey to all those foolish notions and vain alarms which are engendered by ignorance and superstition; and he swallows, without the least hesitation, all the absurdities and childish tales respecting witches, hobgoblins, specters, and apparitions, which have been handed down to him by his forefathers.

While the ignorant man thus gorges his mind with fooleries and absurdities, he spurns at the discoveries of science as impositions on the credulity of mankind, and contrary to reason and common sense. That the sun is a million of times larger than the earth; that light flies from his body at the rate of a hundred thousand miles in the hundredth part of a second; and that the earth is whirling round its axis from day to day with a velocity of a thousand miles every hour, are regarded by him as notions far more improbable and extravagant than the story of the "Wonderful Lamp," and all the other tales of the "Arabian Night's Entertainments." In his hours of leisure from his daily avocations, his thoughts either run wild among the most groveling objects, or sink into sensuality and inanity; and solitude and retirement present no charms to his vacant mind.

While human beings are thus immersed in ignorance, destitute of rational ideas and of a solid substratum of thought, they can never experience those pleasures and enjoyments which flow from the exercise of the understanding, and which correspond to the dignity of a rational and immortal nature.

An enlightened Mind.—On the other hand, the man whose mind is irradiated with the light of substantial science has views, and feelings, and exquisite enjoyments to which the former is an entire stranger. In consequence of the numerous and multifarious ideas he has acquired, he is introduced, as it were, into a new world, where he is entertained with scenes, objects, and movements, of which the mind enveloped in ignorance can form no conception. He can trace back the stream of time to its commencement, and, gliding along its downward course, can survey the most memorable events which have happened in every part of its progress, from the primeval ages to the present day; the rise of empires, the fall of kings, the revolutions of nations, the battles of warriors, and the important events which have followed in their train; the progress of civilization, and of the arts and sciences; the judgments which have been inflicted on wicked nations, the dawnings of Divine mercy toward our fallen race, the manifestation of the Son of God in our nature, the physical changes and revolutions which have taken place in the constitution of our globe; in short, the whole of the leading events in the chain of divine dispensation, from the beginning of the world to the period in which we live.

With his mental eye the enlightened man can survey the terraqueous globe in all its variety of aspects; he can contemplate the continents, islands, and oceans which surround its exterior; the numerous rivers by which it is indented; the lofty ranges of mountains which diversify its surface; its winding caverns; its forests, lakes, and sandy deserts; its whirlpools, boiling springs, and glaciers; its sulphurous mountains, bituminous lakes, and the states and empires into which it is distributed; the tides and currents of the ocean;

the icebergs of the polar regions, and the verdant scenes of the torrid zone.

Sitting at his fireside during the blasts of winter, the enlightened man can survey the numerous tribes of mankind scattered over the various climates of the earth, and entertain himself with views of their manners, customs, religion, laws, trade, manufactures, marriage ceremonies, civil and ecclesiastical governments, arts, sciences, cities, towns, and villages, and the animals peculiar to every region. In his rural walks he can not only appreciate the beneficence of Nature, and the beauties and harmonies of the vegetable kingdom in their exterior aspect, but he can also penetrate into the hidden processes which are going on in the roots, trunks, and leaves of plants and flowers, and contemplate the numerous vessels through which the sap is flowing from their roots through the trunks and branches; the millions of pores through which their odoriferous effluvia exhale; their fine and delicate texture; their microscopical beauties; their orders, genera, and species, and their uses in the economy of nature.

Even when shrouded in darkness and in solitude, where other minds could find no enjoyment, the man of knowledge can entertain himself with the most sublime contemplations. He can trace the huge earth we inhabit flying through the depths of space, carrying along with it its vast population, at the rate of sixty thousand miles every hour, and, by the inclination of its axis, bringing about the alternate succession of summer and winter, of seed-time and harvest. By the aid of his telescope he can transport himself toward the moon, and survey the circular plains, the deep caverns, the conical hills, the lofty peaks, and the rugged and romantic mountain scenery which diversify the surface of this orb of night.

By the help of the same instrument he can range through the planetary system, wing his way through the regions of space along with the swiftest orbs, and trace many of the physical aspects and revolutions which have a relation to distant worlds. He can transport himself to the planet Saturn, and behold a stupendous ring six hundred thousand miles in circumference, revolving in majestic grandeur every ten hours around a globe nine hundred times larger than the earth, while seven moons larger than ours, along with an innumerable host of stars, display their radiance to adorn the firmament of that magnificent world. He can wing his flight through the still more distant regions of the universe, leaving the sun and all his planets behind him, till they appear like a scarcely discernible speck in creation, and contemplate thousands and millions of stars and starry systems beyond the range of the unassisted eye, and wander among the suns and worlds dispersed throughout the boundless dimensions of space.

In his imagination he can fill up those blanks which astronomy has never directly explored, and conceive thousands of systems and ten thousands of worlds beyond all that is visible by the optic tube, stretching out to infinity on every hand, peopled with intelligences of various orders, and all under the superintendence and government of the "King Eternal, Immortal, and Invisible," whose power is omnipotent, and the limit of his dominions past finding out.

It is evident that a mind capable of such excursions and contemplations as I have now supposed must experience enjoyments infinitely superior to those of the individual whose soul is enveloped in intellectual darkness. If substantial happiness is chiefly situated in the mind; if it depends on the multiplicity of objects which lie within the range of its contemplation; if it is augmented by the view of scenes of beauty and sublimity, and displays of infinite intelligence and power; if it is connected with tranquillity of mind, which generally accompanies intellectual pursuits, and the subjugation of the pleasures of sense to the dictates of reason, the enlightened mind must enjoy gratifications as far superior to those of the ignorant as man is superior in station and capacity to the worms of the dust.

In order to illustrate this topic a little further, I shall select a few facts and deductions in relation to science, which demonstrate the interesting nature and delightful tendency of scientific pursuits.

There are several recorded instances of the powerful effect which the study of astronomy has produced upon the human mind. Dr. Rittenhouse, of Pennsylvania, after he had calculated the transit of Venus, which was to happen June 3d, 1769, was appointed, at Philadelphia, with others, to repair to the township of Norriston, and there to observe this planet until its passage over the sun's disc should verify the correctness of his calculations. This occurrence had never been witnessed but twice before by an inhabitant of our earth, and was never to be again seen by any person then living. A phenomenon so rare, and so important in its bearings upon astronomical science, was, indeed, well calculated to agitate the soul of one so alive as he was to the great truths of nature. The day arrived, and there was no cloud on the horizon. The observers, in silence and trembling anxiety, awaited for the predicted moment of observation to arrive. It came, and in the instant of contact, an emotion of joy so powerful was excited in the bosom of Dr. Rittenhouse that he fainted.

Sir Isaac Newton, after he had advanced so far in

his mathematical proof of one of his great astronomical doctrines as to see that the result was to be triumphant, was so affected in view of the momentous truth he was about to demonstrate that he was unable to proceed, and begged one of his companions in study to relieve him, and carry out the calculation. These are striking illustrations, and the effect is perhaps heightened from their connection with a most sublime science, all of whose conclusions stand in open contradiction with those of superficial and vulgar observation.

But the discovery and contemplation of truths in philosophy, chemistry, and the mathematics have, in numerous instances, awakened kindred emotions. The enlightened man sees in every thing he beholds upon the surface of the earth, whether animal or vegetable, and in the very elements themselves, no less than when contemplating the wonders of astronomy, instances innumerable illustrative of the wisdom and beneficence of the Architect, all of which has a direct tendency to increase his happiness. In the invisible atmosphere which surrounds him, where other minds discern nothing but an immense blank, he beholds an assemblage of wonders, and a striking scene of divine wisdom and omnipotence. He views this invisible agent not only as a *material*, but as a *compound* substance, composed of two opposite principles, the one the source of flame and animal life, and the other destructive to both. He perceives the atmosphere as the agent under the Almighty which produces the germination and growth of plants, and all the beauties of the vegetable creation; which preserves water in a liquid state, supports fire and flame, and produces animal heat; which sustains the clouds, and gives buoyancy to the feathered tribes; which is the cause of winds, the vehicle of smells, the medium of sounds, the source of all the pleasures we derive from the harmonies of music, the cause of the universal light and splendor which is diffused around us, and of the advantages we derive from the morning and evening twilight. He contemplates it as the prime mover in a variety of machines, as impelling ships across the ocean, raising balloons to the region of the clouds, blowing our furnaces, raising water from the deepest pits, extinguishing fires, and performing a thousand other beneficent agencies, without which our globe would cease to be habitable. No one can doubt that all these views and contemplations have a direct tendency to enlarge the capacity of the mind, to stimulate its faculties, and to produce rational enjoyment.

But there is another view of this subject which is perhaps still more impressive. The atmosphere, it has been stated, is a compound substance. A knowledge of its elementary principles, which chemistry teaches, introduces its possessor to a new world of happiness. The adaptation of air to respiration, and the influence of a change in the nature or proportion of its elements upon health and longevity, have already been considered.* We have seen that carbonic acid, the vitiating product of respiration, although immediately fatal to animals, constitutes the very life of vegetation; that in the growth of plants the vitiated air is purified and fitted again for the sustenance of animal life; and that, by a beneficent provision of the Creator, animals and vegetables are thus perpetually interchanging kindly offices. It will suffice for our present purpose simply to remind the reader that the atmosphere is composed of the two gases, oxygen and nitrogen, united in the ratio of one to four by volume. Oxygen is a supporter of combustion, nitrogen is not. Increase the proportion of oxygen in the air, and the same substances burn

* See Chapter IV., especially from the 89th page to the 105th.

with increased brilliancy; but diminish the proportion gradually, and they will burn more and more dimly until they become extinct. Iron and steel, as well as wood and the ordinary combustibles, will burn with great brilliancy in pure oxygen.

Water, I may add, is composed of the two gases, oxygen and hydrogen. The former, as we have seen, is a supporter of combustion, and the latter is one of the most combustible substances known. These two gases are nearly two thousand times more voluminous than their equivalent of water, and, when ignited, they *combine with explosive energy.* If, then, the Creator were to decompose the atmosphere that surrounds the earth to the height of forty-five miles, and the water that rests upon its surface, either or both of them, the oxygen, being specifically heavier than the nitrogen or hydrogen, would settle immediately upon the earth, and, coming in contact with fires here and there, its whole surface would, in an instant of time, be enveloped in one general conflagration, and "the day of the Lord," spoken of in the Scriptures, "in which the heavens shall pass away with a great noise, and the elements shall melt with fervent heat, the earth also, and the things therein shall be burned up," would be speedily ushered in. He who understands the first principles of chemical science can not fail to perceive how readily (and in perfect accordance with laws well understood) such a general conflagration would take place were the great Architect simply to resolve these two elements—air and water—into their constituent parts. How full of meaning to such a one are the words of the Psalmist, *The heavens declare the glory of God, and the firmament showeth his handiwork.*

One more illustration must suffice. All fluids, except water, contract in volume as they become colder to the point of congelation. But the point of greatest density in water is about eight degrees above freezing. As the temperature of ALL fluids *increases* above this point, their volume increases. As the temperature of all fluids, with the single exception of WATER, *decreases*, the volume decreases down to the freezing point. Water increases in density as it becomes colder until it reaches the temperature of forty degrees—eight degrees above the freezing point—when it begins to expand. This only exception to the general law of fluids is of greater importance in the economy of nature than most persons are conscious of. As the cold season advances in the temperate and frigid zones, the water in our lakes and rivers is reduced to the temperature of forty degrees; but at this point, by a beneficent provision of an All-wise Providence, the upper substratum becomes specifically lighter, and is converted into a covering of ice, which, resting upon the water beneath, protects it from freezing. Moreover, when water is converted into ice, one hundred and forty degrees of heat are given out, a part of which, entering into the water below, retards the further formation of ice.*

* I may here add, that exactly the *reverse* is true in the *melting* of snow and ice. It requires as much heat to convert these solids into fluids, without at all increasing their temperature, as it does to raise the temperature of water from the freezing point, one hundred and forty degrees, or from thirty-two to one hundred and seventy-two degrees, as indicated by the thermometer. This principle is of vast importance to the world, and particularly to the inhabitants of cold countries, where the ground is covered with snow and ice a part or the whole of the year. The transition from the cold of winter to the heat of summer, in some of the northern climates, takes place within a few days. In these climates, also, there are vast accumulations of snow and ice, which, but for this principle, would be converted into water as soon as the temperature of the atmosphere becomes above thirty-two degrees, which would produce a flood sufficient to inundate and destroy the whole country. But the uniform action of this law renders the melting of snow gradual, and no such accident ensues.

If water, like other fluids, continued to increase in density to the freezing point, the cold air of winter would rob the water of our lakes and rivers of its heat, until the whole was reduced to the temperature of thirty-two degrees; when, but for the circumstance to which we have just alluded, it would be immediately converted into a solid mass of ice from top to bottom, causing instant death to every animal living in it. The lower strata of such a mass of ice would never again become liquefied.

This is a striking proof of the beneficence and design of the Creator in forming water with such an exception to the ordinary laws of nature, and a knowledge of it can hardly fail to exert a most salutary, elevating, and ennobling influence on the mind of its possessor. The field of human happiness, then, with the virtuous seems to enlarge in proportion as a knowledge of the works and laws of the beneficent Creator is extended There is little ground for doubt as to what is GOD'S WILL in relation to the universal education of the family of man, when he has connected with the exercise of mind in the study of his works superior enjoyments and heavenly aspirations.

The various propositions stated and elucidated in this chapter, we think, are as fully established as any moral truths need be, and, we doubt not, they commend themselves to the judgment and conscience of all who have carefully perused the preceding pages, if, indeed, they had not been duly considered and adopted before. If, then, a system of universal education, ju-

---

A similar law is observed in the conversion of *water* into *vapor*, which is of great use in enabling us to cool apartments by sprinkling floors or hanging up moistened cloths. The heat of even a whole city is in like manner greatly moderated by frequently sprinkling the streets. It is on this account that gentle showers in hot weather are so cooling and refreshing.

diciously administered, would dissipate the evils of ignorance, which are legion; if it would greatly increase the productiveness of labor; if it would diminish—not to say exterminate—pauperism and crime; if it would prevent the great majority of fatal accidents that are constantly occurring in every community; if it would save the lives of a hundred thousand children in the United States every year, and as many more puny survivors from dragging out a miserable existence in consequence of being the offspring of ignorant or vicious parents; if it would prevent so much of idiocy, and would humanize those who are born *idiots only*, but have hitherto been permitted, nay, doomed to *die* BRUTES; if it would prevent so much insanity, and would save to society and their family and friends, "clothed and in their right mind," multitudes of every generation who now dwell in mental darkness and gloom; if it would increase the sum total of human happiness in proportion to its excellence, and the number of persons who are brought under its benign influence and uplifting power; if it would do all this—and that this is its legitimate tendency there can be no doubt—it would seem that no enlightened community could be found in any country, and especially that there can be no state in this Union, that would not at once resolve upon maintaining a system of universal education by opening the doors of *improved free schools* to all her sons and daughters, and, if need be, employing agents, vigilant and active, "to go out into the highways and hedges, and compel them to come in." If this is not done, thousands and tens of thousands of every generation will continue to lead cheerless lives, and will go down to their graves like the brute that perisheth, without knowing that He who gave to man life has also, in his goodness, which knows no bounds, provided that in the proper exercise of his faculties man shall find an inexhaustible source of happiness.*

CHAPTER IX.

POLITICAL NECESSITY OF NATIONAL EDUCATION.

In proportion as the structure of a government gives force to public opinion, it is essential that public opinion should be enlightened.—WASHINGTON.

I do not hesitate to affirm not only that a knowledge of the true principles of government is important and useful to Americans, but that it is absolutely indispensable to carry on the government of their choice, and to transmit it to their posterity.—JUDGE STORY.

EVERY succeeding section of the last chapter went to show more and more clearly that, in proportion as the benign influences of a correct education are diffused among and enjoyed by the members of any community, will existing evils of every kind be diminished, and blessings be increased in number and degree. The subject of popular education, then, claims, and should receive, the sympathy and active support of every philanthropist and Christian, without regard to country or clime. We come now to consider a topic in which every patriot, and especially every true American, as such, must feel a lively interest.

Every citizen of our wide-spread country should be fully persuaded that the education of the people is the only permanent basis of national *prosperity* not only, but of national SAFETY. This, in theory, is now con-

* In the annual report of the Trustees of the New England Institution for the Education of the Blind for the year 1834, this beautiful passage occurs: "The expression of one of the pupils, '*that she had never known, before she began to learn, that it was a happiness to be alive,*' may be applied to many."

ceded, and the importance of education is very generally admitted among men, especially in our own country. It is evident, however, that the conviction of its importance is not so deeply inwrought into the mind of society as it ought to be, for it does not manifest itself with all the power of earnest feeling in behalf of education which the subject, in view of its acknowledged weightiness, justly demands.

The objects and advantages of education heretofore considered apply equally to men of every nation and clime, under whatever form of government they may chance to dwell. It is otherwise in regard to the political necessity of popular education. Here a particular training is required to fit men for the government under which they are to live. In despotic governments, the object of popular education is to make good *subjects*, while upon us devolves the higher responsibility of so educating the people that they may become not only good *subjects*, but good SOVEREIGNS—all power originating in and returning to the *sovereign people.*

Only seventy-four years ago, our fathers of the ever-memorable Revolution pledged "fortune, life, and sacred honor" to establish the independence of these United States. Under the fostering care of republican institutions, the tide of population rolled rapidly inland, crossing the Alleganies, sweeping over the vast Valley of the Mississippi, nor resting in its onward course until it settled on the waters of the Columbia and the shores of the Pacific. Previous to the Revolutionary war, the English settlements were confined to the Atlantic coast; now the tide of immigration seems to be to the shores of the Pacific, where states are multiplying and cities springing up as by magic. In a little more than half a century, the states of the Union have increased in number from thirteen to thirty, and in population in a ratio hitherto unprecedented, from three millions to twenty-five millions of souls.

We stand in the same relation to posterity that our ancestors do to us. Each generation has duties of its own to perform; and our duties, though widely different from those of our forefathers, are not less important in their character or less binding in their obligations. It was their duty to found or establish our institutions, and nobly did they perform it. It is our especial and appropriate duty to perfect and perpetuate the institutions we have received at their hands. The boon they would bequeath to the latest posterity can never reach and bless them except through our instrumentality. Upon each present generation rest the duty and the obligation of educating and qualifying for usefulness that which immediately succeeds, upon which, in turn, will devolve a like responsibility. Each succeeding generation will, in the main, be what the preceding has made it. From this responsible agency there is, there can be, no escape.

Trusts, responsibilities, and interests, vaster in amount and more sacred in character than have ever, in the providence of God, been committed to any people, are now intrusted to us. The great experiment of the capacity of man for self-government is being tried anew—an experiment which, wherever it has been tried, has failed, through an incapacity in the people to enjoy liberty without abusing it. We are, I doubt not, now educating the very generation during whose lifetime this great question will be decided. The present generation will, to a great extent, be responsible for the result, whatever it may be. We are, therefore, called upon, as American citizens and Christian philanthropists, to do all that in us lies to secure to this experiment a successful issue; to make *this* the leading nation of the earth, and a model worthy of imitation by all others. Never before this has a nation been planted with so hopeful an opportunity for becoming the universal benefactor of the race.

If for the next fifty years the population of these American States shall continue to increase as during the last fifty, we shall exceed a hundred millions; and in a century, allowing the same ratio of increase, the population will equal that of the Old World. Here, then, is a continent to be filled with innumerable millions of human beings, who may be happy through our wisdom, but who must be miserable through our folly. We may disregard such considerations, but we can not escape the tremendous responsibilities rolling in upon us in view of the relations we sustain to the past and the future. We delight to honor, in *words*, those heroes and martyrs from whom we have received the rich boon of civil and religious liberty. Let us then, in *deeds*, imitate the examples we profess to admire, and contribute our full quota, as individuals and as a generation, toward perfecting and perpetuating the institutions we have received, that they may be enjoyed by those countless millions who are to succeed us in this broad empire.

"In this exigency," to adopt the language of an enlightened practical educator and eminent statesman, "we need far more of wisdom and rectitude than we possess. Preparations for our present condition have been so long neglected, that we now have a double duty to perform. We have not only to propitiate to our aid a host of good spirits, but we have to exorcise a host of evil ones. Every aspect of our affairs, public and private, demonstrates that we need, for their successful management, a vast accession to the common stock of intelligence and virtue. But intelligence and virtue are the product of cultivation and training. They do not spring up spontaneously. We need, therefore, unexampled alacrity and energy in the application of all those influences and means which promise the surest and readiest returns of wisdom and probity, both public and private.

"When the Declaration of Independence was carried into effect, and the Constitution of the United States was adopted, the civil and political relations of the generation then living, and of all succeeding ones, were changed. Men were no longer the same men, but were clothed with new rights and responsibilities. Up to that period, so far as government was concerned, they might have been ignorant; indeed, it has generally been held that where a man's only duty is obedience, it is better that he should be ignorant; for why should a beast of burden be endowed with the sensibilities of a man! Up to that period, so far as government was concerned, a man might have been unprincipled and flagitious. He had no access to the statute-book to alter or repeal its provisions, so as to screen his own violations of the moral law from punishment, or to legalize the impoverishment and ruin of his fellow-beings. But with the new institutions, there came new relations, and an immense accession of powers. New trusts of inappreciable value were devolved upon the old agents and upon their successors, irrevocably.

"With the change in the organic structure of our government, there should have been corresponding changes in all public measures and institutions. For every dollar given by the wealthy or by the state to colleges to cultivate the higher branches of knowledge, a hundred should have been given for primary education. For every acre of land bestowed upon an academy, a province should have been granted to common schools. Select schools for select children should have been discarded, and *universal education* should have joined hands with *universal suffrage*."*

In the simplest form of civil government, there must exist a legislative, a judicial, and an executive department. But no expression of the national will in a system of laws can be sufficiently definite to supersede the necessity of a perpetual succession of Legislatures to supply defects, and to meet emergencies as they arise. However well-informed men may be, and however pure the motives by which they are actuated, all experience hath shown that subjects will come up for consideration that will strike different minds in a variety of forms. This, in a popular government, gives rise to opposing parties. Every man, then, in casting his vote for members of the Legislature, needs to understand what important questions will be likely to come before that branch of the government for settlement, to have examined them in their various bearings, and to have deliberately made up his opinion in relation to the interests involved, in order to vote understandingly; otherwise he will be as likely to oppose as to promote, not only the welfare of the state, but his own most cherished interests.

The same remark that has been made in relation to the legislative department will apply to both the judicial and executive, and to the general government as well as to the several state governments. When the appointed day arrives for deciding the various questions of state and national policy which divide men into opposing parties, there can be no delay. These various and conflicting questions must be decided,

* From "an Oration delivered before the Authorities of the City of Boston, July 4th, 1842, by Horace Mann, Secretary of the Massachusetts Board of Education."

whether much or little preparation has been made, or none at all. And, what is most extraordinary, each voter helps to decide every question which agitates the community as much by not voting as by voting. If the question is so vast or so complicated that any one has not time to examine and make up his mind in relation to it, or if any one is too conscientious to act from conjecture in cases of magnitude, and therefore stays from the polls, another, who has no scruples about acting ignorantly, or from caprice, or malevolence, votes, and, in the absence of the former, decides the question against the right.

However simple our government may be in theory, it has proved, in practice, the most complex government on earth. More questions for legislative interposition, and for judicial exposition and construction, have already arisen under it, ten to one, than have arisen during the same length of time under any other form of government in Christendom. We are a Union of thirty states; a great nation composed of thirty separate nations; and even beyond these, the confederacy is responsible for the fate of vast territories, with their increasing population, and of numerous Indian tribes. Among the component states, there is the greatest variety of customs, institutions, and religions. Then we have the deeper inbred differences of language and ancestry among us, our population being made up of the lineage of all nations. Our industrial pursuits, also, are various; and, with a great natural diversity of soil and climate, they must always continue to be so. Moreover, across the very center of our territory a line is drawn, on one side of which all labor is voluntary, while on the opposite side a system of involuntary servitude prevails.

If, then, general intelligence and popular virtue are

necessary for the successful administration of even the simplest forms of government, and if these qualities are required in a higher and still higher degree in proportion to the complexity of a government, then are both intelligence and virtue necessary in this government to an extent indefinitely beyond what has ever been required in any other. And especially is this true when we consider that our government is representative as it regards the people, and federative as it regards the states; and that, in this respect, it has no precedent on the file of nations. We hence require a double portion of general intelligence and practical wisdom. But men are not born in the possession of these requisites to self-government, neither are they necessarily developed in the growth from infancy to manhood. They are the product of cultivation and training, and can be secured only through good schools opened to and enjoyed by all our youth. The stability of this government requires that universal education should precede universal suffrage.

Under a free government, the intelligence of the people, coupled with their virtue, will be found to be a sure index to a nation's prosperity, and to the individual and social well-being of all who enjoy its protection. God is a being of infinite wisdom and goodness, and no part of his government can be successfully administered except upon the principles of knowledge and virtue. The success that attends a nation of freemen will depend upon the extent to which these are cultivated, and the universality of their dissemination in the body politic. While the cultivation of these will increase the safety of the government, their neglect will hasten its downfall.

Judge Story, in a lecture upon the importance of the science of government as a branch of popular educa tion, has well remarked, that "it is not to rulers and statesman alone that the science of government is important and useful. It is equally indispensable for every American citizen, to enable him to exercise his own rights, to protect his own interests, and to secure the public liberties and the just operations of public authority. A republic, by the very constitution of its government, requires, on the part of the people, more vigilance and constant exertion than any other form of government. The American Republic, above all others, demands from every citizen unceasing vigilance and exertion, since we have deliberately dispensed with every guard against danger or ruin except the intelligence and virtue of the people themselves. It is founded on the basis that the people have wisdom enough to frame their own system of government, and public spirit enough to preserve it; that they can not be cheated out of their liberties, and they will not submit to have them taken from them by force. We have silently assumed the fundamental truth that, as it never can be the interest of the majority of the people to prostrate their own political equality and happiness, so they never can be seduced by flattery or corruption, by the intrigues of faction or the arts of ambition, to adopt any measures which shall subvert them. *If this confidence in ourselves is justified*—and who among Americans does not feel a pride in endeavoring to maintain it?—*let us never forget that it can be justified only by a watchfulness and zeal in proportion to our confidence.* Let us never forget that we must prove ourselves wiser, better, and purer than any other nation ever has yet been, if we are to count upon success. Every other republic has fallen by the discords and treachery of its own citizens. It has been said by one of our own departed statesmen, himself a devout admirer of popular government, that power is perpetually stealing from the many to the few."

The institutions of a republic are endangered by the ignorance of the masses on the one hand, and by intelligent, but unprincipled and vicious aspirants to office and places of emolument on the other. Where these two classes coexist to any considerable extent, the safety of the republic is jeoparded; for they have a strong sympathy with each other, and it is the constant policy of the latter to increase the number of the former. They arouse their passions and stimulate their appetites, and then lead them in a way they know not. A barrel of whisky, or even of hard cider, with a "hurrah!" will control ten to one more of this class of voters than will the soundest arguments of enlightened and honorable statesmen. And yet one of these votes thus procured, when deposited in the ballot-box, counts the same as the vote of a Washington or a Franklin!

There is one remedy, and but one, for this alarming state of things, which prevails to a less or greater extent in almost every community. That remedy is simple. It consists in the establishment of schools for the education of the whole people. These schools, however, should be of a more perfect character than the majority of those which have hitherto existed. In them the principles of morality should be copiously intermingled with the principles of science. Cases of conscience should alternate with lessons in the rudiments. The rule requiring us to do to others as we would that they should do unto us, should be made as familiar as the multiplication table, and our youth should become as familiar with the practical application of the one as of the other. The lives of great and good men should be held up for admiration and example, and especially the life and character of Jesus Christ, as the sublimest pattern of benevölence, of purity, and of self-sacrifice ever exhibited to mortals. In every course of studies, all the practical and preceptive parts of the Gospel should be sacredly inculcated, and all dogmatical theology and sectarianism sacredly excluded. In no school should the Bible be opened to reveal the sword of the polemic, but to unloose the dove of peace.

In connection with the preceding, and in addition to the branches now commonly taught in our schools, the study of *politics*, which has been beautifully defined as *the art of making a people happy*, should be generally introduced. "I am not aware," says an eminent jurist,* "that there are any solid objections which can be urged against introducing the science of government into our common schools as a branch of popular education. If it should be said that it will have a tendency to introduce party creeds and party dogmas into our schools, the true answer is, that the principles of government should be there taught, and not the creeds or dogmas of any party. The principles of the Constitution under which we live; the principles upon which republics generally are founded, by which they are sustained, and through which they must be saved; the principles of public policy, by which national prosperity is secured, and national ruin averted—these certainly are not party creeds or party dogmas, but are fit to be taught at all times and on all occasions, if any thing which belongs to human life and our own condition is fit to be taught. If we wait until we can guard ourselves against every possible chance of abuse before we introduce any system of instruction, we shall wait until the current of time has flowed into the ocean of eternity. There is nothing which ever has been or ever can be taught without some chance of abuse;

* Joseph Story, before the American Institute of Instruction.

nay, without some absolute abuse. Even religion itself, our truest and our only lasting hope and consolation, has not escaped the common infirmity of our nature. If it never had been taught until it could be taught with the purity, simplicity, and energy of the apostolic age, we ourselves, instead of being blessed with the bright and balmy influences of Christianity, should now have been groping our way in the darkness of heathenism, or left to perish in the cold and cheerless labyrinths of skepticism."

Lord Brougham, one of the most powerful advocates of popular education in our day, has made the following remarks, which can not be more fitly addressed to any people than to the citizens of the American States. "A sound system of government," says this transatlantic writer, "requires the people to read and inform themselves upon political subjects; else they are the prey of every quack, every impostor, and every agitator who may practice his trade in the country. If they do not read; if they do not learn; if they do not digest by discussion and reflection what they have read and learned; if they do not qualify themselves to form opinions for themselves, other men will form opinions for them, not according to the truth and the interests of the people, but according to their own individual and selfish interest, which may, and most probably will, be contrary to that of the people at large."

Two very important inquiries here naturally suggest themselves to us: they are, first, whether there is at present in this country a degree of intelligence sufficient for the wise administration of its affairs; and, secondly, whether existing provisions for the education of our country's youth are adequate to the wants of a great and free people, who are endeavoring to demonstrate to the world that great problem of nations—the capability of man for self-government. We judge of the literary attainments of the citizens of a state or of a nation, *as a whole*, by comparing all the individual members thereof with a given standard, and of their arrangements for educating the rising generation by the character of their schools, and the proportion of the population that receive instruction in them. Let us test the existing standard of education in various states of this Union in both of these respects.

Degree of popular Intelligence. — According to the census of 1840,* the total population of the United States was, in round numbers, seventeen millions. Of this number, five hundred and fifty thousand were whites over twenty years of age, who could not read and write. The proportion varies in different states, from one in five hundred and eighty-nine in Connecticut, to one in eleven in North Carolina.

If we exclude, in the estimate, all colored persons, and whites under twenty years of age, the proportion will stand thus: in the United States, one to every twelve is unable to read and write. The proportion varies in the different states, from one in two hundred and ninety-four in Connecticut, which stands the highest, to one in three in North Carolina, which stands the lowest. In Tennessee the proportion is one in four. In Kentucky, Virginia, Georgia, South Carolina, and Arkansas, each, one in five. In Delaware and Alabama, each, one in six. In Indiana, one in seven. In Illinois and Wisconsin, each, one in eight.

* The census for 1850 is now being taken. Whether its results will tell more favorably upon the general interests of education in the United States than those of the last census, remains to be seen. Some of the states during the last ten years have done nobly; others have evidently retrograded. We have also a tide of foreign immigration pouring in upon us hitherto unprecedented, averaging a thousand a day for the past year, all of whom need to be Americanized.

On the brighter end of the scale, next to Connecticut, in which the proportion is one in two hundred and ninety-four, is New Hampshire, in which the proportion is one in one hundred and fifty-nine. In Massachusetts it is one in ninety. In Maine, one in seventy-two. In Vermont, one in sixty-three. Next in order comes Michigan, in which the proportion is one in thirty-nine.*

But these statements in relation to the number of persons in the United States who are unable to read and write, although they give the fearful aggregate of *five hundred and fifty thousand* over twenty years of age who are destitute of these qualifications, it is believed, fail to discover much of gross ignorance that is cherished in various portions of the country; for there is no state in the Union, nor any section of a single state, where men do not wish to be accounted able to read and write. The deputy marshals who took the census received their compensation by the head, and not by the day, for the work done. They therefore traveled from house to house, making the shortest practicable stay at each. More was required of them than

* According to the last census, there were twenty states below Michigan, and only five above her. But even this estimate, favorable as it is in the scale of states, does not allow Michigan an opportunity to appear in her true light, for it is well known that a great proportion of the illiterate population of this state is confined to a few counties. In Mackinaw and Chippewa counties there is one white person over twenty years of age to every five of the entire population that is unable to read and write. In Ottawa, one in fourteen; in Cass, one in twenty-two; in Wayne and Saginaw, each, one in thirty-six. On the other hand, there were eight organized counties in the state in which, according to the census referred to, there was not a single white inhabitant over twenty years of age that was unable to read and write. It is an interesting fact, at least to persons residing in the Northwest, that in Ohio also (on the Western Reserve) there were seven such counties, making fifteen in these two states, while in all New England there were but two—Franklin in Massachusetts, and Essex in Vermont.

could be thoroughly and accurately performed in the time allowed. Their informants were subjected to no test. In the absence of the heads of families, whose information would have been more reliable, the bare word of persons over sixteen years of age was accredited. It is, moreover, well known, that no inconsiderable number of persons gave false information when inquired of by the deputies. From these and other reasons, it is believed that numerous and important errors exist in the census; and this opinion is corroborated by a mass of unquestionable testimony, of which I will introduce a specimen.

The annual message of Governor Campbell, of Virginia, to the Legislature of that state, the year immediately preceding that in which the census was taken, clearly shows that the capacity to read and write in persons over twenty years of age was greatly overestimated in that state. Governor Campbell, after stating that the importance of an efficient system of education, embracing in its comprehensive and benevolent design the whole people, can not be too frequently recurred to, goes on to remark as follows:

"The statements furnished by the clerks of five city and borough courts, and ninety-three of the county courts, in reply to the inquiries addressed to them, ascertain that, of all those who applied for marriage licenses, a large number were unable to write their names. The years selected for this inquiry were those of 1817, 1827, and 1837. The statements show that the applicants for marriage licenses for 1817 amounted to 4682, of whom 1127 were unable to write; 5048 in 1827, of whom the number unable to write was 1166; and in 1837 the applicants were 4614, and of these the number of 1047 were unable to write their names. From which it appears there still exists a deplorable extent of ignorance, and that, in truth, it is hardly less than it was twenty years ago, when the school fund was created. The statements, it will be remembered, are partial, not embracing quite all the counties, and are, moreover, confined to one sex. The education of females, it is to be feared, is in a condition of much greater neglect.

"There are now in the state two hundred thousand children between the ages of five and fifteen. Forty thousand of them are reported to be poor children, and of them only one half to be attending schools. It may be safely assumed that, of those possessing property adequate to the expenses of a plain education, a large number are growing up in ignorance, for want of schools within convenient distances. Of those at school, many derive little or no instruction, owing to the incapacity of the teachers, as well as to their culpable negligence and inattention. Thus the number likely to remain uneducated, and to grow up without just perceptions of their duties, religious, social, and political, is really of appalling magnitude, and such as to appeal with affecting earnestness to a parental Legislature."

If there shall appear any want of agreement between these statements and the returns made by the deputy marshals, no one need be in doubt in relation to which has the strongest claims for credence. These statements were communicated by the governor of a proud state to the Legislature in his annual message. Unlike the statistics collected by the marshals, each case was subjected to an infallible test; for no man who could make a scrawl in the similitude of his name would submit to the mortification of making his mark, and leaving it on record in a written application for a marriage license. The requisition was made upon the officers of the courts, and the evidence, which was of a documentary or judicial character, is the highest known to the law. The result was, that almost one fourth of all the men applying for marriage licenses—more than thirty-three hundred in three years—were unable to write their names! And Governor Campbell clearly intimates an opinion that "the education of females is in a condition of much greater neglect!"

In round numbers, the free white population of Virginia over twenty years of age is three hundred and thirty thousand. One fourth of this number is eighty-two and a half thousand, which, according to the evidence presented by Governor Campbell, is the lowest possible limit at which the minimum of adults unable to read and write can be stated. But the census number is less than fifty-nine thousand, making a difference of nearly twenty-four thousand, or more than forty per cent.

There are several states of about the same rank as Virginia in the educational scale. Kentucky, Tennessee, and North Carolina sink even below her. The last-named state, with a free white population over twenty years of age of less than 210,000, has the appalling number, even according to the census, of 56,609 who are unable to read and write. In other words, forty-two hundred more than one fourth of the whole free population over twenty years of age are, in the educational scale, absolutely *below zero.*

Now if to the five hundred and fifty thousand free white population in the United States over the age of twenty years who are unable to read and write, as shown by the census, we add forty per cent. for its under-estimates, as facts require us to do in the case of Virginia, it would increase the total to seven hundred and seventy thousand. Suppose one fourth of these only are voters—that is, deduct one half for females, and allow that one half of the male moiety is made up of persons either between twenty and twenty-one years of age, or of those who are unnaturalized, which is a most liberal allowance when we consider where the great mass of ignorance belongs, and that the number of ignorant immigrants is much less at the South than at the North—and we have 192,500 voters in the United States who are unable to read and write.

Now, at the presidential election for the same year that the census was taken, when, to use the graphic language of another, "every voter not absolutely in his winding sheet was carried to the polls, when the harvest field was so thoroughly swept that neither stubble nor tares were left for the gleaner," the majority for the successful candidate was 146,081, more than 46,000 less than the estimated number of legal voters at that time in the United States unable to read and write. At this election a larger majority of the electoral votes was given for the successful candidate than was ever given to any other President of the United States, with the exception of Mr. Monroe in 1820, against whom there was but one vote. General Harrison's popular majority, also, was undoubtedly the largest by which any President of the United States has ever been elected, with the exception above mentioned of Mr. Monroe, and perhaps that of General Washington at his second election. And yet this majority, large as it was, was more than 46,000 less than the estimated number of our legal voters who, in the educational scale, are absolutely below zero.

And then it should be borne in mind that hundreds of thousands who are barely able to read and write may never have acquired "a knowledge of the true principles of government," which, in the language of Judge Story, at the head of this chapter, "is not only important and useful to Americans, but is absolutely indispensable to carry on the government of their choice, and to transmit it to posterity." It should also be borne in mind that popular virtue is not less essential to the stability of a free government than is general intelligence. Nay, more; if the liberties of this republic are more endangered by any one class of people than by all others, that class consists of intelligent but unprincipled political aspirants. The connection between ignorance and vice has already been referred to, and is well known among intelligent men; but by none so well, it may be, as by the unprincipled aspirant, who, by pandering to the vicious appetites of the ignorant and the vile, and then by base flattery pronouncing them "highly intelligent, enlightened, and civilized," take advantage of their very want of qualification "to manufacture political capital." These are they to whom Lord Brougham refers when he says, "other men will form opinions for them, not according to truth and the interests of the people, but according to their own individual and selfish interest, which may, and most probably will, be contrary to that of the people at large." We can not, then, avoid coming to the unwelcome and dread conclusion that there is not at present in this country a sufficient degree of intelligence and virtue for the wise, or even the safe administration of its affairs. It remains to consider whether existing provisions for the education of our country's youth are adequate to the wants of the American people.

Existing Provisions for Education.—Of the seventeen millions of persons in the United States, according to the last census, 3,726,080—one in five of the entire population—were free white children between the ages of five and fifteen years. This is the lowest estimate I have ever known made of the ages between which children should regularly attend school. The ages usually stated between which children generally should attend school at least ten months during the year, are from four to sixteen, or from four to eighteen years, and sometimes from four to twenty or twenty-one years.

But what is the actual attendance upon the primary and common schools of the country? It is only 1,845,244, or, to vary the expression and give it more definiteness, the total number of children in attendance upon all our schools, any part of the year, is twenty thousand less than one half of the free-born white children in the United States between the ages of five and fifteen years! And then it should be borne in mind that the same general motives which would lead to an under-statement in regard to the number of persons unable to read and write, would lead to an over-statement in regard to the number of those attending school. The educational statistics of some of the states, made out by competent and faithful school officers, show that the whole number of scholars that attended school any part of the time during the school year 1840–41—the year the census was taken—was several thousand less than the number according to the census.*

If we were to embrace in the estimate the whole number of students in attendance at the universities, colleges, academies, and seminaries of learning of every grade, it would not materially vary the result, for all

* In Massachusetts, according to a statement made by the Secretary of the Board of Education, the whole number of scholars who were in all the public schools any part of the school year 1840–41 was but 155,041, and the average attendance was, in the winter, 116,398, and in the summer, 96,802; while the number given in the census is 158,351, which is greater by 3310 than the entire number that attended school *any part of the year*, according to the returns, and 55,751 more than the average attendance for half of the year.

these taken together are less than one tenth part of the number in attendance upon the common schools. That the number of children attending schools of any grade is less than might be inferred from the foregoing statements, will be apparent when we consider the following facts.

In the United States, taken together as a whole, only one person in ten of the population attends any school whatever any part of the year. Now it is well known that a large number of children under five years of age attend school in many parts of the country, and a much greater number that are over fifteen years of age. I have already said that the entire number of children in attendance upon all our schools is twenty thousand less than one half of the entire number of free-born white children in the United States between the ages of five and fifteen years. This leaves two millions of children uninstructed. We shall have a more just view of the scantiness of our provisions for adequate national education if to this number, appalling as it is, we add the total number of those attending under five and over fifteen in various portions of the country.

Again: no one supposes that in any part of the Union adequate provisions are made for the education of the rising generation, even in a single state. But in the New England states, and in New York and Michigan, one fourth part of the entire population attend school some part of the year. This is twice and a half the general average throughout the Union, and more than five times the average attendance in the majority of the remaining states.

In round numbers, the proportion of the entire population that attend school in the different states of the Union is, according to the census, in Maine, New

Hampshire, and Vermont, each, one in three. In Michigan,* Massachusetts, Connecticut, and New York, the proportion is one in four. In Rhode Island, it is one in five. In Ohio and New Jersey, each, one in six. In Pennsylvania, one in eight. In no other state is the proportion more than one in ten, while in ten states it is less than one in twenty-five.

In fixing this proportion, the nearest whole number has been used. In no state is the proportion in attendance upon the schools as high as one in three. Michigan heads the states in which the proportion is one in four. In this state the proportion is somewhat greater than one in four; it is, however, nearer this than one in three. In the other states the proportion is less than one in four. The states are all arranged according to the size of the fraction, there being less difference in the attendance in Vermont and Michigan than in the latter state and New York.

At the time the last census was taken, Michigan had recently been admitted into the Union, and the state government being but just organized, the school system had only gone partially into operation. According to the census of 1840, the proportion in attendance upon the schools of this state was only one in seven. During the interval from 1840 to 1845, at which time the census of this state was again taken, the population had increased from two hundred and twelve thousand to upward of three hundred thousand, showing an increase of about fifty per cent.; the number of primary schools had increased from less than ten thousand to more than twenty thousand, making an increase of more than one hundred per cent.; and the attendance

* In determining the proportion for this state, the census for 1845 and the school returns for that year were the data used. In the other states I have been obliged to use the census returns of 1840.

upon these schools had advanced from thirty thousand to seventy-six thousand, giving the very remarkable increase of one hundred and fifty per cent. in five years, when, as already stated, the proportion in attendance upon the common schools was more than one in four of the entire population. And during the next two years the number of children in attendance upon the schools increased from seventy-six thousand to one hundred and eight thousand, showing an advance of more than forty per cent. from 1845 to 1847.

It is gratifying to know that this important interest, which underlies all others, is receiving increased attention in various portions of the United States. Among the most striking illustrations that I have noticed of these indications of national improvement, I will instance two.* The following interesting items of fact are gleaned from an address by the superintendent before the public schools of New Orleans, February 22d, 1850—a most befitting day for a school celebration. These statistics strike us more forcibly when we consider that they relate to the metropolis of the South, and to the capital of a state in which, according to the last census, only one person in one hundred received instruction in the primary and common schools of the state. The public schools of the second municipality of New Orleans were established in 1842, comprising at that time less than three hundred pupils. Now the

* My information is derived from the "Southern Journal of Education" for May, 1850—a monthly for the promotion of popular intelligence, published from Knoxville, Tenn.—Samuel A. Jewett, Editor and Publisher. This journal is ably conducted, and has now reached its third volume. This certainly is a very encouraging omen, especially when we consider that it has so long survived in a state where, according to the last census, only one in thirty-three of the entire population attended school. May it long continue to do good service in this important cause.

constant attendance is upward of three thousand—ten times what it was eight years ago. But even this increase, large as it may seem, is not sufficient to constitute the proportion in attendance upon the schools of the state even one in fifty of the entire population.

Kentucky furnishes the other indication of improvement which I propose to notice. In this state, according to the last census, only one in thirty-three of the entire population attended the common schools during any part of the year. The number of children at the present time in that commonwealth, as reported by the second auditor, between the ages of five and sixteen, leaving out the colored children, is one hundred and ninety-three thousand. The number provided with schools, as reported in 1847, was twenty-one thousand; in 1848, thirty-three thousand; and in 1849, eighty-seven thousand; showing a clear advance in two years of sixty-six thousand.* But, with all this improvement, one hundred and five thousand children do not derive any personal benefit from the public school system. In other words, eighteen thousand more children in this state are still growing up without instruction than as yet attend the schools. And the utter inade-

* This improvement well illustrates the advantages resulting to the state from the able and faithful supervision of her public schools. A correspondent of the Baltimore American speaks of the Annual Report of Dr. Robert Breckenridge, Superintendent of Public Instruction, to the General Assembly of Kentucky, as follows: "It is the most important document which has been submitted to that body during the present session, and reflects great credit upon the energy, fidelity, and comprehensive aims of the superintendent in the discharge of his high duties. It is now but two years since Dr. Breckenridge was appointed to the office, and the great service he has rendered to the cause of popular education in the state is strikingly exhibited in the contrast between the present condition of the common schools, and that in which he found them when he received his appointment from the Board of Education."

quacy of the common school privileges of even these will be apparent when it is understood that in the great majority of the districts more than nine tenths of the schools are taught but three months during the year.

We have as yet only considered the great destitution of schools of *any kind*, in which the moiety of the children that attend school at all receive instruction, and the fact that very many of these are kept open but three months during the year.* The inadequacy of existing provisions for the proper education of the rising generation will be more strikingly apparent when we consider the incompetency of, I may perhaps safely say, the majority of persons who are put in charge of the public schools of the country. It is readily conceded that, in those states where education has received most attention, there are many teachers who are thoroughly furnished unto all good works. But it is far otherwise with the majority of teachers even in the more favored states. The testimony of Governor Campbell already quoted, will apply to the teachers of many other states. After speaking of the large number of children in Virginia that "are growing up in ignorance for want of schools within convenient distances," he remarks, that "of those at school, many derive little or no instruction, owing to the incapacity of the teachers, as well as to their culpable negligence and inattention."

President Caldwell, of the University of North Car-

* Even in Massachusetts the average length of time the schools of the state continue is less than eight months, and the average continuance in several of the counties is only five months. The average attendance upon the schools for the time they are kept open is sixty-two per cent. of the number between the ages of four and sixteen years; but in some instances only twenty-six per cent. of the children in a town—about one fourth of the number within the school ages—attend school

olina, in a series of letters on popular education, addressed to the people of that state a few years ago proposes a plan for the improvement of common education. The first and greatest existing evil which he specifies is the want of qualified teachers. Any one who "knows how to read, and write, and cipher," it is said, is regarded as fit to be a "schoolmaster."

"Is a man," remarks President Caldwell, "constitutionally and habitually indolent, a burden upon all from whom he can extract a support? Then there is one way of shaking him off; let us make him a schoolmaster! To teach a school is, in the opinion of many, little else than sitting still and doing nothing. Has any man wasted all his property, or ended in debt by indiscretion and misconduct? The business of school-keeping stands wide open for his reception; and here he sinks to the bottom, for want of capacity to support himself. Has any one ruined himself, and done all he could to corrupt others by dissipation, drinking, seduction, and a course of irregularities? Nay, has he returned from a prison, after an ignominious atonement for some violation of the laws? He is destitute of character, and can not be *trusted;* but presently he opens a school, and the children are seen flocking to it; for, if he is *willing* to act in that capacity—we shall all admit that he can read, write, and cipher to the square root—he will make an excellent schoolmaster. In short, it is no matter what the man is, or what his manners or principles; if he has escaped with his life from the penal code, we have the satisfaction to think that he can still have credit as a schoolmaster."

The Georgia convention of teachers, in a published address, after speaking of the importance of giving a more extended education to our youth *as citizens,* and giving an outline of a liberal system of popular education, go on to remark as follows: "Alas! how far should we be elevated above our present level if all of them were thus enlightened! But how many sons and daughters of free-born Americans are unable to read their native language! How many go to the polls who are unable to read the very charter of their liberties! How many, by their votes, elect men to legislate upon their dearest interests, while they themselves are unable to read even the proceedings of those legislators whom they have empowered to act for them!"

In accounting for this lamentable state of things, the committee of the Convention say, "We seem to forget that first principles are, in education, all-important principles; that primary schools are the places where these principles are to be established, and where such direction will, in all probability, be given to the minds of our children as will decide their future character in life. Hence the idle, and the profane, and the drunken, and the ignorant are employed to impart to our children the first elements of knowledge—are set before them as examples of what literature and science can accomplish! And hence the profession of schoolmaster, which should be the most honorable, is but too often a term of reproach."

That other most unwelcome and dread conclusion, *that existing provisions for popular education in the United States are inadequate to the requirements of a free people*, is, then, in view of all these facts, unavoidably forced upon us.

In the name of Christian philanthropy, in the name of patriotism, then, I inquire whether there is any ground for hope that our free institutions may be transmitted unimpaired to posterity. "With the heroes, and sages, and martyrs of the Revolution," to adopt the language of another, "I believe in the capability of man for self-government, my whole soul thereto most joyously assenting. Nay, if there be any heresy among men, or blasphemy against God, at which the philosopher might be allowed to forget his equanimity, and the Christian his charity, it is the heresy and the blasphemy of believing and avowing that the infinitely good and all-wise Author of the universe persists in creating and sustaining a race of beings who, by a law of their nature, are forever doomed to suffer all the atrocities and agonies of misgovernment, either from the hands of others or from their own. The doctrine of the inherent and necessary disability of mankind for self-government should be regarded not simply with denial, but with abhorrence; not with disproof only, but with execration. To sweep so foul a creed from the precincts of truth, and utterly to consume it, rhetoric should become a whirlwind, and logic fire. Indeed, I have never known a man who desired the establishment of monarchical and aristocratical institutions among us, who had not a mental reservation that, in such case, he and his family should belong to the privileged orders.

"Still, if asked the broad question whether man is capable of self-government, I must answer it conditionally. If by man, in the inquiry, is meant the Fejee Islanders; or the convicts at Botany Bay; or the people of Mexico and of some of the South American Republics, so called; or those as a class, in our own country, who can neither read nor write; or those who can read and write, and who possess talents and an education by force of which they get treasury, or post-office, or bank appointments, and then abscond with all the money they can steal, I answer unhesitatingly that *man*, or rather *such men*, are not fit for self-government.

"But if, on the other hand, the inquiry be whether mankind are not endowed with those germs of intelli gence and those susceptibilities of goodness by which, under a perfectly practicable system of cultivation and training, they are able to avoid the evils of despotism and anarchy, and also of those frequent changes in national policy which are but one remove from anarchy, and to hold steadfastly on their way in an endless career of improvement, then, in the full rapture of that joy and triumph which springs from a belief in the goodness of God and the progressive happiness of man, I answer, THEY ARE ABLE."

PRACTICABILITY OF NATIONAL EDUCATION.

The first duty of government, and the surest evidence of good government, is the encouragement of education. A general diffusion of knowledge is the precursor and protector of republican institutions; and in it we must confide, as the conservative power that will watch our liberties, and guard against fraud, intrigue, corruption, and violence. —DE WITT CLINTON'S *Message to the New York Legislature*, 1826.

If good is to be done, we must bring our minds, as soon as possible, to the confession of the truth, that the education of the people, to be effectual, must here, as elsewhere, to a great extent, be the work of the state; and that an expense, of which all should feel the necessity, and all will share the benefit, must, in a just proportion, be borne by all.—JOHN DUER.

The *desirableness* of national or universal education is now generally admitted in all enlightened communities; but there are some who, honestly no doubt, question its *practicability*. If they provide for the education of their own children, they claim that they have done all that duty or interest requires them to do. They even aver that there is absolute injustice in compelling them to contribute toward the education of the children of others. Now these very persons, when called upon annually by the tax-gatherer to contribute their proportion for the support of paupers—made so by idleness, intemperance, and other vices, which, as we have already seen, result from ignorance—do so cheerfully and ungrudgingly, and without complaining that they support themselves and their families, and that neither duty nor interest requires them to aid in the maintenance of indigent persons in the community.

The Poor Laws of our country, in the case of adults who are unable to support themselves, require merely their maintenance. But with reference to their *children*, more, from the very nature of the case, is needed. Their situation imperatively demands not only a sustenance, but an education that shall enable them in future years to provide for themselves. The same humane reasons which lead civilized communities to provide for the maintenance of indigent adults by legal enactments, bear even more strongly in the case of their children. These require sustenance in common with their parents. But their wants, their necessities, stop not here; neither does the well-being of society with reference to them. Both alike require that such hildren, in common with all others, be so trained as to be enabled not only to provide for themselves when they arrive at mature years, but as shall be necessary to qualify them for the discharge of the duties of citizenship. Then, instead of taxing society for a support, as their parents now do, they will contribute to the elevation of all around, even more largely than society has contributed to their elevation.

Let the necessary provision be made for the education of the children of the poor, in common with al others, and successive generations of the sons of men will steadily progress in knowledge and virtue, and in all that has a tendency to elevate and ennoble human kind. But let their education be neglected, and their rank in society will of necessity be lower, when compared with the better educated and more favored classes, than it would have been only two or three centuries ago, even since the invention of the art of printing in 1440. The reasons are evident. Until after the invention of printing and the multiplication of books, all ranks were, in relation to education, nearly upon a level. But, in the language of the adage, "Knowledge is power;" and, since "knowledge has been increased," those who possess it are elevated, relatively and absolutely, while those who remain in the ignorance of former generations, although their absolute condition in the scale of being is unchanged, occupy, nevertheless, relatively, a lower place in society than they would have done had they lived in the midst of the Dark Ages.

Wherever improved free schools have been maintained, not only are the *children* of the poor in attendance upon them elevated in the scale of intellectual, social, and moral being, but, through their irresistible influence, their degraded and besotted *parents* have been eformed and become law-abiding subjects, when all other means had failed to reach and influence them. Of the truth of this statement I am well persuaded from my own observation. I have also in my possession an abundance of unquestionable testimony to this effect, gathered in cities, towns, and villages which have become celebrated for the maintenance of a high order of public schools. The public, then, on many accounts, are more interested in the right education of poor children than in the preservation of their lives! The latter is carefully provided for. But if this only is done; if their bodies are fed and clothed, without providing for the sustenance of their minds; if we provide for their wants as helpless young animals merely, but neglect to provide for their necessities as spiritual and immortal beings, the probabilities are that such children will become a pest to society, while, in providing for their proper education, we are sure of making them good citizens, of constituting them a blessing to the world that now is, and of brightening their prospects for a blessed immortality in that which is to come.

Bishop Butler, in a sermon preached in Christ Church, London, on charity schools, May 9th, 1745, recognizes the principle that the property of the state should educate the children of the state. "Formerly," says he, "not only the *education* of poor children, but also their *maintenance*, with that of the other poor, were left to voluntary charities. But great changes of different sorts happening over the nation, and charity becoming more cold, or the poor more numerous, it was found necessary to make some legal provision for them. This might, much more properly than charity schools, be called a new scheme;* for, without question, the education of poor children was all along taken care of by voluntary charities, more or less, but obliging us by law to maintain the poor was new in the reign of Queen Elizabeth. Yet, because a change of circumstances made it necessary, its novelty was no reason against it. Now, in that legal provision for the maintenance of the poor, poor children must doubtless have had a part in common with grown people. But this could never be sufficient for children, because their case always requires more than mere maintenance; it requires that they be educated in some proper manner. Wherever there are poor who want to be maintained by charity, there must be poor children, who, besides this, want to be educated by charity; and whenever

* Bishop Butler is here answering the objections of some "people who speak of charity schools as a new-invented scheme, and therefore to be looked upon with suspicion; whereas it is no otherwise new than as the occasion for it is so."

there began to be need of *legal* provision for the *maintenance* of the poor, there must immediately have been need also of some *particular* legal provision in behalf of poor children for their *education*, this not being included in what we call their maintenance."

Not only is it the duty of society to provide *food* for the *minds* as well as sustenance for the bodies of poor children, but their pecuniary interests equally require it; for, as Butler remarks, "if they are not trained up in the way they should go, they will certainly be trained up in the way they should not go, and in all probability will persevere in it, and become miserable themselves and mischievous to society, which, in event, is worse, upon account of both, than if they had been exposed to perish in their infancy."

I have already shown, by unquestionable testimony, that persons who possess the greatest share in the stock of worldly goods are deeply interested in the subject of popular education, as one of *mere insurance;* "that the most effectual way of making insurance upon their property would be to contribute from it enough to sustain an efficient system of common school education, thereby educating the whole mass of mind, and constituting it a police more effective than peace officers or prisons." I might elucidate this subject by illustrations.

It has been estimated that a quarter of a million of dollars has been expended in the county of Philadelphia since 1836 for the suppression of riots occurring within its limits, and in damages occasioned by their outrages and violence, to say nothing of personal injuries and deaths arising from the same cause. Now it will be readily conceded by most persons that half of this sum judiciously expended in organizing and supporting a sufficient police, and in giving the leaders and gangs engaged in those riots an early and suitable education, whereby they would have been taught to think, and feel, and act as rational, moral, and accountable beings, would have prevented the commission of such crimes, together with the sufferings and losses resulting therefrom, and the reproach thus brought upon public and individual character.

Again: The whole number of paupers relieved or supported by public charity in the single state of New York, in the year 1849, according to an authentic statement now before me, was, in round numbers, one hundred thousand, and the entire expense of their support during the year was eight hundred and seven thousand dollars, a sum exceeding by three hundred and forty thousand dollars the amount paid on rate-bills for teacher's wages for educating the seven hundred thousand children of that great state! Of fifty thousand of these paupers, the *causes* of whose destitution have been ascertained, nearly *twenty thousand* are attributable, directly or indirectly, to intemperance, profligacy, licentiousness, and crime! Had even half the amount that is now expended from year to year in their support been judiciously bestowed upon their early mental and moral culture, who can question that, instead of now being a tax upon the communities in which they reside, and a burden to themselves and a grief to their friends, they would not only have provided for their own maintenance, but would have contributed their due proportion to increase the general prosperity of the state.

Great as is her poor-tax, New York contributes annually an immensely greater sum for the support of her criminal police; for the erection of court-houses, and jails, and penitentiaries, and houses of correction; for the arrest, trial, conviction, and punishment of criminals, and for their support in prison and at the various landing-places on their way to the gallows and to a premature and ignominious death. Now, had one half of the money which this state has expended in these two ways been judiciously bestowed in the early education of these unfortunate persons, who can question that the poor and criminal taxes of that state would have been reduced to less than one tenth of what they now are, to say nothing of the fountains of tears that would be thus dried up, and of the untold happiness that would be enjoyed by persons who, in every generation, lead cheerless lives and die ignoble deaths.

Lest some persons may labor under an erroneous impression in relation to this subject, I will give the statistics of education and crime in New York, as derived from official reports, for the last few years. Of 1122 persons—the whole number reported by the sheriffs of the different counties of the state as under conviction and punishment for crime during the year 1847—22 only had a common education, 10 only had a tolerably good education, and only 6 were *well* educated. Of the 1345 criminals so returned in the several counties of the state for the year 1848, 23 only had a common school education, 13 only had a tolerably good education, and only 10 were considered well educated! The returns for other years give like results. Had the whole eleven or thirteen hundred of these convicts been *well educated* instead of only *six* or *ten*—and the moral and religious education of even these was defective—how many of them would society be called upon to support in prisons and penitentiaries? In all probability, as we shall hereafter, I hope, be able to show, NOT ONE. And what is true of the city and county of Philadelphia and of the State of New York, will apply to other cities, counties, and states of this Union.

Once more, and finally: Education, as we have already seen, enables men to subdue their passions, and to improve themselves in the exercise of all the social virtues. Especially have we seen that the educated portions of community, whose moral culture has been duly attended to, are *habitually temperate*, while the appetite of the uncultivated for intoxicating drinks is stronger, and their power of resistance less. Cut off from the sources of enjoyment which are ever open to those whose minds and hearts are cultivated, no wonder they seek for happiness in the gratification of appetite! No wonder that forty thousand of the citizens of the United States annually die drunkards, when we consider that this is only one in twenty of the number who are unable to read and write!

The Hon. Edward Everett has expressed the opinion that the expenses of the manufacture and traffic of intoxicating drinks in the United States exceed annually *one hundred and fifty millions of dollars.* General Cary, in alluding to this statement, says, "This, it is believed, is but an approximation to the cost of these trades to the people. This estimate does not include the money paid by consumers, which is worse than thrown away. An English writer, well versed in statistics, and having access to the most reliable sources of information, says that 'the strong drinks consumed in England alone cost nearly *four hundred millions of dollars annually.*' The expenditure for these sources of all evil in the United States must be equal, at least, to that of England."* Now *one half of this sum would maintain a system of common schools in every state of this Union equal in expense and efficiency to that of Massachusetts or New York.*

* See Tract on "The Liquor Manufacture and Traffic," prepared by request of the National Division of the Sons of Temperance, by S F. Cary, Most Worthy Patriarch.

But I need not extend these observations. Enough I trust, has been said to show that every thing connected with the good of man and the welfare of the race depends upon the attention we bestow in perfecting our systems of public instruction and rendering their blessings universal. I will therefore close what I have to say upon this topic with a summary of the conclusions we have arrived at in the progress of the last two chapters.

We have seen that a good system of common school education—one that is sufficiently comprehensive to embrace all our country's youth in its benevolent design—would free us as a people from a host of evils growing out of popular ignorance; that it would increase the productiveness of labor, as the schools advance in excellence, indefinitely; that it would save to society, in diminishing the number of paupers and criminals, a vast amount of means absorbed in the support of the former, and in bringing the latter to justice, a tax which upon every present generation is more than sufficient for the education of the next succeeding one; that it would prevent the great majority of fatal accidents that are now depopulating communities wherever ignorance prevails; that, by imparting a knowledge of the organic laws, the observance of which is essential to health and happiness, it would save the lives of a hundred thousand children in the United States every year, and that by promoting longevity, in connection with the advantages already enumerated, it would tend more than all other means of state policy to increase at once the wealth and the population of our country; that its legitimate tendency would be to diminish, from generation to generation, not only drunkenness and sensuality in all its Protean forms, but idiocy and insanity, which result from a violation of the laws of our being, which are the laws of God ; that it would, in innumerable ways, tend to diminish the sufferings and mitigate the woes incident to human life, while it would acquaint man with the will of the benevolent Creator, and lead him to cherish an habitual desire to yield obedience thereto ; and that it is the only possible means of perfecting and perpetuating the inestimable boon of civil and religious liberty to the latest generations, and thus securing to the race the maximum of human happiness. Yes, a system of popular education adequate to the requirements of the states of this Union will do all this. None, then, it would seem, can fail to see that true state policy requires the maintenance of improved free schools, good enough for the best, and cheap enough for the poorest, which are a necessary means of universal education.

CHAPTER X.

THE MEANS OF UNIVERSAL EDUCATION.

I would recommend that each state should raise a school fund sufficient for the entire support of the schools; that a suitable school-house and apparatus, with a convenient dwelling-house for the teacher, be furnished by the state for each district; and that every school-house be supplied with a well-qualified teacher, who shall receive from the state a suitable compensation.—John Duer.

Let there be an educational department of the government, and let its details be managed by proper officers, accountable to the representatives of the people.—Dr. Hawks.

We have already considered the nature of education, which has reference to the whole man and to the whole duration of his being. We have seen its importance to individuals and families, to neighborhoods and communities, to states and nations, and that in proportion as it receives attention in any community, will that community become prosperous and happy. We may then very properly inquire after the means to be put in requisition in order to render the blessings of education universal among us. To the consideration of this subject we shall devote the remainder of this work. My first remark is, that

A correct public opinion should be formed. In the language of Bishop Potter, "Our people have absolutely the control over the whole subject of education, not only as it respects their own families, but, to a great extent, in schools and seminaries of learning. If, then, the people were fully awake to its importance and true nature, we should soon have a perfect system, and we should witness results from it for which we now look in vain."

The formation of a correct public opinion is of the utmost importance, for the primary cause of all the defects complained of in education, and the source of all the evils that afflict the community in consequence of its neglect, is *popular indifference.* From this we have more to fear than from all other causes combined. Opposition elicits discussion; and discussion, judiciously conducted, evolves truth; and educational truths brought clearly before the mind of any community will ultimately induce right action. Men may at first be influenced by a comparatively low class of motives, but one which they can appreciate. As they witness the beneficial effects of reform, their motives will gradually become more elevated, and their efforts at improvement more constant; but no important advance can be made without popular enlightenment.

When the majority of the individuals that compose any community come to value education as they ought; when they duly estimate its importance in the various points of view already considered, then will their public servants take more pains to co-operate with them in rendering its blessings universal. Good laws are important as a means of improving our systems of public instruction; but good laws, unsustained by a correct public opinion, will be of no avail. Before any considerable advance can be made either in improving our schools or in causing the attendance upon them to become more general, a good common education—one that shall give us sound minds in sound bodies; one that bestows much attention upon intellectual culture, but more upon the culture of the heart—must come to be ranked among the *necessaries of life.*

Conventions of the friends of education have already done much to correct popular errors in relation to this subject, and have contributed largely to the formation of sound and rational views in relation to its importance in the communities where they have been held. In many instances, however, they have been composed too exclusively of teachers. These should, indeed, be in attendance; but to increase the usefulness of such conventions, and heighten the effect they may be made to produce upon the popular mind, there should also be in attendance members of the several learned professions, statesmen, capitalists, and all the leading minds of the communities in which they are held. In some portions of the country this is now the case, but such instances, I regret to say, are not yet very common among us.

Fourth of July common school celebrations have, within the past few years, become quite common in several states of the Union. This seems peculiarly appropriate, being a practical recognition of the importance of primary schools and universal education in a civil and political point of view. One of the most befitting celebrations of this day which I have ever known was held in Boston eight years ago, when an oration was delivered before the authorities of that city by the Secretary of the Massachusetts Board of Education. The theme of the orator was the importance of national or universal education in a free government as the interest which underlies all others, and as constituting the only means of perfecting and perpetuating to the latest generations the institutions we have received from our fathers, and "a demonstration that our existing means for the promotion of intelligence and virtue are wholly inadequate to the support of a republican government." Such celebrations should be held in every state of this Union, at every recurring anniversary of our national independence, until there can not be found a single individual in all our borders who does not know both his duties and his privileges as a freeman, and who has not virtue enough faithfully to perform the one and temperately to enjoy the other. This, indeed, seems to be in keeping with that most impressive passage of the celebrated Ordinance of the American Congress, adopted July 13th, 1787, which says, "RELIGION, MORALITY, AND KNOWLEDGE BEING NECESSARY TO GOOD GOVERNMENT AND THE HAPPINESS OF MANKIND, SCHOOLS AND THE MEANS OF EDUCATION SHALL FOREVER BE ENCOURAGED."

The twenty-second of February has also been observed, to some extent, in several of the states, by holding such celebrations. Nothing can be more appropriate than these efforts to arouse the popular mind to renewed efforts to improve the common schools of the land, when we consider the import of that portion of the Farewell Address of him, the anniversary of whose birth we celebrate, which relates to popular education. "Promote, as an object of primary importance, institutions for the general diffusion of knowledge." There can be no doubt that WASHINGTON here refers to the maintenance and improvement of common schools as the means of universal education.

The necessity of improving our common schools and of opening wide their doors to all our youth should not only be the theme at school celebrations, at educational conventions, and on the occasion of our national anniversaries, but it should be frequently presented by the civilian and the divine, as well as by the legislator and the journalist, until men generally well understand the importance of education, and are willing to make any sacrifices that may be necessary to secure its advantages to their own children not only, but to all our youth.

PROVISIONS FOR THE SUPPORT OF SCHOOLS.—The provisions which have been made for the support of schools may be reduced to three kinds: first, by means of funds; second, by taxation; third, by a combination of both of these methods.

Connecticut, which has a school fund of more than two millions of dollars, long ago adopted the first plan named. But the inefficiency of her system of public instruction, until within a few years, is proverbial, and affords conclusive evidence that a large school fund is of little or no avail in the absence of a correct public opinion and a due appreciation of the importance of education. The improvements in the schools of that state during the last few years are not in consequence of any increase in her school fund, but because the importance of the subject has been so frequently and impressively presented before the public mind, by means of lectures, public discussions, educational tracts, school journals, and in various other ways, as to overcome that popular indifference which had well-nigh precluded all advance. The late improvements in that state have taken place in spite of the school fund rather than because of any aid derived from it. Dr. Wayland has expressed the opinion that school "funds are valuable as a *condiment*, not as an *aliment;* and that they should never be so large as to render any considerable degree of personal effort on the part of the parent unnecessary." This is true only when a fund is so far relied upon as to slacken personal effort for the improvement of the schools, and to induce parental and popular indifference in relation to them.

The second plan is by taxation, and Massachusetts furnishes an example of it. In most of the counties of this state there are small local funds, the avails of which are added to the amount raised by tax for the support of schools. There are also still less amounts appropriated from the income of the surplus revenue for the purpose of increasing the educational advantages of the children; not to be subtracted from, but to be added to, what the towns would otherwise grant. We may, then, consider the school fund of this state as embracing the entire taxable property of the state, from which such a sum is annually raised by tax as is necessary for the support of the schools. In Vermont, New Hampshire, and Maine, the schools are supported essentially as in Massachusetts, the difference being chiefly in the mode of taxation.

Dr. Wayland, in a letter written some years ago, makes the following remark in relation to the support of schools: "The best legislative provision with which I am acquainted is that of Maine. They have no fund whatever, but oblige every district to raise for education a sum proportioned to the number of its inhabitants or its property. If a town or a district neglects to do this, it is liable to a fine."

In those states whose systems of public instruction

are best administered—which have the best schools, and the greatest proportion of the population in attendance upon them—the schools are generally supported almost entirely by a direct tax, the great principle that THE PROPERTY OF THE STATE SHOULD EDUCATE THE CHILDREN OF THE STATE being practically recognized. It not only appears, then, that large funds are not required for the successful administration of systems of public instruction, but that actually the best schools, and those which are doing most for the correct education of the rising generation, may be found in those states that are destitute of funds, and whose public schools are supported by a direct tax upon the property of the state.

The third plan of supporting schools is a combination of both of the others. New York until within the last year,* Rhode Island, and Michigan may be cited as examples of this plan. Where this plan has been adopted, the districts or townships have generally been required to raise by tax an amount equal to or greater than what has been received from the school fund. Where the expense of supporting the schools has exceeded the whole fund derived from both sources, the balance of the expense has generally been made up by a rate-bill, parents who are able being required to pay in proportion to the number of days their children have attended school. This feature is objectionable even where provision is made for the children of poor parents to attend without charge, for it offers a pecuniary inducement, although the schools be nearly free, to withdraw scholars from attendance upon them for the slightest causes. This plan has obtained very generally in the states northwest of the Ohio River, which have received from the General Confederacy a grant of one

* A year ago the schools of New York were made entirely free by law. See the foot-note on the 267th page of this work.

section, or six hundred and forty acres of land in each township for the support of schools. In some of these states the additional tax is already sufficient, when joined with the avails of the school fund, to render the schools entirely free. If one plan is superior to both of the others, this is, perhaps, entitled to the pre-eminence. The school fund lessens the amount which it is necessary to raise by a direct tax; and still the sum which is levied in this way has a tendency to beget and maintain a lively interest on the part of capitalists in the administration of the educational department, and in the maintenance and improvement of the public schools.

Without a correct public opinion and a due appreciation of the importance of education, either of the three systems named, or any other which may be adopted for the support of schools, will, and, from the very nature of the case, must, be inadequate to meet the necessities of a free people. But let the public be alive to the advantages of education, and rank it first among the necessaries of life, and almost any system will be attended with eminent success. If, then, one system is superior to all others, it is that which is best calculated to beget in the popular mind a realizing sense of the necessity of educating all our youth in good schools. If this can be done in a state which has a large school fund, without diminishing the interest of the people in education, or relaxing their efforts to maintain improved schools, then may such a fund prove serviceable, as it will lessen the general tax. But if the citizens of any state can not be brought to realize the importance of maintaining an elevated standard of common school education, and of rendering its blessings universal, without defraying the whole expense by a direct tax, then will a school fund prove to them a curse, and not a blessing.

Where there is a will there is a way, says the adage. Mr. Duer, as quoted at the head of this chapter, says "I would recommend that each state should raise a fund sufficient for the entire support of the schools; that a suitable school-house and apparatus, with a convenient dwelling-house for the teacher, be furnished by the state for each district; and that every school-house be supplied with a well-qualified teacher, who shall receive from the state a suitable compensation." In this recommendation I fully concur. But with me it is immaterial whether the state raises a separate fund, set apart exclusively for the purposes of education, or regards the entire taxable property of the commonwealth, personal and real, as a general fund from which there shall be drawn annually a sufficient per centage to provide for universal education in free schools. This only do I insist upon, that the people be brought so fully to realize the advantages of a good common education as to place it high on the list of indispensables; then will they provide for rendering its blessings universal. The mode of doing this in any one state may, in view of the peculiar circumstances of a people, be different from that which it would be most advantageous ordinarily to adopt. If there is no other sure way of meeting the expense of common schools, and of begetting and maintaining a deep and abiding interest in popular education, then let the property of the state be regarded as a common fund from which there shall be annually drawn a sum sufficient for the maintenance of improved free schools, in which every child may receive a generous education, as this is the interest first in importance to individuals and families, to neighborhoods and communities, to states and nations.

The state should maintain an Educational Department. The magnitude of the interests involved renders this of the utmost importance. At the head of this department in every state there should be a minister of public instruction—whether he is called school superintendent, school commissioner, secretary of the board of education, or superintendent of public instruction—and he should be allowed time to make himself familiar with all the leading writers on the subject of education, in whatever age or language their works may have been written. Such an officer can not in any other way become qualified for the proper discharge of the duties which pertain to his profession. He should also be allowed time to acquaint himself with the current literature belonging to his department as it emanates from the press; to examine new school-books, and new kinds of school apparatus which claim to possess advantages, that he may be prepared to give to school teachers, school committee-men, and others whose opportunities for examination and investigation are less extended, and many of whom must be inexperienced, such advice as shall enable them judiciously to expend their means for their personal improvement or the improvement of their schools. He should likewise have time and opportunity to become so conversant with the practical operations of different school systems as to be qualified to give such suggestions in official reports as may be of service to the Legislature in perfecting their own, and to subordinate officers in its successful administration. All this would be necessary were we only to consult the pecuniary interests of the state in the judicious expenditure of the means which are annually devoted to the support of common schools. Of how much greater importance is it that there should be such an officer in every state, and that he should enjoy every possible means for increasing his usefulness, when we consider that the successful bestowment of his labors will contribute greatly to increase individual and social happiness, and the general prosperity of the state in all coming generations.

In the further consideration of the means of rendering the blessings of education universal, we shall introduce leading topics in the order in which they naturally suggest themselves.

GOOD SCHOOL HOUSES SHOULD BE PROVIDED.

A school ought to be a noble asylum, to which children will come, and in which they will remain with pleasure; to which their parents will send them with good will.—COUSIN.

If there is one house in the district more pleasantly located, more comfortably constructed, better warmed, more inviting in its general appearance, and more elevating in its influence than any other, that house should be the school-house.—*Michigan School Report*, 1847.

In considering the means of improving our schools, the place where our country's youth receive their first instruction, and where nineteen twentieths of them complete their scholastic training, claims early attention. It is, then, proper to consider the condition of this class of edifices, as they have almost universally been in every part of the United States until within a few years past, and as they now generally are out of those states in which public attention has of late been more especially directed to improvements in education; for, before any people will attempt a reform in this particular, they must see and feel the need of it. Even in the more favored states, comparatively few in number, the improvements in school architecture have been confined mostly to a few localities, and are far from being adequate to the necessities of the case. Did space allow, I would present statements made by school officers in their reports from various states of the Union;

for, however wide the differences may be in common usage, in other respects, there has heretofore been a striking sameness in the appearance of school-houses in every part of the country.

CONDITION OF SCHOOL-HOUSES.—In remarking upon the condition of this class of edifices, as they have heretofore been constructed, and as they are now almost universally found wherever public sentiment has not been earnestly, perseveringly, and judiciously called to their improvement, I will present a few extracts from the official reports of Massachusetts and New York, where greater pains have been taken to ascertain existing defects in schools, with a view to providing the necessary remedies, than in any other two states of this Union.

School-houses in Massachusetts.—The Secretary of the Board of Education of this state, in his report for 1846, remarks in reference to the condition of school-houses in the commonwealth as follows: "For years the condition of this class of edifices throughout the state, taken as a whole, had been growing worse and worse. Time and decay were always doing their work, while only here and there, with wide spaces between, was any notice taken of their silent ravages; and, in still fewer instances, were these ravages repaired. Hence, notwithstanding the improved condition of all other classes of buildings, general dilapidation was the fate of these. Industry, and the increasing pecuniary ability which it creates, had given comfort, neatness, and even elegance to private dwellings. Public spirit had erected commodious and costly churches. Counties, though largely taxed, had yet uncomplainingly paid for handsome and spacious court-houses and public offices. Humanity had been at work, and had made generous and noble provision for the pauper, the blind, the deaf and dumb, the insane. Even jails and houses of correction—the receptacles of felons and other offenders against the laws of God and man—had in many instances been transformed, by the more enlightened spirit of the age, into comfortable and healthful residences. The Genius of Architecture, as if she had made provision for all mankind, extended her sheltering care over the brute creation. Better stables were provided for cattle; better folds for sheep; and even the unclean beasts felt the improving hand of reform. But, in the mean while, the school-houses, to which the children should have been wooed by every attraction, were suffered to go where age and the elements would carry them.

"In 1837, not one third of the public school-houses in Massachusetts would have been considered tenantable by any decent family out of the poor-house or in it. As an inducement to neatness and decency, children were sent to a house whose walls and floors were indeed painted, but they were painted all too thickly by smoke and filth; whose benches and doors were covered with carved work, but they were the gross and obscene carvings of impure hands; whose vestibule, after the Oriental fashion, was converted into a veranda, but the metamorphosis which changed its architectural style consisted in laying it bare of its outer covering. The modesty and chastity of the sexes, at their tenderest age, were to be cultivated and cherished in places which oftentimes were as destitute of all suitable accommodation as a camp or a caravan. The brain was to be worked amid gases that stupefied it. The virtues of generosity and forbearance were to be acquired where sharp discomfort and pain tempt each one to seize more than his own share of relief, and thus to strengthen every selfish propensity.

"At the time referred to, the school-houses in Massachusetts were an opprobrium to the state; and if there be any one who thinks this expression too strong, he may satisfy himself of its correctness by inspecting some of the few specimens of them which still remain.

"The earliest effort at reform was directed to this class of buildings. By presenting the idea of taxation, this measure encountered the opposition of one of the strongest passions of the age. Not only the sordid and avaricious, but even those whose virtue of frugality, by the force of habit, had been imperceptibly sliding into the vice of parsimony, felt the alarm. Men of fortune without children, and men who had reared a family of children and borne the expenses of their education, fancied they saw something of injustice in being called to pay for the education of others, and too often their fancies started into specters of all imaginable oppression and wrong.

"During the five years immediately succeeding the report made by the Board of Education to the Legislature on the subject of school-houses, the sums expended for the erection and repair of this class of buildings fell but little short of *seven hundred thousand dollars.* Since that time, from the best information obtained, I suppose the sum expended on this one item to be about *one hundred and fifty thousand dollars annually.* Every year adds some new improvement to the construction and arrangement of these edifices.

"In regard to this great change in school-houses—it would hardly be too much to call it a *revolution*—the school committees have done an excellent work, or, rather, they have begun it; it is not yet done. Their annual reports, read in open town meeting, or printed and circulated among the inhabitants, afterward embodied in the Abstracts and distributed to the members of the government, to all town and school committees have enlightened and convinced the state."

School-houses in New York.—About ten years ago, special visitors were appointed by the superintendent of common schools in each of the counties of this state, who were requested to visit and inspect the schools, and to report minutely in regard to their state and prospects. The most respectable citizens, without distinction of party, were selected to discharge this duty; and the result of their labors is contained in two reports, made, the one in April, 1840, the other in February, 1841. "It may be remarked, generally," say the visitors of one of the oldest and most affluent towns of the southeastern section of the state, "that the school-houses are built in the old style, are too small to be convenient, and, with one exception, too near the public roads, having generally no other play-ground."—*Report*, 1840, p. 47.

Say the visitors of another large and wealthy town in the central part of the state, "Out of twenty schools visited, ten of the school-houses were in bad repair, and many of them not worth repairing. In none were any means provided for the ventilation of the room. In many of the districts, the school-rooms are too small for the number of scholars. The location of the school-houses is generally pleasant. There are, however, but few instances where play-grounds are attached, and their condition as to privies is very bad. The arrangement of seats and desks is generally very bad, and inconvenient to both scholars and teachers; most of them are without backs."—*Report*, 1840, p. 28.

In another large and populous town in the north-western part of the state, it appears from the report of the visitors that only *five* out of twenty-two school-houses are respectable or comfortable; none have any proper means of ventilation; eight of them are built of logs, and but one of them has a privy.

According to the report from another county, where the evils already enumerated exist, "There is, in general, too little attention to having good and dry wood provided, or a *good supply of any;* or to have a wood-house or shelter to keep it from the storm." This neglect is very common. Another neglect, noticed by many of the visitors, is "the cold and comfortless state in which the children find the school-room, owing to the late hour at which the fire is first made in the morning."

Three years later—and after the appointment of county superintendents in each of the counties of that state, who collected statistics with great care—the Hon. Samuel Young, then state superintendent, after making a minute statement of the number of school-houses constructed of stone, brick, wood, and logs; of their condition as to repair; of the destitution of privies, suitable play-grounds, etc., remarked as follows:

"But 544 out of 9368 houses visited contained more than one room; 7313 were destitute of any suitable play-ground; nearly 6000 were unfurnished with convenient seats and desks; nearly 8000 destitute of the proper facilities for ventilation; *and upward of* 6000 *without a privy of any sort;* while, of the remainder, but about 1000 were provided with privies containing different apartments for male and female pupils! And it is in these miserable abodes of accumulated dirt and filth, deprived of wholesome air, or exposed, without adequate protection, to the assaults of the elements; with no facilities for necessary exercise or relaxation; no convenience for prosecuting their studies; crowded together on benches not admitting of a moment's rest in any position, and debarred the possibility of yielding to the ordinary calls of nature without violent inroads upon modesty and shame, that upward of *two hundred thousand children*, scattered over various parts of the state, are compelled to spend an average period of eight months during each year of their pupilage! Here the first lessons of human life, the incipient principles of morality, and the rules of social intercourse are to be impressed upon the plastic mind. The boy is here to receive the model of his permanent character, and to imbibe the elements of his future career; and here the instinctive delicacy of the young female, one of the characteristic ornaments of the sex, is to be expanded into maturity by precept and example! Is it strange, under such circumstances, that an early and invincible repugnance to the acquisition of knowledge is imbibed by the youthful mind? that the school-house is regarded with unconcealed aversion and disgust, and that parents who have any desire to preserve the health and the morals of their children exclude them from the district school, and provide instruction for them elsewhere?"

A volume might be filled with similar testimony; but one more quotation from another state must suffice. After noticing the common evils already referred to, the superintendent remarks as follows:* "But this notice of *ordinary* deficiencies does not cover the whole ground of error in regard to the situation of school-houses. In some cases they are brought into close connection with positive nuisances. In a case which has fallen under the superintendent's own personal observation, one side of the school-house forms part of the fence of a hog-yard, into which, during the summer, the calves of an extensive dairy establishment have

* First Annual Report of the State Superintendent (Hon. Horace Eaton) of Common Schools, made to the Legislature of Vermont, October, 1846.

been thrown from time to time (disgusting and revolting spectacle!), to be rent and devoured before the eyes of teacher and pupils, except such portions of the mutilated and mangled carcasses as were left by the animals to go to decay, as they lay exposed to the sun and storm. It is true, the windows on the side of the building adjoining the yard were generally observed to be closed, in order to shut out the almost insupportable stench which arose from the decomposing remains. But this closure of the windows could, in no great degree, 'abate the nuisance;' for not a breath of air could enter the house from any direction but it must come saturated with the disgusting and sickening odor that loaded the atmosphere around. It needs no professional learning to tell the deleterious influence upon health which must be exerted by such an agency, operating for continuous hours."

If such evils as have been considered have existed so generally, and still prevail to an alarming extent, even in the states where education has received the most attention, what need must there be for the dissemination of information on this vitally important subject, especially in those states where education has heretofore received less attention! In remarking further upon this subject, I shall consider several leading particulars in the order they naturally suggest themselves. I will, then, commence with the

Location of School-houses.—In comparatively few instances school-houses are favorably located, being situated on dry, hard ground, in a retired though central part of the district, in the midst of a natural or artificial grove. But they are almost universally badly located; exposed to the noise, dust, and danger of the highway; unattractive, if not absolutely repulsive in their external appearance, and built at the least possible expense of material and labor. They are gener ally on one corner of public roads, and sometimes ad jacent to a cooper's shop, or between a blacksmith's shop and a saw-mill. They are not unfrequently placed on an acute angle, where a road forks, and sometimes in turning that angle, the travel is chiefly behind the school-house, leaving it on a small triangle bounded on all sides by public roads.

Occasionally the school-house is situated on a low and worthless piece of ground, with a sluggish stream of water in its vicinity, which sometimes even passes under the house. The comfort, and health even, of children are thus sacrificed to the parsimony of their parents. Scholars very generally step from the school-house directly into the highway. Indeed, school-houses are frequently situated one half in the highway and the other half in the adjacent field, as though they were unfit for either. This is the case even in some of the principal villages of all the states I have ever visited, or from which I have read full reports on the subject.

Strange as it may seem, school-houses are sometimes situated *in the middle of the highway*, a portion of the travel being on each side of them. When the scholars are engaged in their recreations, they are exposed to bleak winds and the inclemency of the weather one portion of the year, and to the scorching rays of the meridian sun another portion. Moreover, their recreations must be conducted in the street, or they trespass upon their neighbors' premises. We pursue a very different policy in locating a church, a court-house, or a dwelling; and should we not pursue an equally wise and liberal policy in locating the *district school-house?*

In the states generally northwest of the River Ohio, six hundred and forty acres of land in every township are appropriated to the support of common schools. Suppose there are ten school districts in a township, this would allow sixty-four acres to every district. It would seem that when the general government has appropriated *sixty-four acres* to create a fund for the encouragement of the schools of a township, that each district might set apart *one acre* as a site for a school-house. Once more: school districts usually contain not less than twenty-five hundred acres of land. Is it, then, asking too much to set apart *one acre* as a site for a school-house, in which the *minds* of the children of the district shall be cultivated, when *twenty-four hundred and ninety-nine* acres are appropriated to feeding and clothing their *bodies?*

I would respectfully suggest, and even *urge* the propriety of locating the school-house on a piece of firm ground of liberal dimensions, and of inclosing the same with a suitable fence. The location should be dry, quiet, and pleasant, and in every respect healthy. The vicinity of places of idle and dissipated resort should by all means be avoided; and, if possible, the site of the school-house should overlook a delightful country, and be surrounded by picturesque scenery. The school yard, at least, should be inclosed not only, but set out with shade trees, unless provided with those of Nature's own planting. It should also be ornamented with beautiful shrubbery, and be made the park of the neighborhood—the pleasantest place for resort within the boundaries of the district. This would contribute largely to the formation of a correct taste on the part of both children and parents. It would also tend to the formation of virtuous habits and the cultivation of self-respect; for the scholars would then enjoy their pastime in a pleasant and healthful yard, where they have a *right* to be, and need no longer be hunted as *trespassers* upon their neighbors' premises, as they now too frequently are.

Size and Construction.—In treating upon the philosophy of respiration at the 92d page of this work, it was stated that, exclusive of entry and closets, where hey are furnished with these appendages, school-houses are not usually larger than twenty by twenty-four feet on the ground, and seven feet in height. The average attendance in houses of these dimensions was estimated at forty-five scholars in the winter. It was also stated that the medium quantity of air that enters the lungs at each inspiration is thirty-six cubic inches, and that respiration is repeated once in three seconds, or twenty times a minute. Now, to say nothing of the inconvenience which so many persons must experience in occupying a house of so narrow dimensions, and making no allowance for the space taken up by desks, furniture, and the scholars themselves, a simple arithmetical computation will show any one that such a room will not contain a sufficient amount of air for the support of life three hours. But I will here simply refer the reader to the fourth chapter of this work, and will not repeat what was there said.

In determining the size of school-houses, due regard should be had to several particulars. There should be a separate entry or lobby for each sex, which Mr. Barnard, in his School Architecture,* very justly says should be furnished with a scraper, mat, hooks or

* "School Architecture," or Contributions to the Improvement of School-houses in the United States, by Henry Barnard, Commissioner of Public Schools in Rhode Island, p. 383. This excellent treatise embodies a mass of most valuable information in relation to school-houses and apparatus. It contains the plans of a great number of the best school-houses in various portions of the United States, and should be consulted by every committee before determining upon a plan for the construction of a valuable school-house.

shelves—both are needed—sink, basin, and towels. A separate entry thus furnished will prevent much confusion, rudeness, and impropriety, and promote the health, refinement, and orderly habits of the children.

The principal room of the school-house, and each such room where there are several departments, should be large enough to allow each occupant a suitable quantity of pure air, which should be at least twice the common amount, or not less than one hundred and fifty cubic feet. There should also be one or more rooms for recitation, apparatus, library, etc., according to the size of the school and the number of scholars to be accommodated.

Every school-room should be so constructed that each scholar may pass to and from his seat without disturbing or in the least incommoding any other one. A house thus arranged will enable the teacher to pass at all times to any part of the room, and to approach each scholar in his seat whenever it may be desirable to do so for purposes of instruction or otherwise. Such an arrangement is of the utmost importance; and without the fulfillment of this condition, no teacher can most advantageously superintend the affairs of a whole school, and especially of a large one.

In determining the details of construction and arrangement for a school-house, due regard must be had to the varying circumstances of country and city, as well as to the number of scholars that may be expected in attendance, the number of teachers to be employed, and the different grades of schools that may be established in a community.

Country Districts.—In country districts, as they have long been situated, and still generally are, aside from separate entries and clothes-rooms for the sexes, there will only be needed one principal school-room, with a smaller room for recitations, apparatus, and other purposes. In arranging and fitting up this room, reference must be had to the requirements of the district; for this one room is to be occupied by children of all ages, for summer and winter schools, and for the secular, but more especially for the religious meetings of the neighborhood. But in its construction primary reference should be had to the convenience of the scholars in school, for it will be used by them more, ten to one, than for all other purposes. Every child, then, even the youngest in school, should be furnished with a seat and desk, at which he may sit with ease and comfort. The seats should each be furnished with a back, and their height should be such as to allow the children to rest their feet comfortably upon the floor. The necessity of this will be apparent by referring to what has been said on the laws of health in the third chapter of this work, at the 68th and following pages.

No one, then, can fail to see the advantages that would result to a densely-settled community from a union of two or more districts for the purpose of maintaining in each a school for the younger children, and of establishing in the central part of the associated districts a school of a higher grade for the older and more advanced children of all the districts thus united.

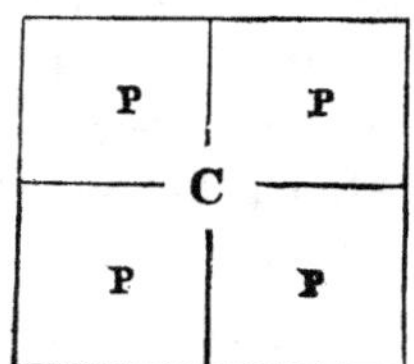

If four districts should be united in this way, they might erect a central house, C, for the larger and more advanced scholars, and four smaller ones, P P P P, for the younger children. The central school might be taught by a male teacher, with female assistants, if needed; but the primary schools, with this arrangement, could be more economically and successfully instructed by females. In several of the states legal provisions are already made for such a consolidation of districts. This would invite a more perfect classification of scholars, and would allow the central school-house to be so constructed, and to have the seats and desks of such a height as to be convenient for the larger grade of scholars, and still be comfortable for other purposes for which it might occasionally be necessary to occupy it. Such an arrangement, while it would obviate the almost insuperable difficulties which stand in the way of proper classification and the thorough government and instruction of schools, would at the same time offer greater inducements to the erection of more comfortable and attractive school-houses.

Cities and Villages.—The plan suggested in the last paragraph may be perfected in cities and villages. For this purpose, where neither the distance nor the number of scholars is too great, some prefer to have all the schools of a district or corporation conducted under the same roof. However this may be, as there will be other places for public meetings of various kinds, each room should be appropriated to a particular department, and be fitted up exclusively for the accommodation of the grade of scholars that are to occupy it. In cities, and even in villages with a population of three or four thousand, it is desirable to establish at least three grades of schools, viz., first, the primary, for the smallest children; second, the intermediate, for those more advanced; and, third, a central high school, for scholars that have passed through the primary and intermediate schools. While this arrangement is favorable to the better classification of the scholars of a village or city, and holds out an inducement to those of the lowest and middle grade of schools to perfect themselves in the various branches of study that are pursued in them respectively as the condition upon which

R

they are permitted to enter a higher grade, it also allows a more perfect adjustment of the seats and desks to the various requirements of the children in their passage through the grade of schools.

New York Free Academy.—In the public schools of the city of New York, two hundred in number, six hundred teachers are employed, and one hundred thousand children annually receive instruction. The Free Academy, which is a public school of the highest grade, and which is represented in our frontispiece, was established by the Board of Education in 1847. The expense of the building, without the furniture, was $46,000, and the annual expense for the salaries of professors and teachers is about $10,000. Out of twenty-four thousand votes cast, twenty thousand were for the establishment of this institution, in which essentially a complete collegiate education may be obtained. No students are admitted to it who have not attended the public schools of the city for at least one full year, nor these until they have undergone a thorough examination and proved themselves worthy. Its influence is not confined to the one hundred or one hundred and fifty scholars who may graduate from it annually, but reaches and stimulates the six hundred teachers, and the hundred thousand children whom they instruct, and thus elevates the common schools of the city *in reality* not only, but places them much more favorably before the public than they otherwise could be.

Smaller cities, and especially villages with a population of but a few thousand, can not, of course, maintain so extended a system of public schools; but they can accomplish essentially the same thing more perfectly, though on a smaller scale. For the benefit of districts in the country and in villages, I will here insert a few plans of school-houses.

Plan of a School-house for fifty-six Scholars.

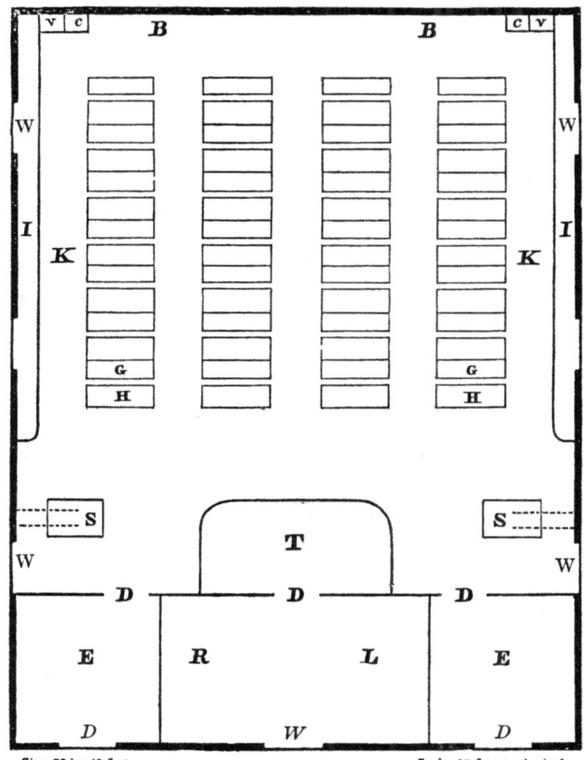

Size, 30 by 40 feet. Scale, 10 feet to the inch.

D D, doors. E E, entries lighted over outer doors, one for the boys and the other for the girls. T, teacher's platform and desk. R L, room for recitation, library, and apparatus, which may be entered by a single door, as represented in the plan, or by two, as in the following plan. S S, stoves with air-tubes beneath. K K, aisles four feet wide—the remaining aisles are each two feet wide. *c v*, chimneys and ventilators. I I, recitation seats. B B, black-board, made by giving the wall a colored hard finish. G H, seats and desks, four feet in length, constructed as represented on the next page. The seat and desk may be made together, and instead of being fastened permanently to the floor, attached in front by a strap hinge, which will admit of their being turned forward while sweeping under and behind them.

Primary and Intermediate Department, on first floor.

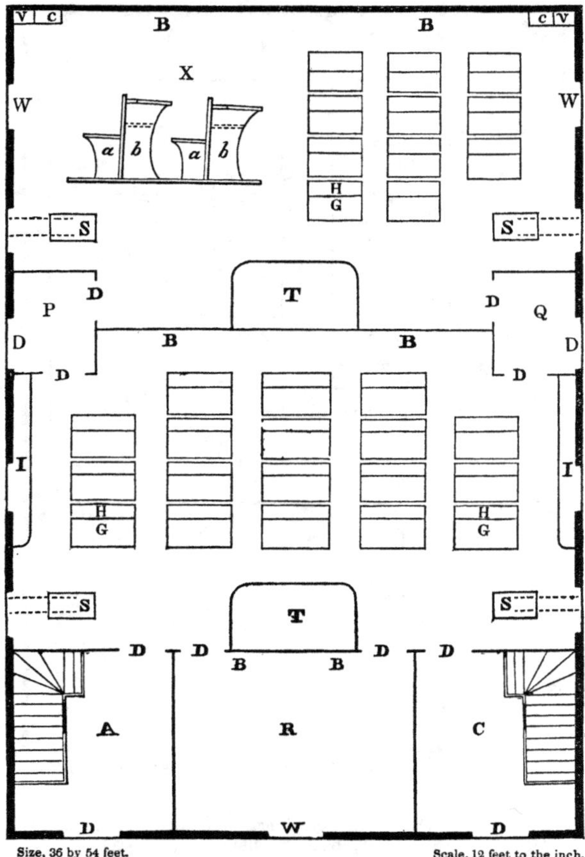

Size, 36 by 54 feet. Scale, 12 feet to the inch.

A, entrance for boys to the High School. C, entrance for girls to High School. P, entrance for boys to the Primary and Intermediate Departments. Q, entrance for girls to the same. D D, doors. W W, windows. T, teacher's platform and desk. G H, desk and seat for two scholars, a section of which is represented at X, in the Primary Department. I I, recitation seats. B B, black-boards. S S, stoves, with air-tubes beneath. *c v*, chimney and ventilator. R, room for recitation library, apparatus, and other purposes.

High School, or Third Department, on second floor.

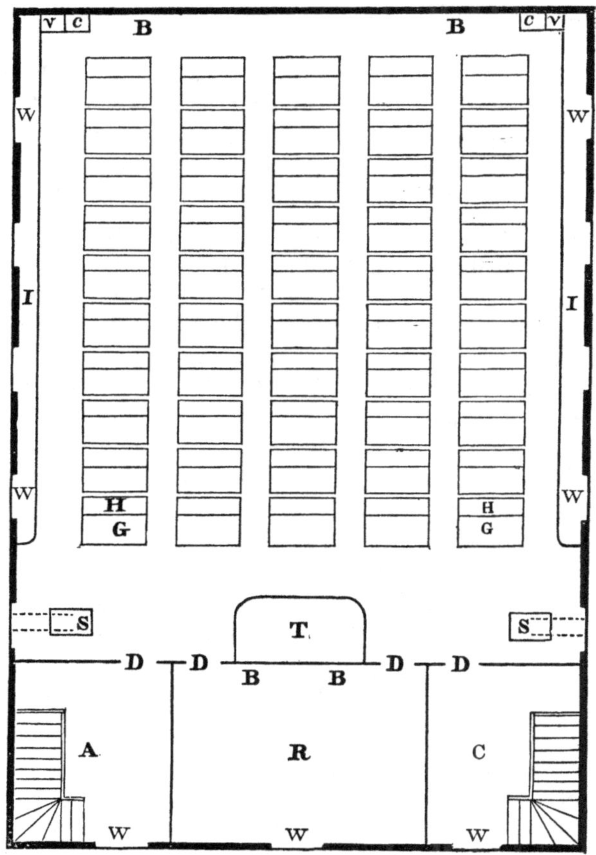

A, entrance for the boys, through the entry below. C, entrance for the girls. G H, desk and seat: aisles from two to three feet wide. D D, doors. W W, windows S S, stoves. *c v*, chimney and ventilator. T, teacher's platform. R, recitation-room. I I, recitation seats in principal room. B B, black-board: as a substitute for the common painted board, a portion of the wall, covered with hard finish, may be painted black; or, what is better, the hard finish itself may be colored before it is put on, by mixing with it lamp-black, wet up with alcohol or sour beer.

Ventilation of School-houses.—We have already seen that in a school-room occupied by forty-five persons, thirty-two thousand four hundred cubic inches of air impart their entire vitality to support animal life *the first minute*, and, mingling with the atmosphere of the room, proportionably deteriorate the whole mass; that the air of crowded school-rooms thus soon becomes entirely unfit for respiration, and that, as the necessary result, the health of both teacher and scholars is endangered; that the scholars gradually lose both the desire and the ability to study, and become more inclined to be disorderly, while the teacher becomes continually more unfit either to teach or govern. Hence the necessity of frequent and thorough ventilation.

The ordinary facilities for ventilating school-rooms consist in opening a door and raising the lower sash of the windows. The only ventilation which has been practiced in the great majority of schools has been entirely accidental, and has consisted in opening and closing the outer door as the scholars enter and pass out of the school-house, before school, during the recesses, and at noon. Ventilation, as such, I may safely say, has not, until within a few years, been practiced in one school in fifty; nor is it at the present time in many parts of the country. It is true, the door has at times been set open a few minutes, and the windows have been occasionally raised, but the object has been either to let the smoke pass out of the room, or to cool it when it has become too warm, not to ventilate it.

Ventilation by opening a door or raising the windows is imperfect, and frequently injurious. A more effectual and safer method of ventilation consists in lowering the upper sash of the window. In very cold or stormy weather, a ventilator in the ceiling may be opened, so as to allow the vitiated air to escape into the attic, in which case there should be a free communication between the attic and the outer air by means of a lattice in the gable, or otherwise. A ventilator may also be constructed in connection with the chimney, by carrying up a partition in the middle, one half of the chimney being used for a smoke flue, and the other half for a ventilator.

But it is often asked, Why is it not just as well to raise the lower sash of the windows as to lower the upper one? In reply I would say, first, lowering the upper sash is *a more effectual method of ventilation.* In a room which is warmed and occupied in cold weather, the warmer and more vitiated portions of the air rise to the upper part of the room, while that which is colder and purer descends. The reason for this may not be readily conceived, especially when we consider that carbonic acid, the vitiating product of respiration, is specifically heavier than common air. Three considerations, however, will make it apparent. 1. Gases of different specific gravity mix uniformly, under favorable circumstances. 2. The carbonic acid which is exhaled from the lungs at about blood heat is hence rarefied, and specifically lighter than the air in the room, which inclines it to ascend. 3. The ingress of cold and heavier air from without is chiefly through apertures near the base of the room. Raising the lower sash of the windows allows a portion of the purer air of the room to pass off, while the more vitiated air above is retained. Lowering the upper sash allows the impure air above to escape, while the purer air below remains unchanged.

Lowering the upper sash is also the *safer method of ventilation.* It not only allows the impure air more readily to escape, but provides also for the more uniform diffusion of the pure air from without, which takes its place through the upper part of the room. The renovated air will gradually settle upon the heads of the scholars, giving them a purer air to breathe, while the comfort of the body and lower extremities will remain undisturbed. This is as it should be; for warm feet and cool heads contribute alike to physical comfort and clearness of mind. Raising the lower sash of the windows endangers the health of scholars, exposing those who sit near them to colds, catarrhs, etc. Indeed, when it is very cold or stormy, it is unsafe to ventilate by lowering the upper sash of the windows. At such times, provision should be made for the escape of impure air at the upper part of the room, and for the introduction of pure air at the lower part, as will be shown while treating upon the means of warming.

Means of Warming.—Next in importance to pure air in a school-room is the maintenance of an even temperature. This is an indispensable condition of health, comfort, and successful labor. It is one, however, that is very generally disregarded; or, perhaps I should say, one that is not often enjoyed. School-houses are generally warmed by means of stoves, some of which are in a good condition, and supplied with dry, seasoned wood. The instances, however, in which such facilities for warming exist, are comparatively few. It is much more common to see cracked and broken stoves, the doors without either hinges or latch, with rusty pipe of various sizes. Green wood, also, and that which is old and partially decayed, either drenched with rain or covered with snow during inclement weather, is much more frequently used for fuel than sound, seasoned wood, protected from the weather by a suitable wood-house. With this state of things, it is exceedingly difficult to kindle a fire, which burns poorly, at best, when built. Fires, moreover, are frequently built so late, that the house does not become comfortably warm at the time appointed for commencing school. These neglects are the fruitful source of much discomfort and disorder. The temperature is fluctuating; the room is filled with smoke a considerable part of the ime, especially in stormy weather; and the school is l able to frequent interruptions, in fastening together and tying up stove-pipe, etc., etc.

This may seem a little like exaggeration. I know full well there are many noble exceptions. But in a large majority of instances some of these inconveniences exist; and the most of them coexist much more frequently than persons generally are aware of. I speak from the personal observation of several thousand schools in different states, and from reliable information in relation to the subject from various portions of the country. I have myself many times heard trustees and patrons, who have visited their school with me for the first time in several years, say, "We ought to have some dry wood to kindle with; I didn't know as it was so smoky: we must get some new pipe; really, our stove is getting dangerous," etc. And some of the boys have relieved the embarrassment of their parents by saying, "It don't smoke near so bad to-day as it does sometimes!"

The principal reason why the stoves in our schoolhouses are so cracked and broken, and why the pipes are so rusty and open, lies in the circumstance that green wood, or that which is partially decayed and saturated with moisture, is used for fuel, instead of good seasoned wood, protected from the inclemency of the weather by a suitable wood-house. There are at least three reasons why this is poor policy. 1. It takes double the amount of wood. A considerable portion of the otherwise sensible heat becomes latent, in the conversion of ice, snow, and moisture into steam. 2. The steam thus generated cracks the stove and rusts the pipe, so that they will not last one half as long as though dry wood from a wood-house were used. 3. It is impossible to preserve an even temperature. Sometimes it is too cold, and at other times it is too warm; and this, with such means of warming, is unavoidable. Scores of teachers have informed me that, in order to keep their fires from going out, it was necessary to have their stoves constantly full of wood, and even to lay wood upon the stove, that a portion of it might be seasoning while the rest was burning. Aside from the inconvenience of a fluctuating temperature, this is an unseemly and filthy practice, and one that generates very offensive and injurious gases.

Again: I have frequently heard the following and similar remarks: "The use of stoves in our school-houses is a great evil;" "Stoves are unhealthy in our school-houses, or in any other houses," etc. This idea being somewhat prevalent, and stoves being generally used in our school-houses, their influence upon health becomes a proper subject for consideration.

Combustion, whether in a stove or fire-place, consists in a chemical union of the *oxygen gas* of the atmosphere with *carbon*, the combustible part of the wood or coal used for fuel. Carbonic acid, the vitiating product of combustion, does not, however, ordinarily deteriorate the atmosphere of the room, but, mingling with the smoke, escapes through the stove-pipe or chimney.

The stove, in point of economy, is far superior to the open fire-place as ordinarily constructed. When the latter is used, it has been estimated that nine tenths of the heat evolved ascends the chimney, and only one tenth, or, according to Rumford and Franklin, only one fifteenth, is radiated from the front of the fire into the room. Four-fold more fuel is required to warm a room by a fire-place than when a stove is used. Oxygen is, of course, consumed in a like proportion, and hence, when the open fire-place is used, there is necessarily a four-fold greater ingress of cold air to supply combustion than where a stove is employed.

And, what is of still greater importance, when a fire-place is used, it is impossible to preserve so uniform a temperature throughout the room as when a stove is employed. When a fire-place is used, the cold air is constantly rushing through every crevice at one end of the room to supply combustion at the other end. Hence the scholars in one part of the room suffer from cold, while those in the opposite part are oppressed with heat. The stove may be set in a central part of the room, whence the heat will radiate, not in one direction merely, but in all directions. In addition to this, as we have already seen, only one fourth as much air is required to sustain combustion, on both of which accounts a much more even and uniform temperature can be maintained throughout a room where a stove is used than where a fire-place is employed.

But whence, then, has arisen the prevailing opinion that stoves are unhealthy? There are two sources of mischief, either of which furnishes a sufficient foundation for this popular fallacy. The first has already been referred to, and consists simply in the almost total neglect of proper ventilation. The other lies in the circumstance that school-rooms are generally kept too warm. In addition to the inconvenience of too high a temperature, the aqueous vapor existing in the atmosphere in its natural and healthful state is dispersed, and the air of the room becomes too dry. The evil being seen, the remedy is apparent. Reduce the temperature of the room to its proper point, and supply the deficiency of aqueous vapor by an evaporating dish partially filled with pure water. If this is not done, the dry and over-heated air, which is highly absorbent of moisture in every thing with which it comes in contact, not only creates a disagreeable sensation of dryness on the surface of the body, but in passing over the delicate membrane of the throat, creates a tickling, induces a cough, and lays the foundation for pulmonary disease, especially when ventilation is neglected. The water in the evaporating dish should be frequently changed, and kept free from dirt and other impurities. Care also should be taken not to create more moisture than the air naturally contains, otherwise the effect will be positively injurious.

The evil complained of is attributable mainly to the maintenance of a too high temperature. Were a thermometer placed in many of our school-rooms—and a school-house should never be without one in every occupied apartment—instead of indicating a suitable temperature, say sixty-two or sixty-five degrees, or even a summer temperature, it would not unfrequently rise above blood heat. The system is thus not only enfeebled and deranged by breathing an infectious atmosphere, but the debility thence arising is considerably increased in consequence of too high a temperature. The two causes combined eminently predispose the system to disease. The change from inhaling a fluid poison at blood heat, to inhaling the purer air without at the freezing point or below, is greater than the system can bear with impunity.

A uniform temperature, which is highly important, can be more easily and more effectually maintained where a stove is employed, furnished with a damper, and supplied with dry, hard wood, than where a fire-place is used. In the former case the draft may be regulated, in the latter it can not be. A great amount of air enters into combustion even where a stove is used. A greater quantity enters into the combustion where a fire-place is used, in proportion to the increased amount of wood consumed. Much of the heated air, also, where an open fire-place is used, mingling with the smoke, passes off through the chimney, and its place is supplied by an ingress of cold air at the more distant portions of the room. There is hence not only a great waste of fuel, but a sacrifice of comfort, health, and life.

But even where a stove is used there is a constant ingress of cold air through cracks and defects in the floor, doors, windows, and walls, which causes it to be colder in the outer portions of the room than in the central portions and about the stove. The evil is the same in kind as that already referred to in speaking of fire-places, but less in degree. This evil, however, may be almost entirely obviated by a very simple arrangement, which will also do much to render ventilation at once more effectual and safe, especially in very cold and inclement weather. The arrangement is as follows:

Immediately beneath the floor—and in case the school-house is two stories high, between the ceiling and the floor above—insert a tube from four to six inches in diameter, according to the size of the rooms, the outer end communicating with the external air by means of an orifice in the under-pinning or wall of the house, and the other, by means of an angle, passing upward through the floor beneath the stove. This part of the tube should be furnished with a register, so as to admit much or little air, as may be desirable. This simple arrangement will reverse the ordinary currents of air in a school-room. The cold air, instead of entering at the crevices in the outer part of the room, where it is coldest, enters directly beneath the stove, where it is warmest. It thus moderates the heat immediately about the stove, and being warmed as it enters, and mingling with the heated air, establishes currents toward the walls, and gradually finds its way out at the numerous crevices through which the cold air previously entered. If these are not sufficient for the purpose, several ventilators should be provided in distant parts of the room, as already suggested. This simple arrangement, then, provides for the more even dissemination of heat through all parts of the room, and thus secures a more uniform temperature, and, at the same time, provides a purer air for respiration, contributes greatly to the comfort and health of the scholars, and fulfills several important conditions which are essential to the most successful prosecution of their studies, and to the maintenance and improvement of social and moral, as well as intellectual and physical health.

By inclosing the stove on three sides in a case of sheet iron, leaving a space of two or three inches between the case and the stove for an air chamber, the air will become more perfectly warmed before entering the room at the top of the case. The best mode, however, of warming and ventilating large school-houses is by pure air heated in a furnace placed in the basement. The whole house can in this way be warmed without any inconvenience to the school from maintaining the fires, on account of either noise, dust, or smoke. But as this mode of warming can not be advantageously adopted except in very large schools, it will not often be found desirable out of cities and large villages.

Library and Apparatus.—I have already said that every school-house should have a room for recitations library, and apparatus. In country districts where but one teacher is employed in a school, it will perhaps generally be found convenient to conduct the majority of the recitations in the principal school-room. But even where this practice obtains, there is still urgent necessity for a room for a library, apparatus, and other purposes.

Several of the states have carried into successful operation the noble system of District Libraries. These, in the single state of New York, already contain nearly two millions of volumes. In some of the new states the system of Township Libraries has been adopted, which, on some accounts, is better adapted to a sparse population with limited means. These, in the State of Michigan, already contain one hundred thousand volumes. The director of each school district draws from the township library every three months the number of books his district is entitled to. These, for the time being, constitute the district library, and each citizen in the township is thus allowed the use of all the books in the township library.

Now, whichever of these systems is adopted, the school-house is the appropriate depository of the library. There are many reasons for this. It is central. It is the property of the district. During term-time it is visited daily by members from perhaps every family in the district. There may, and should be, a time fixed, at least once a week, when the library will be open, the librarian or his assistant being in attendance, at which time books may be returned and drawn anew. For this purpose, and on all accounts, no place can be so appropriate and free from objection as the school-house. The library may also be opened one or more evenings in the week, and especially during the winter, when evenings are long, as a district reading-room.

Moreover, should a District Lyceum be established, the use of a well-selected library, which will always be at hand, and of appropriate apparatus for the illustration of scientific lectures, will contribute greatly to increase both the popularity and the usefulness of the institution.

With such an arrangement, the children of the district would most assuredly be much more benefited by the instructions they would receive. The school would also possess many attractions for adults of both sexes, and by the co-operation of the wise and the good, its refining, purifying, and regenerating influences may be brought effectually to bear upon every family and every individual within the boundaries of the district. Then will the idea of Cousin be realized, who says, "A school ought to be a noble asylum, to which children will come, and in which they will remain with pleasure; to which their parents will send them with good will;" and, I will add, one whose uplifting influence both children and parents will constantly feel.

Such a room as I have described will also be found important for various other purposes, as a commodious place for retirement in case of sudden indisposition, a place where a teacher may see a patron or a friend in private, should it be at any time desirable, or a parent his child. It would also be of great service in giving the teacher an opportunity to see scholars in private, for various purposes, as well as in affording a convenient room for scholars to retire to, with the permission of the teacher, for mutual instruction.

That able and judicious advocate of popular enlightenment, and eminently successful school fficer, the Honorable Henry Barnard, does not over-estimate the importance of district libraries. In speaking of the benefits they confer upon a community, he says, "Wherever such libraries have existed, especially in connection with the advantages of superior schools and an educated ministry, they have called forth talent and virtue, which would otherwise have been buried in poverty and ignorance, to elevate, bless, and purify society. The establishment of a library in every school-house will bring the mighty instrument of good books to act more directly and more broadly on the entire population of a state than it has ever yet done; for it will open the fountains of knowledge, without money and without price, to the humble and the elevated, the poor and the rich."

Appurtenances to School-houses.—There are, perhaps, in the majority of school-houses, a pail for water, a cup, a broom, and a chair for the teacher. Some one or more of these are frequently wanting. I need hardly say, every school-house should be supplied with them all. In addition to these, every school-house should be furnished with the following articles: 1. An evaporating dish for the stove, which should be supplied with clean pure water. 2. A thermometer, by which the temperature of the room may be regulated. 3. A clock, by which the time of beginning and closing school, and conducting all its exercises, may be governed. 4. A shovel and tongs. 5. An ash-pail and an ash-house For want of these, much filth is frequently suffered to accumulate in and about the school-house, and not unfrequently the house itself takes fire and burns down. 6. A wood-house, well supplied with seasoned wood. 7. A well, with provisions not only for drinking, but for the cleanliness of pupils. 8. And last, though not least, in this connection, two privies, in the rear of the school-house, separated by a high close fence, one for the boys and the other for the girls. For want of these indispensable appendages of civilization, the delicacy of children is frequently offended, and their morals corrupted

Nay, more, the unnatural detention of the *fæces*, when nature calls for an evacuation, is frequently the foundation for chronic diseases, and the principal cause of permanent ill health, resulting not unfrequently in premature death. The accommodations in this respect provided by a district in a country village of the Northwest, whose schools have become celebrated, are none too ample. Two octagonal privies are provided—one for each sex—each of which has seven apartments. These are cleansed every two weeks, regularly, and oftener, if necessary.

Mr. Barnard, in treating upon the external arrangements of school-houses, has the following sensible remarks: "The building should not only be located on a dry, healthy, and pleasant site, but be surrounded by a yard, of never less than half an acre, protected by a neat and substantial inclosure. This yard should be large enough in front for all to occupy in common for recreation and sport, and planted with oaks, elms, maples, and other shady trees, tastefully arranged in groups and around the sides. In the rear of the building, it should be divided by a high and close fence, and one portion, appropriately fitted up, should be assigned exclusively for the use of boys, and the other for girls. Over this entire arrangement the most perfect neatness, seclusion, order, and propriety should be enforced, and every thing calculated to defile the mind, or wound the delicacy or the modesty of the most sensitive, should receive attention in private, and be made a matter of parental advice and co-operation.

"In cities and populous districts, particular attention should be paid to the play-ground, as connected with the physical education of children. In the best-conducted schools, the play-ground is now regarded as the *uncovered* school-room, where the real dispositions and habits of the pupils are more palpably developed, and can be more wisely trained, than under the restraint of an ordinary school-room. These grounds are provided with circular swings, and are large enough for various athletic games. To protect the children in their sports in inclement weather, in some places, the school-house is built on piers; in others, the basement story is properly fitted up, and thrown open as a play-ground."

A good and substantial room, well fitted up, and properly warmed in cold weather, in which children may conduct their sports, under the supervision of a teacher or monitor, is of the utmost importance; and especially is this true of all schools for small children. Such a room is, indeed, for these, hardly less important than the school-room. Among other things, it should be supplied with dumb-bells,* see-saws, weights and measures of various kinds, etc., etc. These are important for both boys and girls; but, as they are uncommon, it may be well to suggest the proper mode of using them, and the advantages they confer.

Dumb-bells may be used, in connection with the sports enumerated in the third chapter, for developing and strengthening the chest and improving the health. I would refer any who question the fitness of such exercises to what has been said on the subject at the 77th and following pages, and especially to the testimony of Dr. Caldwell there introduced.

See-saws, in addition to the benefits that result from the exercise, are attractive, and may be rendered highly instructive. For this purpose, the plank or board

* Dumb-bells are usually made of cast iron, and sometimes of bell-metal, of the shape indicated by the figure, and should weigh from two to ten pounds each, according to the strength of the person using them.

used should be well hung and properly balanced. The distance from the fulcrum or point of support should be accurately graduated, and marked in feet and inches. Then, knowing the weight of one scholar, the weights of all the others may be ascertained by their relative distances from the fulcrum when they exactly balance. These interesting experiments may be tried by any child as soon as he understands the ground rules of arithmetic, and the simple fact that, for two children to balance, the product of the weight of one multiplied into his distance from the fulcrum will exactly equal the product of the weight of the other into his distance from the fulcrum. Such simple experiments, when thus mingled with sports, and made interesting to young children, serve the double purpose of attaching them to the school, and of fixing in their minds the habit of observation and experiment, and of understanding the why and wherefore, which will be of incalculable service to them all the way through life.

Weights and measures serve the same general purpose, and may be rendered well-nigh as useful as slates and black-boards. Thousands of children recite every year the table, "four gills make a pint, two pints make a quart, four quarts make a gallon," etc., month in and month out, without any distinct idea of what constitutes a gill or a quart, or even knowing which of the two is the greater. But let these measures be once introduced into the experimental play-room, and let the child, under the supervision of the teacher or monitor, actually *see* that four gills make a pint, etc., and he will learn the table with ten-fold greater pleasure than he otherwise would, and in one tenth the time.

The same general remark will apply to the other tables of weight and measure, to experimental philosophy, and to nearly every branch of study pursued in the common schools of our country. I have but one other general remark to make on this subject, and that is in relation to the

INFLUENCE OF SCHOOL-HOUSES.—Cicero observes that the face of a man will be tinged by the sun, for whatever purpose he walks abroad; so, by daily associations, the minds of all persons are influenced, and their characters permanently affected, by scenes with which they are familiar; and especially is this true during the impressive periods of childhood and youth. Many persons seem to think that school-masters and school-mistresses do all the teaching in our schools. But it is not so. Fellow-students, neighbors, and citizens teach, by precept and by example; and especially do *school-houses teach.* And oh! what lessons of degradation, pollution, and ruin they sometimes impart! as he can not fail to be convinced who remembers the testimony already introduced in relation to their condition.

I have seen the fond parent accompany his lovely child of four summers to the school the first day of its attendance. The child had seen pictures of school-houses in books. Pictures, if not always pretty, usually please children. It was so in this case. The child, anxious to go to school, talked of the school-house on the way. There arrived, the parent passed his innocent little one into the care of the teacher, with a few remarks, and was about to retire, when the child, clinging to him, said, pathetically and energetically, "Pa! pa!! I don't want to stay in this ugly old house; I am afraid it will fall down on me: I want to go home to our own pretty parlor." But the parent, breaking away from his child, leaves it in tears, with a sad heart. How cruel to do such violence to the tender feelings of innocent children! And how baneful the influence! The school, instead of being a comfortable, pleasant, and delightful place, as it should be, is to the child positively offensive, and the school-house a dreary prison. "Just as the twig is bent, the tree's inclined." The child learns to hate school, to hate instruction, and all that is good. He soon becomes the practiced truant. In a few years he arrives at manhood; but, instead of being a blessing to his family and a useful member of society, he too frequently drags out a wretched life, in ignorance and penury, dividing it between the poor-house and jail, and terminating it, peradventure, upon the gallows.

It needs the pen of a ready writer duly to portray the influence of neglected school-houses. Parents seem to have forgotten that, *while men sleep, the enemy comes and sows tares;* that if good school-houses do not *elevate*, neglected ones will *pollute* their children. I have already alluded, in the language of others, to the representations of vulgarity and obscenity that meet the eye in every direction. But I am constrained to add, that, during the intermissions, and before school, "certain lewd fellows of the baser sort" sometimes lecture in the hearing of the school generally, boys and girls, large and small, illustrating their subject by these vulgar delineations.

But why are these things so? And how may they be remedied? Different persons will answer these questions variously. But when we bear in mind that, in architectural appearance, school-houses have very generally more resembled barns, sheds for cattle, or mechanic shops, than Temples of Science; that windows are broken; that benches are mutilated; that desks are cut up; that wood is unprovided; that out-buildings are neglected; that obscene images and vulgar delineations meet the eye within and without; that, in fine, their very appearance is so contemptible, that scholars feel themselves degraded in being obliged to occupy them; when we bear in mind all these things, and then consider that the impressive minds of children are necessarily and permanently affected by scenes with which they become familiar, we can not wonder that they yield themselves to such influences, and consent to increase their degradation by multiplying the abominations with which they are surrounded. And especially shall we cease to wonder at the existence of these things, when we consider that scholars are very often unfurnished with suitable employment; that the younger scholars are frequently urged on by the example and influence of the older ones; and that teachers are sometimes employed who are so far lost to shame as to countenance these disgusting and corrupting practices by engaging in them themselves!

A knowledge of the cause suggests the remedy. Let, then, the school-house be commodious and cleanly; inviting in its appearance, and elevating in its influence. Let every member of the school, at all times, be furnished with entertaining and profitable employment. Let the corrupting influence of bad example be at once and forever removed. And, finally, let the services of a well-qualified teacher, of good morals, correct example, and who is scrupulously watchful, be invariably secured.

But if the mean appearance of our school-houses is one reason why they are so defaced, it may be asked, why do not our *churches*, which are frequently among the most elegant specimens of architecture, escape the pollution? The reason is evident. The foul *habit* is contracted in the unseemly school-house, and it becomes so established that it is very difficult to suspend its exercise even in the Temple of God. Were our school-houses, in point of neatness and architecture, equal to our churches, the evil in question would soon become less prevalent, and, with judicious supervision, we might safely predict its early extinction.

I would not suggest that too much pains are taken to make our churches pleasant and comfortable, but I do protest that there is a great and unwise disproportion in the appearance of our churches and school-houses. It is frequently the case in villages and country neighborhoods, that the expense of the former is from fifty to eighty times the value of the latter. The *appearance* of our school-houses is an important consideration. If we would cultivate the *beastly* propensities of our youth, we have but to provide them places of instruction resembling the *hovels* which our cattle occupy, and the work is well begun. On the contrary, if we would take into the account the whole duration of our being, and the cultivation and right development of the nobler faculties of our nature, while the animal propensities are allowed to remain in a quiescent state, and *adapt means to ends,* our school-houses should be pleasant and tasteful. Every thing offensive should be separated from them, and no pains should be spared to give them an inviting aspect and an elevating influence.

It is easier to make children good than to reform wicked men. It is cheaper to construct commodious school-houses, with pleasant yards and suitable appurtenances, than to erect numerous jails and extensive prisons. George B. Emerson, in a lecture on moral education, speaks to the point. "In regard to the lower animal propensities," says he, "the only safe principle is, that nothing should be allowed which has a tendency, directly or indirectly, to excite them. In many places there prevails an alarming and criminal indifference upon this point. It is one toward which the attention of the teacher should be carefully directed. No sound should be suffered from the lips; no word, or figure, or mark should be allowed to reach the eyes, to deface the wall of the house or out-house, which could give offense to the most sensitive delicacy. This is the teacher's business. He must not be indifferent to it. He has no right to neglect it. He can not transfer it to another. He, and he only, is responsible.* It is impossible to be over-scrupulous in this matter. And the committee should see that the teacher does his duty; otherwise all his lessons in duty are of no avail, and the school, instead of being a source of purity, delicacy, and refinement, becomes a fountain of corruption,

* I would by no means free parents from responsibility in this matter. They, if any class, may be said to be "alone responsible;" but, in fact, all who are intrusted with the care of children share in the responsibility. *Secret vice,* in the opinion of those who have had occasion to remark the extent to which it is practiced, from colleges and the higher seminaries of learning down to the common school, and even in the nursery before the child is sent to school, prevails to an alarming extent. It is often the principal, and, in many instances, the sole cause of a host of evils that are commonly attributed to hard study, among which are impaired nutrition, and general lassitude and weakness, especially of the loins and back; loss of memory, dullness of apprehension, and both indisposition and incapacity for study; dizziness, affections of the eyes, headaches, etc., etc. Secret vice in childhood and youth is also a fruitful source of *social vice* later in life, and of excesses even within the pale of wedlock, ruinous alike to the parties themselves and to their offspring. Licentiousness in some of its forms, as we have frequently had occasion to see, from the highest testimony introduced into the text in various passages, in addition to the evils here referred to, sometimes leads to the most driveling idiocy, and to insanity in its worst forms. All, then, who have the charge of children, and especially parents and teachers, should exercise a rational familiarity with them on this delicate but important subject. They should give them timely counsel in relation to the temptations to which they may be exposed, apprise them of the evils that follow in the train of disobedience, and endeavor, by kindly advice and friendly admonition, to infix in their minds a delicate sense of honor, an abhorrence for this whole class of vice, and a determination never to entertain a thought of indulging the appetite for sex except within the pale of wedlock, and in accordance with God's own appointment.

throwing out poisonous waters, and rendering the moral influence more pestiferous than that fabled fountain of old, over which no creature of heaven could fly and escape death."

In conclusion, on this subject, I would say, if there is one house in the district more pleasantly located, more comfortably constructed, better warmed, and more inviting in its general appearance, and more elevating in its influence than any other, that house should be the school-house.

WELL-QUALIFIED TEACHERS SHOULD BE EMPLOYED.

All the provisions heretofore described would be of none effect if we took no pains to procure for the public school thus constituted an able master, and worthy of the high vocation of instructing the people. It can not be too often repeated, that it is the master that makes the school.—GUIZOT.

Society can never feel the power of education until it calls into exercise a class of effective educators.—LALOR.

One of the surest signs of the regeneration of society will be the elevation of the art of teaching to the highest rank in the community.—CHANNING.

We come next to the consideration of *school teachers;* for, in order to have good schools, we want not merely good school-houses. These, as already seen, are of the utmost importance ; but, to insure success, *we must have good teachers in those houses.* And here, were I addressing myself exclusively to the members of this profession, it would be appropriate to dwell in detail upon the requisite qualifications of teachers. But this would be foreign from my present design.*

Among the many excellent works already before the public, I would name the following, which the practical teacher may profitably consult: THE SCHOOL AND THE SCHOOLMASTER, by Dr. Potter and G. B. Emerson; THEORY AND PRACTICE OF TEACHING, by D. P. Page; THE

It has not been my intention in any thing I have yet said, nor will it be in any thing I may hereafter urge, to overlook the importance of domestic education. Napoleon once said to an accomplished French lady that the old systems of education were good for nothing, and inquired what was wanting for the proper training of young persons in France. With keen discernment and great truth, she replied, in one word—Mothers. This reply forcibly impressed the emperor, and he exclaimed, "Behold an entire system of education! You must make *mothers* that know how to train their children." I may add, we want mothers not only, but *fathers* too, qualified for the great work of training their offspring aright; for parents are readily admitted to be the natural educators of their children. But the literary training of children has always been accomplished chiefly by delegation; and not only the literary, but, to a great extent, the moral and religious.

This course has been adopted on account of the situation of families; many parents being unable to teach their children themselves, and others lacking the necessary leisure to carry forward a systematic and thorough course of instruction. This course is dictated by policy; for the children of a whole neighborhood may be better taught, and at less expense, in good schools, than in their respective families. This course has also been adopted as a matter of necessity; for the great-

School Teacher's Manual, by Henry Dunn; The Teacher, by Jacob Abbott; The Teacher's Manual, by Thomas H. Palmer; The Teacher Taught, by Emerson Davis; Slate and Black-board Exercises, by Wm. A. Alcott; Lectures on Education, by Horace Mann; Corporal Punishment, by Lyman Cobb; Confessions of a Schoolmaster, by Wm. A. Alcott; The Teacher's Institute, by Wm. B. Fowle, The True Relation of the Sexes, by John Ware. These are also useful to parents. A more extended list, with tables of contents, may be found in Barnard's School Architecture, p. 279 to 288.

ness of the work of education requires, in order to carry it forward successfully, that it should be studied as a profession. The teacher then engages jointly with the parent in the work of education, and with him shares its toils, its responsibilities, and its delights.

From the greatness of the teacher's work, as we have already considered it—training, as he should, his youthful charge for respectability, usefulness, and happiness in this life, and for everlasting felicity in that which is to come—we may infer what should be his qualifications. And we remark, in the general, that the business of

School teaching should rank among the learned professions. The teacher should well understand the nature of the subjects of education, as physical, intellectual, and moral beings. The education of children can not safely be intrusted to persons who are not practically acquainted with human physiology, and with mental science as based thereon. The most serious physical evils frequently result from allowing incompetent persons to exercise the functions of this high and responsible vocation.

In addition to a thorough knowledge of all the branches in which a teacher is expected to give instruction, and an acquaintance with those collateral branches that have a bearing upon them, the instructor of youth should possess the rare attainment of *aptness to teach.* It will be of little avail if the teacher has become familiar with all wisdom, unless he can readily communicate instruction to others. Paul, in speaking of the qualifications of bishops, says, among other things, they should be "apt to teach." This attainment is no less important for schoolmasters than for bishops. It is especially important that the teacher should be well acquainted with intellectual philosophy and moral science. This is necessary, in order to enable him to judge correctly of character, and to teach, and govern, and train his charge aright. But these attainments can never be made until teaching is elevated to the rank of a profession.

The lawyer is required to devote a series of years o a regular course of classical study and professional reading before he can find employment in a case in which a few dollars only are pending. With this we find no fault. But it should not be forgotten that the teacher's calling is as much more important than the ordinary exercise of the lègal profession, as the imperishable riches of mind are more valuable than the corruptible treasures of earth.

We seek out from among us men of sound discretion and good report to enact laws for the government of the state and nation. And with this, too, we find no fault. It is right and proper that we should do so. But it should be borne in mind that it is the teacher's high prerogative not only so to instruct and train the rising generation that they shall rightly understand law, but to infix in their minds the principles of justice and equity, the attainment of which is the high aim of legislation. While our legislators enact laws for the government of the people, the well-qualified and faithful schoolmaster prepares those under his charge to govern themselves. Without the teacher's conservative influence, under the best legislation, the great mass of the people will be lawless; while the tendency of his labors is to qualify the rising generation, who constitute our future freemen and our country's hope, to render an enlightened, a cheerful, and a ready obedience to the high claims of civil law. The well-qualified, faithful teacher, then, becomes the right arm of the legislator.

The physician is required to become thoroughly acquainted with the anatomy and physiology of the human body; in a word, to become acquainted with "the house I live in;" to understand the diseases to which we are subject, and their proper treatment, before he is allowed to extract a tooth, to open a vein, or administer the simplest medicine. Nor with this do we find fault, for we justly prize the body. It is the habitation of the immortal mind. When in health, it is the mind's servant, and ready to do its biddings; but darken its windows by disease, and it becomes the mind's prison-house. But while the physician, whom we honor and love, is required to make these attainments before he is permitted *even to repair* "the house I live in," should not he who teaches the MASTER of the house be entitled to a respectable rank in society?

It is common, in the various branches of the Church universal, for men who feel themselves called of God to preach the Gospel to obtain a collegiate education, and then devote several years to professional study, before exercising the functions of the sacred office; and this has been required by popular opinion. And heretofore, I may add, the efforts of the minister have been directed chiefly to the *reformation of adults* whose early training has been imperfectly attended to, and to the building up of a religious character where no correct early foundation has been laid, when the time and energies of a people upon whom labor is bestowed are devoted chiefly to absorbing secular pursuits. The competent and faithful teacher, on the contrary, enters upon the discharge of his duties under circumstances widely different, and with infinitely better prospects of success. Jesus said, *Suffer the little children to come unto me, and forbid them not; for of such is the kingdom of God.* These are they upon whom the teacher is called to bestow labor. He remembers that Solomon the wise has said, *Train up a child in the way he should go, and when he is old he will not depart from it;* and he confidently expects that, with proper parental co-operation, if he faithfully discharges his duty, and directs his efforts in accordance with the will of the Great Teacher, his youthful charge, when arrived at the years of accountability, and in all future life, will be like "the child Samuel, who grew on, and was in favor both with the Lord and also with men." No wonder, then, that Channing should say, "One of the surest signs of the regeneration of society will be *the elevation of teaching to the highest rank in the community.*"

The clerical profession can never equal that of the teacher in moral sublimity and prospective usefulness until religious teachers come to direct their attention chiefly to the correct early education of the young in the Sabbath-schools, but more especially in the common schools of our country. Then, and not till then, will it be entitled to the pre-eminence.

Should any teacher, in view of the immense responsibilities of his calling, be disposed to inquire, as all well may, *Who is sufficient for these things?* we would say to him, in the language of Wirt, "Let your motto be *Perseverando vinces*—by perseverance thou wilt overcome. Practice upon it, and you will be convinced of its value by the distinguished pre-eminence to which it will lead you." Especially will this be true in case the anxious teacher faithfully complies with the Divine direction, *If any man lack wisdom, let him ask of God, that giveth to all men liberally, and upbraideth not; and it shall be given him.*

Parents and citizens generally should be impressed with the truth of the maxim, "As is the teacher, so will be the school." They should desire for their own children, and for all others, teachers whose intellectual, social, and moral habits are, in all respects, what they are willing their children should form. They should, at least, be well apprised of this fact: If the teacher is not, in these respects, what they would have their children become, their children will be likely to become *what the teacher is.*

There is a story of a German schoolmaster, which shows the low notions that may be entertained of education. Stouber, the predecessor of Oberlin, the pastor of Waldbach, on his arrival at the place, desired to be shown to the principal school-house. He was conducted into a miserable cottage, where a number of children were crowded together, without any occupation. He inquired for the master. "There he is," said one, as soon as silence could be obtained, pointing to a withered old man, who lay on a little bed in one corner. "Are you the master, my friend?" asked Stouber. "Yes, sir." "And what do you teach the children?" "Nothing, sir." "Nothing! how is that?" "Because," replied the old man, "I know nothing myself." "Why, then, were you appointed the schoolmaster?" "Why, sir, I had been taking care of the Waldbach pigs a number of years, and when I got too old and infirm for that employment, they sent me here to take care of the children."

This anecdote may evince a degree of stupidity not to be met with in this country. We are, however, very far from being as careful in the selection of teachers as we ought to be. Unworthy teachers frequently find employment. I refer not to teachers whose literary qualifications are insufficient, although, as we have already seen, there are quite too many such. I refer now more particularly to those who are disqualified for the office because of moral obliquity.

Teachers are sometimes employed who are habitual Sabbath breakers; who are accustomed to the use of vulgar and profane language; who frequent the gambling table; who habitually use tobacco, in several of its forms, and that in the school-house! nay, more, who even teach the despicable habit to their children during school hours! Several emperors have prohibited the use of this filthy weed in their respective kingdoms, under the severest penalties. The pope has made a bull to excommunicate all those who use tobacco in the churches. One of the most numerous of the Protestant sects once prohibited the use of tobacco in their society; but so strong is this filthy habit, especially when formed in early life, that this society has backslidden and given up this excellent rule.

Since writing the above, I have noticed an article headed "Tobacco-using Ministers," which has appeared in several highly-reputable and widely-circulating periodicals, from which it appears that a large annual conference of divines of the same order, among other resolutions, have adopted one recommending "that the ministers refrain from the use of tobacco in all its forms, especially in the house of worship."

In commenting upon this action, a religious paper observes, that "by 'tobacco in all its forms' we suppose is meant chewing, smoking, and snuffing. But can it be possible that a minister, whose duty it is to recommend purity, and whose example should be cleanliness, can need conference resolutions to dissuade him from a practice so filthy and disgusting? And do they even carry this inconsistency into the 'house of worship?' So it seems!" But such is the severity of the strictures in the article referred to, that, although just, I forbear inserting them.

It has been suggested that, while Robinson Crusoe

was alone on his island, he may have had a right to smoke, snuff, or chew; but that, when his man Friday came, "a decent regard for the opinions of mankind"—as the Declaration of Independence has it—should have debarred him at once from further indulgence.

One who has enjoyed large opportunities of observing, and who is scrupulous to a proverb, has remarked, that "the ministerial profession is probably the most offending in this particular. The Scriptures have much to say about keeping the *body* pure. Had tobacco been known to the Hebrews, who can doubt that it would have been among the articles prohibited by the Levitical law? St. Paul beseeches the Romans, by the mercies of God, to present their *bodies* 'a living sacrifice, holy and acceptable.' To the Corinthians he says, 'Know ye not that ye are the temple of God, and that the spirit of God dwelleth in you? If any man defile the temple of God, him will God destroy; for the temple of God is holy, *which temple ye are.*' He commands them to glorify God in their *body* as well as in their spirit; for 'know ye not,' says he, 'that your *body* is the temple of the Holy Ghost?' What sort of a 'temple of the Holy Ghost' is he, every atom and molecule of whose physical system is saturated and stenched with the vile fetor of tobacco; whose every vesicle is distended by its foul gases; whose brain and marrow are begrimed and blackened with its sooty vapors and effluxions; all whose pores jet forth its malignant stream like so many hydrants; whose prayers are breathed out, not with a *sweet*, but with a *foul*-smelling savor; who baptizes infants with a hand which itself needs literal baptism and purification as by fire; and who carries to the bed-side of the dying an odor which, if the 'immaterial essence' could be infected by any earthly virus, would subject the departed soul to quarantine before it could enter the gates of heaven?"*

"Touch not, taste not, handle not," is the only safe rule in relation to all vicious practices; and especially is it true of this habit, which we can not call *beastly*, for there is not a *natural* beast in creation that indulges in it. I therefore congratulate my countrymen in view of the prospect before us of ultimately being freed from this disgusting and filthy habit, for the Board of Education in some of our cities have already wisely adopted the rule of employing no teachers who use tobacco in any form. Let this rule become universal among us, and the next generation will be comparatively free from the use of that repulsive weed, which only one of all created beings takes to naturally. Wherever else the filthy practice may be allowed, it ought never to be permitted in a house consecrated to the sacred work of educating the rising generation. And just look at the immense expenditure in this coun-

* A female teacher in the Bay State, in 1847, addressed the following inquiry through the columns of the Massachusetts Common School Journal:

"I have been laboring for the last year in a large school, and have endeavored, according to the best of my ability, to inculcate habits of neatness among the pupils, especially to break them of the filthy habit of spitting upon the floor. I have often told them *gentlemen* never do it. But at a recent visit of the committee, an individual, who has been elected by the town to superintend the educational interests of the rising generation, *spit* the dirty juice of his *tobacco* quid upon the floor of my school-room with apparent self-complacency.

"Shall I say to the children that this person is *not* a *gentleman*, and thus destroy his influence? or shall I pass it over in silence, and thus leave them to draw the natural inference that all I have said on the subject is only a woman's whim?"

Mr. Mann, the editor, gave a full reply through the Journal, from which I have here quoted part of a paragraph. He closes by offering a prize of the "eternal gratitude of all decent men" to the discoverer of a remedy or antidote for the evil.

try for the support of this pernicious habit. It is said, on good authority, that for *smoking* merely we pay annually a tax of ten millions of dollars, which is a much greater sum than is paid to the teachers of all the public schools in the United States.

But to return: teachers are sometimes employed who are addicted to inebriety; who are notorious libertines, and unblushingly boast of the number of their victims. But I will not extend this dark catalogue. Comment is unnecessary. My fellow-countrymen, who have carefully perused and properly weighed the preceding considerations, I doubt not, will concur with me in the opinion that there is no station in life—no, not excepting even the clerical office, that, in order to be well filled, so much demands purity of heart, simplicity of life, Christian courtesy, and every thing that will ennoble man, and beautify and give dignity to the human character, as that of the primary school-teacher. He influences his pupils in the formation of habits and character, by precept, it is true, but chiefly by example. His example, then, should be such, that, if strictly followed by his pupils, it will lead them aright in all things, astray in nothing. It should be his chief concern to allure to brighter worlds on high, and himself lead the way. Then, and not till then, will he be prepared to magnify and fill his office.

But, it may be said, we have not a sufficiency of well-qualified teachers, according to this standard, to take the charge of all, or of any considerable part of our schools. This is very readily admitted. Some such, however, there are. These should be employed. Their influence will be felt by others. The present generation of teachers may be much improved by means of teachers' associations and teachers' institutes. By the establishment of normal schools, or teachers' seminaries, a higher grade of teachers may be trained up and qualified to take the charge of the next generation of scholars. These institutions have been established in several of the European states, in New England and New York, and more recently in Michigan, by the several State Legislatures, and to some extent in other states. "Those seminaries for training masters," says Lord Brougham, "are an invaluable gift to mankind, and lead to the indefinite improvement of education." In remarking upon their advantages, the same high authority says, "These training seminaries would not only teach the masters the branches of learning and science they are now deficient in, but would teach them what they know far less—the didactic art—the mode of imparting the knowledge which they have or may acquire; the best mode of training and dealing with children in all that regards both temper, capacity, and habits, and the means of stirring them to exertion, and controlling their aberrations."

Normal schools are essential to the complete success of any system of popular education. The necessity for their establishment can not fail to be apparent to any one at all competent to judge, when he considers the early age at which young persons of both sexes generally enter upon the business of school-teaching—or, perhaps I may more appropriately say, of "keeping" school; for the majority of them can hardly be regarded as competent to *teach.*

For the purpose of being more specific, and of impressing, if possible, upon the mind of the reader, the necessity of professional instruction, the author trusts he will be pardoned for introducing a few paragraphs from a report made nine years ago as county superintendent of common schools in the State of New York, and which was printed at that time in the Assembly documents of that state. The author, at the time referred to, exercised a general supervision over more than twenty thousand children, aided in the examination of the teachers of twenty large townships, and visited and inspected their schools. Nine years' additional experience—four of which have been devoted to the supervision of the schools of a large state, and a considerable portion of the remaining time to the visitation of schools in different states—has convinced him that the condition of common schools, and the qualifications of teachers in those states of the Union where increased attention has not been bestowed upon the subject within a few years past, are not in advance of what they were at that time in the county referred to. The paragraphs introduced are included within brackets.

[LITERARY QUALIFICATIONS.—Some of the teachers possess a very limited knowledge of the branches usually taught in our common schools. This is true even of a portion of those who have bestowed considerable attention upon some of the higher branches of study. There is in our common schools, and indeed in our higher schools, an undue anxiety to advance rapidly. A score of persons may be heard speaking of the number of their recitations, of their rapid progress, and perhaps of skipping difficulties, while hardly *one* will speak of progressing *understandingly*, and comprehending *every principle* as he proceeds. When students speak of their progress in study, their first qualifying word should be *thorough*, after which, if they please, they may add *rapid*.

The following circumstances, that have occurred in classes of both ladies and gentlemen who have presented themselves for examination as candidates for teaching, illustrate the nature and extent of the evil. I have more than once received, in answer to the question

'What is language?" the following reply: "Language is an *unlimited sense*." I have met with some experienced teachers, holding two or three town certificates, who did not know one half of the marks and pauses used in writing. They could, indeed, generally recite the answers in the spelling-book with some degree of accuracy; but when the marks have been pointed out, and their names and use have been asked, teachers *in service* have sometimes mistaken the note of *interrogation* for a *parenthesis*, and made other as gross errors. In answer to the question "What is arithmetic?" I have several times received the following reply: "It is the *art of science*," etc. Sometimes this constitutes the entire reply. In one instance *four fifths* of the class united in this answer. The terms sum, remainder, product, and quotient are frequently applied indiscriminately in the four ground rules of arithmetic. There are, hence, three chances for them to be used erroneously where there is one chance for them to be correctly applied. The following expressions are common: *Add* up and set down the *remainder; subtract* and set down the *quotient; multiply* and write down the *sum; divide* and write down the *product*, etc.: never so much as thinking that sum belongs to addition; remainder, to subtraction; product, to multiplication; and quotient, to division. In attending the examination of such teachers, any person of discernment will soon become satisfied that with them "language is an unlimited sense;" that "arithmetic is the art *of* science;" and that grammar, too, is "the art of science;" for the same answer has been given to the question, "What is grammar?" I introduce these things, not for the purpose of ridiculing any portion of our teachers, but to exemplify the extent of the evil under consideration.

The majority of teachers manifest a tolerable familiarity with the branches usually taught in our common schools. They have not, however, generally studied more than one author on the same subject.

A portion of our teachers, it gives me pleasure to add, are not only superior scholars in the common English branches, but they have made respectable attainments in philosophy, astronomy, chemistry, algebra, Latin, etc. All of these branches are successfully taught in a few of our schools.

School Government.—There is, perhaps, as wide a difference in the administration of government in our common schools as in any other particular connected with them. Good government requires the healthful exercise of a rare combination of good qualities. But this can not reasonably be expected in inexperienced youth, who, instead of being guided by enlightened moral sentiment, have not only never subjected *themselves* to government, but are totally unacquainted with the principles upon which it should be administered. About one third of our schools are tolerably well governed. A portion of them are under a wise and parental supervision, the government being uniformly mild, and at the same time efficient. But indecision, rashness, and inefficiency are far more common. Sometimes teachers resolve to have no whispering, leaving seats, asking questions, etc., among any of the scholars, and severely punish every detected offender. Soon a portion of the patrons justly manifest dissatisfaction. Then all attempts to govern the school are unwisely given up. Many teachers thus rashly fly from one extreme of government to the other, without stopping to test the "golden mean," or even appearing to bestow a single thought upon the subject.

Again: the feelings of the teacher have been outraged by having frequently witnessed severity, and even cruelty, in government; and, in studiously avoiding them, he has inadvertently adopted a lax government, if government it may be called. The latter may be the more amiable extreme, but it is hardly the less fatal. I have heard scholars say in the presence of such a teacher, "We have a good teacher, who gives us all the good advice we need, and then lets us do as we please;" and then I have witnessed whispering, talking, chewing gum and throwing it about the house, passing from seat to seat, playing with tops and whirls, tossing wads of wet paper about the house and to the ceiling, cutting images upon the desks, imitating the practice of botanic physicians, exhibiting and passing from one to another roots and herbs, and discoursing upon their properties, chasing mice about the house, and in some instances slaying them, and practicing sundry other antics too numerous to be mentioned. Good advice was freely given, but it was disregarded with impunity.

Government in school, as elsewhere, should be mild but efficient. The teacher should speak kindly, but with authority. Every request should meet with a ready compliance. The scholars will not only fear to disobey such a teacher, but will, at the same time, respect, and even love him. This is not only good theory, but is susceptible of being reduced to practice. It is, indeed, exemplified in many of our schools, as a visit to them will clearly manifest. I know of no one thing in school government more mischievous in its tendency than the habit of speaking several times without being obeyed.

Mode of Instruction.—In some schools the instruction is thorough and systematic. In them the scholars generally learn *principles*, and understand, and are able to explain, all that they pass over. But this is the case in comparatively few schools. Scholars generally are poorly instructed, and understand very imperfectly what they profess to have learned. I will give a few illustrations:

First. Scholars are frequently introduced to the twenty-six letters of the alphabet four times a day for several weeks in succession, without making a single acquaintance. They occasionally become so familiar with their names and order as to repeat them down and back, as well without the book as with it, before learning a single letter.

This method of instruction is as unphilosophical as it is unsuccessful. Were I to be introduced to twenty-six strangers, and were my introducer to pronounce their names in rapid succession down and back, giving me merely an opportunity of pronouncing them after him, I should hardly expect to form a *single acquaintance with twenty-six introductions.* But were he to introduce me to one, and give me an opportunity of shaking hands with him, of conversing with him, of observing his features, etc.; and were he then to introduce me to another, in like manner, with the privilege of shaking hands again with the first, before my introduction to the third; and were he thus to introduce me to them all successively, I might form *twenty-six acquaintances with one introduction.*

The application is readily made. Introduce the abecedarian to but *one* letter at first. Describe it to him familiarly. Fix its contour distinctly in his mind. Compare it with things with which he is acquainted, if it will admit of such comparison. It might be well to make the letter upon a slate or black-board. When he shall have become acquainted with *one* letter so as to know it any where, introduce him to another. After he becomes acquainted with the second, let him again point out the first. As he learns new letters, he will thus retain a knowledge of those he has previously learned. It is immaterial where we commence, provided two conditions are fulfilled. It would be well to have the first letters as simple in their construction, and as easily described, as possible. It would be well, also, to have them so selected as to combine and form simple words, with which the child is familiar. He will thus become encouraged in his first efforts.

Suppose we commence with O, and tell the child that it is *round;* that it is shaped like the *button* on his coat, or like a *penny*, which might be shown to him. After the child has become somewhat familiar with its *shape* and *name*, suppose we inquire what there was on the breakfast table shaped like O. It may be necessary to name a few articles, as knives, forks, spoons, plates. Before there is time to proceed further, the child, in nine cases out of ten, will say, "The *plates* look like O." Suppose we next take X, which may be represented by crossing the fore-fingers, or two little sticks. We can now teach the child that these two letters, combined, spell *ox*. We might then tell him a familiar story about *oxen;* that we put a *yoke* on them; that they draw the cart, etc.; and that *cart-wheels* are *great* O's. Suppose we take B next. We might tell the child that it is a straight line with two bows on the right side of it, and that it is shaped some like the *ox-yoke*. We might then instruct him that these three letters, B, O, and X, combined, spell *box;* that its top and sides are rectangles, and that its ends are squares, if they are so. The child has now learned three letters, two words, and a score of ideas. He, moreover, likes to go to school. Any other method in which children would be equally interested might be pursued instead of this, which is only introduced as a *specimen* of the manner in which the alphabet has been successfully taught.* Better methods may be devised.

Second. The Roman notation table is sometimes taught after the same manner. After spelling, I have heard the teacher say to the class, One I.? to which the scholar at the head would reply, one; and the exercise would continue through the class, as follows: two I.'s? two; three I.'s? three; IV.? four; and so on, to two X.'s? twenty; three X.'s? twenty-one. No, says the teacher, *thirty.* Thus corrected, the class went through the entire table, without making another mistake. The thought occurred to me that they did not *know* their lesson, though they had *recited* it, making but *one* mistake. With the permission of the teacher, I inquired of the class, "What does IV. stand for?" None of them could tell. I then inquired, "What do VII. stand for?" They all shook their heads. I next inquired, "What does IX. stand for?" and the teacher remarked, "*They have just got it learnt the other way; they ha'n't learnt it that way yet.*" They had all learned to *count;* they hence recited correctly to twenty; and when told that three X.'s stand for *thirty* instead of *twenty-one,* they passed on readily to forty, fifty, sixty, etc., without making another mistake. And this, too, is but a *specimen* of the evil.

In teaching this table, the child should be instructed,

* Since these suggestions were first given to the public, several excellent books for children have been published, constructed on a similar plan to that here recommended. It will generally be found advantageous to teach the vowels first, and then to teach such consonants as combine with the *long sound* of the vowel; as, for example, first o; then g, h, l, n, and s, when the child can read go, ho, lo, no, and so. After this, e may be learned, and then b, m, and s, when the child can read be, bee, me, and see. Then these may be combined as see me; lo, see me; see me ho; lo, see me ho, etc. The idea is, that every letter and combination of letters be used as fast they are learned.

in the beginning, that there are but seven letters used, by which all numbers may be represented; that when standing alone, I. represents *one;* V., *five;* X., *ten;* L., *fifty;* C., *one hundred;* D., *five hundred;* and M., *one thousand.* The child should next be taught that, as often as a letter is repeated, so many times its *value* is repeated; thus, X. represents *ten;* two X.'s, *twenty;* three X.'s, *thirty,* etc.; that when a letter representing a *less* number is placed *after* one representing a *greater,* its value is to be *added;* thus, VII. represent *seven;* LX., *sixty,* etc.; that when a letter representing a *less* number is placed *before* one representing a *greater,* its value is to be *subtracted;* thus, IV. represents *four;* IX., *nine;* XL., *forty,* etc. When the child understands what is here presented, he has the key to the whole matter. He is acquainted with the principle upon which the tables are constructed, and a little practice will enable him to apply it, as well to what is *not* in the table as to what *is* in it. I have known scholars study that table faithfully *four months,* and then have but an imperfect knowledge of what was *in the book.* I have known others who, with *one hour's* study, after *five minutes'* instruction in the principles here laid down, understood the table perfectly, and could recite it, without making a single mistake, even before they had studied the whole of it *once over.*

Third. The manner in which *reading* is generally taught is hardly superior to the modes of instruction already considered. In many instances, commendable effort is made to secure correct pronunciation, and a proper observance of the inflections and pauses. But there is a great lack in *understanding* what is read. When visiting schools, with the permission of the teacher, I usually interrogate reading classes with reference to the meaning of what they have read. Occasionally I receive answers that give satisfactory evidences of correct instruction. Generally, however, the scholars have no distinct idea concerning the author's meaning. They, astonished, sometimes say, "I didn't know as the *meaning* has any thing to do with reading; I try to pronounce the words right, and mind the stops." Teachers sometimes say their scholars are poor readers, and it takes all their attention to pronounce their words correctly. They therefore do not wish to have them *try* to *understand* what they read, thinking it would be a hinderance to them. They occasionally justify themselves in the course they pursue, saying, "I don't have time to question my classes on their reading, nor hardly time to look over and correct mistakes." At the same time they will read three or four times around, twice a day or oftener. The idea prevails extensively, judging from the practice of teachers, that the value of their services depends upon the extent of the various exercises of the school. If the classes can read several times around, twice a day, and spell two or three pages, teachers frequently think they have done well, even though one half of the mistakes in reading are uncorrected, and one fourth or more of the words in the spelling lessons are misspelled, to say nothing of understanding what is read. The majority of schools might be very much improved by conducting them upon the principle that "what is worth doing at all is worth doing well." I am fully satisfied that it is incomparably better for classes to read *once* around, *once* a day, and *understand* what they read, than to read *four* times around, *four* times a day, *without understanding* their lessons. Scholars should, indeed, never be allowed to read what is beyond their comprehension; and great pains should be taken to see that they actually understand every lesson, and every book read. The early formation of such a habit will be of incalculable value in after life.

I will introduce one extract from my note-book by way of illustration. The reader will please observe that it relates to neither a back district nor an inexperienced teacher.

"This is one of the oldest and most important districts in town. The school is taught by an experienced and highly-reputable teacher. The first class in the English Reader read the section entitled '*The Journey of a Day; a Picture of Human Life.*' Obidah had been contemplating the beauties of nature, visiting cascades, viewing prospects, etc., and in these amusements the hours passed away uncounted, till 'day vanished from before him, and a sudden tempest gathered around his head;' when, it is said, 'he beheld through the brambles the *glimmer of a taper*.' I inquired of the class, 'What is a taper?' No one replied. I added, 'It is either the sun, a light, a house, or a man,' whereupon one replied, 'the sun;' another, 'a house;' another still, 'a house;' and still another, 'a man.' I next inquired, 'What does glimmer mean?' No reply being given, I added, 'It either means a light, the shadow, the top, or the bottom.' They then replied successively as follows: 'Top, shadow, bottom,' which would give their several ideas of the phrase, 'the glimmer of a taper,' as follows: The shadow of a house. The top of a man. The bottom of the sun, etc. It should be borne in mind, the class had just read that this 'taper' was discovered after 'day had vanished from sight.'"

This example is selected from among more than a hundred, scores of which are more striking illustrations than the one introduced, which is selected because it occurred in the first class of an important school, taught by an experienced and highly-reputable teacher.

The habit of reading without understanding originates mainly in the circumstance that the books put into the hands of children are to them uninteresting. The style and matter are often above their comprehension. It is impossible, for example, for children at an early age to understand the English Reader, a work which frequently constitutes their only reading-book (at least in school) when but seven years of age. The English Reader is an *excellent book*, and would grace the library of any gentleman. But it requires a better knowledge of language, and more maturity of mind than is often possessed by children ten years old, to understand it, and to be interested in its perusal. Hence its use induces the habit of "pronouncing the words and minding the stops," with hardly a single successful effort to arrive at the idea of the author. To this early-formed habit may be traced the prevailing indifference, and, in some instances, *aversion* to reading, manifested not only in childhood, but in after life.

The matter and style of the reading-book should be adapted to the capacity and taste of the learner. The teacher should see that it is well understood, and then it can hardly prove uninteresting, or be otherwise than well read. Children should read less in school than they ordinarily do, and greater pains should be taken to have them understand every sentence, and word even, of what they do read. They will thus become more interested in their reading, and read much more extensively, not only while young, but in after life, and with incomparably more profit.

Fourth. I have heard several classes in geography bound states and counties with a considerable degree of accuracy, when none of them could point to the north, south, east, or west. Indeed, a portion of them were not aware that these terms relate to the four cardinal points of the compass. Still more: some of them say that "geography is a description of the earth," but they do not know as they ever *saw* the earth. They have no idea that *they live upon it.* Scholars in grammar frequently think that the only object of the study is to enable them to recite the definitions and rules, and to *parse.* They do not look for any assistance in thinking, speaking, or writing correctly, neither do they expect any aid therefrom in understanding what they read.

Classes in arithmetic not unfrequently think the principal object in pursuing that science is to be able to *do the sums* according to the rule, and perhaps to *prove* them. Propose to them a practical question for solution, and their reply is, "That isn't in the arithmetic." Some one more courageous may say, "If you'll tell me what rule it is in, I'll try it!" Practical questions should be added by the teacher, till the class can readily apply the principles of each rule to the ordinary transactions of business in which they are requisite. Generally, in grammar, arithmetic, and elsewhere, there is too much inquiry, *comparatively,* after the *how,* and too little after the *why.*]

Now if these paragraphs, descriptive of the condition of common schools and the qualifications of teachers at the commencement of the educational reform in New York, are applicable to those states of the Union whose provisions for general education are not equal to what hers then were, nothing can be plainer than that there exists an imperative demand for the establishment of normal schools in every part of the Union. Massachusetts has three; but her provisions in this respect are not adequate to her necessities.

Union schools, and systems of graded schools in cities and villages, should possess a normal characteristic; that is, young men and women who have the requisite natural and acquired ability should be employed as assistants in the lower departments, and should sustain essentially the relation of *apprenticed teachers*, to be promoted or discontinued according as they shall prove themselves worthy or otherwise. In the public schools of the city of New York there are about two hundred teachers of this description. These and all the less experienced teachers meet at a stated time every week for the purpose of receiving normal instruction from a committee of teachers whose instructions are adapted to their wants. A similar feature has been adopted in other cities, and in many villages, and should become universal among us.

In connection with the suggestions I have just introduced from a former report, I wish to say, I know of no reform which is more needed in our schools than that of rendering instruction at once *thorough* and *practical.* The suggestion in the note on the 428th page, in relation to teaching the alphabet, will admit of general application. As fast as principles are learned, they should be applied. Practical questions for the exercise of the student should be interspersed with the lessons in all our text-books, when the nature of the subject will admit of it. When these are not given by the author, they should be supplied by the teacher.

I will illustrate by an example. Several years ago a teacher had the charge of a class in natural philosophy. There were no questions in the text-book used for the exercise of the student, as here recommended. In treating upon the hydraulic press, the author said, in relation to the force to be obtained by its use, "If a pressure of two tons be given to a piston, the diameter of which is only a quarter of an inch, the force transmitted to the other piston, if three feet in diameter, would be upward of forty thousand tons." The teacher inquired of the class, How much upward of forty thousand tons would the pressure be? Not one in a large class was prepared to answer the question. Some of the scholars laughed outright at the idea of asking such a question. After a few familiar remarks by the teacher, the class was dismissed. This question, however, constituted a part of their review lesson. The next day found it solved by every member of the class. Several of the scholars said to the teacher that they had derived more practical information in relation to natural philosophy from the solution of this one question, than they had previously acquired in studying it several quarters.

In treating upon the velocity of falling bodies, such questions as the following might be asked: Suppose a body in a vacuum falls sixteen feet the first second, how far will it fall the first three seconds? How far will it fall the next three seconds? How much further will it fall during the ninth second than in the fifth? If this paragraph should be read by any teacher or student of natural philosophy who has not been accustomed thus to apply principles, the author would suggest that it may be found pleasant and perhaps profitable to pause and solve these questions before reading further.

The importance of reducing immediately to practice every thing that is learned, is no less essential in moral and religious education than in physical or intellectual. Indeed, any thing short of this is jeoparding one's dearest interests; for "to him that knoweth to do good and doeth it not, to him it is sin." The practical educator should bear in mind that man is susceptible of progression in his moral and religious nature as well as in his physical and intellectual. "Cease to do evil; learn to do well," is the Divine command. He who does only the former has but a negative goodness. The practice of the latter is essential to the healthful condition of the soul. It is important that we seek earnestly to be "cleansed from secret faults." Without this, our progress in excellence will at best be slow. While "the way of the wicked is as darkness, and they stumble at they know not what," it is nevertheless true that "the path of the just is as the shining light, that shineth more and more unto the perfect day."

Understanding what we do of the nature of man, the subject of education, and knowing that "the fear of the Lord is the beginning of wisdom," and that the Great Teacher, who "taught as one having authority," hath said, "Seek ye first the kingdom of God and his righteousness," can we regard it any thing less than consummate folly to enter upon the work of education in the open neglect of these precepts? Should we not rather cheerfully comply with them, and do what we can to encourage all teachers, and all who receive instruction, to regard this law of progression, so that, while their physical and intellectual natures are being cultivated and developed, they may not remain "babes" in the practice of morality and the Christian virtues, but "grow in grace and in the knowledge of the Lord and Savior Jesus Christ?"

We can not expect the student will excel his teacher, if indeed he equals him, in merely intellectual pursuits; much less can we reasonably look for superior attainments in morals and religion. If, then, the teacher would secure the most perfect obedience of his scholars from the highest motives, he must show them that he himself cheerfully and habitually complies, in heart and in life, with all the precepts of the Great Teacher, with whom is lodged all authority, and from whom he derives his. When the members of a school become convinced that their teacher habitually asks wisdom of the Supreme Educator, whose will he aims constantly to do, they will feel almost irresistibly urged to yield obedience to the precepts of Christianity, and, with suitable encouragement, will take upon themselves the easy yoke of Christ.*

Even common arithmetic, when well taught, and illustrated by judiciously constructed examples, may be made not only more practical than it has usually been heretofore, but while the student is becoming acquainted with the science of numbers, it may be rendered an efficient instrumentality in showing the advantages of knowledge and virtue, and the expense and burden to the community of ignorance and crime, thus promoting the great work of moral culture, as is beautifully illustrated by the following examples, selected from a recent treatise on that subject:

"In the town of Bury, England, with an estimated population of twenty-five thousand, the expenditure for beer and spirits, in the year 1836, was estimated at £54,190. If this was 24 per cent. of the entire loss, resulting from the waste of money, ill health, loss of labor, and the other evils attendant upon intoxication, what was the average loss from intemperance, for each man, woman, and child in the place, estimating the pound sterling at $4.80. Ans. $43.332."

* In a former chapter, the necessity of moral and religious education was dwelt upon at length. The importance of the Scriptures as a text-book, containing as they do the only perfect code of morals known to man, and the objections sometimes urged against their use, were duly considered. I wish here simply to add, that their exclusion from our schools would be even more sectarian than their perverted use; for the atheistical plan, which forbids the entrance of the Bible into multitudes of our schools, under the pretense of excluding sectarianism, shuts out Christianity, and establishes the influence of *a single sect*, that would dethrone the Creator, and break up every bond of social order.

This one example may do more, in many instances, toward establishing young men who may be engaged in its solution in habits of total abstinence, than a score of lectures on temperance, or as many lessons on domestic or political economy. The following, also, may more effectually check existing abuses of some of the laws of health and longevity than a month's study of physiology and moral science: "It has been estimated that a man, in a properly ventilated room, can work twelve hours a day with no greater inconvenience than would be occasioned by ten hours' work in a room badly ventilated; and that, where there is proper ventilation, a man may gain ten years' good labor on account of unimpaired health. According to this estimate, what is the loss in thirty years to each individual in a badly-ventilated work-shop, valuing the labor at ten cents per hour? Ans. $5008." What an astonishing result! Five thousand and eight dollars moneyed loss to each individual who respires impure air, estimating labor at but ten cents an hour.

Now suppose this loss occurs only in the case of the eight hundred thousand adults in the United States who are unable to read and write—and it must accrue to a much greater number of persons—and *one fourth of the annual loss would be sufficient to maintain an efficient system of common schools in every state of the Union the entire year.*

It has sometimes been said, even by individuals occupying high stations in society, that persons of the second or third order of intellect make the best school-teachers. But in the light of what has been said, this statement needs but be made to prove its fallacy. In order properly to fill the teachers' office, we need men and women of the first order of intellect, brought to a high state of cultivation. A well-qualified and faithful school-teacher earns, and of right ought to receive, a salary equal to that paid to the clergyman, or received by the members of the other learned professions. He who can teach a good school can ordinarily engage with proportionate success in more lucrative pursuits. So true is this remark, that scarcely a man can be found that has attained to any considerable eminence as a teacher, who has not been repeatedly solicited, and perhaps strongly *tempted*, to relinquish teaching and engage in pursuits less laborious and more profitable. Many yield to this temptation, and hence much of the best talent has been attracted to the other professions. School committees, however, can generally secure the services of teachers of any grade of qualifications they desire, upon the simple condition of offering an adequate remuneration.

We have said, as is the teacher so will be the school. We might add, as are the wages, so ordinarily is the teacher. Let it be understood that in any township, county, or state, a high order of teachers is called for, and that an adequate remuneration will be given, and the demand will be supplied. Well-qualified teachers will be called in from abroad until competent ones can be trained up at home. Here, as in other departments of labor, as is the demand, so will be the supply.

The best means which citizens can employ to give character and stability to the vocation of the teacher is to select competent and worthy individuals to take the charge of their schools, and then pay them so liberally that they can have no pecuniary inducement to change their employment. Let this be generally done, and teaching will soon be raised, in public estimation, to the rank of a learned profession; and the *fourth learned profession*—the vocation of the practical educator—will be taken up for life by as great a proportion of men and women eminent for talent, cultivation, and moral worth, as either of the other three professions have ever been able to boast.

SCHOOLS SHOULD CONTINUE THROUGH THE YEAR.

Schools should be kept open at least ten full months during the year; in other words, *the entire year*, with the usual quarterly or semi-annual vacations.—*Michigan School Report.*

It is not enough that good school-houses be provided and well-qualified teachers be employed. Our schools should be kept open a sufficient length of time during the year to make their influence strongly and most favorably felt. The work of instruction, while it is going forward, should be the business of both teachers and scholars. If children are habituated to industry, to close application, to hard study, and to good personal, social, and moral habits during the period of their attendance upon school, these habits will be favorably felt in after life, in the development of characters whose possessors will be at once respectable and useful members of society, and a blessing to the age in which they live. On the contrary, if children are allowed to attend an indifferent school three months during the year, to work three months, to play three months, and are permitted to spend the remaining three months in idleness, the influence of this course will be felt, and it will be likely to give character to their future lives.

Under such circumstances, the good, if any, that children will receive while attending an indifferent school one fourth of the year, will be more than counterbalanced by the evil influences that surround them during the half of the year they devote to play and idleness. We can not reasonably expect that children brought up under such unfavorable and distracting influences will become even respectable members of society, much less that they will be a blessing to the generation in which they live.

In villages and densely-settled neighborhoods schools should be kept open at least ten full months during the year; in other words, *the entire year*, with the usual quarterly or semi-annual vacations; and, if possible, they should not, under any circumstances, be continued less than eight months. And, I may add, the same teacher should be retained in the charge of a school, wherever practicable, from year to year. The teacher occupies, for the time being, the place of the parent. But what kind of government and discipline should we expect in a family where a new step-father or step-mother is introduced and invested with parental authority every six months, and where the children are left in orphanage half of the year! Much more may we inquire, what kind of instruction and educational training may we reasonably expect in a large school whose wants are no better provided for! A school-teacher should be selected with as great care as the minister of the parish; and when selected, the services of the one should be continued as uninterruptedly and permanently as those of the other. Then will be beautifully illustrated this interesting truth: It is easier, cheaper, and pleasanter incomparably, and infinitely more effectual, rightly to train the rising generation, than it is to reform men grown old in sin.

Lalor, in his prize essay on education, published ten years ago in London, has recorded a kindred sentiment in this very beautiful and highly-expressive language: "The school-master alone, going forth with the power of intelligence and a moral purpose among the infant minds of the community, can stop the flood of vice and crime at its source, by repressing in childhood those wild passions which are its springs. Nay, often will the mature mind, hard as adamant against the terrors of the law and the contempt of society, be softened to tears of penitence by the innocence of its educated child speaking unconscious reproof."

EVERY CHILD SHOULD ATTEND SCHOOL.

The plan of this nation was not, and is not, to see how many *individuals* we can raise up who shall be distinguished, but to see how high, by free schools and free institutions, we can raise the *great mass* of population.—REV. JOHN TODD.

I promised God that I would look upon every Prussian peasant child as a being who could complain of me before God if I did not provide for him the best education, as a man and a Christian, which it was possible for me to provide.—SCHOOL-COUNSELOR DINTER.

Good school-houses may be built, well-qualified teachers may be employed, and schools may be kept open the entire year, but all this will not secure the correct education of the people, unless those schools are *patronized;* patronized, not by a few persons, not by one half, or three fourths even of a community, but by the *whole community.* As was said in a former chapter, there is no safety but in the education of the masses. A few vile persons will taint and infect a whole neighborhood. In the graphic language of the Scriptures, *One sinner destroyeth much good.*

The better portions of the community every where provide for the education of their children. If they are not instructed at home, they are sent to good schools, public or private, where their education is well looked after. Unfortunately, those children whose education is most neglected at home are the very ones, usually, that are sent least to school, and when at all, to the poorest schools.

But how shall the evil in question be remedied? How shall we secure the attendance of children generally at the schools, provided good ones are established? In the first place, diligent effort should be made to arouse the public mind to an appreciation of the importance and necessity of universal attendance. This will go far toward remedying the evil. It should be made every where unpopular, and be regarded as dishonorable in a member of our social compact, and unworthy of a citizen of a free state, to bring up a child without giving him such an education as shall fit him for the discharge of the duties of an American citizen.

But there is a portion of almost every community who feel hardly able to allow their children the necessary time to pursue an extended course of common school education, and who are really unable to clothe them properly, furnish them with useful books, and pay their tuition. This class, although comparatively small, is not unimportant. The legal provisions made for such children vary in different states. Wherever the free school principle is adopted, their tuition is of course provided for. This provision in some instances extends further. The statutes of Michigan relating to primary schools make it the duty of the district board to exempt from the payment of teachers' wages not only, but from providing fuel for the use of the district, all such persons residing therein as in their opinion ought to be exempted, and to admit the children of such persons to the school free of charge not only, but the district board is authorized to purchase, *at the expense of the district,* such books as may be necessary for the use of children thus admitted by them to the district school. The entire expense incurred for tuition, fuel, and books, in such cases, is assumed by the district, and paid by a tax levied upon the property thereof.

We have now arrived at an interesting crisis. We have exhausted the legal provision, generous as it is, and yet the blessing of universal education is not secured to those who will succeed us. Good schools may every where be established, in which the wealthy, and those in comfortable circumstances, may educate their children. Provision—yes, generous provision, though but just—has been made to meet the expense of tuition and books for the children of indigent parents. Still, they may not sufficiently appreciate an education to send their children; or, if this be not so, they may keep them at home from motives of delicacy, being unable to clothe them decently. How shall such cases be met? How shall we actually bring such children into the peaceable possession and enjoyment of a good common school education, that rich legacy which noble-minded legislators have bequeathed to them, and which is the inalienable right of every son and daughter of this republic?

Legislation has already, in many of the states, done much—perhaps all that can be reasonably expected, at least, until a good common education shall be better appreciated by the community at large, and be ranked, as it ought to be, among the *necessaries of life.* The work, then, must be consummated chiefly by the united and well-directed efforts of benevolent and philanthropic individuals.

Benevolent females—and especially Christian mothers, who have long been pre-eminently distinguished for their successful efforts in protecting the innocent, administering to the wants of the necessitous, and reclaiming the wanderer from the paths of vice—have felt the claims of this innocent and unoffending portion of the community, and have, in some instances, organized themselves into associations to meet those claims.

Benevolent and Christian females can doubtless accomplish more, by visiting the poor and needy in their respective school districts, and making known unto them their privileges, and encouraging and assisting them, if need be, to avail themselves of these privileges, than by the same expenditure of time and means in any other way. They have long and very generally been accustomed to clothe the children of the destitute, and accompany them to the Sunday-school, and there teach them those things which pertain to their present and everlasting well-being, and have thus accomplished incalculable good ; but by co-operating with the civil authorities in securing the attendance of every child in their respective districts at the *improved common school,* they can hardly fail to accomplish vastly more.

Several associations have been formed for this noble purpose, and many children who, but for their fostering care, would have remained at their cheerless homes, have, by this labor of love, been sought out, properly cared for, and led to the common school, that fountain of intellectual life, and of social and moral culture, which is alike open to all. Gentlemen should every where encourage the formation of such associations, and, when formed, should offer every facility in their power to increase their usefulness. Clergymen might help forward such benevolent labors, where they are entered upon, by preaching occasionally from that good text, *Help those women.*

But there are two classes of our fellow-citizens—perhaps I should say fellow-beings—who, notwithstanding the abundant legal provisions to which I have referred, and the utmost that the benevolent and philanthropic can accomplish by voluntary effort, will utterly refuse to give their children such an education as we have been contemplating. These are, first, men in comfortable circumstances, who have so much blindness of mind, and such an utter disregard for the welfare of their offspring, as to deprive them of the advantages of even a common school education ; and, secondly, those who have such an obduracy of heart as absolutely to refuse to allow their children to attend school, and who, although the abundant provisions of the law are made known unto them, in meekness and love, by "man's guardian angel," prove utterly incorrigible.

Such persons are unworthy to sustain the parental relation, and the safety of the community requires that the forfeiture be claimed, and that the right of control be transferred from such unnatural parents to the civil authorities ; for, as Kent says, "A parent who sends his son into the world uneducated, and without skill in any art or science, does a great injury to mankind as well as to his own family, for he defrauds the community of a useful citizen, and bequeaths to it a nuisance." How true is it that "the mobs, the riots, the burnings, the lynchings perpetrated by the *men* of the present day, are perpetrated because of their vicious or defective education when *children!* We see and feel the havoc and the ravage of their tiger passions now, when they are full grown, but it was years ago that they were whelped and suckled."

In the very expressive language of Macaulay, the right to HANG includes the right to EDUCATE. This is not a strange nor a new idea. It long ago entered into civil codes in the Old World, not only, but in the New. In Prussia, when a parent refuses, without satisfactory excuse, to send his child to school the time required by law, he is cited before the court, tried, and, if he refuses compliance, the child is taken from him and sent to *school*, and the father to *prison.*

Similar laws were enacted and *enforced* by our New

England fathers more than two hundred years ago, which history informs us were attended with the most beneficial results.* Although their descendants of the present generation should blush for their degeneracy, still we should be encouraged from an increasing disposition of late to return to these salutary restraints and needful checks upon ignorance and crime. Said the Honorable Josiah Quincy, Jr., late mayor of the city of Boston, in his inaugural address, "I hold that the state has a right to compel parents to take advantage of the means of educating their children. If it can punish them for crime, it should surely have the power of preventing them from committing it, by giving them the habits and the education that are the surest safeguards." Similar sentiments have been recently promulgated by the heads of the school departments of several states in their official reports, and by governors in their annual messages; and we have much reason for believing that the time is not distant when an enlightened public sentiment shall demand the re-enactment of these most salutary laws of our ancestors.

COMPULSORY ATTENDANCE UPON SCHOOL.—Since the preceding paragraphs were prepared for the printer, the author has received the statutes and resolves of the Massachusetts Legislature of 1850, relating to education, which recognize the principle here contended for.

* The following paragraph is from the Massachusetts Colony Laws of 1642; "Forasmuch as the good education of children is of singular behoof and benefit to any commonwealth, and whereas many parents and masters are too indolent and negligent of their duty in that kind, it is ordered that the select-men of every town in the several precincts and quarters, where they dwell, shall have a vigilant eye over their brethren and neighbors, to see, first, that none of them shall suffer so much barbarism in any of their families as not to teach, by themselves or others, their children and apprentices so much learning as may enable them perfectly to read the English tongue, and knowledge of the capital laws, upon penalty of *twenty shillings* for each neglect therein."

Each of the several cities and towns in that commonwealth is "authorized and empowered to make all needful provisions and arrangements concerning habitual truants, and children not attending school, without any regular and lawful occupation, growing up in ignorance, between the ages of six and fifteen years; and, also, all such ordinances and by-laws respecting such children as shall be deemed most conducive to their welfare and the good order of such city or town; and there shall be annexed to such ordinances suitable penalties, not exceeding, for any one breach, a fine of twenty dollars."

It is made the duty of the "several cities and towns availing themselves of the provisions of this act, to appoint, at the annual meetings of said towns, or annually by the mayor and aldermen of said cities, three or more persons, who alone shall be authorized to make the complaints, in every case of violation of said ordinances or by-laws, to the justice of the peace, or other judicial officer, who, by said ordinances, shall have jurisdiction in the matter, which persons thus appointed shall alone have authority to carry into execution the judgments of said justices of the peace, or other judicial officer."

It is further provided that "the said justices of the peace, or other judicial officer, shall, in all cases, at their discretion, in place of the fine aforesaid, be authorized to order children proved before them to be growing up in truancy, and without the benefit of the education provided for them by law, to be placed, for such periods of time as they may judge expedient, in such institution of instruction, or house of reformation, or other suitable situation, as may be assigned or provided for the purpose in each city or town availing itself of the powers herein granted."

This principle has been incorporated into several municipal codes. Children in the city of Boston, under sixteen years of age, whose "parents are dead, or, if living, do, frcm vice, or any other cause, neglect to provide suitable employment for, or to exercise salutarv control over" them, may be sent by the court to the house of reformation. By the late act, establishing the State Reform School, male convicts under sixteen years of age may be sent to this school from any part of the commonwealth, to be there "instructed in piety and morality, and in such branches of useful knowledge as shall be adapted to their age and capacity." The inmates may be bound out; but, in executing this part of their duty, the trustees "shall have scrupulous regard to the religious and moral character of those to whom they are bound, to the end that they may secure to the boys the benefit of a good example, and wholesome instruction, and the sure means of improvement in virtue and knowledge, and thus the opportunity of becoming intelligent, moral, useful, and happy citizens of the commonwealth."

The Massachusetts State Reform School is designed to be a "school for the instruction, reformation, and employment of juvenile offenders." Any boy under sixteen years of age, "convicted of any offense punishable by imprisonment other than for life," may be sentenced to this school. Here he may be kept during the term of his sentence; or he may be bound out as an apprentice; or, in case he proves incorrigible, he may be sent to prison, as he would originally have been but for the existence of this school.

The buildings erected are sufficiently large for three hundred boys. Attached to the establishment is a large farm, the cost of all which, when the buildings are completed and furnished, and the farm stocked and provided with agricultural implements, it is estimated will be about one hundred thousand dollars. A citizen of that state has given twenty-two thousand five hundred dollars to this institution, partly to defray past expenses and partly to form a fund for its future benefit.

"In visiting this noble institution, one can not but think how closely it resembles, in spirit and in purpose, the mission of Him who came to seek and to save that which was lost; and yet, in traversing its spacious halls and corridors, the echo of each footfall seems to say that one tenth part of its cost would have done more in the way of prevention than its whole amount can accomplish in the way of reclaiming, and would, besides, have saved a thousand pangs that have torn parental hearts, and a thousand more wounds in the hearts of the children themselves, which no human power can ever wholly heal. When will the state learn that it is better to spend its units for prevention than tens and hundreds for remedy? How long must the state, like those same unfortunate children, suffer the punishment of THEIR existence before IT will be reformed?"

Kindred institutions have existed in several of our principal cities for a quarter of a century, among which are the House of Reformation for Juvenile Delinquents in New York, the House of Refuge in Philadelphia, and the House of Reformation in Boston. Considering the degradation of their parents, the absence of correct early instruction, and the corrupting influences to which the children sent to these institutions have been exposed, becoming generally *criminals* before any effort has been made by the humane for their correct educational training, one may well wonder at the success which has crowned the efforts that have been put forth in their behalf, for the greater part of them *are effectually and permanently reformed.* This, however, only shows more clearly the power of education, and the advantages that may be derived from the establishment and maintenance of improved common schools throughout our country.

But how are these reforms effected? The means are simple, and are slightly different from those already described for the correct training of unoffending children. Take, for instance, the House of Reformation in the City of New York. In the first place, they have a good school-house, embracing nearly all the modern improvements. The yard and play-ground are of ample dimensions, and are inclosed by a substantial fence. This constitutes a barrier beyond which the children, once within, can not pass. But the clean gravel-walks, the beautiful shade-trees, the green grass-plats, the sparkling fountains, the ornamental flower-garden, all conspire to render the place delightful. It is, indeed, a prison in one sense, but the children seem hardly to know it. Then, again, well-qualified teachers and superintendents are employed. The spirit which actuates them is that of love. By proving themselves the friends of the children, the children become their friends, and are hence easily governed, considering their former neglect. Being well instructed, they love study, and generally make commendable progress. Their habits are regular, and they are constantly employed. A portion of the day is devoted to study; another portion to industrial pursuits; and still another to recreation and amusements. Strict obedience is required. This may be yielded at first from restraint, but ultimately from love. The love of kind and faithful teachers, the love of approving consciences, the love of right, the love of God, separately and conjointly influence them, until they can say ultimately of a truth, "*The love of Christ constraineth us.*'

Their industrial habits are of incalculable benefit to them. They all learn some trade, and acquire the habits and the skill requisite to constitute them producers, and thus practically conform to this fundamental law, "*that if any man would not work, neither should he eat.*" The other conditions that have been stated as essential to success are also complied with, the scholars being kept under the influence of good teachers, and of the same teachers from year to year during their continuance in the institution.

The well-qualified and eminently successful teacher who has long been connected with the Refuge in New York, in a late report says, "The habits of industry which the children here acquire will be of incalculable benefit to them through life. Yet we look upon the School Department as the greatest of all the means employed to save our youthful charge from ignorance and vice. As it is the mind and the heart that are mostly depraved, so we must act mostly upon the mind and the heart to eradicate this depravity.

"The education here is a *moral* education. We do endeavor, it is true, by all the powers we possess, to impress upon the mind the great importance of a good education; and not only to *impress* it upon the mind, but to assist the mind to act, that it may obtain it. But our principal aim is to fan into life the almost dying spark of virtue, and kindle anew the moral feelings, that they may glow with fresh ardor, and shine forth again in the beauty of innocence. Our object is not to store the memory with facts, but to elevate the soul; not to think for the children, but to teach them to think for themselves; to describe the road, and put them in the way; never to hint what they have been, nor what they are, but to point them continually to what they may be.

"*We feel assured that our labor will not be lost.* Judging the future from the past, we are sanguine in our belief that our toils have left an impress upon the mind which time can not efface. Scarcely a week passes but our hearts are cheered and animated, and our eyes are gladdened at the sight of those whom we taught in by-gone years, who bid no fairer then to cheer us than those with whom we labor now. Yet they are saved—saved to themselves; saved to society; saved to their friends—who, but for this Refuge, would have poisoned the moral atmosphere of our land, and breathed around them more deadly effluvia than that of the fabled Upas."

The success which has attended well-directed efforts for the reformation of juvenile delinquents, and *evening free schools* for the education of adults of all ages whose early education has been neglected, ought to inspire the friends of human improvement with increased confidence in the redeeming power of a correct early education, such as every state in this Union may provide for all her children. When this confidence is begotten, and when a good common education comes to be generally regarded as the birth-right of every child in the community, then may the friends of free institutions and of indefinite human advancement look for the more speedy realization of their long-cherished hopes. For one generation the community must be doubly taxed—once in the reformation of juvenile delinquents, and in the education of ignorant adults in evening schools, and again in the correct training of all our children in improved schools. This done, each succeeding generation will come upon the stage under more favorable circumstances than the preceding, and each present generation will be better prepared to educate that which is to follow, to the end of time.

THE REDEEMING POWER OF COMMON SCHOOLS.

If all our schools were under the charge of teachers possessing what I regard as the right intellectual and moral qualifications, and if all the children of the community were brought under the influence of these schools for ten months in the year, I think that the work of training up THE WHOLE COMMUNITY to intelligence and virtue would soon be accomplished, as completely as any human end can be obtained by human means.—REV. JACOB ABBOTT.

I might here introduce a vast amount of incontrovertible evidence to show that, if the attendance of all the children in any commonwealth could be secured at such improved common schools as we have been contemplating for ten months during the year, from the age of four to that of sixteen years, they would prove competent to the removal of ninety-nine one hundredths of the evils with which society is now infested in one generation, and that they would ultimately redeem the state from social vices and crimes.

The Hon. Horace Mann, late Secretary of the Massachusetts Board of Education, issued a circular in 1847, in which he raised the question now under consideration. This circular was sent out to a large number of the most experienced and reputable teachers in the Northern and Middle States, all of whom were pleased to reply to it. Each reply corroborates the position here stated; and, taken together *as a whole*, they are entitled to implicit credence. The whole correspondence is too voluminous to be here exhibited; I can not, however, forbear introducing a few illustrative passages.

Says Mr. Page, the late lamented principal of the New York State Normal School, "Could I be connected with a school furnished with all the appliances you name; where all the children should be constant attendants upon my instruction for a succession of years; where all my fellow-teachers should be such as you suppose; and where all the favorable influences described in your circular should surround me and cheer me, even with my moderate abilities as a teacher, I should scarcely expect, after the first generation submitted to the experiment, to fail *in a single case* to secure the results you have named."

Mr. Solomon Adams, of Boston, who has been engaged in the profession of teaching twenty-four years, remarks as follows: "Permit me to say that, in very many cases, after laboring long with individuals almost against hope, and sometimes in a manner, too, which I can now see was not always wise, I have never had a case which has not resulted in some good degree according to my wishes. The many kind and voluntary testimonials given years afterward by persons who remembered that they were once my wayward pupils, are among the pleasantest and most cheering incidents of my life. So uniform have been the results, when I have had a fair trial and time enough, that I have unhesitatingly adopted the motto, *Never despair.* Parents and teachers are apt to look for too speedy results from the labors of the latter. The moral nature, like the intellectual and physical, is long and slow in reaching the full maturity of its strength. I was told a few years since by a person who knew the history of nearly all my pupils for the first five years of my labor, that not one of them had ever brought reproach upon himself or mortification upon friends by a bad life. I can not now look over the whole of my pupils, and find one who had been with me long enough to receive a decided impression, whose life is not honorable and useful. I find them in all the learned professions and in the various mechanical arts. I find my female pupils scattered as teachers through half the states of the Union, and as the wives and assistants of Christian missionaries in every quarter of the globe.

"So far, therefore, as my own experience goes, so far as my knowledge of the experience of others extends, so far as the statistics of crime throw any light upon the subject, I confidently expect that ninety-nine in a hundred, and I think even more, with such means of education as you have supposed, and with such Divine favor as we are authorized to expect, would become good members of society, the supporters of order, and law, and truth, and justice, and all righteousness."

The Rev. Jacob Abbott, who has been engaged in the practical duties of teaching for about ten years in the cities of Boston and New York, and who has had under his care about eight hundred pupils of both sexes, and of all ages from four to twenty-five, has expressed in a long letter the sentiment placed at the head of this section. "If all our schools were under the charge of teachers possessing what I regard as the right intellectual and moral qualifications, and if all the children of the community were brought under the influence of these schools for ten months in the year, I think the work of training up THE WHOLE COMMUNITY to intelligence and virtue would soon be accomplished as completely as any human end can be obtained by human means."

Mr. Roger S. Howard, of Vermont, who has been engaged in teaching about twenty years, remarks, among other things, as follows: "Judging from what I have seen and do know, if the conditions you have mentioned were strictly complied with; if the attendance of the scholars could be as universal, constant, and long-continued as you have stated; if the teachers were men and women of those high intellectual and moral qualities—apt to teach, and devoted to their work, and favored with that blessing which the word and providence of God teach us always to expect upon our honest, earnest, and well-directed efforts in so good a cause—on these conditions and under these circumstances, I do not hesitate to express the opinion that the failures need not be—would not be one per cent."

Miss Catharine E. Beecher, of Brattleboro, Vermont, who has been engaged directly and personally as a teacher about fifteen years, in Hartford, Connecticut, and Cincinnati, Ohio, and who has had the charge of not less than a thousand pupils from every state in the Union, after stating these and other considerations, remarks as follows: "I will now suppose that it could be so arranged that, in a given place, containing from ten to fifteen thousand inhabitants, in any part of the country where I ever resided, *all* the children at the age of four shall be placed six hours a day, for twelve years, under the care of teachers having the same views that I have, and having received that course of training for their office that any state in this Union can secure to the teachers of its children. Let it be so arranged that all these children shall remain till sixteen under these teachers, and also that they shall spend their lives in this city, and I have no hesitation in saying I do not believe that *one*, no, NOT A SINGLE ONE, would fail of proving a respectable and prosperous member of society; nay, more, I believe every one would, at the close of life, find admission into the world of endless peace and love. I say this solemnly, deliberately, and with the full belief that I am upheld by such imperfect experimental trials as I have made, or seen made by others; but, more than this, that I am sustained by the authority of Heaven, which sets forth this grand paliadium of education, '*Train up a child in the way he should go, and when he is old he will not depart from it.*'

"This sacred maxim surely sets the Divine *imprimatur* to the doctrine that *all* children *can* be trained up in the way they should go, and that, when so trained, they will not depart from it. Nor does it imply that education *alone* will secure eternal life without supernatural assistance; but it points to the true method of securing this indispensable aid.

"In this view of the case, I can command no language strong enough to express my infinite longings that my countrymen, who, as legislators, have the control of the institutions, the laws, and the wealth of our *physically* prosperous nation, should be brought to see that they now have in their hands the power of securing to *every* child in the coming generation a life of virtue and usefulness here, and an eternity of perfected bliss hereafter. How, then, can I express, or imagine, the awful responsibility which rests upon them, and which hereafter they must bear before the great Judge of nations, if they suffer the present state of things to go on, bearing, as it does, thousands and hundreds of thousands of helpless children in our country to hopeless and irretrievable ruin!"

Testimony similar to the preceding might be multiplied to almost any extent. Enough, however, I trust, has been said to remove any doubts in relation to the redeeming power of education which the reader may have previously entertained. Universal education, we have seen, constitutes the most effectual and the only sure means of securing to individuals and communities, to states and nations, exemption from all avoidable evils of whatever kind, and the possession of a competency of this world's goods, with the ability and disposition so to enjoy them as most to augment human happiness.

Yes, education, and nothing short of it, will dissipate the evils of ignorance; it will greatly increase the productiveness of labor, and make men more moral, industrious, and skillful, and thus diminish pauperism and crime, while at the same time it will indefinitely augment the sum total of human happiness. By diminishing the number of fatal accidents that are constantly occurring in every community, and securing to the rising generation such judicious physical and moral treatment as shall give them sound minds in sound bodies, it will lay an unfailing foundation for general prosperity, will greatly promote longevity, and will thus, in both of these and in many other ways, do more to increase the population, wealth, and universal well-being of the thirty states of this Union than all other means of state policy combined.

At the late Peace Convention at Paris to consider the practicability and necessity of a Congress of Nations to adjust national differences, composed of about fifteen hundred members, picked men from every Christian nation, Victor Hugo, the President of the Convention, on taking the chair, made an address that was received with great applause, in which the following passages occur:

"A day will come when men will no longer bear arms one against the other; when appeals will no longer be made to war, but to civilization! The time will come when the cannon will be exhibited as an old instrument of torture, and wonder expressed how such a thing could have been used. A day, I say, will come when the United States of America and the United States of Europe will be seen extending to each other the hand of fellowship across the ocean, and when we shall have the happiness of seeing every where the majestic radiation of universal concord."

That such a time will come, every heart that glows with Christian benevolence must earnestly desire and fervently pray. But we can not hope to attain the end without the use of the necessary means. So glorious a result as this, that has become an object of universal desire throughout Christendom, must follow when the conditions upon which it depends are complied with. What these are there can be little room for doubt. Let, then, every friend of Universal Peace seek it in the use of the appropriate means—*Universal Education.*

The same remark will apply to every form of Christian benevolence and universal philanthropy; for, as has been well remarked, in universal education, every "follower of God and friend of human kind" will find the only sure means of carrying forward that particular reform to which he is devoted. In whatever department of philanthropy he may be engaged, he will find that department to be only a segment of the great circle of beneficence of which *Universal Education* is the center and circumference; and that he can most successfully promote the permanent advancement of his most cherished interest in securing the establishment of, and attendance upon, IMPROVED SCHOOLS FREE TO ALL.

INDEX.

THE END.

NOTICES OF THE FIRST EDITION.

FROM a large number of extended notices of the first edition, we have space only for the following extracts:

We have read most of the works of this character which have been published in this country, and while we feel that comparisons are commonly odious, we are free to acknowledge that we have not before read a book which so ably discusses almost every topic connected with popular education. * * Take it as a whole, we have never before seen its equal.—*Joseph McKeen, LL. D., Superintendent of Common Schools for the City and County of New York, and Editor of the New York Journal of Education.*

We commend the work, not merely as a useful manual for teachers and school committees, but as one TO BE READ BY THE PEOPLE—every man, woman, and child of whom is interested in the subject of which it treats.—*Methodist Quarterly Review.*

A valuable treatise on the subject to which it is devoted, discussing it, in its various details, with great comprehensiveness of view, with a rich copiousness of illustration, and with excellent common sense.—*New York Tribune.*

No greater service could be done to the commonwealth than to put a copy of this work into every one of its families.—*Michigan Farmer.*

It is a rich concentration of the best principles on the noblest of subjects; and the man who can make its truths familiar to the minds and operative upon the actions of our people, is their highest benefactor.—*Rev. D. D. Wheden, D. D.*

Every Parent should have a copy of it. Each Teacher of our youth should be familiar with its whole contents. I do not know of a book upon that subject, in the world, which is so proper to be used as a text-book in all our higher seminaries.—*Rev. E. Cheever, D. D.*

It is a work for circulation; and the friends of free education could hardly do a better thing than to set the volume freely at work in the community at large.—*New York Evangelist.*

It may properly be regarded as a FAMILY BOOK, furnishing an amount of varied instruction and entertainment to the intelligent households of our countrymen, for which they will be sincerely grateful.—*Christian Quarterly Review.*

This is truly a national work, and should be in the hands of every educator throughout the land. We cannot speak too highly of it, and earnestly recommend it to the careful perusal of all interested in the educational reforms of the day.—*Teachers' Advocate.*

This is a most able and elaborate treatise, embracing physical, moral, and intellectual education, with the proper training of the five senses. It is the philosophy of the free-school system, and should be widely read.—*Democratic Quarterly Review.*

The various topics introduced are most happily illustrated. The work should find a place in every family.—*Mich. Christian Herald.*

We feel confident that no person interested in the subject can peruse this volume without obtaining new views of his duties toward his offspring, and of the means which should be employed to advance their moral and intellectual welfare.—*Boston Journal.*

The author takes a philosophic, and at the same time a clear and practical common-sense view of his subject. He is evidently acquainted not only with general theories of education, but also with the minute details of teaching. His plans of school-houses are admirable, and his instructions to teachers minute and comprehensive.—*Pittsburg Saturday Visitor.*

This valuable work has been some time before the public, but like other *Standard Productions*, it is rising in esteem the longer it is known. During the last fifteen months, we have consulted no work of the kind, as a book of reference, so frequently, and always with a higher idea of its value, as a digest of facts and statistics.—*Ohio Journal of Education.*

The volume before us is certainly the most complete, elaborate, and practical disquisition on education we have yet seen.—*New Orleans Bee.*

In the production of this volume the author has given commendable proof of his industry, good sense, and thorough acquaintance with an interest on which he rightly judges that the future prosperity of the American Republic essentially depends.—*Harpers' Magazine.*

If its principles pervaded our school systems, we should have a basis for future prosperity not to be realized in any other way.—*Rev. J. Holmes Agnew, D. D.*

I am highly pleased with its practical common-sense character; I believe in its general orthodoxy, and feel more confidence in recommending it to the public, than any other work on the subject with which I am acquainted. I would that every teacher in our State—nay, in *the whole country*—were in the possession of your book. Hardly less valuable is the work for *families* in general.—*J. W. Bulkley, Esq., City Superintendent of Schools, Brooklyn, N. Y.*

It is admirably calculated to advance the best interests of the present and coming generations. Hence, I hope it may be universally read, and duly regarded. Its highly interesting facts, just principles, correct reasoning, and pleasing style, must secure for it an extensive patronage. It should be found in every family, and in every library, private and public, and should be studied in all our schools of learning. —*Rev. Dr. O. C. Comstock, formerly Chaplain to Congress, Superintendent of Public Instruction, &c., &c.*

It embodies an immense amount of valuable information. It suggests right methods of culture for hand and head and heart; for promoting health and worth and happiness. It advocates the doctrine of the *right* of man to receive, and the *duty* of society to bestow that culture. The array of authorities by which its arguments are supported confers great strength on its positions. * * I feel confident that no parent or teacher can fail to derive great benefit from a candid consideration of its contents, and that in presenting it to the public the author has done a service to his country.—*Isaac Sams, President of the Ohio State Teachers' Association.*

Three or four chapters, at the commencement of the book, are devoted to the subject of physical education, and the education of the senses. These are topics of great importance, but so generally neglected that the earnestness with which the author dwells upon them, and the excellent practical precepts he lays down, gives the work a peculiar value in our eyes.—*Littell's Living Age.*

This work should be in the hands of every parent who regards his own welfare, that of his children, or the future well-being of his country. The plain common-sense man who takes it up and reads it at his clean and quiet hearth, will find it philosophical, but not abstruse, and will meet in it no line or word that he cannot fully comprehend, and will be startled in it by no attempt at pedantry or display of learning. Let all such buy and read it, depending upon it that they cannot better charm the ears of the wife and children, through a winter's evening, than by reading to them aloud from its pages.—*Detroit Advertiser.*

We know of no practical book that has given us so much pleasure. The author's views of education are of such a sound, practical, common-sense order, that they cannot fail to receive the attention of the country in this age of progress.—*Monthly Hesperian.*

We have been highly interested and profited by a careful perusal of its pages. It is designed for parents and teachers, and for young persons of both sexes. Mr. Mayhew's name is intimately identified with the cause of popular education in this country, and we believe that in the production of this work he has furnished to the world an enduring monument of his enlightened zeal and rare talents, so freely and effectually devoted to the cause of public instruction.—*U. S. Miscellany and Teachers' Manual.*

This is not a new work; but it is one that will never be old. Most works in a few years become insipid, or are supplanted by some new improvement; but we are inclined to the opinion that it will be a long time before this work is superseded. So long as there are men to be trained physically and mentally, so long will there be a necessity for this inestimable work, which is a credit to the author and the age. We have been astonished at its richness. Every page has an excellence. —*Monthly Literary Miscellany.*

This is an exceedingly valuable work, and should be read by all parents and teachers—all school-committee men and legislators. The author regards children as animals gifted with intellect, instead of intellects wasted on animals. He advocates the education of the whole compound being, and consequently talks very differently from the old-fashioned lecturers about cultivating the mind and teaching the young idea how to shoot. He talks about bathing-tubs, and soap and water as essential means of education. He preaches the importance of food and air. He enters into the philosophy of educating the whole body as a substratum for educating mind.—*Boston Chronotype.*

We commend this work to the study of all who feel an interest in education. The subject is thoroughly canvassed, and we sincerely wish that every man in Kentucky would read it.—*Louisville Courier.*

The author clearly shows how education dissipates the evils of ignorance, increases the productiveness of labor, diminishes pauperism and crime, and advances the great end of life—human happiness.—*Hunt's Merchants' Magazine.*

It certainly should be numbered among the effects of every school teacher, and should also find a place in every family library.—*Coldwater Sentinel.*

Mr. Mayhew is a clear-headed, intelligent man, and has written a sensible book on Education. His views on the importance of harmony in physical, intellectual, and moral training, are judicious and well expressed. * * * On the whole subject of Christian education, distinctively as such, without which all other culture would be worse than useless, the public sentiment needs to be corrected.—*Church Quarterly Review.*

We find that, for worth and ability, this work even surpasses our anticipations. It has no superior in point of plain, practical *good sense*; while it more fully, and as ably, discusses the general bearings of universal education, as any that has yet appeared. It is truly a masterly exposition of the subject of popular education, as applied to the individual and associated interests of our people. It is not of worth to the teacher alone, but is of such a character as to make it of the first importance that every school and family library be supplied with a copy. Discussing, as it does, the general subject of education, it is peculiarly *the work* to be *studied* by the whole people. It must meet with a very wide circulation, as it ought; especially will every friend of education secure a copy.—*Eclectic Journal of Education.*

THE NATIONAL SERIES OF READERS.

COMPLETE IN TWO INDEPENDENT PARTS.

I.

THE NATIONAL READERS.

By PARKER & WATSON.

No. 1.—National Primer, ... *64 pp., 16mo,*
No. 2.—National First Reader, . . . *128 pp., 16mo,*
No. 3.—National Second Reader, . . *224 pp., 16mo,*
No. 4.—National Third Reader, . . *288 pp., 12mo,*
No. 5.—National Fourth Reader, . . *432 pp., 12mo,*
No 6.—National Fifth Reader, . . *600 pp., 12mo,*

National Elementary Speller, . . . *160 pp., 16mo,*
National Pronouncing Speller, . . . *188 pp., 12mo,*

II.

THE INDEPENDENT READERS.

By J. MADISON WATSON.

The Independent First (or Primary) Reader, *80 pp., 16mo,*
The Independent Second Reader, . *160 pp., 16mo,*
The Independent Third Reader, . . *240 pp., 16mo,*
The Independent Fourth Reader, . . *264 pp., 12mo,*
The Independent Fifth Reader, . . *336 pp., 12mo,*
The Independent Sixth Reader, . . *474 pp., 12mo,*

The Independent Child's Speller (Script), *80 pp., 16mo,*
The Independent Youth's Speller (Script), *168 pp., 12mo,*
The Independent Spelling Book, . . *160 pp., 16mo,*

***** The Readers constitute two complete and entirely distinct series, either of which is adequate to every want of the best schools. The Spellers may accompany either Series.**

PARKER & WATSON'S NATIONAL READERS.

The salient features of these works which have combined to render them so popular may be briefly recapitulated as follows:

1. **THE WORD-BUILDING SYSTEM.**—This famous progressive method for young children originated and was copyrighted with these books. It constitutes a process with which the beginner with *words* of one letter is gradually introduced to additional lists formed by prefixing or affixing single letters. and is thus led almost insensibly to the mastery of the more difficult constructions. This is one of the most striking modern improvements in methods of teaching.

2. **TREATMENT OF PRONUNCIATION.**—The wants of the youngest scholars in this department are not overlooked. It may be said that from the first lesson the student by this method need never be at a loss for a prompt and accurate rendering of every word encountered.

3. **ARTICULATION AND ORTHOEPY** are considered of primary importance.

4. **PUNCTUATION** is inculcated by a series of interesting *reading lessons*, the simple perusal of which suffices to fix its principles indelibly upon the mind.

5. **ELOCUTION.** Each of the higher Readers (3d, 4th and 5th) contains elaborate, scholarly, and thoroughly practical treatises on elocution. This feature alone has secured for the series many of its warmest friends.

6. **THE SELECTIONS** are the crowning glory of the series. Without exception it may be said that no volumes of the same size and character contain a collection so diversified, judicious, and artistic as this. It embraces the choicest gems of English literature, so arranged as to afford the reader ample exercise in every department of style. So acceptable has the taste of the authors in this department proved, not only to the educational public but to the reading community at large, that thousands of copies of the Fourth and Fifth Readers have found their way into public and private libraries throughout the country, where they are in constant use as manuals of literature, for reference as well as perusal.

7. **ARRANGEMENT.** The exercises are so arranged as to present constantly alternating practice in the different styles of composition, while observing a definite plan of progression or gradation throughout the whole. In the higher books the articles are placed in formal sections and classified topically, thus concentrating the interest and inculcating a principle of association likely to prove valuable in subsequent general reading.

8. **NOTES AND BIOGRAPHICAL SKETCHES.** These are full and adequate to every want. The biographical sketches present in pleasing style the history of every author laid under contribution.

9. **ILLUSTRATIONS.** These are plentiful, almost profuse, and of the highest character of art. They are found in every volume of the series as far as and including the Third Reader.

10. **THE GRADATION** is perfect. Each volume overlaps its companion preceding or following in the series, so that the scholar, in passing from one to another, is only conscious, by the presence of the new book, of the transition.

11. **THE PRICE** is reasonable. The National Readers contain more matter than any other series in the same number of volumes published. Considering their completeness and thoroughness they are much the cheapest in the market.

12. **BINDING.** By the use of a material and process known only to themselves, in common with all the publications of this house, the National Readers are warranted to outlast any with which they may be compared—the ratio of relative durability being in their favor as two to one.

WATSON'S INDEPENDENT READERS.

This Series is designed to meet a general demand for smaller and cheaper books than the National Series proper, and to serve as well for intermediate volumes of the National Readers in large graded schools requiring more books than one ordinary series will supply.

Beauty. The most casual observer is at once impressed with the unparalleled mechanical beauty of the Independent Readers. The Publishers believe that the æsthetic tastes of children may receive no small degree of cultivation from their very earliest school books, to say nothing of the importance of making study attractive by all such artificial aids that are legitimate. In accordance with this view, not less than $25,000 was expended in their preparation before publishing, with a result which entitles them to be considered "The Perfection of Common School Books."

Selections. They contain, of course, none but entirely new selections. These are arranged according to a strictly progressive and novel method of developing the elementary sounds in order in the lower numbers, and in all, with a view to topics and general literary style. The mind is thus led in fixed channels to proficiency in every branch of good reading, and the evil results of 'scattering' as practised by most school-book authors, avoided.

The Illustrations, as may be inferred from what has been said, are elegant beyond comparison. They are profuse in every number of the series from the lowest to the highest. This is the only series published of which this is true.

The Type is semi-phonetic, the invention of Prof. Watson. By it every letter having more than one sound is clearly distinguished in all its variations without in any way mutilating or disguising the normal form of the letter.

Elocution is taught by prefatory treatises of constantly advancing grade and completeness in each volume, which are illustrated by wood-cuts in the lower books, and by black-board diagrams in the higher. Prof. Watson is the first to introduce Practical Illustrations and Black-board Diagrams for teaching this branch.

Foot Notes on every page afford all the incidental instruction which the teacher is usually required to impart. Indices of words refer the pupil to the place of their first use and definition. The Biographies of Authors and others are in every sense excellent.

Economy. Although the number of pages in each volume is fixed at the minimum, for the purpose recited above, the utmost amount of matter available without overcrowding is obtained in the space. The pages are much wider and larger than those of any competitor and contain *twenty per cent* more matter than any other series of the same type and number of pages.

All the Great Features. Besides the above all the popular features of the National Readers are retained except the Word-Building system. The latter gives place to an entirely new method of progressive development, based upon some of the best features of the Word System, Phonetics and Object Lessons.

NATIONAL READERS.

ORIGINAL AND "INDEPENDENT" SERIES

SPECIMEN TESTIMONIALS.

From D. H. HARRIS, *Supt. Public Schools, Hannibal, Mo.*

The National Series of Readers are now in use in our public schools, and I regard them *the best* that I have ever examined or used.

From HON. J. K. JILLSON, *Supt. of Education, State of South Carolina.*

I have carefully examined your new and beautiful Series of Readers known as "The Independent Readers," and do not hesitate to recommend it as the finest and most excellent ever presented to the public.

From D. N. ROOK, *Sec. of School Board, Williamsport, Pa.*

I would say that Parker & Watson's Series of Readers and Spellers give the best satisfaction in our schools of any Series of Readers and Spellers that have ever been used. There is nothing published for which we would exchange them

From PROF. H. SEELE, *New Braunfels Academy, Texas.*

I recommend the National Readers for four good reasons: (1.) The printing, engraving, and binding is excellent. (2.) They contain choice selections from English Literature. (3.) They inculcate good morals without any sectarian bias. (4.) They are truly *National*, because they teach pure patriotism and not sectional prejudice.

From S. FINDLEY, *Supt. Akron Schools, Ohio.*

We use no others, and have no desire to. They give entire satisfaction. We like the freshness and excellence of the selections. We like the biographical notes and the definitions at the foot of the page. We also like the white paper and clear and beautiful type. In short, we do not know where to look for books which would be so satisfactory both to teachers and pupils.

From PRES. ROBERT ALLYN, *McKendree College, Ill.*

Since my connection with this college, we have used in our preparatory department the Series of Readers known as the "National Readers," compiled by Parker & Watson, and published by Messrs. A. S. Barnes & Co. They are *excellent*; afford choice selections; contain the right system of elocutionary instruction, and are well printed and bound so as to be serviceable as well as interesting. I can commend them as among the excellent means used by teachers to make their pupils proficient in that noblest of school arts, GOOD READING.

From W. T. HARRIS, *Supt. Public Schools, St. Louis, Mo.*

I have to admire these excellent selections in prose and verse, and the careful arrangement which places first what is easy of comprehension, and proceeds gradually to what is difficult. I find the lessons so arranged as to bring together different treatments of the same topic, thereby throwing much light on the pupil's path, and I doubt not adding greatly to his progress. The proper variety of subjects chosen, the concise treatise on elocution, the beautiful typography and substantial binding—all these I find still more admirable than in the former series of National Readers, which I considered *models* in these respects.

From H. T. PHILLIPS, Esq., *of the Board of Education, Atlanta, Ga.*

The Board of Education of this city have selected for use in the public schools of Atlanta the entire series of your Independent Readers, together with Steele's Chemistry and Philosophy. As a member of the Board, and of the Committee on Text-books, the subject of Readers was referred to me for examination. I gave a pretty thorough examination to ten (10) different series of Readers, and in endeavoring to arrive at a decision upon the sole question of merit, and entirely independent of any extraneous influence, I very cordially recommended the Independent Series. This verdict was approved by the Committee and adopted by the Board.

From Report of REV. W. T. BRANTLY, D.D., *late Professor of Belles Lettres, University of Georgia, on "Text-Books in Reading," before the Teachers' Convention of Georgia, May 4, 1870.*

The *National Series*, by Parker & Watson, is deserving of its high reputation. The Primary Books are suited to the weakest capacity; whilst those more advanced supply instructive illustration on all that is needed to be known in connection with the art.

WATSON'S CHILD'S SPELLER.

THE INDEPENDENT CHILD'S SPELLER.

This unique book, published in 1872, is the first to be consistently printed in imitation of writing: that is, it teaches orthography as we use it. It is for the smallest class of learners, who soon become familiarized with words by their forms, and learn to read writing while they spell.

EXTRACT FROM THE PREFACE.

Success in teaching English orthography is still exceptional, and it must so continue until the principles involved are recognized in practice. Form is foremost: the eye and the hand must be trained to the formation of words; and since spelling is a part of writing, the written form only should be used. The laws of mental association, also—especially those of resemblance, contrast, and contiguity in time and place—should receive such recognition in the construction of the text-book as shall insure, whether consciously or not, their appropriate use and legitimate results. Hence, the spelling-book, properly arranged, is a necessity from the first; and, though primers, readers, and dictionaries may serve as aids, it can have no competent substitute.

Consistently with these views, the words used in the Independent Child's Speller have such original classifications and arrangements in columns—in reference to location, number of letters, vowel sounds, alphabetic equivalents, and consonant terminations—as exhibit most effectively their formation and pronunciation. The vocabulary is strictly confined to the simple and significant monosyllables in common use. He who has mastered these may easily learn how to spell and pronounce words of more than one syllable.

The introduction is an illustrated alphabet in script, containing twenty-six pictures of objects, and their names, commencing both with capitals and small letters. Part First embraces the words of one, two, and three letters; Part Second, the words of four letters; and Part Third, other monosyllables. They are divided into short lists and arranged in columns, the vowels usually in line, so as to exhibit individual characteristics and similarity of formation. The division of words into paragraphs is shown by figures in the columns. Each list is immediately followed by sentences for reading and writing, in which the same words are again presented with irregularities of form and sound. Association is thus employed, memory tested, and definition most satisfactorily taught.

Among the novel and valuable features of the lessons and exercises, probably the most prominent are their adaptedness for young children and their being printed in exact imitation of writing. The author believes that hands large enough to spin a top, drive a hoop, or catch a ball, are not too small to use a crayon, or a slate and pencil; that the child's natural desire to draw and write should not be thwarted, but gratified, encouraged, and wisely directed; and that since the written form is the one actually used in connection with spelling in after-life, the eye and the hand of the child should be trained to that form from the first. He hopes that this little work, designed to precede all other spelling-books and conflict with none, may satisfy the need so universally recognized of a fit introduction to orthography, penmanship, and English composition.

The National Readers and Spellers.

THEIR RECORD.

These books have been adopted by the School Boards, or official authority, of the following important States, cities, and towns—in most cases for exclusive use

The State of Missouri. **The State of Kentucky.**
The State of Alabama.
The State of Florida. **The State of North Carolina.**
The State of Delaware. **The State of Louisiana.**

New York.
New York City.
Brooklyn.
Buffalo.
Albany.
Rochester.
Troy.
Syracuse.
Elmira.
&c., &c.

Pennsylvania.
Reading.
Lancaster.
Erie.
Scranton.
Carlisle.
Carbondale.
Westchester.
Schuylkill Haven.
Williamsport.
Norristown.
Bellefonte.
Wilkesbarre.
&c., &c.

New Jersey.
Newark.
Jersey City.
Paterson.
Trenton.
Camden.
Elizabeth.
New Brunswick.
Phillipsburg.
Orange.
&c., &c.

Delaware.
Wilmington.

D. C.
Washington.

Illinois.
Chicago.
Peoria.
Alton.
Springfield.
Aurora.
Galesburg.
Rockford.
Rock Island.
&c., &c.

Wisconsin.
Milwaukee.
Fond du Lac.
Oshkosh.
Janesville.
Racine.
Watertown.
Sheboygan.
La Crosse.
Waukesha.
Kenosha.
&c., &c.

Michigan.
Grand Rapids.
Kalamazoo.
Adrian.
Jackson.
Monroe.
Lansing.
&c., &c.

Ohio.
Toledo.
Sandusky.
Conneaut.
Chardon.
Hudson.
Canton.
Salem.
&c., &c.

Indiana.
New Albany.
Fort Wayne.
Lafayette.
Madison.
Logansport.
Indianapolis.

Iowa.
Davenport.
Burlington.
Muscatine.
Mount Pleasant.
&c.

Nebraska.
Brownsville.
Lincoln.
&c.

Oregon.
Portland.
Salem.
&c.

Virginia.
Richmond.
Norfolk.
Petersburg.
Lynchburg.
&c.

South Carolina
Columbia.
Charleston.

Georgia.
Savannah.

Louisiana.
New Orleans.

Tennessee
Memphis

The *Educational Bulletin* records periodically all new points gained

SCHOOL-ROOM CARDS.

Baade's Reading Case,

A frame containing movable cards, with arrangement for showing one sentence at a time, capable of 28,000 transpositions.

Eureka Alphabet Tablet

Presents the alphabet upon the Word Method System, by which the child will learn the alphabet in nine days, and make no small progress in reading and spelling in the same time.

National School Tablets, 10 Nos.

Embrace reading and conversational exercises, object and moral lessons, form, color, &c. A complete set of these large and elegantly illustrated Cards will embellish the school-room more than any other article of furniture.

READING.

Fowle's Bible Reader

The narrative portions of the Bible, chronologically and topically arranged, judiciously combined with selections from the Psalms, Proverbs, and other portions which inculcate important moral lessons or the great truths of Christianity. The embarrassment and difficulty of reading the Bible itself, by course, as a class exercise, are obviated, and its use made feasible, by this means.

North Carolina First Reader
North Carolina Second Reader
North Carolina Third Reader

Prepared expressly for the schools of this State, by C. H. Wiley, Superintendent of Common Schools, and F. M. Hubbard, Professor of Literature in the State University.

Parker's Rhetorical Reader

Designed to familiarize Readers with the pauses and other marks in general use, and lead them to the practice of modulation and inflection of the voice.

Introductory Lessons in Reading and Elocution

Of similar character to the foregoing, for less advanced classes.

High School Literature

Admirable selections from a long list of the world's best writers, for exercise in reading, oratory, and composition. Speeches, dialogues, and model letters represent the latter department.

ORTHOGRAPHY.

SMITH'S SERIES

Supplies a speller for every class in graded schools, and comprises the most complete and excellent treatise on English Orthography and its companion branches extant.

1. Smith's Little Speller .

First Round in the Ladder of Learning.

2. Smith's Juvenile Definer

Lessons composed of familiar words grouped with reference to similar signification or use, and correctly spelled, accented, and defined.

3. Smith's Grammar-School Speller

Familiar words, grouped with reference to the sameness of sound of syllables differently spelled. Also definitions, complete rules for spelling and formation of derivatives, and exercises in false orthography.

4. Smith's Speller and Definer's Manual

A complete *School Dictionary* containing 14,000 words, with various other useful matter in the way of Rules and Exercises.

5. Smith's Etymology—Small, and Complete Ed's.

The first and only Etymology to recognize the *Anglo-Saxon* our *mother tongue;* containing also full lists of derivatives from the Latin, Greek, Gaelic, Swedish, Norman, &c., &c ; being, in fact, a complete etymology of the language for schools.

Sherwood's Writing Speller
Sherwood's Speller and Definer
Sherwood's Speller and Pronouncer

The Writing Speller consists of properly ruled and numbered blanks to receive the words dictated by the teacher, with space for remarks and corrections. The other volumes may be used for the dictation or ordinary class exercises.

Price's English Speller

A complete spelling-book for all grades, containing more matter than "Webster," manufactured in superior style, and sold at a lower price—consequently the cheapest speller extant.

Northend's Dictation Exercises

Embracing valuable information on a thousand topics, communicated in such a manner as at once to relieve the exercise of spelling of its usual tedium, and combine it with instruction of a general character calculated to profit and amuse.

Wright's Analytical Orthography

This standard work is popular, because it teaches the elementary sounds in a plain and philosophical manner, and presents orthography and orthoepy in an easy, uniform system of analysis or parsing.

Fowle's False Orthography

Exercises for correction.

Page's Normal Chart

The elementary sounds of the language for the school-room walls.

ORTHOGRAPHY—Continued.

Barber's Complete Writing Speller

"The Student's Own Hand-Book of Orthography, Definitions, and Sentences, consisting of Written Exercises in the Proper Spelling, Meaning, and Use of Words." (Published 1873.) This differs from Sherwood's and other Writing Spellers in its more comprehensive character. Its blanks are adapted to writing whole sentences instead of detached words, with the proper divisions for numbering, corrections, etc. Such aids as this, like Watson's Child's Speller and Sherwood's Writing Speller, find their *raison d'être* in the postulate that the art of correct spelling is dependent upon written, and not upon spoken language, for its utility, if not for its very existence. Hence the indirectness of purely oral instruction.

Pooler's Test Speller

The best collection of "hard words" yet made. The more uncommon ones are fully defined, and the whole are *arranged alphabetically* for convenient reference. The book is designed for Teachers' Institutes and "Spelling Schools," and is prepared by an experienced and well-known conductor of Institutes.

ETYMOLOGY.

Smith's Complete Etymology,
Smith's Condensed Etymology,

Containing the Anglo-Saxon, French, Dutch, German, Welsh, Danish, Gothic, Swedish, Gaelic, Italian, Latin, and Greek Roots, and the English words derived therefrom accurately spelled, accented, and defined.

From HON. JNO. G. MCMYNN, *late State Superintendent of Wisconsin.*

I wish every teacher in the country had a copy of this work.

From PRIN. WM. F. PHELPS, *Minn. State Normal.*

The book is superb—just what is needed in the department of etymology and spelling.

From PROF. C. H. VERRILL, *Pa. State Normal School.*

The Etymology (Smith's) which we procured of you we like much. It is the best work for the class-room we have seen.

From HON. EDWARD BALLARD, *Supt. of Common Schools, State of Maine.*

The author has furnished a manual of singular utility for its purpose.

DICTIONARY.

The Topical Lexicon,

This work is a School Dictionary, an Etymology, a compilation of synonyms, and a manual of general information. It differs from the ordinary lexicon in being arranged by topics instead of the letters of the alphabet, thus realizing the apparent paradox of a "Readable Dictionary." An unusually valuable school book.

ENGLISH GRAMMAR.

CLARK'S DIAGRAM SYSTEM.

Clark's Easy Lessons in Language,

Published 1874. Contains illustrated object-lessons of the most attractive character, and is couched in language freed as much as possible from the dry technicalities of the science.

Clark's Brief English Grammar,

Published 1872. Part I. is adapted to youngest learners, and the whole forms a complete "brief course" in one volume, adequate to the wants of the common school.

Clark's Normal Grammar,

Published 1870, and designed to take the place of Prof. Clark's veteran "Practical" Grammar, though the latter is still furnished upon order. The Normal is an entirely new treatise. It is a full exposition of the system as described below, with all the most recent improvements. Some of its peculiarities are—A happy blending of SYNTHESES with ANALYSES; thorough Criticisms of common errors in the use of our Language; and important improvements in the Syntax of Sentences and of Phrases.

Clark's Key to the Diagrams,

Clark's Analysis of the English Language, ·

Clark's Grammatical Chart,

The theory and practice of teaching grammar in American schools is meeting with a thorough revolution from the use of this system. While the old methods offer proficiency to the pupil only after much weary plodding and dull memorizing, this affords from the inception the advantage of *practical Object Teaching*, addressing the eye by means of illustrative figures; furnishes association to the memory, its most powerful aid, and diverts the pupil by taxing his ingenuity. Teachers who are using Clark's Grammar uniformly testify that they and their pupils find it the most interesting study of the school course.

Like all great and radical improvements, the system naturally met at first with much unreasonable opposition. It has not only outlived the greater part of this opposition, but finds many of its warmest admirers among those who could not at first tolerate so radical an innovation. All it wants is an impartial trial to convince the most skeptical of its merit. No one who has fairly and intelligently tested it in the school-room has ever been known to go back to the old method. A great success is already established, and it is easy to prophecy that the day is not far distant when it will be the *only system of teaching English Grammar.* As the SYSTEM is copyrighted, no other text-books can appropriate this obvious and great improvement.

Welch's Analysis of the English Sentence,

Remarkable for its new and simple classification, its method of treating connectives, its explanations of the idioms and constructive laws of the language, etc.

Clark's Diagram English Grammar.

TESTIMONIALS.

From J. A. T. DURNIN, *Principal Dubuque R. C. Academy, Iowa.*

In my opinion, it is well calculated by its system of analysis to develop those rational faculties which in the old systems were rather left to develop themselves, while the memory was overtaxed, and the pupils discouraged.

From B. A. COX, *School Commissioner, Warren County, Illinois.*

I have examined 150 teachers in the last year, and those having studied or taught Clark's System have universally stood fifty per cent. better examinations than those having studied other authors.

From M. H. B. BURKET, *Principal Masonic Institute, Georgetown, Tennessee.*

I traveled two years amusing myself in instructing (exclusively) Grammar classes with Clark's system. The first class I instructed fifty days, but found that this was more time than was required to impart a theoretical knowledge of the science. During the two years thereafter I instructed classes only *thirty* days each. Invariably I proposed that unless I prepared my classes for a more thorough, minute, and accurate knowledge of English Grammar than that obtained from the ordinary books and in the ordinary way in from one to two years, I would make no charge. I never failed in a solitary case to far exceed the hopes of my classes, and made money and character rapidly as an instructor.

From A. B. DOUGLASS, *School Commissioner, Delaware County, New York.*

I have never known a class pursue the study of it under a *live* teacher, that has not succeeded; I have never known it to have an opponent in an educated teacher who had *thoroughly* investigated it; I have never known an *ignorant* teacher to examine it; I have never known a teacher who has used it, to try any other.

From J. A. DODGE, *Teacher and Lecturer on English Grammar, Kentucky.*

We are tempted to assert that it foretells the dawn of a brighter age to our mother-tongue. Both pupil and teacher can fare sumptuously upon its contents, however highly they may have prized the manuals into which they may have been initiated, and by which their expressions have been moulded.

From W. T. CHAPMAN, *Superintendent Public Schools, Wellington, Ohio.*

I regard Clark's System of Grammar the best published. For teaching the analysis of the English Language, it surpasses any I ever used.

From F. S. LYON, *Principal South Norwalk Union School, Connecticut.*

During ten years' experience in teaching, I have used six different authors on the subject of English Grammar. I am fully convinced that Clark's Grammar is better calculated to make thorough grammarians than any other that I have seen.

From CATALOGUE OF ROHRER'S COMMERCIAL COLLEGE, *St. Louis, Missouri.*

We do not hesitate to assert, without fear of successful contradiction, that a better knowledge of the English language can be obtained by this system in six weeks than by the old methods in as many months.

From A. PICKETT, *President of the State Teachers' Association, Wisconsin.*

A thorough experiment in the use of many approved authors upon the subject of English Grammar has convinced me of the superiority of Clark. When the pupil has completed the course, he is left upon a foundation of *principle*, and not upon the *dictum* of the author.

From GEO. F. MCFARLAND, *Prin. McAllisterville Academy, Juniata Co., Penn.*

At the first examination of public-school teachers by the county superintendent, when one of our student teachers commenced analyzing a sentence according to Clark, the superintendent listened in mute astonishment until he had finished, then asked what that meant, and finally, with a very knowing look, said such work wouldn't do here, and asked the applicant to parse the sentence right, and gave the lowest certificates to all who barely mentioned Clark. Afterwards, I presented him with a copy, and the next fall he permitted it to be partially used, while the third of last fall, he openly commended the system, and appointed three of my best teachers to explain it at the two Institutes and one County Convention held since September.

☞ For further testimony of equal force, see the **Publishers' Special Circular**, or current numbers of the **Educational Bulletin.**

GEOGRAPHY.

NATIONAL GEOGRAPHICAL SYSTEM.

THE SERIES.

I. Monteith's First Lessons in Geography,
II. Monteith's New Manual of Geography,
II. McNally's System of Geography,

INTERMEDIATE OR ALTERNATE VOLUMES.

1*. Monteith's Introduction to Geography,
2*. Monteith's Physical and Political Geography,

ACCESSORIES.

Monteith's Wall Maps 2 sets (see page 15),
Monteith's Manual of Map-Drawing (Allen's System)
Monteith's Map-Drawing and Object-Lessons,
Monteith's Map-Drawing Scale,

1. PRACTICAL OBJECT TEACHING. The infant scholar is first introduced to *a picture* whence he may derive notions of the shape of the earth, the phenomena of day and night, the distribution of land and water, and the great natural divisions, which mere words would fail entirely to convey to the untutored mind. Other pictures follow on the same plan, and the child's mind is called upon to grasp no idea without the aid of a pictorial illustration. Carried on to the higher books, this system culminates in Physical Geography, where such matters as climates, ocean currents, the winds, peculiarities of the earth's crust, clouds and rain, are pictorially explained and rendered apparent to the most obtuse. The illustrations used for this purpose belong to the highest grade of art.

2. CLEAR, BEAUTIFUL, AND CORRECT MAPS. In the lower numbers the maps avoid unnecessary detail, while respectively progressive, and affording the pupil new matter for acquisition each time he approaches in the constantly enlarging circle the point of coincidence with previous lessons in the more elementary books. In the Physical and Political Geography the maps embrace many new and striking features. One of the most effective of these is the new plan for displaying on each map the relative sizes of countries not represented, thus obviating much confusion which has arisen from the necessity of presenting maps in the same atlas drawn on different scales. The maps of "McNally" have long been celebrated for their superior beauty and completeness. This is the only school-book in which the attempt to make a *complete* atlas *also clear and distinct*, has been successful. The map *coloring* throughout the series is also noticeable. Delicate and subdued tints take the place of the startling glare of inharmonious colors which too frequently in such treatises dazzle the eyes, distract the attention, and serve to overwhelm the names of towns and the natural features of the landscape.

GEOGRAPHY—Continued.

3. THE VARIETY OF MAP-EXERCISE. Starting each time from a different basis, the pupil in many instances approaches the same fact no less than *six times*, thus indelibly impressing it upon his memory. At the same time, this system is not allowed to become wearisome—the extent of exercise on each subject being graduated by its relative importance or difficulty of acquisition.

4. THE CHARACTER AND ARRANGEMENT OF THE DESCRIPTIVE TEXT. The cream of the science has been carefully culled, unimportant matter rejected, elaboration avoided, and a brief and concise manner of presentation cultivated. The orderly consideration of topics has contributed greatly to simplicity. Due attention is paid to the facts in history and astronomy which are inseparably connected with, and important to the proper understanding of geography—and *such only* are admitted on any terms. In a word, the National System teaches geography as a science, pure, simple, and exhaustive.

5. ALWAYS UP TO THE TIMES. The authors of these books, editorially speaking, never sleep. No change occurs in the boundaries of countries, or of counties, no new discovery is made, or railroad built, that is not at once noted and recorded, and the next edition of each volume carries to every school-room the new order of things.

6. SUPERIOR GRADATION. This is the only series which furnishes an available volume for every possible class in graded schools. It is not contemplated that a pupil must necessarily go through every volume in succession to attain proficiency. On the contrary, *two* will suffice, but *three* are advised; and, if the course will admit, the whole series should be pursued. At all events, the books are at hand for selection, and every teacher, of every grade, can find among them one *exactly suited* to his class. The best combination for those who wish to abridge the course consists of Nos. 1, 2, and 3, or where children are somewhat advanced in other studies when they commence geography, Nos. 1*, 2, and 3. Where but *two* books are admissible, Nos. 1* and 2*, or Nos. 2 and 3, are recommended.

7. FORM OF THE VOLUMES AND MECHANICAL EXECUTION. The maps and text are no longer unnaturally divorced in accordance with the time-honored practice of making text-books on this subject as inconvenient and expensive as possible. On the contrary, all map questions are to be found on the page opposite the map itself, and each book is complete in one volume. The mechanical execution is unrivalled. Paper and printing are everything that could be desired, and the binding is—A. S. Barnes & Company's.

8. MAP-DRAWING. In 1869 the system of Map-Drawing devised by Professor Jerome Allen was secured *exclusively* for this series. It derives its claim to originality and usefulness from the introduction of a *fixed unit of measurement* applicable to every Map. The principles being so few, simple and comprehensive, the subject of Map-Drawing is relieved of all practical difficulty. (In Nos. 2, 2*, and 3, and published separately.)

9. ANALOGOUS OUTLINES. At the same time with Map-Drawing was also introduced (in No. 2) a new and ingenious variety of Object Lessons, consisting of a comparison of the outlines of countries with familiar objects pictorially represented.

GEOGRAPHY—Continued.

MONTEITH'S INDEPENDENT COURSE.

Elementary Geography

Comprehensive Geography (with 103 Maps)

☞ These volumes are not revisions of old works—not an addition to any series—but are entirely new productions—each by itself complete, independent, comprehensive, yet simple, brief, cheap, and popular; or, taken together, the most admirable "series" ever offered for a common-school course. They present the following features, skillfully interwoven—the student learning all about one country at a time.

LOCAL GEOGRAPHY, or the Use of Maps. Important features of the Maps are the coloring of States as objects, and the ingenious system for laying down a much larger number of names for reference than are found on any other Maps of same size—and without crowding.

PHYSICAL GEOGRAPHY, or the Natural Features of the Earth, illustrated by the original and striking ***Relief Maps,*** being bird's-eye views or photographic pictures of the Earth's surface.

DESCRIPTIVE GEOGRAPHY, including the Physical; with some account of Governments, and Races, Animals, etc.

HISTORICAL GEOGRAPHY, or a brief summary of the salient points of history, explaining the present distribution of nations, origin of geographical names, etc.

MATHEMATICAL GEOGRAPHY, including ASTRONOMICAL, which describes the Earth's position and character among planets; also the Zones, Parallels, etc.

COMPARATIVE GEOGRAPHY, or a system of analogy, connecting new lessons with the previous ones. Comparative sizes and latitudes are shown on the margin of each Map, and all countries are measured in the "*frame of Kansas.*"

TOPICAL GEOGRAPHY, consisting of questions for review, and testing the student's general and specific knowledge of the subject, with suggestions for *Geographical Compositions.*

ANCIENT GEOGRAPHY. A section devoted to this subject, with Maps, will be appreciated by teachers. It is seldom taught in our common schools, because it has heretofore required the purchase of a separate book.

GRAPHIC GEOGRAPHY, or MAP-DRAWING by Allen's "Unit of Measurement" system (now almost universally recognized as without a rival) is introduced throughout the lessons, and not as an appendix.

CONSTRUCTIVE GEOGRAPHY, or GLOBE-MAKING. With each book a set of Map Segments is furnished, with which each student may make his own Globe by following the directions given.

RAILROAD GEOGRAPHY, with a grand Map illustrating routes of travel in the United States. Also, a "Tour in Europe."

MAP DRAWING.

Monteith's Map-Drawing Made Easy.

A neat little book of outlines and instructions, giving the "corners of States" in suitable blanks, so that Maps can be drawn by unskillful hands from any atlas; with instructions for written exercises or compositions on geographical subjects, and Comparative Geography.

Monteith's Manual of Map-Drawing (Allen's System).

The only consistent plan, by which all Maps are drawn on one scale. By its use much time may be saved, and much interest and accurate knowledge gained.

Monteith's Map-Drawing and Object Lessons.

The last-named treatise, bound with Mr. Monteith's ingenious system for committing outlines to memory by means of pictures of living creatures and familiar objects. Thus, South America resembles a dog's head; Cuba, a lizard; Italy, a boot; France, a coffee-pot; Turkey, a turkey, etc., etc.

Monteith's Map-Drawing Scale.

A ruler of wood, graduated to the "Allen fixed unit of measurement."

WALL MAPS.

Monteith's Pictorial Chart of Geography.

The original drawing for this beautiful and instructive chart was greatly admired in the publisher's "exhibit" at the Centennial Exhibition of 1876. It is *a picture* of the Earth's surface with every natural feature displayed, teaching also physical geography, and especially the mutations of water. The uses to which man puts the earth and its treasures and forces, as Agriculture, Mining, Manufacturing, Commerce, and Transportation are also graphically portrayed so that the young learner gets a realistic idea of "the world we live in," which weeks of book-study might fail to convey.

Monteith's School Maps, 8 Numbers.

The "School Series" includes the Hemispheres (2 Maps), United States, North America, South America, Europe, Asia, Africa.—Price, $2.50 each.

Each map is 28 × 34 inches, beautifully colored, has the names all laid down, and is substantially mounted on canvas with rollers.

Monteith's Grand Maps, 8 Numbers.

The "Grand Series" includes the Hemispheres (1 Map), United States, South America, Europe, Asia, Africa, The World on Mercator's Projection, and Physical Map of the World.—Price, $5.00 each. Size 42 × 52 inches, names laid down, colored, mounted, &c.

Monteith's Sunday School Maps,

Including a Map of Paul's Travels ($5.00), one of Ancient Canaan ($3.00), and Modern Palestine ($3.00), or Palestine and Canaan together ($5.00).

MONTEITH'S GEOGRAPHIES

Have been adopted, by official authority, for the schools of the following States and Cities—in most cases for *exclusive* and uniform use.

California, Tennessee, Iowa, Arkansas, North Carolina,
Missouri, Texas, Louisiana, Florida, Kansas,
Alabama, Vermont, Oregon, Minnesota, Mississippi.

Cities.—New York City, Brooklyn, Chicago, New Orleans, Buffalo, Richmond, Jersey City, Hartford, Worcester, San Francisco, Louisville, Newark, Milwaukee, Charleston, Rochester, Mobile, Syracuse, Memphis, Salt Lake City, Nashville, Utica, Wilmington, Trenton, Norfolk, Norwich, Lockport, Dubuque, Galveston, Portland, Savannah, Indianapolis, Springfield, Wheeling, Toledo, Bridgeport, St. Paul, Vicksburg, &c.

Monteith & McNally's National Geographies.

CRITICAL OPINIONS.

From R. A. ADAMS, *Member of Board of Education, New York.*

I have found, by examination of the Book of Supply of our Board, that considerably the largest number of any series now used in our public schools is the National, by Monteith and McNally.

From BRO. PATRICK, *Chief Provincial of the Vast Educational Society of the* CHRISTIAN BROTHERS *in the United States.*

Having been convinced for some time past that the series of Geographies in use in our schools were not giving satisfaction, and came far short of meeting our most reasonable expectations, I have felt it my imperative duty to examine into this matter, and see if a remedy could not be found.

Copies of the different Geographies published in this country have been placed at our command for examination. On account of other pressing duties we have not been able to give as much time to the investigation of all these different series as we could have desired; yet we have found enough to convince us that there are many others better than those we are now using; but we cheerfully give our most decided preference, above all others, to the National Series, by Monteith & McNally.

Their easy gradation, their thoroughly practical and independent character, their comprehensive completeness as a full and accurate system, the wise discrimination shown in the selection of the subject matter, the beautiful and copious illustrations, the neat cut type, the general execution of the works, and *other excellencies*, will commend them to the friends of education everywhere.

From the "HOME MONTHLY," *Nashville, Tenn.*

MONTEITH'S AND MCNALLY'S GEOGRAPHIES.—Geography is so closely connected with Astronomy, History, Ethnology, and Geology, that it is difficult to define its limits in the construction of a text-book. If the author confines himself strictly to a description of the earth's surface, his book will be dry, meager, and unintelligible to a child. If, on the other hand, he attempts to give information on the cognate sciences, he enters a boundless field, and may wander too far. It seems to us that the authors of the series before us have hit on the happy medium between too much and too little. *The First Lessons*, by applying the system of object-teaching, renders the subject so attractive that a child, just able to read, may become deeply interested in it. The second book of the course enlarges the view, but still keeps to the maps and simple descriptions. Then, in the third book, we have Geography combined with History and Astronomy. A general view of the solar system is presented, so that the pupil may understand the earth's position on the map of the heavens. The first part of the fourth book treats of Physical Geography, and contains a vast amount of knowledge compressed into a small space. It is made bright and attractive by beautiful pictures and suggestive illustrations, on the principle of object-teaching. The maps in the second part of this volume are remarkably clear, and the map exercises are copious and judicious. In the fifth and last volume of the series, the whole subject is reviewed and systematized. This is strictly a Geography. Its maps are beautifully engraved and clearly printed. The map exercises are full and comprehensive. In all these books the maps, questions and descriptions are given in the same volume. In most geographies there are too many details and minute descriptions—more than any child out of purgatory ought to be required to learn. The power of memory is overstrained; there is confusion—no clearly defined idea is formed in the child's mind. But in these books, in brief, pointed descriptions, and constant use of bright, accurate maps, the whole subject is photographed on the mind.

MATHEMATICS.

DAVIES' NATIONAL COURSE.

ARITHMETIC.

1. Davies' Primary Arithmetic,
2. Davies' Intellectual Arithmetic,
3. Davies' Elements of Written Arithmetic, .
4. Davies' Practical Arithmetic,
5. Davies' University Arithmetic.

TWO BOOK SERIES.

1. First Book in Arithmetic, Primary and Mental.
2. Complete Arithmetic.

ALGEBRA.

1. Davies' New Elementary Algebra,
2. Davies' University Algebra,
3. Davies' New Bourdon's Algebra.

GEOMETRY.

1. Davies' Elementary Geometry and Trigonometry,
2. Davies' Legendre's Geometry,
3. Davies' Analytical Geometry and Calculus,
4. Davies' Descriptive Geometry,
5. Davies' New Calculus,

MENSURATION.

1. Davies' Practical Mathematics and Mensuration,
2. Davies' Elements of Surveying,
3. Davies' Shades, Shadows, and Perspective,

MATHEMATICAL SCIENCE.

Davies' Grammar of Arithmetic,
Davies' Outlines of Mathematical Science,
Davies' Nature and Utility of Mathematics,
Davies' Metric System,
Davies & Peck's Dictionary of Mathematics,

DAVIES' NATIONAL COURSE of MATHEMATICS.

ITS RECORD.

In claiming for this series the first place among American text-books, of whatever class, the Publishers appeal to the magnificent record which its volumes have earned during the *thirty-five years* of Dr. Charles Davies' mathematical labors. The unremitting exertions of a life-time have placed *the modern series* on the same proud eminence among competitors that each of its predecessors has successively enjoyed in a course of constantly improved editions, now rounded to their perfect fruition—for it seems almost that this science is susceptible of no further demonstration.

During the period alluded to, many authors and editors in this department have started into public notice, and by borrowing ideas and processes original with Dr. Davies, have enjoyed a brief popularity, but are now almost unknown. Many of the series of to-day, built upon a similar basis, and described as "modern books," are destined to a similar fate; while the most far-seeing eye will find it difficult to fix the time, on the basis of any data afforded by their past history, when these books will cease to increase and prosper, and fix a still firmer hold on the affection of every educated American.

One cause of this unparalleled popularity is found in the fact that the enterprise of the author did not cease with the original completion of his books. Always a practical teacher, he has incorporated in his text-books from time to time the advantages of every improvement in methods of teaching, and every advance in science. During all the years in which he has been laboring, he constantly submitted his own theories and those of others to the practical test of the class-room—approving, rejecting, or modifying them as the experience thus obtained might suggest. In this way he has been able to produce an almost perfect series of class-books, in which every department of mathematics has received minute and exhaustive attention.

Upon the death of Dr. Davies, which took place in 1876; his work was immediately taken up by his former pupil and mathematical associate of many years, Prof. W. G. Peck, LL.D., of Columbia College. By him the original Series is kept carefully revised and not allowed in any way to fall behind the times.

Davies' System is the acknowledged National Standard for the United States, for the following reasons:—

1st. It is the basis of instruction in the great national schools at West Point and Annapolis.

2d. It has received the *quasi* endorsement of the National Congress.

3d. It is exclusively used in the public schools of the National Capital.

4th. The officials of the Government use it as authority in all cases involving mathematical questions.

5th. Our great soldiers and sailors commanding the national armies and navies were educated in this system. So have been a majority of eminent scientists in this country. All these refer to "Davies" as authority.

6th. A larger number of American citizens have received their education from this than from any other series.

7th. The series has a larger circulation throughout the whole country than any other, being *extensively used in every State in the Union.*

Davies' National Course of Mathematics.

TESTIMONIALS.

From L. VAN BOKKELEN, *State Superintendent Public Instruction, Maryland.*

The series of Arithmetics edited by Prof. Davies, and published by your firm, have been used for many years in the schools of several counties, and the city of Baltimore, and have been approved by teachers and commissioners.

Under the law of 1865, establishing a uniform system of Free Public Schools, these Arithmetics were unanimously adopted by the State Board of Education, after a careful examination, and are now used in all the Public Schools of Maryland.

These facts evidence the high opinion entertained by the School Authorities of the value of the series theoretically and practically.

From HORACE WEBSTER, *President of the College of New York.*

The undersigned has examined, with care and thought, several volumes of Davies' Mathematics, and is of the opinion that, as a whole, it is the most complete and best course for Academic and Collegiate instruction, with which he is acquainted.

From DAVID N. CAMP, *State Superintendent of Common Schools, Connecticut.*

I have examined Davies' Series of Arithmetics with some care. The language is clear and precise; each principle is thoroughly analyzed, and the whole so arranged as to facilitate the work of instruction. Having observed the satisfaction and success with which the different books have been used by eminent teachers, it gives me pleasure to commend them to others.

From J. O. WILSON, *Chairman Committee on Text-Books, Washington, D. C.*

I consider Davies' Arithmetics decidedly superior to any other series, and in this opinion I am sustained, I believe, by the entire Board of Education and Corps of Teachers in this city, where they have been used for several years past.

From JOHN L. CAMPBELL, *Professor of Mathematics, Wabash College, Indiana.*

A proper combination of abstract reasoning and practical illustration is the chief excellence in Prof. Davies' Mathematical works. I prefer his Arithmetics, Algebras, Geometry and Trigonometry to all others now in use, and cordially recommend them to all who desire the advancement of sound learning.

From MAJOR J. H. WHITTLESEY, *Government Inspector of Military Schools.*

Be assured, I regard the works of Prof. Davies, with which I am acquainted, as by far the best text-books in print on the subjects which they treat. I shall certainly encourage their adoption wherever a word from me may be of any avail.

From T. McC. BALLANTINE, *Prof. Mathematics Cumberland College, Kentucky.*

I have long taught Prof. Davies' Course of Mathematics, and I continue to like their working.

From JOHN McLEAN BELL, B. A., *Prin. of Lower Canada College.*

I have used Davies' Arithmetical and Mathematical Series as text-books in the schools under my charge for the last six years. These I have found of great efficacy in exciting, invigorating, and concentrating the intellectual faculties of the young.

Each treatise serves as an introduction to the next higher, by the similarity of its reasonings and methods; and the student is carried forward, by easy and gradual steps, over the whole field of mathematical inquiry, and that, too, in a *shorter* time than is usually occupied in mastering a single department. I sincerely and heartily recommend them to the attention of my fellow-teachers in Canada.

From D. W. STEELE, *Prin. Philekoian Academy, Cold Springs, Texas.*

I have used Davies' Arithmetics till I know them nearly by heart. A better series of school-books never were published. I have recommended them until they are now used in all this region of country.

PECK'S ARITHMETICS.

By the Prof. of Mathematics at Columbia College, New York.

1. Peck's First Lessons in Numbers,

Embracing all that is usually included in what are called Primary and Intellectual Arithmetics; proceeding gradually from object lessons to abstract numbers; developing Addition and Subtraction simultaneously: with other attractive novelties.

2. Peck's Manual of Practical Arithmetic,

An excellent "Brief" course, conveying a sufficient knowledge of Arithmetic for ordinary business purposes.

It is thoroughly "practical," because the author believes the Theory cannot be studied with advantage until the pupil has acquired a certain facility in combining numbers, which can only be had by practice.

3. Peck's Complete Arithmetic,

The whole subject—theory and practice—presented within very moderate limits. This author's most remarkable faculty of mathematical treatment is comprehended in three words: System, Conciseness, Lucidity. The directness and simplicity of this work cannot be better expressed than in the words of a correspondent who adopted the book at once, because, as he said, it is "free from that *juggling with numbers*" practiced by many authors.

From the "Galaxy," New York.

In the "Complete Arithmetic" each part of the subject is logically developed. First are given the necessary definitions; second, the explanations of such signs (if any) as are used; third, the principles on which the operation depends; fourth, an exemplification of the manner in which the operation is performed, which is so conducted that the reason of the rule which is immediately thereafter deduced is made perfectly plain; after which follow numerous graded examples and corresponding practical problems. All the parts taken together are arranged in logical order. The subject is treated as a whole, and not as if made up of segregated parts. It may seem a simple remark to make that (for example) addition is in principle one and the same everywhere, whether employed upon simple or compound numbers, fractions, etc., the only difference being in the *unit* involved; but the number of persons who understand this practically, compared to the number who have studied arithmetic, is not very great. The student of the "Complete Arithmetic" cannot fail to understand it. All the principles of the science are presented within moderate limits. Superfluity of matter—to supplement defective definitions, to make clear faulty demonstrations and rules expressed either inaccurately or obscurely, to make provision for a multiplicity of cases for which no provision is requisite—has been carefully avoided. The definitions are plain and concise; the principles are stated clearly and accurately; the demonstrations are full and complete; the rules are perspicuous and comprehensive; the illustrative examples are abundant and well fitted to familiarize the student with the application of principles to the problems of science and of every-day life.

☞ The Definitions constitute the power of the book. We have never seen them excelled for clearness and exactness.—*Iowa School Journal.*

MATHEMATICS—Continued.

PECK'S HIGHER COURSE.

Peck's Manual of Algebra,

Bringing the methods of Bourdon within the range of the Academic Course.

Peck's Manual of Geometry,

By a method purely practical, and unembarrassed by the details which rather confuse than simplify science.

Peck's Practical Calculus,

Peck's Analytical Geometry,

Peck's Elementary Mechanics,

Peck's Mechanics, with Calculus,

The briefest treatises on these subjects now published. Adopted by the great Universities; Yale, Harvard, Columbia, Princeton, Cornell, &c.

ARITHMETICAL EXAMPLES.

Reuck's Examples in Denominate Numbers,

Reuck's Examples in Arithmetic,

These volumes differ from the ordinary arithmetic in their peculiarly *practical* character. They are composed mainly of examples, and afford the most severe and thorough discipline for the mind. While a book which should contain a complete treatise of theory and practice would be too cumbersome for every-day use, the insufficiency of *practical* examples has been a source of complaint.

HIGHER MATHEMATICS.

Macnie's Algebraical Equations,

Serving as a complement to the more advanced treatises on Algebra, giving special attention to the analysis and solution of equations with numerical coefficients.

Church's Elements of Calculus,

Church's Analytical Geometry,

Church's Descriptive Geometry, 2 vols.,

These volumes constitute the "West Point Course" in their several departments.

Courtenay's Elements of Calculus,

A standard work of the very highest grade.

Hackley's Trigonometry,

With applications to navigation and surveying, nautical and practical geometry and geodesy.

PENMANSHIP.

Beers' System of Progressive Penmanship. Per dozen

This "round hand" system of Penmanship in twelve numbers, commends itself by its simplicity and thoroughness. The first four numbers are primary books. Nos. 5 to 7, advanced books for boys. Nos. 8 to 10, advanced books for girls. Nos. 11 and 12, ornamental penmanship. These books are printed from steel plates (engraved by McLees), and are unexcelled in mechanical execution. Large quantities are annually sold.

Beers' Slated Copy Slips, per set

All beginners should practice, for a few weeks, slate exercises, familiarizing them with the form of the letters, the motions of the hand and arm, &c., &c. These copy slips, 32 in number, supply all the copies found in a complete series of writing-books, at a trifling cost.

Payson, Dunton & Scribner's Copy-B'ks. P. doz.,

The National System of Penmanship, in three distinct series—(1) Common School Series, comprising the first six numbers; (2) Business Series, Nos. 8, 11, and 12; (3) Ladies' Series, Nos. 7, 9, and 10.

Fulton & Eastman's Chirographic Charts,

To embellish the school room walls, and furnish class exercise in the elements of Penmanship.

Payson's Copy-Book Cover, per hundred

Protects every page except the one in use, and furnishes "lines" with proper slope for the penman, under. Patented.

National Steel Pens, Card with all kinds

Pronounced by competent judges the perfection of American-made pens, and superior to any foreign article.

SCHOOL SERIES.	
School Pen, per gross,	$ 60
Academic Pen, do	63
Fine Pointed Pen, per gross	70
POPULAR SERIES.	
Capitol Pen, per gross,	1 00
do do pr. box of 2 doz.	25
Bullion Pen (imit. gold) pr. gr.	75
Ladies' Pen do	63
Index Pen, per gross	75
BUSINESS SERIES.	
Albata Pen, per gross,	40
Bank Pen, do	70
Empire Pen, do	70
Commercial Pen, per gross	60
Express Pen, do	75
Falcon Pen, do	70
Elastic Pen, do	75

Stimpson's Scientific Steel Pen, per gross $1 50

One forward and two backward arches, ensuring great strength, well-balanced elasticity, evenness of point, and smoothness of execution. One gross in twelve contains a Scientific Gold Pen.

Stimpson's Ink-Retaining Holder, per doz. 1 50

A simple apparatus, which does not get out of order, withholds at a single dip as much ink as the pen would otherwise realize from a dozen trips to the inkstand, which it supplies with moderate and easy flow.

Stimpson's Gold Pen, $3 00; with Ink Retainer 4 50

Stimpson's Penman's Card, $0 25

One dozen Steel Pens (assorted points) and Patent Ink-retaining Pen holder.

HISTORY.

Monteith's Youth's History.

A History of the United States for beginners. It is arranged upon the catechetical plan, with illustrative maps and engravings, review questions, dates in parentheses (that their study may be optional with the younger class of learners), and interesting Biographical Sketches of all persons who have been prominently identified with the history of our country.

Willard's United States, School and University Editions.

The plan of this standard work is chronologically exhibited in front of the title-page; the Maps and Sketches are found useful assistants to the memory, and dates, usually so difficult to remember, are so systematically arranged as in a great degree to obviate the difficulty. Candor, impartiality, and accuracy, are the distinguishing features of the narrative portion.

Willard's Universal History.

The most valuable features of the "United States" are reproduced in this. The peculiarities of the work are its great conciseness and the prominence given to the chronological order of events. The margin marks each successive era with great distinctness, so that the pupil retains not only the event but its time, and thus fixes the order of history firmly and usefully in his mind. Mrs. Willard's books are constantly revised, and at all times written up to embrace important historical events of recent date.

Lancaster's English History,

By the Master of the Stoughton Grammar School, Boston. The most practical of the "brief books." Though short, it is not a bare and uninteresting outline, but contains enough of explanation and detail to make intelligible the *cause and effect* of events. Their relations to the history and development of the American people is made specially prominent.

Willis' Historical Reader,

Being Collier's Great Events of History adapted to American schools. This rare epitome of general history, remarkable for its charming style and judicious selection of events on which the destinies of nations have turned, has been skillfully manipulated by Prof. Willis, with as few changes as would bring the United States into its proper position in the historical perspective. As reader or text-book it has few equals and no superiors.

Berard's History of England,

By an authoress well known for the success of her History of the United States. The social life of the English people is felicitously interwoven, as in fact, with the civil and military transactions of the realm.

Ricord's History of Rome

Possesses the charm of an attractive romance. The Fables with which this history abounds are introduced in such a way as not to deceive the inexperienced, while adding materially to the value of the work as a reliable index to the character and institutions, as well as the history of the Roman people.

Hanna's Bible History.

The only compendium of Bible narrative which affords a connected and chronological view of the important events there recorded, divested of all superfluous detail.

Summary of History; American, French and English.

A well-proportioned outline of leading events, condensing the substance of the more extensive text-book in common use into a series of statements so brief, that every word may be committed to memory, and yet so comprehensive that it presents an accurate though general view of the whole continuous life of nations.

Marsh's Ecclesiastical History.

Affording the History of the Church in all ages, with accounts of the pagan world during Biblical periods, and the character, rise, and progress of all Religions, as well as the various sects of the worshipers of Christ. The work is entirely non-sectarian, though strictly catholic. A separate volume contains carefully prepared QUESTIONS for class use.

BARNES' ONE-TERM HISTORY.

A Brief History of the United States,

This is probably the MOST ORIGINAL SCHOOL-BOOK published for many years, in any department. A few of its claims are the following:

1. Brevity.—The text is complete for Grammar School or intermediate classes, in 290 12mo pages, large type. It may readily be completed, if desired, in one term of study.

2. Comprehensiveness.—Though so brief, this book contains the pith of all the wearying contents of the larger manuals, and a great deal more than the memory usually retains from the latter.

3. Interest has been a prime consideration. Small books have heretofore been bare, full of dry statistics, unattractive. This one is charmingly written, replete with anecdote, and brilliant with illustration.

4. Proportion of Events.—It is remarkable for the discrimination with which the different portions of our history are presented according to their importance. Thus the older works being already large books when the civil war took place, give it less space than that accorded to the Revolution.

5. Arrangement.—In six epochs, entitled respectively, Discovery and Settlement, the Colonies, the Revolution, Growth of States, the Civil War, and Current Events.

6. Catch Words.—Each paragraph is preceded by its leading thought in prominent type, standing in the student's mind for the whole paragraph.

7. Key Notes.—Analogous with this is the idea of grouping battles, etc. about some central event, which relieves the sameness so common in such descriptions, and renders each distinct by some striking peculiarity of its own.

8. Foot Notes.—These are crowded with interesting matter that is not strictly a part of history proper. They may be learned or not, at pleasure. They are certain in any event to be read.

9. Biographies of all the leading characters are given in full in foot-notes.

10. Maps.—Elegant and distinct Maps from engravings on copper-plate, and beautifully colored, precede each epoch, and contain all the places named.

11. Questions are at the back of the book, to compel a more independent use of the text. Both text and questions are so worded that the pupil must give intelligent answers IN HIS OWN WORDS. "Yes" and "No" will not do.

12. Historical Recreations.—These are additional questions to test the student's knowledge, in review, as: "What trees are celebrated in our history?" "When did a fog save our army?" "What Presidents died in office?" "When was the Mississippi our western boundary?" "Who said, 'I would rather be right than President?'" etc.

13. The Illustrations, about seventy in number, are the work of our best artists and engravers, produced at great expense. They are vivid and interesting, and mostly upon subjects never before illustrated in a school-book.

14. Dates.—Only the leading dates are given in the text, and these are so associated as to assist the memory, but at the head of each page is the date of the event first mentioned, and at the close of each epoch a summary of events and dates.

15. The Philosophy of History is studiously exhibited—the causes and effects of events being distinctly traced and their interconnection shown.

16. Impartiality.—All sectional, partisan, or denominational views are avoided. Facts are stated after a careful comparison of all authorities without the least prejudice or favor.

17. Index.—A verbal index at the close of the book perfects it as a work of reference.

It will be observed that the above are all particulars in which School Histories have been signally defective, or altogether wanting. Many other claims to favor it shares in common with its predecessors.

BARNES' ONE-TERM HISTORY—Continued.

From PROF. WM. F. ALLEN, *State Univ. of Wisconsin.*

I think the author of the new "Brief History of the United States" has been very successful in combining brevity with sufficient fullness and interest. *Particularly*, he has avoided the excessive number of names and dates that most histories contain. Two features that I like *very much* are the *anecdotes* at the foot of the page and the "*Historical Recreations*" in the Appendix. The latter, I think, is quite a *new* feature, and the other is *very* well executed.

From S. G. WRIGHT, *Assist.-Supt. Pub. Inst., Kansas.*

It is with extreme pleasure we submit our recommendation of the "Brief History of the United States." It meets the needs of young and older children, combining concision with perspicuity, and if "brevity is the soul of wit," this "Brief History" contains not only that well-chosen ingredient, but wisdom sufficient to enlighten those students who are wearily longing for a "new departure" from certain old and uninteresting presentations of fossilized writers. We congratulate a progressive public upon a progressive book.

From HON. NEWTON BATEMAN, *Supt. Pub. Inst., Illinois.*

Barnes' One-Term History of the United States is an exceedingly attractive and spirited little book. Its claim to several new and valuable features seems well founded. Under the form of six well-defined Epochs, the History of the United States is traced tersely, yet pithily, from the earliest times to the present day. A good map precedes each epoch, whereby the history and geography of the period may be studied together, *as they always should be.* The syllabus of each paragraph is made to stand in such bold relief, by the use of large, heavy type, as to be of much *mnemonic* value to the student. The book is written in a sprightly and piquant style, the interest never flagging from beginning to end—a rare and difficult achievement in works of this kind.

From the "Chicago Schoolmaster" (Editorial).

A thorough examination of Barnes' Brief History of the United States brings the examiner to the conclusion that it is a superior book in almost every respect. The book is neat in form, and of good material. The type is clear, large, and distinct. The facts and dates are correct. The arrangement of topics is just the thing needed in a history text-book. By this arrangement the pupil can see at once what he is expected to do. The topics are well selected, embracing the leading ideas or principal events of American history. . . . The book as a whole is much superior to any I have examined. So much do I think this, that I have ordered it for my class, and shall use it in my school. (Signed) B. W. BAKER.

A Brief History of France,

By the author of the "Brief United States," with all the attractive features of that popular work (which see), and new ones of its own.

It is believed that the history of France has never before been presented in such brief compass, and this is effected without sacrificing one particle of interest. The book reads like a romance, and, while drawing the student by an irresistible fascination to his task, impresses the great outlines indelibly upon the memory.

Gilman's First Steps in General History,

A "suggestive outline" of rare compactness. Each country is treated by itself, and the United States receive special attention. Frequent Maps, contemporary events in Tables, References to Standard Works for fuller details, and a minute Index constitute the "Illustrative Apparatus." From no other work that we know of can so succinct a view of the world's history be obtained. Considering the necessary limitation of space, the style is surprisingly vivid, and at times even ornate. In all respects a charming, though not the less practical, text-book.

Gilman's "Seven Historic Ages,"

This book is written in the style used by a father talking with his children on the progress of history. As one Age after another is taken up, the author brings before the young reader the prominent men and characteristic events by which it is to be remembered. The object is to stimulate the pupil in school or the child at home to study history, to think of it as a lively picture of the doings of men, and not as a dead list of uninteresting dates.

Baker's Brief History of Texas,

On the plan of "Barnes' Brief Histories," with Constitution of the State, for Schools.

DRAWING.

Chapman's American Drawing Book,

The standard American text-book and authority in all branches of art. A compilation of art principles. A manual for the amateur, and basis of study for the professional artist. Adapted for schools and private instruction.

CONTENTS.—"Any one who can Learn to Write can Learn to Draw."—Primary Instruction in Drawing.—Rudiments of Drawing the Human Head.—Rudiments in Drawing the Human Figure.—Rudiments of Drawing.—The Elements of Geometry.—Perspective.—Of Studying and Sketching from Nature.—Of Painting.—Etching and Engraving.—Of Modeling.—Of Composition.—Advice to the American Art-Student. The work is of course magnificently illustrated with all the original designs.

Chapman's Elementary Drawing Book,

A Progressive Course of Practical Exercises, or a text-book for the training of the eye and hand. It contains the elements from the larger work, and a copy should be in the hands of every pupil; while a copy of the "American Drawing Book," named above, should be at hand for reference by the class.

The Little Artist's Portfolio,

25 Drawing Cards (progressive patterns), 25 Blanks, and a fine Artist's Pencil, all in one neat envelope.

Clark's Elements of Drawing,

A complete course in this graceful art, from the first rudiments of outline to the finished sketches of landscape and scenery.

Fowle's Linear and Perspective Drawing,

For the cultivation of the eye and hand, with copious illustrations and directions for the guidance of the unskilled teacher.

Monk's Drawing Books—Six Numbers, per set,

Each book contains *eleven* large patterns, with opposing blanks. No. 1. Elementary Studies. No. 2. Studies of Foliage. No. 3. Landscapes. No. 4. Animals, I. No. 5. Animals, II. No. 6. Marine Views, etc.

Allen's Map-Drawing, Scale,

This method introduces a new era in Map-Drawing, for the following reasons:—1. It is a system. This is its greatest merit.—2. It is easily understood and taught.—3. The eye is trained to exact measurement by the use of a scale.—4. By no special effort of the memory, distance and comparative size are fixed in the mind.—5. It discards useless construction of lines.—6. It can be taught by any teacher, even though there may have been no previous practice in Map-Drawing.—7. Any pupil old enough to study Geography can learn by this System, in a short time, to draw accurate maps.—8. The System is not the result of theory, but comes directly from the school-room. It has been thoroughly and successfully tested there, with all grades of pupils.—9. It is economical, as it requires no mapping plates. It gives the pupil the ability of rapidly drawing accurate maps.

Ripley's Map-Drawing,

Based on the Circle. One of the most efficient aids to the acquirement of a knowledge of Geography is the practice of map-drawing. It is useful for the same reason that the best exercise in orthography is the *writing* of difficult words. Sight comes to the aid of hearing, and a double impression is produced upon the memory. Knowledge becomes less mechanical and more intuitive. The student who has sketched the outlines of a country, and dotted the important places, is little likely to forget either. The impression produced may be compared to that of a traveller who has been over the ground, while more comprehensive and accurate in detail.

BOOK-KEEPING.

Folsom's Logical Book-keeping,
Folsom's Blanks to Book-keeping,

This treatise embraces the interesting and important discoveries of Prof. Folsom (of the Albany "Bryant & Stratton College"), the partial enunciation of which in lectures and otherwise has attracted so much attention in circles interested in commercial education.

After studying business phenomena for many years, he has arrived at the positive laws and principles that underlie the whole subject of Accounts; finds that the science is based in *Value* as a generic term; that value divides into *two classes* with varied species; that all the exchanges of values are reducible to nine equations; and that all the results of all these exchanges are limited to *thirteen* in number.

As accounts have been universally taught hitherto, without setting out from a radical analysis or definition of values, the science has been kept in great obscurity, and been made as difficult to impart as to acquire. On the new theory, however, these obstacles are chiefly removed. In reading over the first part of it, in which the governing laws and principles are discussed, a person with ordinary intelligence will obtain a fair conception of the *double entry* process of accounts. But when he comes to study thoroughly these laws and principles as there enunciated, and works out the examples and memoranda which elucidate the *thirteen results* of business, the student will neither fail in readily acquiring the science as it is, nor in becoming able intelligently to apply it in the interpretation of business.

Smith & Martin's Book-keeping,
Smith & Martin's Blanks,

This work is by a practical teacher and a practical book-keeper. It is of a thoroughly popular class, and will be welcomed by every one who loves to see theory and practice combined in an easy, concise, and methodical form.

The Single Entry portion is well adapted to supply a want felt in nearly all other treatises, which seem to be prepared mainly for the use of wholesale merchants, leaving retailers, mechanics, farmers, etc., who transact the greater portion of the business of the country, without a guide. The work is also commended, on this account, for general use in Young Ladies' Seminaries, where a thorough grounding in the simpler form of accounts will be invaluable to the future housekeepers of the nation.

The treatise on Double Entry Book-keeping combines all the advantages of the most recent methods, with the utmost simplicity of application, thus affording the pupil all the advantages of actual experience in the counting-house, and giving a clear comprehension of the entire subject through a judicious course of mercantile transactions.

The shape of the book is such that the transactions can be presented as in actual practice; and the simplified form of Blanks—three in number—adds greatly to the ease experienced in acquiring the science.

NATURAL SCIENCE.

FAMILIAR SCIENCE.

Norton & Porter's First Book of Science,

By eminent Professors of Yale College. Contains the principles of Natural Philosophy, Astronomy, Chemistry, Physiology, and Geology. Arranged on the Catechetical plan for primary classes and beginners.

Chambers' Treasury of Knowledge,

Progressive lessons upon—*first*, common things which lie most immediately around us, and first attract the attention of the young mind; *second*, common objects from the Mineral, Animal, and Vegetable kingdoms, manufactured articles, and miscellaneous substances; *third*, a systematic view of Nature under the various sciences. May be used as a Reader or Text-book.

NATURAL PHILOSOPHY.

Norton's First Book in Natural Philosophy,

By Prof. NORTON, of Yale College. Designed for beginners. Profusely illustrated, and arranged on the Catechetical plan.

Peck's Ganot's Course of Nat. Philosophy,

The standard text-book of France, Americanized and popularized by Prof. PECK, of Columbia College. The most magnificent system of illustration ever adopted in an American school-book is here found. For intermediate classes.

Peck's Elements of Mechanics,

A suitable introduction to Bartlett's higher treatises on Mechanical Philosophy, and adequate in itself for a complete academical course.

Bartlett's SYNTHETIC, AND ANALYTIC, Mechanics,

Bartlett's Acoustics and Optics,

A system of Collegiate Philosophy, by Prof. BARTLETT, of West Point Military Academy.

Steele's 14 Weeks Course in Philos. (see p. 34)

Steele's Philosophical Apparatus,

Adequate to performing the experiments in the ordinary text-books. The articles will be sold separately, if desired. See special circular for details.

GEOLOGY.

Page's Elements of Geology,

A volume of Chambers' Educational Course. Practical, simple, and eminently calculated to make the study interesting.

Emmons' Manual of Geology,

The first Geologist of the country has here produced a work worthy of his reputation.

Steele's 14 Weeks Course (see p. 34)

Steele's Geological Cabinet,

Containing 125 carefully selected specimens. In four parts. Sold separately, if desired. See circular for details.

Peck's Ganot's Popular Physics.

TESTIMONIALS.

From PROF. ALONZO COLLIN, *Cornell College, Iowa.*

I am pleased with it. I have decided to introduce it as a text-book.

From H. F. JOHNSON, *President Madison College, Sharon, Mi..*

I am pleased with Peck's Ganot, and think it a magnificent book.

From PROF. EDWARD BROOKS, *Pennsylvania State Normal School.*

So eminent are its merits, that it will be introduced as the text-book upon ele mentary physics in this institution.

From H. H. LOCKWOOD, *Professor Natural Philosophy U. S. Naval Academy.*

I am so pleased with it that I will probably add it to a course of lectures given to the midshipmen of this school on physics.

From GEO. S. MACKIE, *Professor Natural History University of Nashville, Tenn.*

I have decided on the introduction of Peck's Ganot's Philosophy, as I am satisfied that it is the best book for the purposes of my pupils that I have seen. combining simplicity of explanation with elegance of illustration.

From W. S. MCRAE, *Superintendent Vevay Public Schools, Indiana.*

Having carefully examined a number of text-books on natural philosophy, I do not hesitate to express my decided opinion in favor of Peck's Ganot. The matter, style, and illustration eminently adapt the work to the popular wants.

From REV. SAMUEL MCKINNEY, D.D., *Pres't Austin College, Huntsville, Texas.*

It gives me pleasure to commend it to teachers. I have taught some classes with it as our text, and must say, for simplicity of style and clearness of illustration, I have found nothing as yet published of equal value to the teacher and pupil.

From C. V. SPEAR, *Principal Maplewood Institute, Pittsfield, Mass.*

I am much pleased with its ample illustrations by plates, and its clearness and simplicity of statement. It covers the ground usually gone over by our higher classes, and contains many fresh illustrations from life or daily occurrence, and new applications of scientific principles to such.

From J. A BANFIELD, *Superintendent Marshall Public Schools, Michigan.*

I have used Peck's Ganot since 1862, and with increasing pleasure and satisfaction each term. I consider it superior to any other work on physics in its adaptation to our high schools and academies. Its illustrations are superb— better than three times their number of pages of fine print.

From A. SCHUYLER, *Prof. of Mathematics in Baldwin University, Berea, Ohio.*

After a careful examination of Peck's Ganot's Natural Philosophy, and an actual test of its merits as a text-book, I can heartily recommend it as admirably adapted to meet the wants of the grade of students for which it is intended. Its diagrams and illustrations are *unrivaled.* We use it in the Baldwin University.

From D. C. VAN NORMAN, *Principal Van Norman Institute, New York.*

The Natural Philosophy of M. Ganot, edited by Prof. Peck, is, in my opinion, the best work of its kind, for the use intended, ever published in this country. Whether regarded in relation to the natural order of the topics, the precision and clearness of its definitions, or the fullness and beauty of its illustrations, it is certainly, I think, an advance.

☞ For many similar testimonials, see current numbers of the Illustrated Educational Bulletin.

NATURAL SCIENCE—Continued.

CHEMISTRY.

Porter's First Book of Chemistry,

Porter's Principles of Chemistry,

The above are widely known as the productions of one of the most eminent scientific men of America. The extreme simplicity in the method of presenting the science, while exhaustively treated, has excited universal commendation.

Darby's Text-Book of Chemistry,

Purely a Chemistry, divesting the subject of matters comparatively foreign to it (such as heat, light, electricity, etc.), but usually allowed to engross too much attention in ordinary school-books.

Gregory's Chemistry, (Organic and Inorganic, each)

The science exhaustively treated. For colleges and medical students.

Steele's Fourteen Weeks Course,

A successful effort to reduce the study to the limits of a *single term.* (See page 34.)

Steele's Chemical Apparatus,

Adequate to the performance of all the important experiments.

BOTANY.

Thinker's First Lessons in Botany,

For children. The technical terms are largely dispensed with in favor of an easy and familiar style adapted to the smallest learner.

Wood's Object-Lessons in Botany,

Wood's American Botanist and Florist,

Wood's New Class-Book of Botany,

The standard text-books of the United States in this department. In style they are simple, popular, and lively; in arrangement, easy and natural; in description, graphic and strictly exact. The Tables for Analysis are reduced to a perfect system. More are annually sold than of all others combined.

Wood's Plant Record,

A simple form of Blanks for recording observations in the field.

Wood's Botanical Apparatus,

A portable Trunk, containing Drying Press, Knife, Trowel, Microscope, and Tweezers, and a copy of Wood's Plant Record—composing a complete outfit for the collector.

Willis's Flora of New Jersey,

"*Catalogus Plantarum in Nova Cæsarea repertarum.*" This remarkable flora is of great interest to all botanists, and the Jersey Pines have been termed "the Mecca to which every young botanist hopes some day to make a pilgrimage." This work is indispensable to those botanizing on the ground, and is the most useful book of reference ever published for collectors in all parts of the country. It contains also a Botanical Directory, with addresses of living American botanists.

Young's Familiar Lessons,

Combining simplicity of diction with some degree of technical and scientific knowledge for intermediate classes. Specially adapted for Texas and the Southwest.

Darby's Southern Botany,

Embracing general Structural and Physiological Botany, with vegetable products, and descriptions of Southern plants, and a complete Flora of the Southern States.

NATURAL SCIENCE—Continued.

WOOD'S BOTANIES.

TESTIMONIALS.

From PROF. RICHARD OWEN, *University of Indiana.*

I am well pleased with the evidence of philosophical method exhibited in the general arrangement, as well as with the clearness of the explanations, the ready intelligibility of the analytical tables, and the illustrative aid furnished by the numerous and excellent wood-cuts. I design using the work as a text-book with my next class.

From PRIN. B. R. ANDERSON, *Columbus Union School, Wisconsin.*

I have examined several works with a view to recommending some good text-book on Botany, but I lay them all aside for "Wood's Botanist and Florist." The arrangement of the book is in my opinion excellent, its style fascinating and attractive, its treatment of the various departments of the science is thorough, and last, but far from unimportant, I like the topical form of the questions to each chapter. It seems to embrace the entire science. In fact, I consider it a complete, attractive, and exhaustive work.

From M. A. MARSHALL, *New Haven High School, Conn.*

It has all the excellencies of the well-known Class-Book of Botany by the same author in a smaller book. By a judicious system of condensation, the size of the Flora is reduced one-half, while no species are omitted, and many new ones are added. The descriptions of species are very brief, yet sufficient to identify the plant, and, when taken in connection with the generic description, form a complete description of the plant. The book as a whole will suit the wants of classes better than anything I have yet seen. The adoption of the Botanist and Florist would not require the exclusion of the Class-Book of Botany, as they are so arranged that both might be used by the same class.

From PROF. G. H. PERKINS, *University of Vermont and State Agricultural College.*

I can truly say that the more I examine Wood's Class-Book, the better pleased I am with it. In its illustrations, especially of particulars not easily observed by the student, and the clearness and compactness of its statements, as well as in the territory its flora embraces, it appears to me to surpass any other work I know of. The whole science, so far as it can be taught in a college course, is well presented and rendered unusually easy of comprehension. The mode of analysis is excellent, avoiding as it does to a great extent those microscopic characters which puzzle the beginner, and using those that are obvious as far as possible. I regard the work as a most admirable one, and shall adopt it as a text-book another year.

AGRICULTURE.

Pendleton's Scientific Agriculture,

A text-book for colleges and schools; treats of the following topics: Anatomy and Physiology of Plants; Agricultural Meteorology; Soils as related to Physics; Chemistry of the Atmosphere; of Plants; of Soils; Fertilizers and Natural Manures; Animal Nutrition, etc. By E. M. PENDLETON, M. D., Prof. of Agriculture in the University of Georgia.

From President A. D. WHITE, *Cornell University.*

Dear Sir: I have examined your "Text-book of Agricultural Science," and it seems to me excellent in view of the purpose it is intended to serve. Many of your chapters interested me especially, and all parts of the work seem to combine scientific instruction with practical information in proportions dictated by sound common sense.

From President ROBINSON, *of Brown University.*

It is scientific in method as well as in matter, comprehensive in plan, natural and logical in order, compact and lucid in its statements, and must be useful both as a text-book in Agricultural colleges, and as a hand-book for intelligent planters and farmers.

NATURAL SCIENCE—Continued.

PHYSIOLOGY.

Jarvis' Elements of Physiology,

Jarvis' Physiology and Laws of Health,

The only books extant which approach this subject with a proper view of the true object of teaching Physiology in schools, viz., that scholars may know how to take care of their own health. In bold contrast with the abstract *Anatomies*, which children learn as they would Greek or Latin (and forget as soon), to *discipline the mind*, are these text-books, using the *science* as a secondary consideration, and only so far as is necessary for the comprehension of the *laws of health.*

Hamilton's Vegetable and Animal Physiology,

The two branches of the science combined in one volume lead the student to a proper comprehension of the Analogies of Nature.

Steele's Fourteen Weeks Course,

In the popular style, avoiding technical and purely scientific formulas. It contains beautiful and vivid illustrations, some of them colored, and a blackboard analysis of the skeleton. The sections on diseases and accidents, and their prompt home treatment, give the book great practical value (see p. 34).

ASTRONOMY.

Willard's School Astronomy,

By means of clear and attractive illustrations, addressing the eye in many cases by analogies, careful definitions of all necessary technical terms, a careful avoidance of verbiage and unimportant matter, particular attention to analysis, and a general adoption of the simplest methods. Mrs. Willard has made the best and most attractive *elementary* Astronomy extant.

McIntyre's Astronomy and the Globes,

A complete treatise for intermediate classes. Highly approved.

Bartlett's Spherical Astronomy,

The West Point course, for advanced classes, with applications to the current wants of Navigation, Geography, and Chronology.

Steele's Fourteen Weeks Course,

Reduced to a single term, and better adapted to school use than any work heretofore published. Not written for the information of scientific men, but for the inspiration of youth, the pages are not burdened with a multitude of figures which no memory could possibly retain. The whole subject is presented in a clear and concise form. (See p. 34.)

NATURAL HISTORY.

Carll's Child's Book of Natural History,

Illustrating the Animal, Vegetable, and Mineral Kingdoms, with applicatien to the Arts. For beginners. Beautifully and copiously illustrated.

ZOOLOGY.

Chambers' Elements of Zoology,

A complete and comprehensive system of Zoology, adapted for academic instruction, presenting a systematic view of the Animal Kingdom as a portion of external Nature.

Steele's Fourteen Weeks Course,

Notable for its superb and entertaining illustrations, which include every animal named; blackboard tables of classification and tabular review of the whole animal kingdom; interesting and characteristic facts and anecdotes; directions for collecting and preserving specimens, etc., etc. (See p. 34.)

Jarvis' Physiology and Laws of Health.

TESTIMONIALS.

From SAMUEL B. McLANE, *Superintendent Public Schools, Keokuk, Iowa.*

I am glad to see a really good text-book on this much neglected branch. This is clear, concise, accurate, and eminently adapted to the *class-room.*

From WILLIAM F. WYERS, *Principal of Academy, West Chester, Pennsylvania.*

A thorough examination has satisfied me of its superior claims as a text-book to the attention of teacher and taught. I shall introduce it at once.

From H. R. SANFORD, *Principal of East Genesee Conference Seminary, N. Y.*

"Jarvis' Physiology" is received, and fully met our expectations. We immediately adopted it.

From ISAAC T. GOODNOW, *State Superintendent of Kansas—published in connection with the "School Law."*

"Jarvis' Physiology," a common-sense, practical work, with just enough of anatomy to understand the physiological portions. The last six pages, on Man's Responsibility for his own health, are worth the price of the book.

From D. W. STEVENS, *Superintendent Public Schools, Fall River, Mass.*

I have examined Jarvis' "Physiology and Laws of Health," which you had the kindness to send to me a short time ago. In my judgment it is far the best work of the kind within my knowledge. It has been adopted as a text-book in our public schools.

From HENRY G. DENNY, *Chairman Book Committee, Boston, Mass.*

The very excellent "Physiology" of D. Jarvis I had introduced into our High School, where the study had been temporarily dropped, believing it to be by far the best work of the kind that had come under my observation; indeed, the reintroduction of the study was delayed for some months, because Dr. Jarvis' book could not be had, and we were unwilling to take any other.

From PROF. A. P. PEABODY, D.D., LL.D., *Harvard University.*

* * I have been in the habit of examining school-books with great care, and I hesitate not to say that, of all the text-books on Physiology which have been given to the public, Dr. Jarvis' deserves the first place on the score of accuracy, thoroughness, method, simplicity of statement, and constant reference to topics of practical interest and utility.

From JAMES N. TOWNSEND, *Superintendent Public Schools, Hudson, N. Y.*

Every human being is appointed to take charge of his own body; and of all books written upon this subject, I know of none which will so well prepare one to do this as "Jarvis' Physiology"—that is, in so small a compass of matter. It considers the pure, simple *laws of health* paramount to science; and though the work is thoroughly scientific, it is divested of all cumbrous technicalities, and presents the subject of physical life in a manner and style really charming. It is unquestionably the best text-book on physiology I have ever seen. It is giving great satisfaction in the schools of this city, where it has been adopted as the standard.

From L. J. SANFORD, M.D., *Prof. Anatomy and Physiology in Yale College*

Books on human physiology, designed for the use of schools, are more generally a failure perhaps than are school-books on most other subjects.

The great want in this department is met, we think, in the well-written treatise of Dr. Jarvis, entitled "Physiology and Laws of Health." * * The work is not too detailed nor too expansive in any department, and is clear and concise in all. It is not burdened with an excess of anatomical description, nor rendered discursive by many zoological references. Anatomical statements are made to the extent of qualifying the student to attend, understandingly, to an exposition of those functional processes which, collectively, make up health; thus the laws of health are enunciated, and many suggestions are given which, if heeded, will tend to its preservation.

☞ For further testimony of similar character, see current numbers of the Illustrated Educational Bulletin.

NATURAL SCIENCE.

"FOURTEEN WEEKS" IN EACH BRANCH.

By J. DORMAN STEELE, A. M.

Steele's 14 Weeks Course in Chemistry (New Ed.)
Steele's 14 Weeks Course in Astronomy
Steele's 14 Weeks Course in Philosophy
Steele's 14 Weeks Course in Geology
Steele's 14 Weeks Course in Physiology
Steele's 14 Weeks Course in Zoology

Our Text-Books in these studies are, as a general thing, dull and uninteresting. They contain from 400 to 600 pages of dry facts and unconnected details. They abound in that which the student cannot learn, much less remember. The pupil commences the study, is confused by the fine print and coarse print, and neither knowing exactly what to learn nor what to hasten over, is crowded through the single term generally assigned to each branch, and frequently comes to the close without a definite and exact idea of a single scientific principle.

Steele's Fourteen Weeks Courses contain only that which every well-informed person should know, while all that which concerns only the professional scientist is omitted. The language is clear, simple, and interesting, and the illustrations bring the subject within the range of home life and daily experience. They give such of the general principles and the prominent facts as a pupil can make familiar as household words within a single term. The type is large and open; there is no fine print to annoy; the cuts are copies of genuine experiments or natural phenomena, and are of fine execution.

In fine, by a system of condensation peculiarly his own, the author reduces each branch to the limits of a single term of study, while sacrificing nothing that is essential, and nothing that is usually retained from the study of the larger manuals in common use. Thus the student has rare opportunity to *economize his time*, or rather to employ that which he has to the best advantage.

A notable feature is the author's charming "style," fortified by an enthusiasm over his subject in which the student will not fail to partake. Believing that Natural Science is full of fascination, he has moulded it into a form that attracts the attention and kindles the enthusiasm of the pupil.

The recent editions contain the author's "Practical Questions" on a plan never before attempted in scientific text-books. These are questions as to the nature and cause of common phenomena, and are not directly answered in the text, the design being to test and promote an intelligent use of the student's knowledge of the foregoing principles.

Steele's General Key to his Works.

This work is mainly composed of Answers to the Practical Questions and Solutions of the Problems in the author's celebrated "Fourteen Weeks Courses" in the several sciences, with many hints to teachers, minor Tables, &c. Should be on every teacher's desk.

Steele's 14 Weeks in each Science.

TESTIMONIALS.

From L. A. Bikle, *President N. C. College.*

I have not been disappointed. Shall take pleasure in introducing this series.

From J. F. Cox, *Prest. Southern Female College, Ga.*

I am much pleased with these books, and expect to introduce them.

From J. R. Branham, *Prin. Brownsville Female College, Tenn.*

They are capital little books, and are now in use in our institution.

From W. H. Goodale, *Professor Readville Seminary, La.*

We are using your 14 Weeks Course, and are much pleased with them.

From W. A. Boles, *Supt. Shelbyville Graded School, Ind.*

They are as entertaining as a story book, and much more improving to the mind.

From S. A. Snow, *Principal of High School, Uxbridge, Mass.*

Steele's 14 Weeks Courses in the Sciences are a perfect success.

From John W. Doughty, *Newburg Free Academy, N. Y.*

I was prepared to find Prof. Steele's Course both attractive and instructive. My highest expectations have been fully realized.

From J. S. Blackwell, *Prest. Ghent College, Ky.*

Prof. Steele's unexampled success in providing for the wants of academic classes, has led me to look forward with high anticipations to his forthcoming issue.

From J. F. Cook, *Prest. La Grange College, Mo.*

I am pleased with the neatness of these books and the delightful diction. I have been teaching for years, and have never seen a lovelier little volume than the Astronomy.

From M. W. Smith, *Prin. of High School, Morrison, Ill.*

They seem to me to be admirably adapted to the wants of a public school, containing, as they do, a sufficiently comprehensive arrangement of elementary principles to excite a healthy thirst for a more thorough knowledge of those sciences.

From J. D. Bartley, *Prin. of High School, Concord, N. H.*

They are just such books as I have looked for, viz., those of interesting style, not cumbersome and filled up with things to be omitted by the pupil, and yet sufficiently full of facts for the purpose of most scholars in these sciences in our high schools; there is nothing but what a pupil of average ability can thoroughly master.

From Alonzo Norton Lewis, *Principal of Parker Academy, Conn.*

I consider Steele's Fourteen Weeks Courses in Philosophy, Chemistry, &c., the *best* school-books that have been issued in this country.

As an introduction to the various branches of which they treat, and especially for that numerous class of pupils who have not the time for a more extended course, I consider them *invaluable.*

From Edward Brooks, *Prin. State Normal School, Millersville, Pa.*

At the meeting of Normal School Principals, I presented the following resolution, which was unanimously adopted: "*Resolved,* That Steele's 14 Weeks Courses in Natural Philosophy and Astronomy, or an amount equivalent to what is contained in them, be adopted for use in the State Normal Schools of Pennsylvania." The works themselves will be adopted by at least three of the schools, and, I presume, by them all.

LITERATURE.

Gilman's First Steps in English Literature,

The character and plan of this exquisite little text-book may be best understood from an analysis of its contents:

INTRODUCTION. Chapter I, Historical; II, Definition of Terms; III, Languages of Europe, with Chart.

PERIOD OF IMMATURE ENGLISH, with Chart. Chapter IV, Original English; V, Broken English; VI, Dead English; VII, Reviving English.

PERIOD OF MATURE ENGLISH, with Chart. Chapter VIII, The Italian Influence; IX, Puritan Influence; X, French Influence; XI, Age of Pope; XII, Age of Johnson; XIII, Age of Poetical Romance; XIV, Age of Prose Romance.

The volume concludes with a Chart of Bible Translations, a Bibliography or Guide to General Reading, and other aids to the student.

Cleveland's Compendiums,

ENGLISH LITERATURE. AMERICAN LITERATURE.
ENGLISH LITERATURE OF THE XIXTH CENTURY.

In these volumes are gathered the cream of the literature of the English-speaking people for the school-room and the general reader. Their reputation is national. More than 125,000 copies have been sold.

Boyd's English Classics,

MILTON'S PARADISE LOST. THOMSON'S SEASONS.
YOUNG'S NIGHT THOUGHTS. POLLOK'S COURSE OF TIME.
COWPER'S TASK, TABLE TALK, &C. LORD BACON'S ESSAYS.

This series of annotated editions of great English writers, in prose and poetry, is designed for critical reading and parsing in schools. Prof. J. R. Boyd proves himself an editor of high capacity, and the works themselves need no encomium. As auxiliary to the study of Belles Lettres, etc., these works have no equal.

Pope's Essay on Man,

Pope's Homer's Iliad,

The metrical translation of the great poet of antiquity, and the matchless "Essay on the Nature and State of Man," by ALEXANDER POPE, afford superior exercise in literature and parsing.

ÆSTHETICS.

Huntington's Manual of the Fine Arts,

A view of the rise and progress of Art in different countries, a brief account of the most eminent masters of Art, and an analysis of the principles of Art. It is complete in itself, or may precede to advantage the critical work of Lord Kames.

Boyd's Kames' Elements of Criticism,

The best edition of this standard work; without the study of which none may be considered proficient in the science of the Perceptions. No other study can be pursued with so marked an effect upon the taste and refinement of the pupil.

CLEVELAND'S COMPENDIUMS.

TESTIMONIALS.

From the New Englander.

This is the very best book of the kind we have ever examined.

From GEORGE B. EMERSON, Esq., *Boston.*

The Biographical Sketches are just and discriminating; the selections are admirable, and I have adopted the work as a text-book for my first class.

From PROF. MOSES COIT TYLER, *of the Michigan University.*

I have given your book a thorough examination, and am greatly delighted with it; and shall have great pleasure in directing the attention of my classes to a work which affords so admirable a bird's-eye view of recent "English Literature."

From the Saturday Review.

It acquaints the reader with the characteristic method, tone, and quality of all the chief notabilities of the period, and will give the careful student a better idea of the recent history of English Literature than nine educated Englishmen in ten possess.

From the Methodist Quarterly Review, New York.

This work is a transcript of the best American mind; a vehicle of the noblest American spirit. No parent who would introduce his child to a knowledge of our country's literature, and at the same time indoctrinate his heart in the purest principles, need fear to put this manual in the youthful hand.

From REV. C. PEIRCE, *Principal, West Newton, Mass.*

I do not believe the work is to be found from which, within the same limits, so much interesting and valuable information in regard to English writers and English literature of every age, can be obtained; and it deserves to find a place in all our high schools and academies, as well as in every private library.

From the Independent.

The work of selection and compilation—requiring a perfect familiarity with the whole range of English literature, a judgment clear and impartial, a taste at once delicate and severe, and a most sensitive regard to purity of thought or feeling—has been better accomplished in this than in any kindred volume with which we are acquainted.

POLITICAL ECONOMY.

Champlin's Lessons on Political Economy,

An improvement on previous treatises, being shorter, yet containing everything essential, with a view of recent questions in finance, etc., which is not elsewhere found.

From J. L. BOTHWELL, *Prin. Public School No. 14, Albany, N. Y.*

I have examined Champlin's Political Economy with much pleasure, and shall be pleased to put it into the hands of my pupils. In quantity and quality I think it superior to anything that I have examined.

From PRES. N. E. COBLEIGH, *East Tennessee Wesleyan University.*

An examination of Champlin's Political Economy has satisfied me that it is the book I want. For brevity and compactness, division of the subject, and clear statement, and for appropriateness of treatment, I consider it a better text-book than any other in the market.

From the Evening Mail, New York.

A new interest has been imparted to the science of political economy since we have been necessitated to raise such vast sums of money for the support of the government. The time, therefore, is favorable for the introduction of works like the above. This little volume of two hundred pages is intended for beginners, for the common school and academy. It is intended as a basis upon which to rear a more elaborate superstructure. There is nothing in the principles of political economy above the comprehension of average scholars, when they are clearly set forth. This seems to have been done by President Champlin in an easy and graceful manner.

ELOCUTION.

Thwing's Vocal Culture.

A Drill-Book for voice and gesture, by Rev. Prof. Thwing, of Brooklyn Tabernacle Lay College. Price 50 cts.

Taverner Graham's Reasonable Elocution,

Based upon the belief that true Elocution is the right interpretation of THOUGHT, and guiding the student to an intelligent appreciation, instead of a merely mechanical knowledge, of its rules.

Zachos' Analytic Elocution.

All departments of elocution—such as the analysis of the voice and the sentence, phonology, rhythm, expression, gesture, etc.—are here arranged for instruction in classes, illustrated by copious examples.

Sherwood's Self Culture.

Self-culture in reading, speaking, and conversation—a very valuable treatise to those who would perfect themselves in these accomplishments.

SPEAKERS.

Northend's Little Orator—Child's Speaker.

Two little works of the same grade but different selections, containing simple and attractive pieces for children under twelve years of age.

Northend's Young Declaimer.

Northend's National Orator.

Two volumes of Prose, Poetry, and Dialogue, adapted to intermediate and grammar classes respectively.

Northend's Entertaining Dialogues.

Extracts eminently adapted to cultivate the dramatic faculties, as well as entertain an audience.

Swett's Common School Speaker.

Selections from recent literature.

Raymond's Patriotic Speaker,

A superb compilation of modern eloquence and poetry, with original dramatic exercises. Nearly every eminent *living* orator is represented, without distinction of place or party.

COMPOSITION AND RHETORIC.

Brookfield's First Book in Composition,

Making the cultivation of this important art feasible for the smallest child. By a new method, to induce and stimulate thought.

Boyd's Composition and Rhetoric.

This work furnishes all the aid that is needful or can be desired in the various departments and styles of composition, both in prose and verse.

Day's Art of Rhetoric,

Noted for exactness of definition, clear limitation, and philosophical development of subject; the large share of attention given to Invention, as a branch of Rhetoric, and the unequalled analysis of style.

MIND AND MORALS.

Mahan's Intellectual Philosophy

The subject exhaustively considered. The author has evinced learning, candor, and independent thinking.

Mahan's Science of Logic

A profound analysis of the laws of thought. The system possesses the merit of being intelligible and self consistent. In addition to the author's carefully elaborated views, it embraces results attained by the ablest minds of Great Britain, Germany, and France, in this department.

Boyd's Elements of Logic

A systematic and philosophic condensation of the subject, fortified with additions from Watts, Abercrombie, Whately, &c.

Watts on the Mind

The Improvement of the Mind, by Isaac Watts, is designed as a guide for the attainment of useful knowledge. As a text-book it is unparalleled; and the discipline it affords cannot be too highly esteemed by the educator.

Peabody's Moral Philosophy

A short course; by the Professor of Christian Morals, Harvard University—for the Freshman Class and for High Schools.

Fletcher's Practical Ethics

A topical analysis of each of the Virtues and Graces, furnishing outlines for the pupil to illustrate from his own experience or reading.

Alden's Text-Book of Ethics

For young pupils. To aid in systematizing the ethical teachings of the Bible, and point out the coincidences between the instructions of the sacred volume and the sound conclusions of reason.

Willard's Morals for the Young

Lessons in conversational style to indicate the elements of moral philosophy. The study is made attractive by narratives and engravings.

GOVERNMENT.

Howe's Young Citizen's Catechism

Explaining the duties of District, Town, City, County, State, and United States Officers, with rules for parliamentary and commercial business.

Young's Lessons in Civil Government

A comprehensive view of Government, and abstract of the laws showing the rights, duties, and responsibilities of citizens.

Mansfield's Political Manual

This is a complete view of the theory and practice of the General and State Governments, designed as a text-book. The author is an esteemed and able professor of constitutional law, widely known for his sagacious utterances in the public press.

Martin's Civil Government

Emanating from Massachusetts State Normal School. Historical and statistical. Each chapter summarized by a succinct statement of underlying principles on which good government is based.

MODERN LANGUAGE.

Illustrated Language Primers,

FRENCH AND ENGLISH. GERMAN AND ENGLISH.
SPANISH AND ENGLISH.

The names of common objects properly illustrated and arranged in easy lessons.

Ledru's French Fables,

Ledru's French Grammar,

Ledru's French Reader,

The author's long experience has enabled him to present the most thoroughly practical text-books extant, in this branch. The system of pronunciation (by phonetic illustration) is original with this author, and will commend itself to all American teachers, as it enables their pupils to secure an absolutely correct pronunciation without the assistance of a native master. This feature is peculiarly valuable also to "self-taught" students. The directions for ascertaining the gender of French nouns—also a great stumbling-block—are peculiar to this work, and will be found remarkably competent to the end proposed. The criticism of teachers and the test of the school-room is invited to this excellent series, with confidence.

Worman's French Echo,

To teach conversational French by actual practice, on an entirely new plan, which recognizes the importance of the student learning *to think* in the language which he speaks. It furnishes an extensive vocabulary of words and expressions in common use, and suffices to free the learner from the embarrassments which the peculiarities of his own tongue are likely to be to him, and to make him thoroughly familiar with the use of proper idioms.

Worman's German Echo,

On the same plan. See Worman's German Series, page 42.

Pujol's Complete French Class-Book,

Offers, in one volume, methodically arranged, a complete French course—usually embraced in series of from five to twelve books, including the bulky and expensive Lexicon. Here are Grammar, Conversation, and choice Literature—selected from the best French authors. Each branch is thoroughly handled; and the student, having diligently completed the course as prescribed, may consider himself, without further application, *au fait* in the most polite and elegant language of modern times.

Pujol's French Grammar, Exercises, Reader,

These volumes contain Part I, Parts II and III, and Part IV of the Complete Class-Book respectively, for the convenience of scholars and teachers. The Lexicon is bound with each part.

Maurice-Poitevin's Grammaire Francaise,

American schools are at last supplied with an American edition of this famous text-book. Many of our best institutions have for years been procuring it from abroad rather than forego the advantages it offers. The policy of putting students who have acquired some proficiency from the ordinary text-books, into a Grammar written in the vernacular, cannot be too highly commended. It affords an opportunity for finish and review at once; while embodying abundant practice of its own rules.

Joynes' French Pronunciation,

Willard's Historia de los Estados Unidos,

The History of the United States, translated by Professors TOLON and DE TORNOS, will be found a valuable, instructive, and entertaining reading-book for Spanish classes.

Pujol's Complete French Class-Book.

TESTIMONIALS.

From PROF. ELIAS PEISSNER, *Union College.*

I take great pleasure in recommending Pujol and Van Norman's French Class-Book, as there is no French grammar or class-book which can be compared with it in completeness, system, clearness, and general utility.

From EDWARD NORTH, *President of Hamilton College.*

I have carefully examined Pujol and Van Norman's French Class-Book, and am satisfied of its superiority, for college purposes, over any other heretofore used. We shall not fail to use it with our next class in French.

From A. CURTIS, *Pres't of Cincinnati Literary and Scientific Institute.*

I am confident that it may be made an instrument in conveying to the student, in from six months to a year, the art of speaking and writing the French with almost native fluency and propriety.

From HIRAM ORCUTT, A. M., *Prin. Glenwood and Tilden Ladies' Seminaries.*

I have used Pujol's French Grammar in my two seminaries, exclusively, for more than a year, and have no hesitation in saying that I regard it the best text-book in this department extant. And my opinion is confirmed by the testimony of Prof. F. De Launay and Mademoiselle Marindin. They assure me that the book is eminently accurate and practical, as tested in the school-room.

From PROF. THEO. F. DE FUMAT, *Hebrew Educational Institute, Memphis, Tenn.*

M. Pujol's French Grammar is one of the best and most practical works. The French language is chosen and elegant in style—modern and easy. It is far superior to the other French class-books in this country. The selection of the conversational part is very good, and will interest pupils; and being all completed in only one volume, it is especially desirable to have it introduced in our schools.

From PROF. JAMES H. WORMAN, *Bordentown Female College, N. J.*

The work is upon the same plan as the text-books for the study of French and English published in Berlin, for the study of those who have not the aid of a teacher, and these books are considered, by the first authorities, the best books. In most of our institutions, Americans teach the modern languages, and heretofore the trouble has been to give them a text-book that would dispose of the difficulties of the French pronunciation. This difficulty is successfully removed by P. and Van N., and I have every reason to believe it will soon make its way into most of our best schools.

From PROF. CHARLES S. DOD, *Ann Smith Academy, Lexington, Va.*

I cannot do better than to recommend "Pujol and Van Norman." For comprehensive and systematic arrangement, progressive and thorough development of all grammatical principles and idioms, with a due admixture of theoretical knowledge and practical exercise, I regard it as superior to any (other) book of the kind.

From A. A. FORSTER, *Prin. Pinehurst School, Toronto, C. W.*

I have great satisfaction in bearing testimony to M. Pujol's System of French Instruction, as given in his complete class-book. For clearness and comprehensiveness, adapted for all classes of pupils, I have found it superior to any other work of the kind, and have now used it for some years in my establishment with great success.

From PROF. OTTO FEDDER, *Maplewood Institute, Pittsfield, Mass.*

The conversational exercises will prove an immense saving of the hardest kind of labor to teachers. There is scarcely any thing more trying in the way of teaching language, than to rack your brain for short and easily intelligible bits of conversation, and to repeat them time and again with no better result than extorting at long intervals a doubting "oui," or a hesitating "non, monsieur"

☞ **For further testimony of a similar character, see special circular, and current numbers of the Educational Bulletin.**

GERMAN.

A COMPLETE COURSE IN THE GERMAN.

By JAMES H. WORMAN, A. M.

Worman's Elementary German Grammar
Worman's Complete German Grammar

These volumes are designed for intermediate and advanced classes respectively. Though following the same general method with "Otto" (that of 'Gaspey'), our author differs essentially in its application. He is more practical, more systematic, more accurate, and besides introduces a number of invaluable features which have never before been combined in a German grammar.

Among other things, it may be claimed for Prof. Worman that he has been *the first* to introduce in an American text-book for learning German, a system of analogy and comparison with other languages. Our best teachers are also enthusiastic about his methods of inculcating the art of speaking, of understanding the spoken language, of correct pronunciation; the sensible and convenient original classification of nouns (in four declensions), and of irregular verbs, also deserves much praise. We also note the use of heavy type to indicate etymological changes in the paradigms, and, in the exercises, the parts which specially illustrate preceding rules.

Worman's Elementary German Reader
Worman's Collegiate German Reader

The finest and most judicious compilation of classical and standard German Literature. These works embrace, progressively arranged, selections from the masterpieces of Goethe, Schiller, Korner, Seume, Uhland, Freiligrath, Heine, Schlegel, Holty, Lenau, Wieland, Herder, Lessing, Kant, Fichte, Schelling, Winkelmann, Humboldt, Ranke, Raumer, Menzel, Gervinus, &c., and contains complete Goethe's "Iphigenie," Schiller's "Jungfrau;" also, for instruction in modern conversational German, Benedix's "Eigensinn."

There are besides, Biographical Sketches of each author contributing, Notes, explanatory and philological (after the text), Grammatical References to all leading grammars, as well as the editor's own, and an adequate Vocabulary.

Worman's German Echo

Consists of exercises in colloquial style entirely in the German, with an adequate vocabulary, not only of words but of idioms. The object of the system developed in this work (and its companion volume in the French) is to break up the laborious and tedious habit of *translating the thoughts*, which is the student's most effectual bar to fluent conversation, and to lead him to *think in the language in which he speaks*. As the exercises illustrate scenes in actual life, a considerable knowledge of the manners and customs of the German people is also acquired from the use of this manual.

Worman's German Copy-Books, 3 Numbers,

On the same plan as the most approved systems for English penmanship, with progressive copies.

Worman's German Grammars.

TESTIMONIALS.

From Prof. R. W. JONES, *Petersburg Female College, Va.*

From what I have seen of the work it is almost certain *I shall introduce it* into this institution.

From Prof. G. CAMPBELL, *University of Minnesota.*

A valuable addition to our school-books, and will find many friends, and do great good.

From Prof. O. H P. CORPREW, *Mary Military Inst, Md.*

I am better pleased with them than any I have ever taught. I have already ordered through our booksellers.

From Prof. R. S. KENDALL, *Vernon Academy, Conn.*

I at once put the Elementary Grammar into the hands of a class of beginners, and have used it *with great satisfaction.*

From Prof. D. E. HOLMES, *Berlin Academy, Wis.*

Worman's German works are *superior.* I shall use them hereafter in my German classes.

From Prof. MAGNUS BUCHHOLTZ, *Hiram College, Ohio.*

I have examined the Complete Grammar, and find it *excellent.* You may rely that it will be used here.

From Prin. THOS. W. TOBEY, *Paducah Female Seminary, Ky.*

The Complete German Grammar is worthy of an extensive circulation. It is *admirably adapted* to the class-room. I shall use it.

From Prof. ALEX. ROSENSPITZ, *Houston Academy, Texas.*

Bearer will take and pay for 3 dozen copies. Mr. Worman deserves the approbation and esteem of the teacher and the thanks of the student.

From Prof. G. MALMENE, *Augusta Seminary, Maine.*

The Complete Grammar cannot fail to *give great satisfaction* by the simplicity of its arrangement, and by its completeness.

From Prin. OVAL PIRKEY, *Christian University, Mo.*

Just such a series as is positively necessary. I do hope the author will succeed as well in the French, &c., as he has in the German.

From Prof. S. D. HILLMAN, *Dickinson College, Pa.*

The class have lately commenced, and my examination thus far warrants me in saying that I regard it as *the best* grammar for instruction in the German.

From Prin. SILAS LIVERMORE, *Bloomfield Seminary, Mo.*

I have found a classically and scientifically educated Prussian gentleman whom I propose to make German instructor. I have shown him both your German grammars. He has expressed *his approbation* of them generally.

From Prof. Z. TEST, *Howland School for Young Ladies, N. Y.*

I shall introduce the books. From a cursory examination I have no hesitation in pronouncing the Complete Grammar *a decided improvement* on the text-books at present in use in this country.

From Prof. LEWIS KISTLER, *Northwestern University, Ill.*

Having looked through the Complete Grammar with some care I must say that you have produced *a good book;* you may be awarded with this gratification—that your grammar promotes the facility of learning the German language, and of becoming acquainted with its rich literature.

From Pres. J. P. ROUS, *Stockwell Collegiate Inst., Ind.*

I supplied a class with the Elementary Grammar, and it gives *complete satisfaction.* The conversational and reading exercises are well calculated to illustrate the principles, and lead the student on an easy yet thorough course. I think the Complete Grammar equally attractive.

THE CLASSICS.

LATIN.

Silber's Latin Course,

The book contains an Epitome of Latin Grammar, followed by Reading Exercises, with explanatory Notes and copious References to the leading Latin Grammars, and also to the Epitome which precedes the work. Then follow a Latin-English Vocabulary and Exercises in Latin Prose Composition, being thus complete in itself, and a very suitable work to put in the hands of one about to study the language.

Searing's Virgil's Æneid,

It contains only the first six books of the Æneid. 2. A very carefully constructed Dictionary. 3. Sufficiently copious Notes. 4. Grammatical references to four leading Grammars. 5. Numerous Illustrations of the highest order, 6. A superb Map of the Mediterranean and adjacent countries. 7. Dr. S. H. Taylor's "Questions on the Æneid." 8. A Metrical Index, and an Essay on the Poetical Style. 9. A photographic *fac simile* of an early Latin M.S. 10. The text according to Jahn, but paragraphed according to Ladewig. 11. Superior mechanical execution.

"Have examined it with great pleasure and can safely say it is the best edition of Virgil with which I am acquainted."—PROF. LESLIE WAGGENER, *Bethel College, Ky.*

"Am *very* much pleased. In following points think it surpasses: instructive illustrations, pointed and sensible notes where they are convenient to use, and a vocabulary that gives the *derivation of Latin words.*"—PRIN. E. L. RICHARDSON, *Addison Union School, N. Y.*

"A fine specimen of art, and edited in a *masterly manner.*"—SUPT. W. C. ROTE, *Lawrence Public Schools, Kansas.*

"Of Searing's Virgil I cannot speak in too high terms. While as a text-book it contains as many excellences as any I have ever seen, the fineness of the paper and the beauty of typography and exceeding neatness make it an ornament for the centre-table."—PRIN. E. C. SPALDING, *Nunda Academy, N. Y.*

☞ *For further testimonials, see page 45.*

Blair's Latin Pronunciation,

An inquiry into the proper sounds of the Language during the Classical Period. By Prof. Blair, of Hampden Sidney College, Va.

GREEK.

Crosby's Greek Grammar,

Crosby's Xenophon's Anabasis,

MYTHOLOGY.

Dwight's Grecian and Roman Mythology.

School edition, University edition,

A knowledge of the fables of antiquity, thus presented in a systematic form, is as indispensable to the student of general literature as to him who would peruse intelligently the classical authors. The mythological allusions so frequent in literature are readily understood with such a Key as this.

SEARING'S VIRGIL.

SPECIMEN FRAGMENTS OF LETTERS.

"I adopt it gladly."—PRIN. V. DABNEY, *Loudoun School, Va.*

"I like Searing's Virgil."—PROF. BRISTOL, *Ripon College, Wis.*

"Meets my desires very thoroughly."—PROF. CLARK, *Berea College, Ohio.*

"Superior to any other edition of Virgil."—PRES. HALL, *Macon College, Mo.*

"Shall adopt it at once."—PRIN. B. P. BAKER, *Searcy Female Institute, Ark.*

"Your Virgil is a *beauty*."—PROF. W. H. DE MOTTE, *Illinois Female College.*

"After use, I regard it the best."—PRIN. G. H. BARTON, *Rome Academy, N. Y.*

"We like it better every day."—PRIN. R. K. BUEHRLE, *Allentown Academy, Pa.*

"I am delighted with your Virgil."—PRIN. W. T. LEONARD, *Pierce Academy, Mass.*

"Stands well the test of class-room."—PRIN. F. A. CHASE, *Lyons Col. Inst., Iowa.*

"I do not see how it can be improved."—PRIN. N. F. D. BROWNE, *Charl. Hall, Md.*

"The most complete that I have seen."—PRIN. A. BROWN, *Columbus High School, Ohio.*

"Our Professor of Language very highly approves."—SUPT. J. G. JAMES, *Texas Military Institute.*

"It responds to a want long felt by teachers. It is beautiful and complete."—PROF. BROOKS, *University of Minnesota.*

"The ideal edition. We want a few more classics of the same sort."—PRIN. C. F. P. BANCROFT, *Lookout Mountain Institute, Tenn.*

"I certainly have never seen an edition so complete with important requisites for a student, nor with such fine text and general mechanical execution."—PRES. J. R. PARK, *University of Deseret, Utah.*

"It is charming both in its design and execution. And, on the whole, I think it is the best thing of the kind that I have seen."—PROF. J. DE F. RICHARDS, *Pres. pro tem. of University of Alabama.*

"In beauty of execution, in judicious notes, and in an adequate vocabulary, it merits all praise. I shall recommend its introduction."—PRES. J. K. PATTERSON, *Kentucky Agricultural and Mechanical College.*

"Containing a good vocabulary and judicious notes, it will enable the industrious student to acquire an accurate knowledge of the most interesting part of Virgil's works."—PROF. J. T. DUNKLIN, *East Alabama College.*

"It wants no element of completeness. It is by far the best classical text-book with which I am acquainted. The notes are just right. They help the student when he most needs help."—PRIN. C. A. BUNKER, *Caledonia Grammar School, Vt.*

"I have examined Searing's Virgil with interest, and find that it more nearly meets the wants of students than that of any other edition with which I am acquainted. I am able to introduce it to some extent at once."—PRIN. J. EASTER, *East Genesee Conference Seminary.*

"I have been wishing to get a sight of it, and it exceeds my expectations. It is a beautiful book in every respect, and bears evidence of careful and critical study. The engravings add instruction as well as interest to the work. I shall recommend it to my classes."—PRIN. CHAS. H. CHANDLER, *Glenwood Ladies' Seminary.*

"A. S. Barnes & Co. have published an edition of the first six books of Virgil's Æneid, which is superior to its predecessors in several respects. The publishers have done a good service to the cause of classical education, and the book deserves a large circulation."—PROF. GEORGE W. COLLORD, *Brooklyn Polytechnic, N. Y.*

"My attention was called to Searing's Virgil by the fact of its containing a vocabulary which would obviate the necessity of procuring a lexicon. But use in the class-room has impressed me most favorably with the accuracy and just proportion of its notes, and the general excellence of its grammatical suggestions. The general character of the book in its paper, its typography, and its engravings is highly commendable, and the fac-simile manuscript is a valuable feature. I take great pleasure in commending the book to all who do not wish a complete edition of Virgil. It suits our short school courses admirably."—HENRY L. BOLTWOOD, *Master of Princeton High School, Ill.*

RECORDS.

Cole's Self-Reporting Class-Book,

For saving the Teacher's labor in averaging. At each opening are a full set of Tables showing any scholar's standing at a glance and entirely obviating the necessity of computation.

Tracy's School-Record, Pocket edition,

For keeping a simple but exact record of Attendance, Deportment, and Scholarship. The larger edition contains also a Calendar, an extensive list of Topics for Compositions and Colloquies, Themes for Short Lectures, Suggestions to Young Teachers, etc.

Brooks' Teacher's Register,

Presents at one view a record of Attendance, Recitations, and Deportment for the whole term.

Carter's Record and Roll-Book,

This is the most complete and convenient Record offered to the public. Besides the usual spaces for General Scholarship, Deportment, Attendance, etc., for each name and day, there is a space in red lines enclosing six minor spaces in blue for recording Recitations.

National School Diary,

A little book of blank forms for weekly report of the standing of each scholar, from teacher to parent. A great convenience.

REWARDS.

National School Currency,

A little box containing certificates in the form of Money. The most entertaining and stimulating system of school rewards. The scholar is paid for his merits and fined for his shortcomings. Of course the most faithful are the most successful in business. In this way the use and value of money and the method of keeping accounts are also taught. One box of Currency will supply a school of fifty pupils.

TACTICS.

The Boy Soldier,

Complete Infantry Tactics for Schools, with illustrations, for the use of those who would introduce this pleasing relaxation from the confining duties of the desk.

CHARTS.

McKenzie's Elocutionary Chart,

Baade's Reading Case,

This remarkable piece of school-room furniture is a receptacle containing a number of primary cards. By an arrangement of slides on the front, one sentence at a time is shown to the class. Twenty-eight thousand transpositions may be made, affording a variety of progressive exercises which no other piece of apparatus offers. One of its best features is, that it is so exceedingly simple as not to get out of order, while it may be operated with one finger.

Marcy's Eureka Tablet,

A new system for the Alphabet, by which it may be taught without fail in nine lessons.

Scofield's School Tablets,

On Five Cards, exhibiting Ten Surfaces. These Tablets teach Orthography, Reading, Object-Lessons, Color, Form, etc.

Watson's Phonetic Tablets,

Four Cards, and Eight Surfaces; teaching Pronunciation and Elocution phonetically—for class exercises.

Page's Normal Chart,

The whole science of Elementary Sounds tabulated. By the author of Page's Theory and Practice of Teaching.

Clark's Grammatical Chart,

Exhibits the whole Science of Language in one comprehensive diagram.

Davies' Mathematical Chart,

Mathematics made simple to the eye.

Monteith's Reference Maps, School series, Grand series,

Eight Numbers. Mounted on Rollers. Names all laid down in small type. so that to the pupil at a short distance they are Outline Maps, while they serve as *their own key* to the teacher.

Willard's Chronographers,

Historical. Four Numbers. Ancient Chronographer; English Chronographer; American Chronographer; Temple of Time (general). Dates and Events represented to the eye.

APPARATUS.

Harrington's Geometrical Blocks,

These patented blocks are *hinged*, so that each form can be dissected.

Harrington's Fractional Blocks,

Steele's Chemical Apparatus,

Steele's Philosophical Apparatus, (see p.28)

Steele's Geological Cabinet, (see p.28)

Wood's Botanical Apparatus, (see p.30)

Bock's Physiological Apparatus,

MUSIC.

The National School Singer,

Bright, new music for the day school, embracing Song Lessons, Exercise Songs, Songs of Study, Order, Promptness and Obedience, of Industry and Nature, Patriotic and Temperance Songs, Opening and Closing Songs; in fact, everything needed in the school-room. By an eminent Musician and Composer.

Jepson's Music Readers. 3 vols.

These are not books from which children simply learn songs, parrot-like, but teach the subject progressively—the scholar learning to read music by methods similar to those employed in teaching him to read printed language. Any teacher, however ignorant of music, provided he can, upon trial, simply sound the scale, may teach it without assistance, and will end by being a good singer himself. The "Elementary Music Reader," or first volume, fully develops the system. The two companion volumes carry the same method into the higher grades, but their use is not essential.

The First Reader is also published in three parts, at 30 cents each, for those who prefer them in that form.

Bartley's Songs for the School.

A selection of appropriate Hymns of an unsectarian character, carefully classified and set to popular and "singable" Tunes, for opening and closing exercises. The Secular Department is full of bright and well selected music.

Nash & Bristow's Cantara,

The first volume is a complete musical text-book for schools of every grade. No. 2 is a choice selection of Solos and Part Songs. The authors are Directors of Music in the public schools of New York City, in which these books are the standard of instruction.

The Polytechnic

Collection of Part Songs for High and Normal Schools and Clubs. This work contains a quantity of exceedingly valuable material, heretofore accessible only in sheet form or scattered in numerous and costly works. The collection of "College Songs" is a very attractive feature.

Curtis' Little Singer,—School Vocalist,

Kingsley's School-Room Choir,—Young Ladies' Harp,

Hager's Echo (A Cantata).

DEVOTION.

Brooks' School Manual of Devotion,

This volume contains daily devotional exercises, consisting of a hymn, selections of Scripture for alternate reading by teacher and pupils, and a prayer. Its value for opening and closing school is apparent.

Brooks' School Harmonist,

Contains appropriate *tunes* for each hymn in the "Manual of Devotion" described above.

A. S. BARNES & CO.'S CATALOGUE.

DEPARTMENT OF GENERAL LITERATURE.

PRICES INCLUDING POSTAGE.

THE TEACHERS' LIBRARY.

Object Lessons—Welch, - - - - - - $1 00

This is a complete exposition of the popular modern system of "object-teaching," for teachers of primary classes.

Theory and Practice of Teaching—Page, - - 1 50

This volume has, without doubt, been read by two hundred thousand teachers, and its popularity remains undiminished—large editions being exhausted yearly. It was the pioneer, as it is now the patriarch, of professional works for teachers.

The Graded School—Wells, - - - - - - 1 25

The proper way to organize graded schools is here illustrated. The author has availed himself of the best elements of the several systems prevalent in Boston, New York, Philadelphia, Cincinnati, St. Louis, and other cities.

The Normal—Holbrook, - - - - - - 1 50

Carries a working school on its visit to teachers, showing the most approved methods of teaching all the common branches, including the technicalities, explanations, demonstrations, and definitions introductory and peculiar to each branch.

School Management—Holbrook, - - - - - 1 50

Treating of the Teacher's Qualifications; How to overcome Difficulties in Self and Others; Organization; Discipline; Methods of inciting Diligence and Order; Strategy in Management; Object Teaching.

The Teachers' Institute—Fowle, - - - - - 1 25

This is a volume of suggestions inspired by the author's experience at institutes, in the instruction of young teachers. A thousand points of interest to this class are most satisfactorily dealt with.

Schools and Schoolmasters—Dickens, - - - - 1 25

Appropriate selections from the writings of the great novelist.

The Metric System—Davies, - - - - - 1 50

Considered with reference to its general introduction, and embracing the views of John Quincy Adams and Sir John Herschel.

The Student; The Educator—Phelps, - - each, 1 50

The Discipline of Life—Phelps, - - - - - 1 75

The authoress of these works is one of the most distinguished writers on education, and they cannot fail to prove a valuable addition to the School and Teachers' Libraries, being in a high degree both interesting and instructive.

A Scientific Basis of Education—Hecker, - - 2 50

Adaptation of study and classification by temperaments.

Teachers' Hand-Book — Phelps - - - - - $1 50

By WM. F. PHELPS, Principal of Minnesota State Normal School. Embracing the objects, history, organization and management of Teachers' Institutes, followed by Methods of Teaching, in detail, for all the fundamental branches. Every young teacher, every practical teacher, every experienced teacher even, needs this book.

From the New York Tribune.

"The discipline of the school should prepare the child for the discipline of life. The country schoolmaster, accordingly, holds a position of vital interest to the destiny of the republic, and should neglect no means for the wise and efficient discharge of his significant functions. This is the key-note of the present excellent volume. In view of the supreme importance of the teacher's calling, Mr. Phelps has presented an elaborate system of instruction in the elements of learning, with a complete detail of methods and processes, illustrated with an abundance of practical examples and enforced by judicious counsels, which may serve as an aid to the teacher in the performance of his arduous duties, and in the attainment of the highest excellence in his profession. The author's directions may not always be accepted without challenge by experienced instructors, who, however, are encouraged to think for themselves; but they are always suggestive, and cannot fail to be of signal value to those who are just entering upon their profession and beginning to comprehend its difficulties, as well as to discover its secrets."

American Education — Mansfield - - - - - 1 50

A treatise on the principles and elements of education, as practised in this country, with ideas towards distinctive republican and Christian education.

American Institutions — De Tocqueville - - - - 1 50

A valuable index to the genius of our Government.

Universal Education — Mayhew - - - - - 1 75

The subject is approached with the clear, keen perception of one who has observed its necessity, and realized its feasibility and expediency alike. The redeeming and elevating power of improved common schools constitutes the inspiration of the volume.

Higher Christian Education — Dwight - - - - 1 50

A treatise on the principles and spirit, the modes, directions and results of all true teaching; showing that right education should appeal to every element of enthusiasm in the teacher's nature.

Oral Training Lessons — Barnard - - - - - 1 00

The object of this very useful work is to furnish material for instructors to impart orally to their classes, in branches not usually taught in common schools, embracing all departments of Natural Science and much general knowledge.

Lectures on Natural History — Chadbourne - - 75

Affording many themes for oral instruction in this interesting science—especially in schools where it is not pursued as a class exercise.

Outlines of Mathematical Science — Davies - - 1 00

A manual suggesting the best methods of presenting mathematical instruction on the part of the teacher, with that comprehensive view of the whole which is necessary to the intelligent treatment of a part, in science.

Nature and Utility of Mathematics — Davies - - 1 50

An elaborate and lucid exposition of the principles which lie at the foundation of pure mathematics, with a highly ingenious application of their results to the development of the essential idea of the different branches of the science.

Mathematical Dictionary — Davies and Peck - - 4 00

This cyclopædia of mathematical science defines, with completeness, precision, and accuracy, every technical term; thus constituting a popular treatise on each branch, and a general view of the whole subject.

Liberal Education of Women—Orton . . *$1 50

Treats of "the demand and the method;" being a compilation of the best and most advanced thought on this subject, by the leading writers and educators in England and America. Edited by a Professor in Vassar College.

Education Abroad—Northrop *1 50

A thorough discussion of the advantages and disadvantages of sending American children to Europe to be educated; also, Papers on Legal Prevention of Illiteracy, Study and Health, Labor as an Educator, and other kindred subjects. By the Hon. Secretary of Education for Connecticut.

The Teacher and the Parent—Northend . . *1 50

A treatise upon common-school education, designed to lead teachers to view their calling in its true light, and to stimulate them to fidelity.

The Teachers' Assistant—Northend *1 50

A natural continuation of the author's previous work, more directly calculated for daily use in the administration of school discipline and instruction.

School Government—Jewell *1 50

Full of advanced ideas on the subject which its title indicates. The criticisms upon current theories of punishment and schemes of administration have excited general attention and comment.

Grammatical Diagrams—Jewell *1 00

The diagram system of teaching grammar explained, defended, and improved. The curious in literature, the searcher for truth, those interested in new inventions, as well as the disciples of Prof. Clark, who would see their favorite theory fairly treated, all want this book. There are many who would like to be made familiar with this system before risking its use in a class. The opportunity is here afforded.

The Complete Examiner—Stone *1 25

Consists of a series of questions on every English branch of school and academic instruction, with reference to a given page or article of leading text-books where the answer may be found in full. Prepared to aid teachers in securing certificates, pupils in preparing for promotion, and teachers in selecting review questions.

School Amusements—Root *1 50

To assist teachers in making the school interesting, with hints upon the management of the school-room. Rules for military and gymnastic exercises are included. Illustrated by diagrams.

Institute Lectures—Bates *1 50

These lectures, originally delivered before institutes, are based upon various topics in the departments of mental and moral culture. The volume is calculated to prepare the will, awaken the inquiry, and stimulate the thought of the zealous teacher.

Method of Teachers' Institutes—Bates . . . *75

Sets forth the best method of conducting institutes, with a detailed account of the object, organization, plan of instruction, and true theory of education on which such instruction should be based.

History and Progress of Education *1 50

The systems of education prevailing in all nations and ages, the gradual advance to the present time, and the bearing of the past upon the present in this regard, are worthy of the careful investigation of all concerned in education.

THE SCHOOL LIBRARY.

The two elements of instruction and entertainment were never more happily combined than in this collection of standard books. Children and adults alike will here find ample food for the mind, of the sort that is easily *digested*, while not degenerating to the level of modern romance.

LIBRARY OF LITERATURE.

Milton's Paradise Lost. Boyd's Illustrated Ed., $1 60

Young's Night Thoughts . . . . do. . . 1 60

Cowper's Task, Table Talk, &c. . do. . . 1 60

Thomson's Seasons . . . . do. . . 1 60

Pollok's Course of Time . . . . do. . . 1 60

These works, models of the best and purest literature, are beautifully illustrated, and notes explain all doubtful meanings.

Lord Bacon's Essays (Boyd's Edition) . . . 1 60

Another grand English classic, affording the highest example of purity in language and style.

The Iliad of Homer. Translated by Pope. . . 80

Those who are unable to read this greatest of ancient writers in the original, should not fail to avail themselves of this metrical version.

Compendium of Eng. Literature—Cleveland, 2 25

English Literature of XIXth Century do. 2 25

Compendium of American Literature do. 2 25

Nearly one hundred and fifty thousand volumes of Prof. Cleveland's inimitable compendiums have been sold. Taken together they present a complete view of literature. To the man who can afford but a few books these will supply the place of an extensive library. From commendations of the very highest authorities the following extracts will give some idea of the enthusiasm with which the works are regarded by scholars:

With the Bible and your volumes one might leave libraries without very painful regret.—The work cannot be found from which in the same limits so much interesting and valuable information may be obtained.—Good taste, fine scholarship, familiar acquaintance with literature, unwearied industry, tact acquired by practice, an interest in the culture of the young, and regard for truth, purity, philanthropy and religion are united in Mr. Cleveland.—A judgment clear and impartial, a taste at once delicate and severe.—The biographies are just and discriminating.—An admirable bird's-eye view.—Acquaints the reader with the characteristic method, tone, and quality of each writer.—Succinct, carefully written, and wonderfully comprehensive in detail, etc., etc.

Milton's Poetical Works—Cleveland . . . 2 25

This is the very best edition of the great Poet. It includes a life of the author, notes, dissertations on each poem, a faultless text, and is *the only* edition of Milton with a complete verbal Index.

LIBRARY OF HISTORY.

Seven Historic Ages—Gilman, - - - - - $1 00

Or, Talks about Kings, Queens, and Barbarians. These delightful sketches of notable events stir the imagination of the young reader, and give him a taste for further historical reading. Illustrated.

Outlines of General History—Gilman, - - - - 1 25

The number of facts which the author has compressed into these outline sketches is really surprising; the chapters on the Middle Ages and Feudalism afford striking examples of his power of succinct but comprehensive statement. In his choice of representative periods and events in the histories of Nations he shows very sound judgment, and his characterization of conspicuous historical figures is accurate and impartial.

Great Events of History—Collier, - - - - - 1 50

This celebrated work, edited for American readers by Prof. O. R. Willis, gives, in a series of pictures, a pleasantly readable and easily remembered view of the Christian era. Each chapter is headed by its central point of interest to afford association for the mind. Delineations of life and manners at different periods are interwoven. A geographical appendix of great value is added.

History of England—Lancaster, - - - - - 1 50

An arrangement of the essential facts of English History in the briefest manner consistent with clearness. With a fine Map.

History of Liberty—Aiken, - - - - - - 1 00

Explaining the growth of the "fair consummate flower" of freedom in America as the result of centuries of trial and experience in the Old World.

Critical History of the Civil War—Mahan, - - 3 00

A logical analysis of campaigns and battles, and the causes of victory and defeat. By Dr. Asa Mahan, first President of Oberlin College. Dr. Mahan never forgets that history is "philosophy teaching by examples," and his work should be a text-book for American youth.

History of Europe—Alison, - - - - - - 2 50

A reliable and standard work, which covers with clear, connected, and complete narrative the eventful occurrences of the years A. D. 1789 to 1815, being mainly a history of the career of Napoleon Bonaparte.

History of Rome—Ricord, - - - - - - 1 75

An entertaining narrative for the young. Illustrated. Embracing successively, The Kings; The Republic; The Empire.

Ecclesiastical History—Marsh, - - - - - - 2 00

A history of the Church in all ages, with a comprehensive review of all forms of religion from the creation of the world. No other source affords, in the same compass, the information here conveyed.

History of the Ancient Hebrews—Mills, - - - - 1 75

The record of "God's people" from the call of Abraham to the destruction of Jerusalem; gathered from sources sacred and profane.

The Mexican War—Mansfield, - - - - - 1 50

A history of its origin, and a detailed account of its victories; with official despatches, the treaty of peace, and valuable tables. Illustrated.

Early History of Michigan—Sheldon, - - - - 2 50

A work of value and deep interest to the people of the West. Compiled under the supervision of Hon. Lewis Cass. Portraits.

History of Texas—Baker, - - - - - - 1 25

A pithy and interesting resumé. Copiously illustrated. The State constitution and extracts from the speeches and writings of eminent Texans are appended.

NEW LIBRARY OF HISTORY.

Barnes' Centenary History, - - - - - *$6 00

"*One Hundred Years of American Independence.*" This superbly illustrated work, by the author of "Barnes' Brief Histories" (for schools), is appropriately issued in the "centennial year" (1876). An extended Introduction brings down the history from the earliest times. The leading idea is to make American History *popular* for the masses, and especially with the young. The style is therefore life-like and vivid, carrying the reader along by the sweep of the story as in a novel, so that when he begins an account of an important event he cannot very well lay down the book until he finishes.

Lamb's History of New York City.

One of the most important works ever issued. It opens with a brief outline of the condition of the old world prior to the settlement of the new, and proceeds to give a careful analysis of the two great Dutch Commercial Corporations to which New York owes its origin. It sketches the rise and growth of the little colony on Manhattan Island; describes the Indian Wars with which it was afflicted; gives color and life to its Dutch rulers; paints its subjugation by the English, its after vicissitudes, the Revolution of 1689; in short, it leads the reader through one continuous chain of events down to the American Revolution. Then, gathering up the threads, the author gives an artistic and comprehensive account of the progress of the City, in extent, education, culture, literature, art, and political and commercial importance, during the last century. Prominent persons are introduced in all the different periods, with choice bits of family history, and glimpses of social life. The work contains maps of the City in the different decades, and several rare portraits from original paintings, which have never before been engraved. The illustrations, about 250 in number, are all of an interesting and highly artistic character.

The work is now being published, by subscription only, in about 30 parts, at 50 cents each.

Carrington's Battles of the Revolution, - - - $6 00

A careful description and analysis of every engagement of the War for Independence, with topographical charts prepared from personal surveys by the author, a veteran officer of the U. S. Army, and Professor of Military Science in Wabash College.

Baker's Texas Scrap-Book, - - - - - $5 00

Comprising the History, Biography, Literature, and Miscellany of Texas and its people. A valuable collection of material, anecdotical and statistical, which is not to be found in any other form. The work is handsomely illustrated. (Sheep, $6.00.)

LIBRARY OF REFERENCE.

Home Cyclopædia of Literature and Fine Arts, - $3 00

A complete index to all terms employed in belles lettres, philosophy, theology, law, mythology, painting, music, sculpture, architecture, and all kindred arts.

The Rhyming Dictionary—Walker, - - - 1 25

A serviceable manual to composers, being a complete index of allowable rhymes.

The Topical Lexicon—Williams, - - - - 1 75

The useful terms of the English language *classified by subjects* and arranged according to their affinities of meaning, with etymologies, definitions, and illustrations. A very entertaining and instructive work.

Mathematical Dictionary—Davies and Peck, - - 4 00

A thorough compendium of the science, with illustrations and definitions.

www.ingramcontent.com/pod-product-compliance
Lightning Source LLC
LaVergne TN
LVHW021310110826
845150LV00003B/538
9781425558420